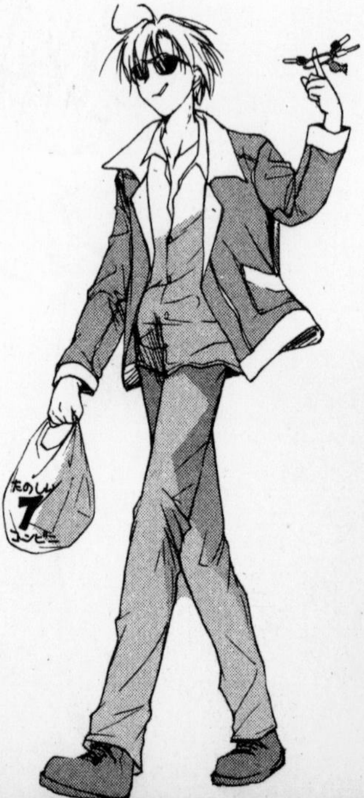
たのしい
7
コンビニ

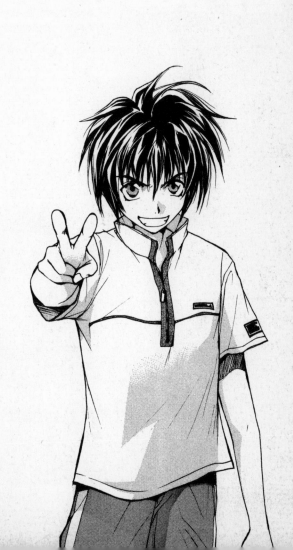

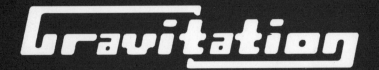

Volume 11

By
Maki Murakami

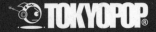

HAMBURG // LONDON // LOS ANGELES // TOKYO

Gravitation Vol. 11
Created by Maki Murakami

Translation - Ray Yoshimoto
English Adaptation - Jamie S. Rich
Copy Editors - Troy Lewter and Suzanne Waldman
Retouch and Lettering - Paul Tanck
Production Artist - Vicente Rivera, Jr.
Cover Design - Seth Cable

Editor - Paul Morrissey
Digital Imaging Manager - Chris Buford
Pre-Press Manager - Antonio DePietro
Production Managers - Jennifer Miller and Mutsumi Miyazaki
Art Director - Matt Alford
Managing Editor - Jill Freshney
VP of Production - Ron Klamert
Editor-in-Chief - Mike Kiley
President and C.O.O. - John Parker
Publisher and C.E.O. - Stuart Levy

A 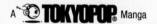 Manga

TOKYOPOP Inc.
5900 Wilshire Blvd. Suite 2000
Los Angeles, CA 90036

E-mail: info@TOKYOPOP.com
Come visit us online at www.TOKYOPOP.com

ISBN: 1-59532-414-3

First TOKYOPOP printing: April 2005
10 9 8 7 6 5 4 3 2 1
Printed in the USA

THE MEMBERS OF THE GRAVITATION BAND

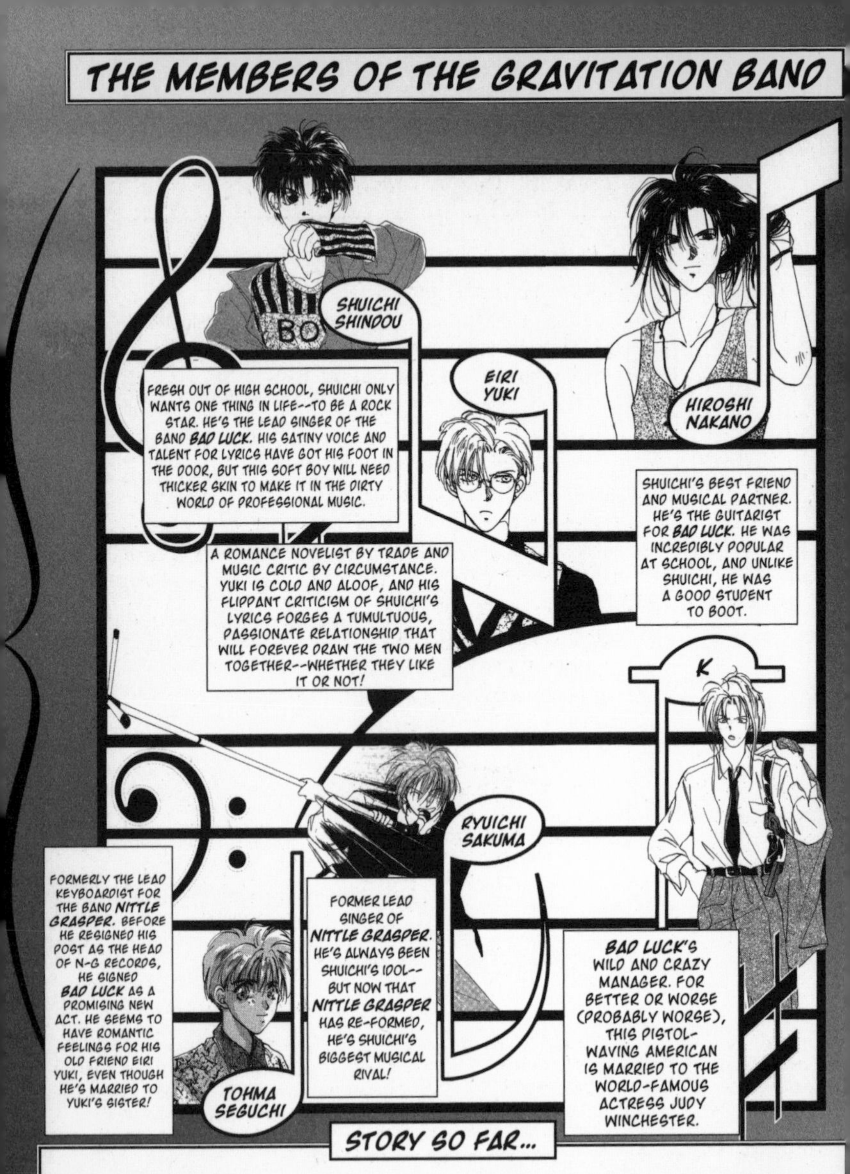
SHUICHI SHINDOU
HIROSHI NAKANO
EIRI YUKI
K
RYUICHI SAKUMA
TOHMA SEGUCHI

SHUICHI SHINDOU: FRESH OUT OF HIGH SCHOOL, SHUICHI ONLY WANTS ONE THING IN LIFE--TO BE A ROCK STAR. HE'S THE LEAD SINGER OF THE BAND ***BAD LUCK***. HIS SATINY VOICE AND TALENT FOR LYRICS HAVE GOT HIS FOOT IN THE DOOR, BUT THIS SOFT BOY WILL NEED THICKER SKIN TO MAKE IT IN THE DIRTY WORLD OF PROFESSIONAL MUSIC.

HIROSHI NAKANO: SHUICHI'S BEST FRIEND AND MUSICAL PARTNER. HE'S THE GUITARIST FOR ***BAD LUCK***. HE WAS INCREDIBLY POPULAR AT SCHOOL, AND UNLIKE SHUICHI, HE WAS A GOOD STUDENT TO BOOT.

EIRI YUKI: A ROMANCE NOVELIST BY TRADE AND MUSIC CRITIC BY CIRCUMSTANCE. YUKI IS COLD AND ALOOF, AND HIS FLIPPANT CRITICISM OF SHUICHI'S LYRICS FORGES A TUMULTUOUS, PASSIONATE RELATIONSHIP THAT WILL FOREVER DRAW THE TWO MEN TOGETHER--WHETHER THEY LIKE IT OR NOT!

TOHMA SEGUCHI: FORMERLY THE LEAD KEYBOARDIST FOR THE BAND ***NITTLE GRASPER***. BEFORE HE RESIGNED HIS POST AS THE HEAD OF N-G RECORDS, HE SIGNED ***BAD LUCK*** AS A PROMISING NEW ACT. HE SEEMS TO HAVE ROMANTIC FEELINGS FOR HIS OLD FRIEND EIRI YUKI, EVEN THOUGH HE'S MARRIED TO YUKI'S SISTER!

RYUICHI SAKUMA: FORMER LEAD SINGER OF ***NITTLE GRASPER***. HE'S ALWAYS BEEN SHUICHI'S IDOL--BUT NOW THAT ***NITTLE GRASPER*** HAS RE-FORMED, HE'S SHUICHI'S BIGGEST MUSICAL RIVAL!

K: ***BAD LUCK'S*** WILD AND CRAZY MANAGER. FOR BETTER OR WORSE (PROBABLY WORSE), THIS PISTOL-WAVING AMERICAN IS MARRIED TO THE WORLD-FAMOUS ACTRESS JUDY WINCHESTER.

STORY SO FAR...

YOSHIKI, YUKI KITAZAWA'S YOUNGER BROTHER (OR IS THAT SISTER?), HAS ARRIVED IN JAPAN. IN THE AFTERMATH, TOHMA LAYS DOWN THE LAW BY SUSPENDING K AND FIRING SAKANO. AMIDST THE ENSUING CHAOS, RAGE ENDS UP BECOMING ***BAD LUCK'S*** NEW MANAGER. MEANWHILE, IN A "SHOCK TREATMENT" EFFORT TO CURE EIRI'S TRAUMA OVER HIS DARK PAST WITH YUKI KITAZAWA, YOSHIKI IMPERSONATES THE ELDER YUKI AND CONFRONTS EIRI. INSPIRED BY THIS ENCOUNTER, EIRI BEGINS TO EXPRESS HIMSELF TOWARDS SHUICHI WITH A BIT MORE HONESTY. AND AS IF THAT WEREN'T ENOUGH, WHILE ALL THIS IS GOING ON, ***BAD LUCK*** IS ORDERED TO RELEASE ***FIVE*** SINGLES IN ***FIVE*** WEEKS!! SHUICHI IS FIRED UP AND READY TO TAKE ON THE CHALLENGE, BUT RYUICHI SUDDENLY MAKES A BOLD STATEMENT TO SAKANO, WHO HAS RE-EMERGED AS THE MANAGER OF ***BAD LUCK'S*** HEROES TURNED RIVALS--THE CLASSIC TECHNO BAND ***NITTLE GRASPER!*** THE OLD-TIMERS ARE GOING TO ONE-UP ***BAD LUCK*** BY KICKING OUT THE SAME AMOUNT OF SINGLES IN ONLY ***THREE*** WEEKS!

CONTENTS

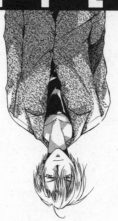

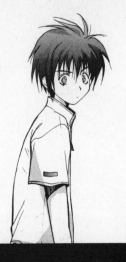

GRAVITATION

Gravitation

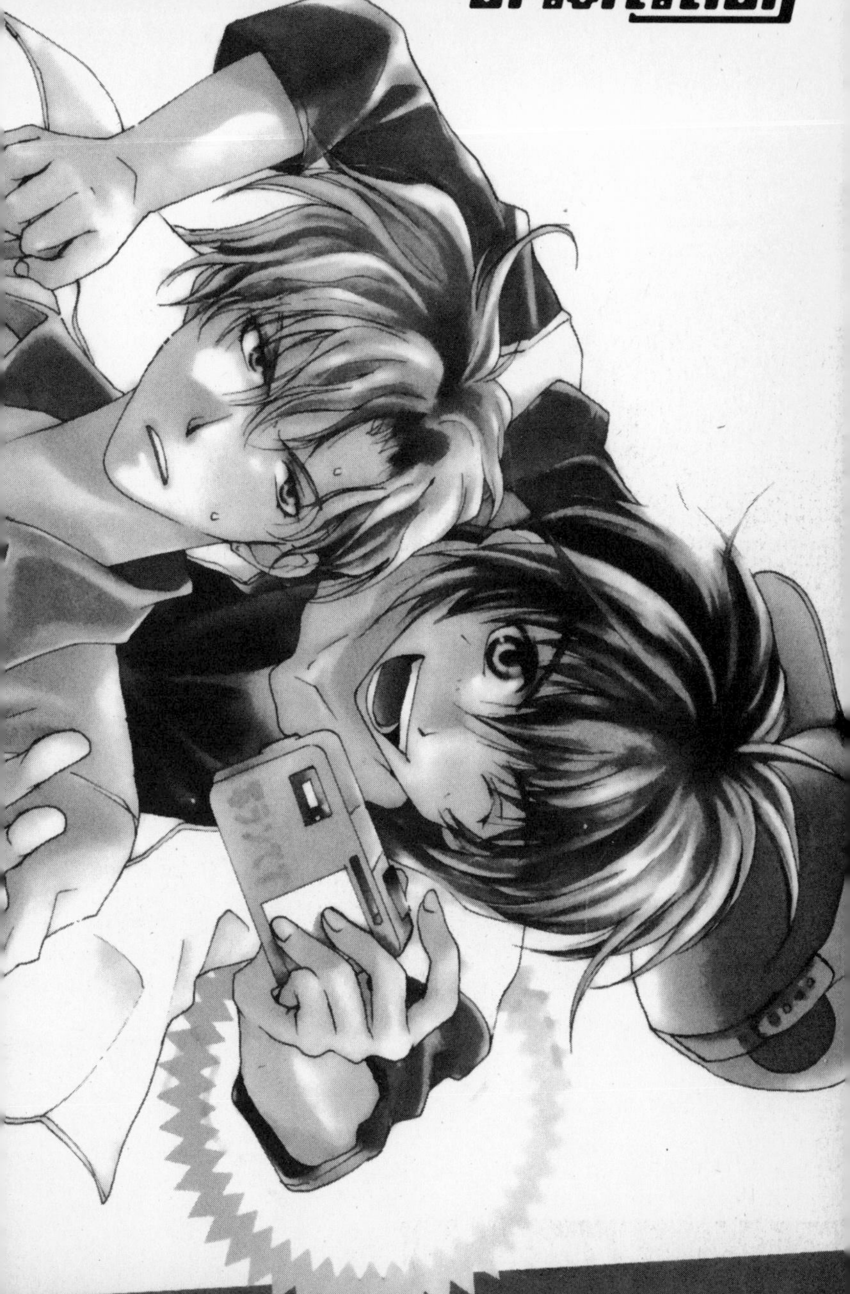

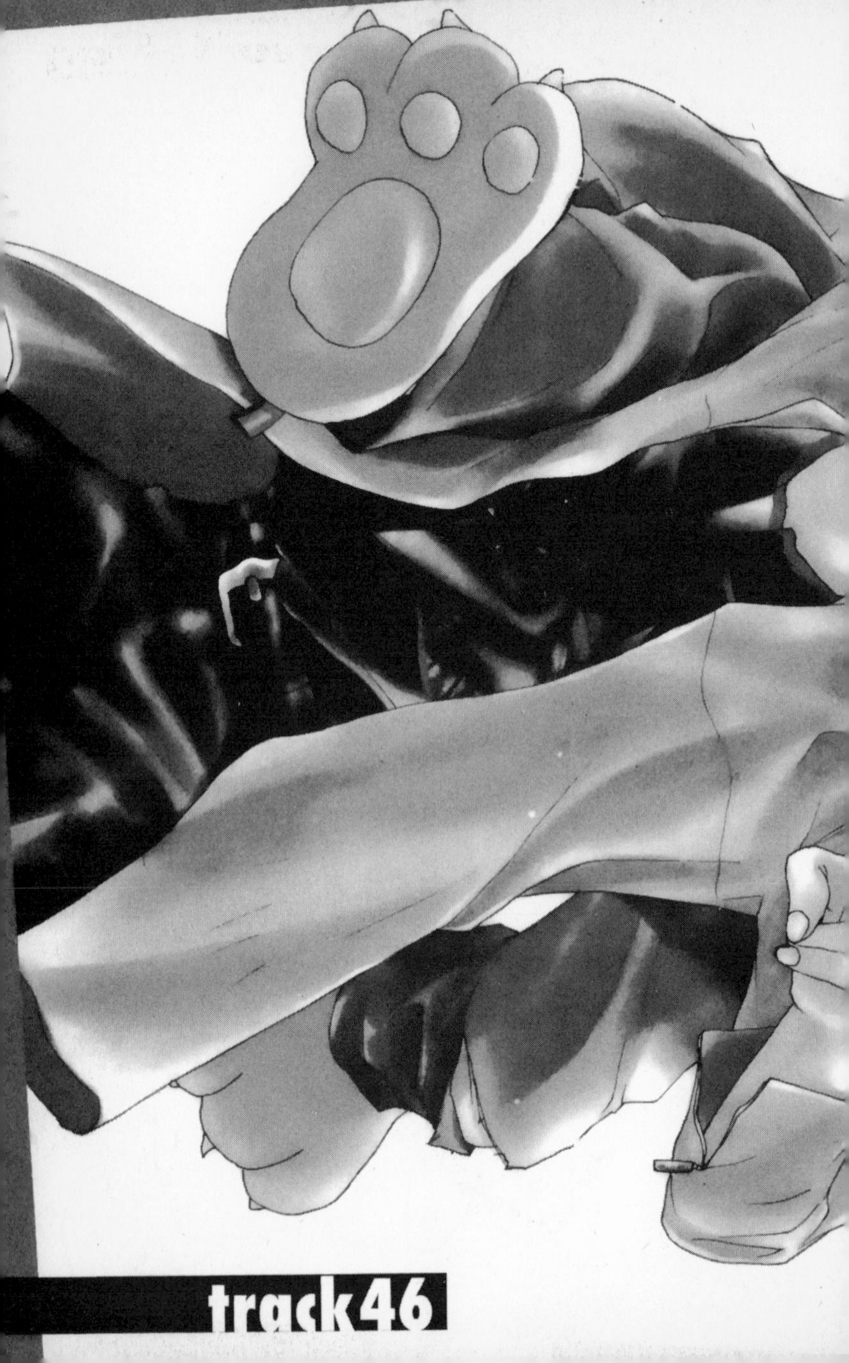
track46

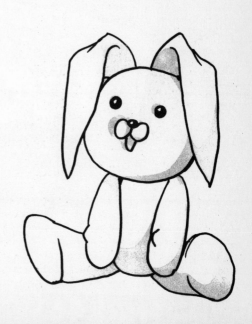

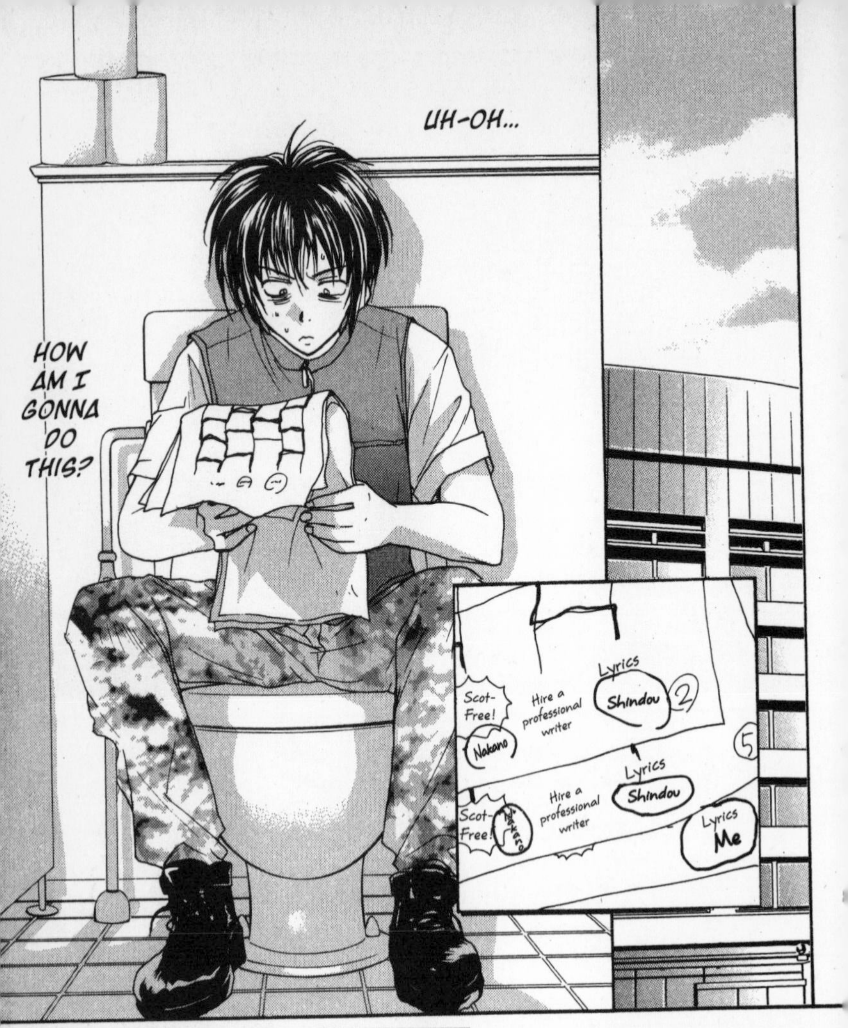
UH-OH...
Lyrics
Shindou
2
Hire a professional writer
Scot-Free!
Nakano
5
Lyrics
Shindou
Hire a professional writer
Scot-Free!
Nakano
Lyrics
Me
HOW AM I GONNA DO THIS?

ABOUT GRAVITATION TRACK 46

Hello! Long time no see! This is your favorite female manga artist here, who also raises a breed of grasshopper named Tonosama Batta. (Ugh!) Yup, you guessed it--it's me, Maki Murakami. Or maybe I'm not...maybe I'm actually a guy... (Double ugh!) Anyway, I present to you the 46th chapter of *Gravitation*. This manga just keeps going, and going, and going... And just when you think it's coming to an end, it doesn't! Oh, the anxiety of it all...ugh!! We're into a new storyline now, so I hope you'll like it. I'll try to heat up all this cold anxiety with *Gravitation's* new direction. Cheers!

p.s. - Then again, if it doesn't work and you have a hard time reading this one, I'm sorry. Boy, it sure is cold in here...

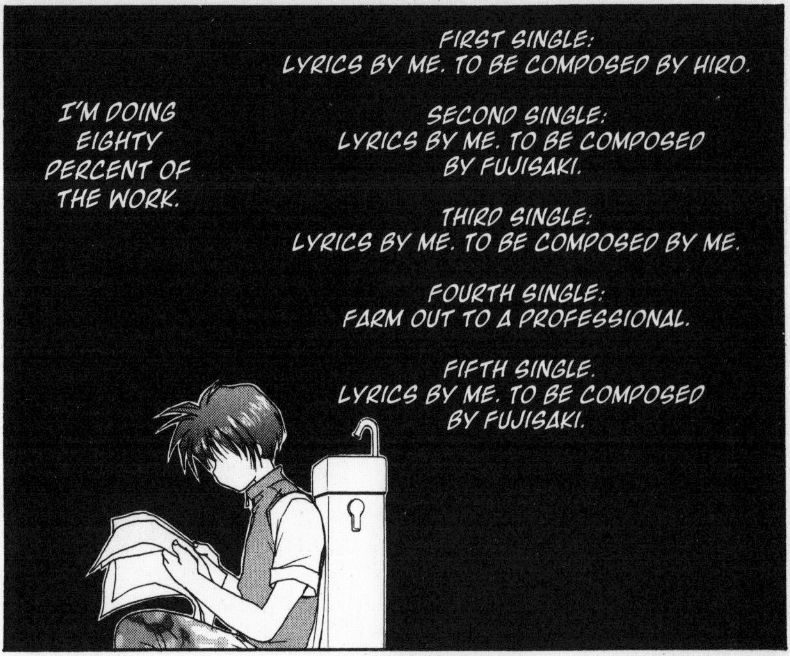
FIRST SINGLE:
LYRICS BY ME. TO BE COMPOSED BY HIRO.
SECOND SINGLE:
LYRICS BY ME. TO BE COMPOSED BY FUJISAKI.
THIRD SINGLE:
LYRICS BY ME. TO BE COMPOSED BY ME.
FOURTH SINGLE:
FARM OUT TO A PROFESSIONAL.
FIFTH SINGLE.
LYRICS BY ME. TO BE COMPOSED BY FUJISAKI.
I'M DOING EIGHTY PERCENT OF THE WORK.

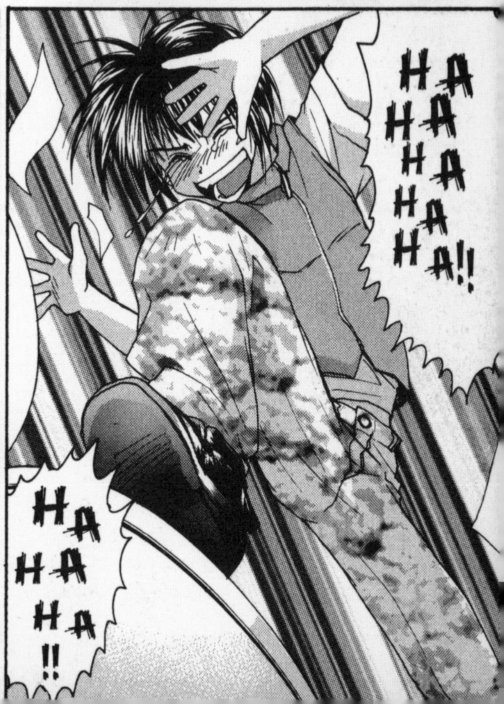
HA HA HA HA HA HA HA HA HA HA!!
HA HA HA HA HA HA !!

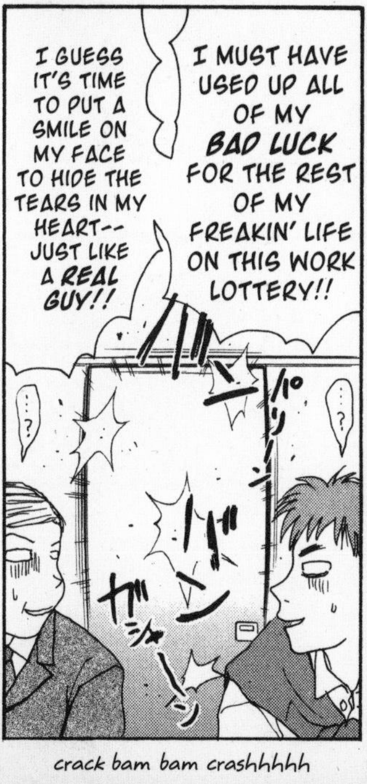
I MUST HAVE USED UP ALL OF MY **BAD LUCK** FOR THE REST OF MY FREAKIN' LIFE ON THIS WORK LOTTERY!!
I GUESS IT'S TIME TO PUT A SMILE ON MY FACE TO HIDE THE TEARS IN MY HEART--JUST LIKE A **REAL GUY!!**
...?
...?

crack bam bam crashhhhh

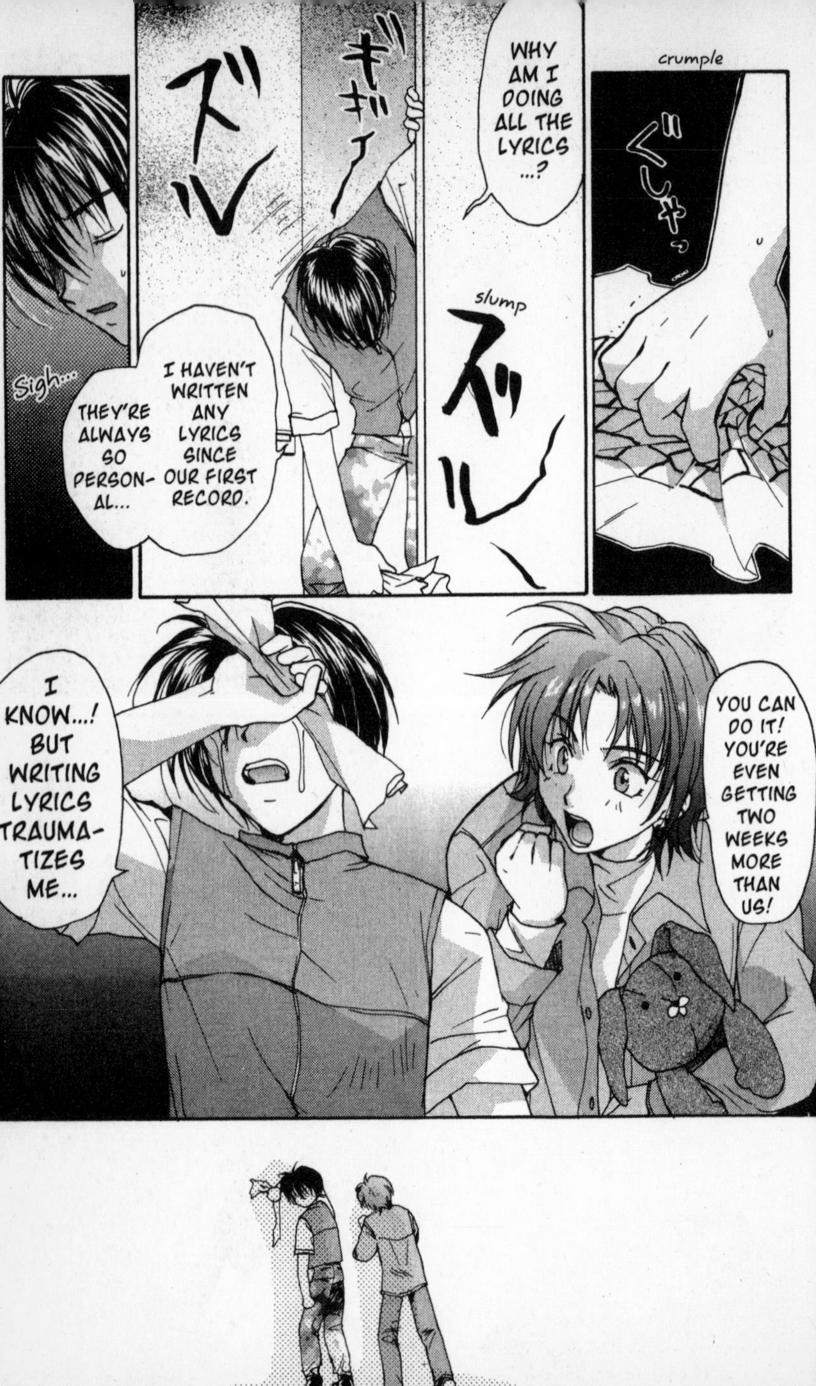
crumple
ぐしゃっ
WHY AM I DOING ALL THE LYRICS ...?
slump
ズッル
ギィ
ズル
I HAVEN'T WRITTEN ANY LYRICS SINCE OUR FIRST RECORD.
THEY'RE ALWAYS SO PERSON-AL...
Sigh...
YOU CAN DO IT! YOU'RE EVEN GETTING TWO WEEKS MORE THAN US!
I KNOW...! BUT WRITING LYRICS TRAUMA-TIZES ME...

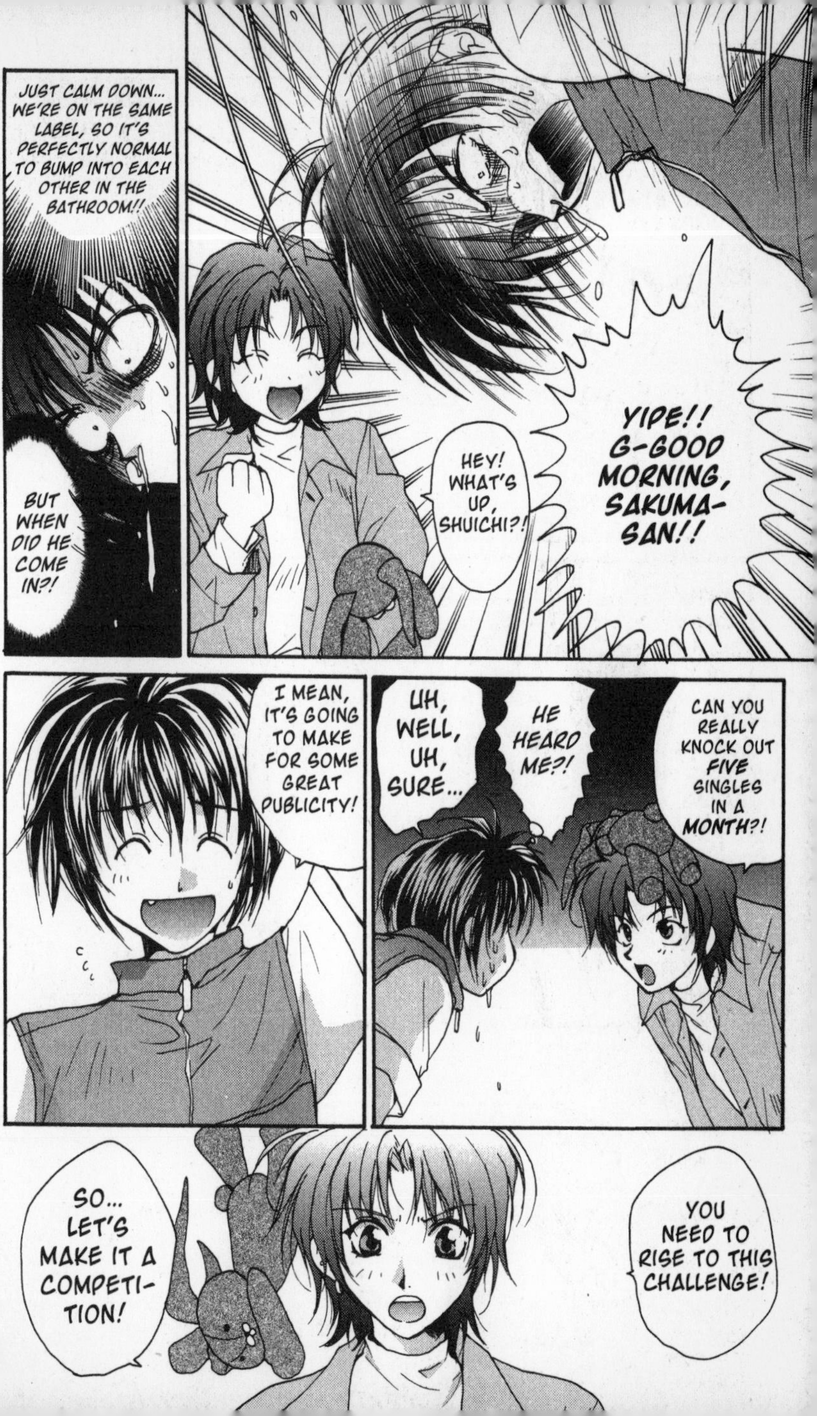
YIPE!! G-GOOD MORNING, SAKUMA-SAN!!
HEY! WHAT'S UP, SHUICHI?!
JUST CALM DOWN... WE'RE ON THE SAME LABEL, SO IT'S PERFECTLY NORMAL TO BUMP INTO EACH OTHER IN THE BATHROOM!!
BUT WHEN DID HE COME IN?!
CAN YOU REALLY KNOCK OUT FIVE SINGLES IN A MONTH?!
HE HEARD ME?!
UH, WELL, UH, SURE...
I MEAN, IT'S GOING TO MAKE FOR SOME GREAT PUBLICITY!
YOU NEED TO RISE TO THIS CHALLENGE!
SO... LET'S MAKE IT A COMPETITION!

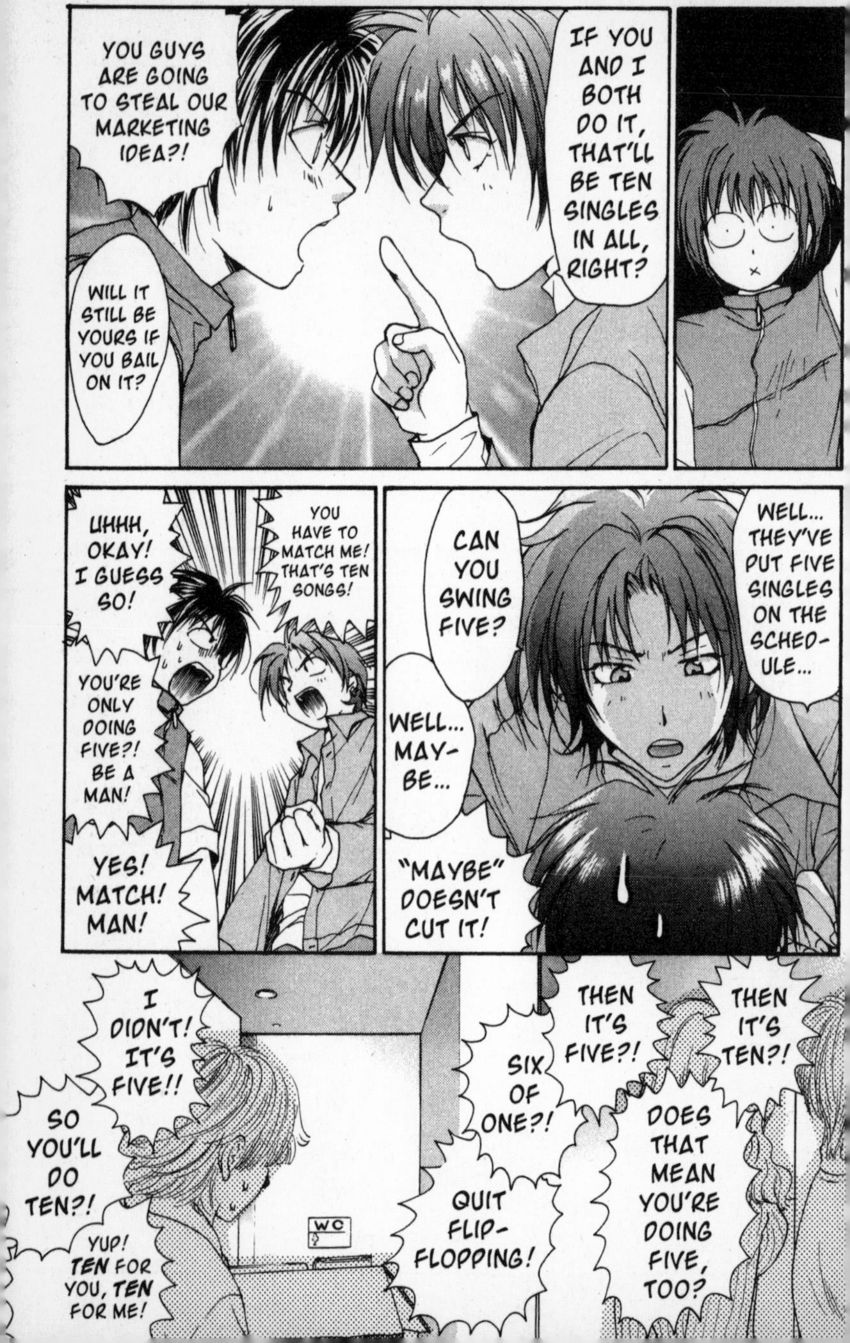
IF YOU AND I BOTH DO IT, THAT'LL BE TEN SINGLES IN ALL, RIGHT?
YOU GUYS ARE GOING TO STEAL OUR MARKETING IDEA?!
WILL IT STILL BE YOURS IF YOU BAIL ON IT?
WELL... THEY'VE PUT FIVE SINGLES ON THE SCHED-ULE...
CAN YOU SWING FIVE?
WELL... MAY-BE...
"MAYBE" DOESN'T CUT IT!
YOU HAVE TO MATCH ME! THAT'S TEN SONGS!
UHHH, OKAY! I GUESS SO!
YOU'RE ONLY DOING FIVE?! BE A MAN!
YES! MATCH! MAN!
THEN IT'S TEN?!
THEN IT'S FIVE?!
SIX OF ONE?!
DOES THAT MEAN YOU'RE DOING FIVE, TOO?
QUIT FLIP-FLOPPING!
I DIDN'T! IT'S FIVE!!
SO YOU'LL DO TEN?!
YUP! **TEN** FOR YOU, **TEN** FOR ME!
WC

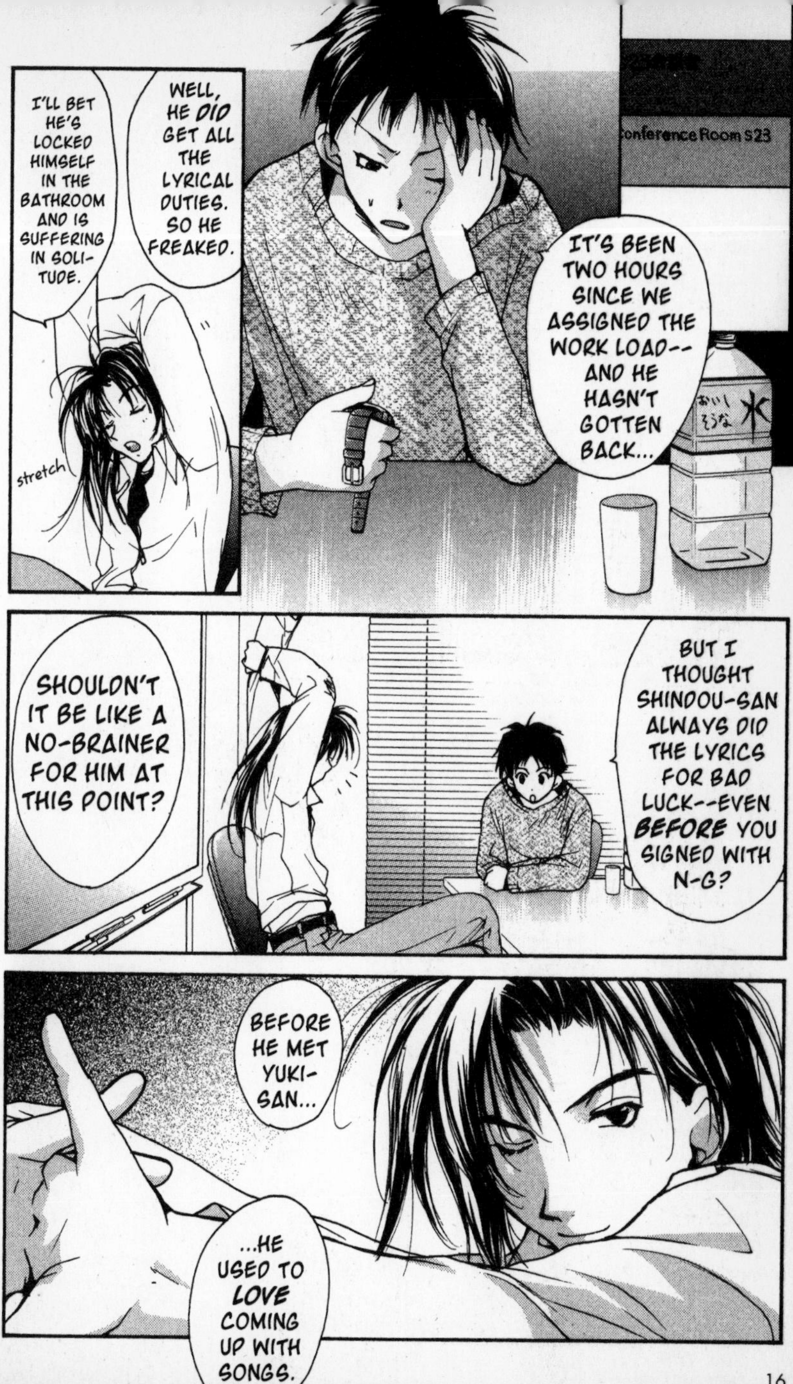
Conference Room S23
IT'S BEEN TWO HOURS SINCE WE ASSIGNED THE WORK LOAD-- AND HE HASN'T GOTTEN BACK...
おいしそうな 水
WELL, HE *DID* GET ALL THE LYRICAL DUTIES. SO HE FREAKED.
I'LL BET HE'S LOCKED HIMSELF IN THE BATHROOM AND IS SUFFERING IN SOLI- TUDE.
stretch
BUT I THOUGHT SHINDOU-SAN ALWAYS DID THE LYRICS FOR BAD LUCK--EVEN ***BEFORE*** YOU SIGNED WITH N-G?
SHOULDN'T IT BE LIKE A NO-BRAINER FOR HIM AT THIS POINT?
BEFORE HE MET YUKI- SAN...
...HE USED TO ***LOVE*** COMING UP WITH SONGS.

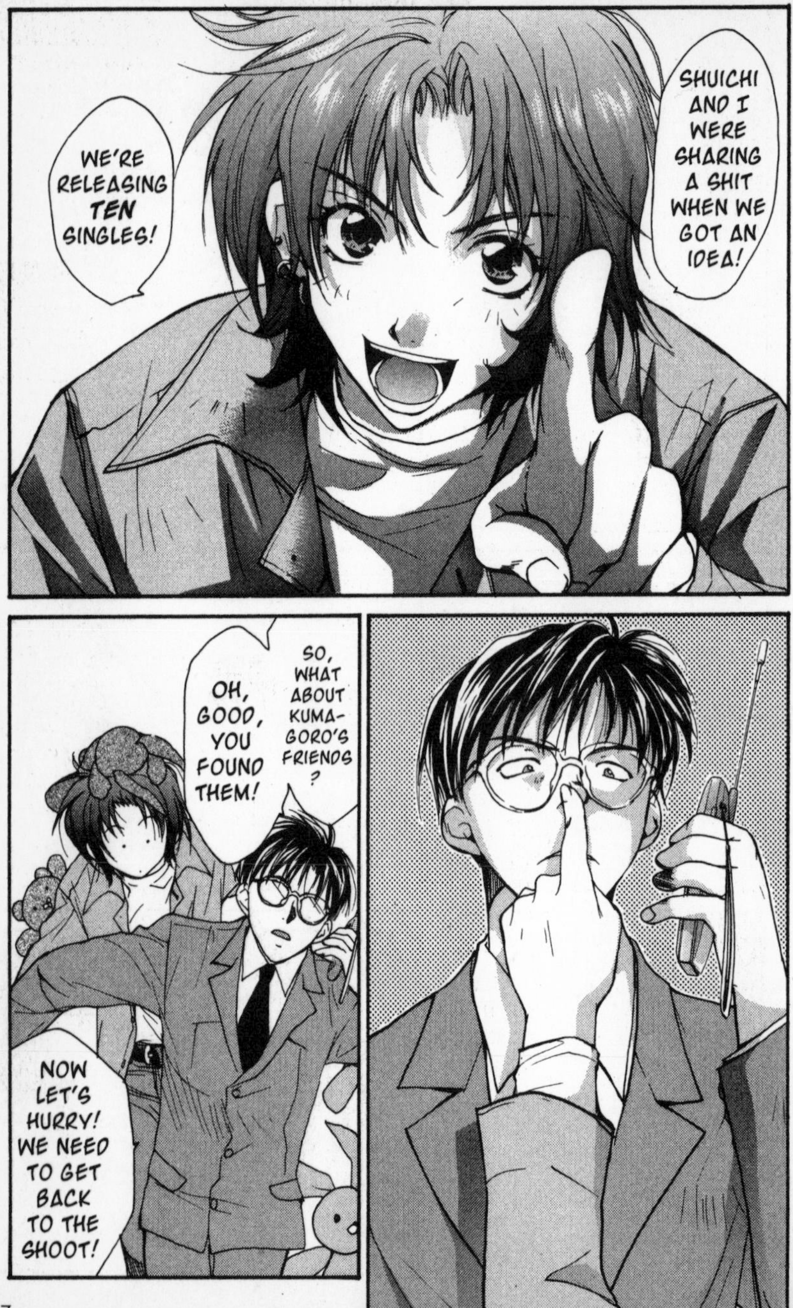
SHUICHI AND I WERE SHARING A SHIT WHEN WE GOT AN IDEA!
WE'RE RELEASING *TEN* SINGLES!
SO, WHAT ABOUT KUMA-GORO'S FRIENDS?
OH, GOOD, YOU FOUND THEM!
NOW LET'S HURRY! WE NEED TO GET BACK TO THE SHOOT!

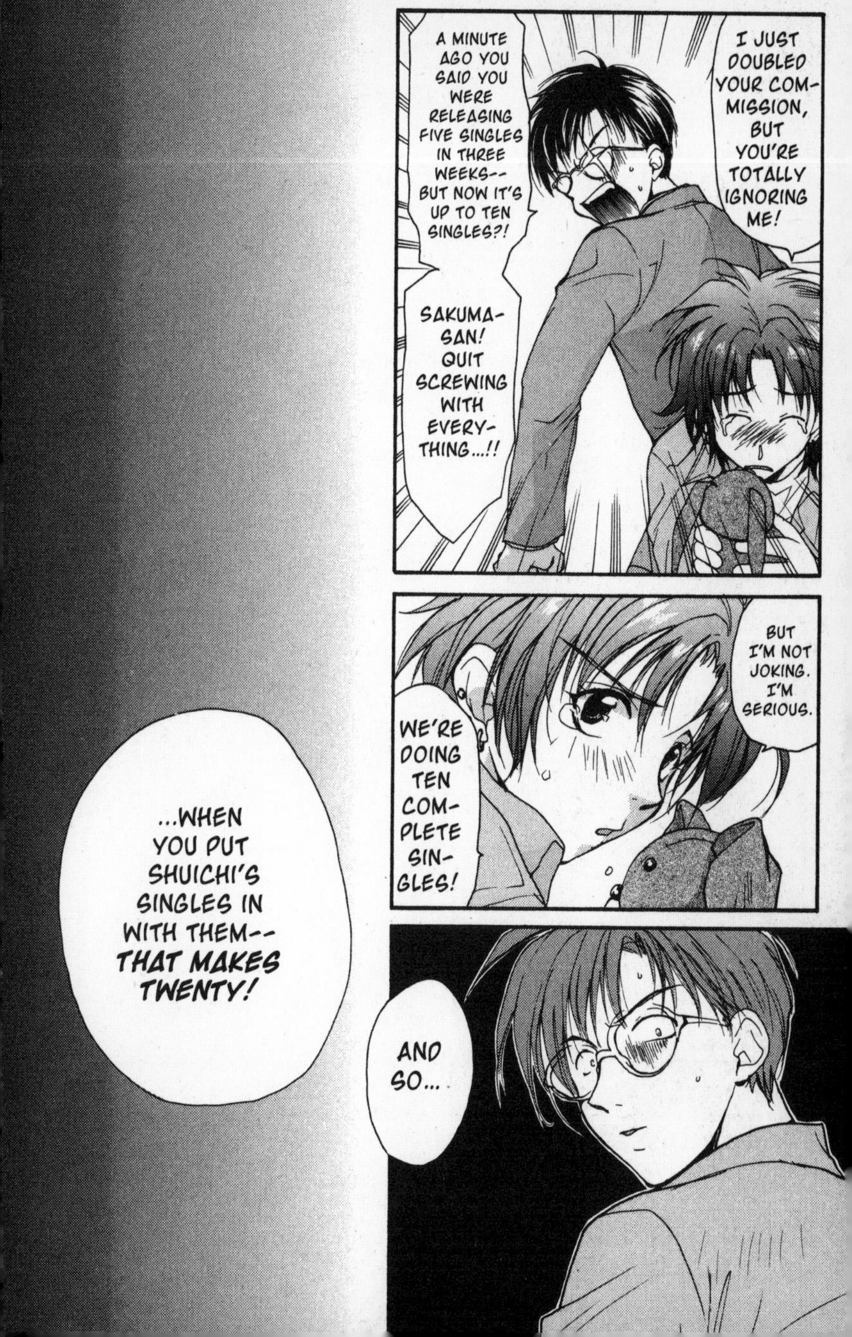
I JUST DOUBLED YOUR COM-MISSION, BUT YOU'RE TOTALLY IGNORING ME!
A MINUTE AGO YOU SAID YOU WERE RELEASING FIVE SINGLES IN THREE WEEKS--BUT NOW IT'S UP TO TEN SINGLES?!
SAKUMA-SAN! QUIT SCREWING WITH EVERY-THING...!!
BUT I'M NOT JOKING. I'M SERIOUS.
WE'RE DOING TEN COM-PLETE SIN-GLES!
AND SO...
...WHEN YOU PUT SHUICHI'S SINGLES IN WITH THEM--
THAT MAKES TWENTY!

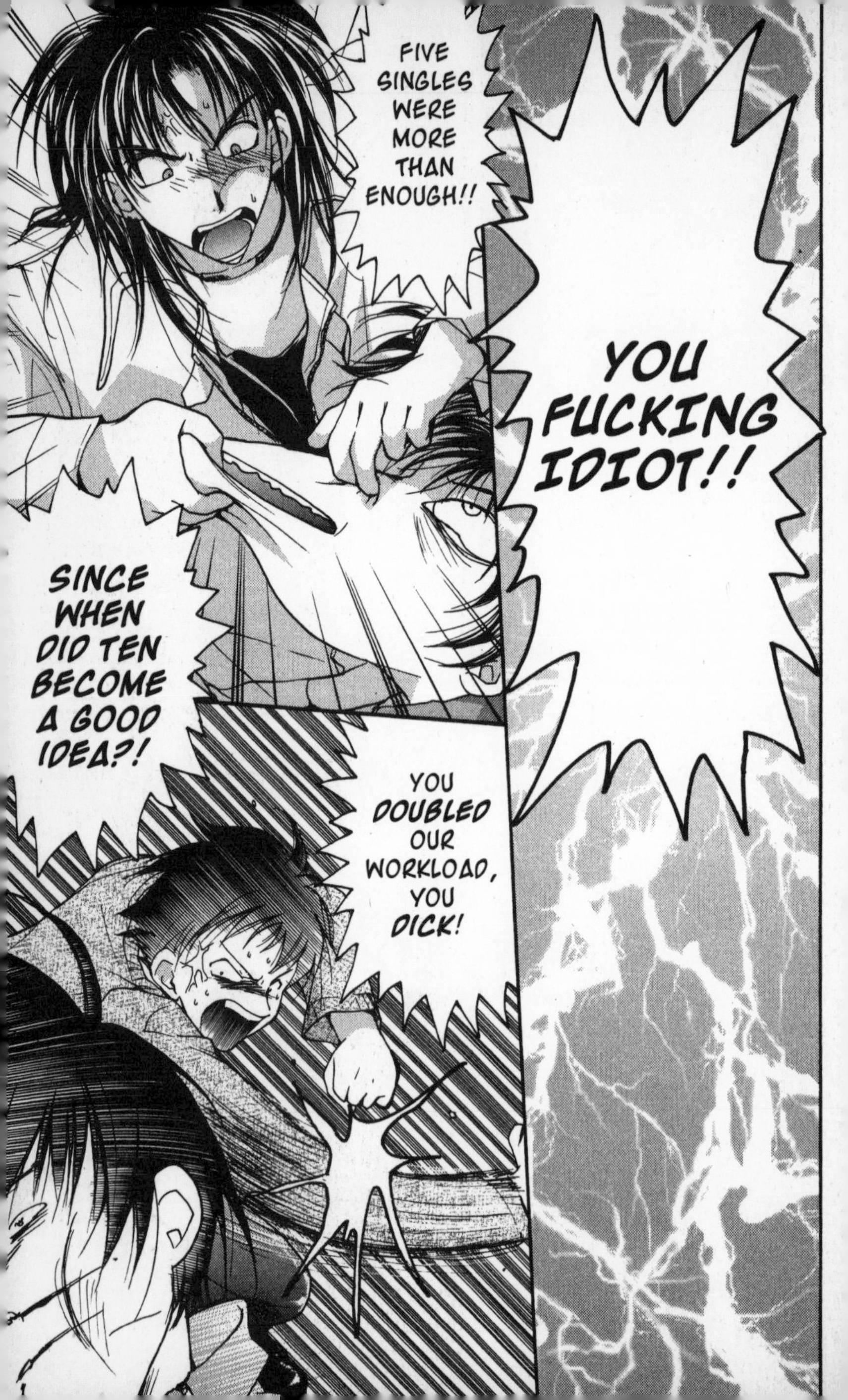

YOU FUCKING IDIOT!!
FIVE SINGLES WERE MORE THAN ENOUGH!!
SINCE WHEN DID TEN BECOME A GOOD IDEA?!
YOU DOUBLED OUR WORKLOAD, YOU DICK!

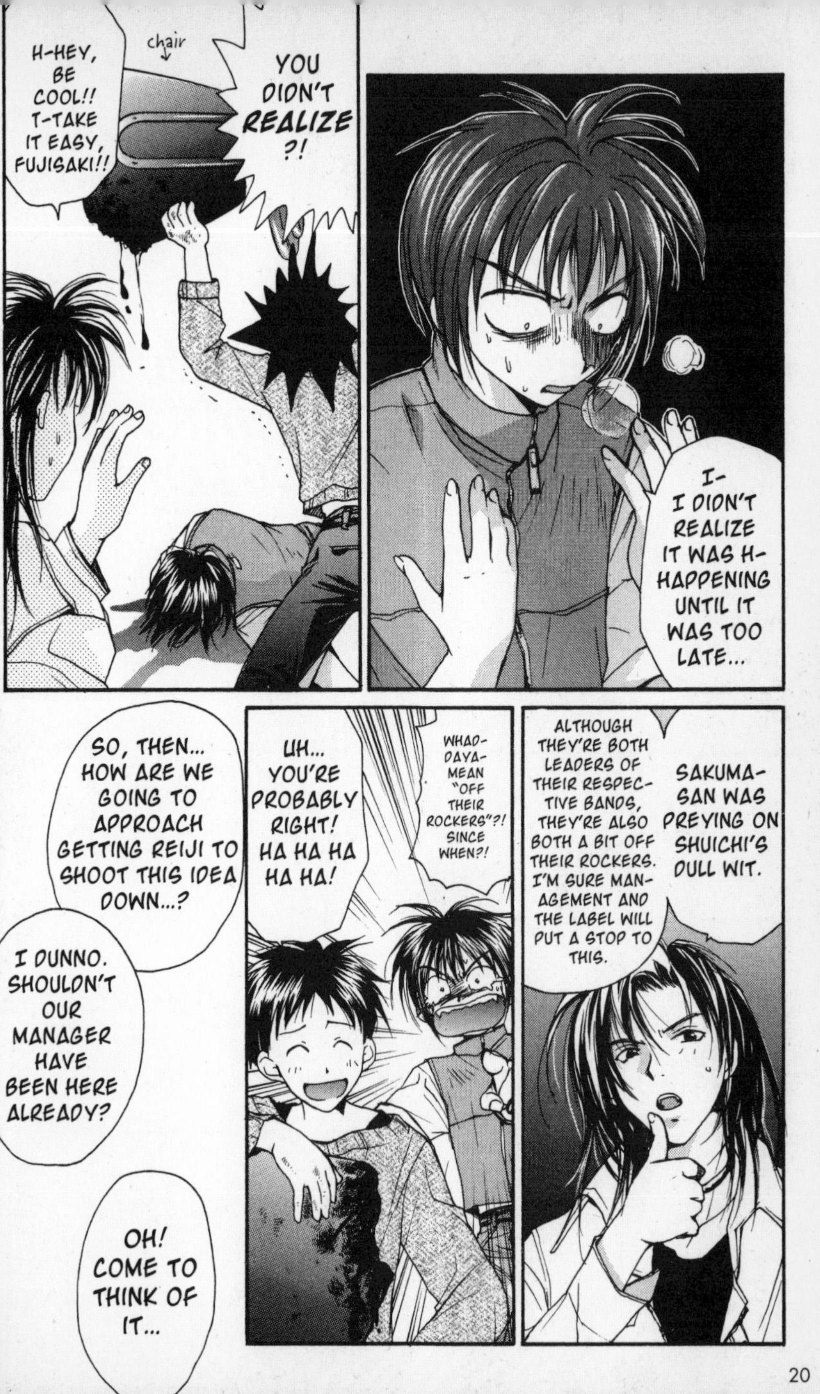

I- I DIDN'T REALIZE IT WAS H-HAPPENING UNTIL IT WAS TOO LATE...
YOU DIDN'T REALIZE?!
chair
H-HEY, BE COOL!! T-TAKE IT EASY, FUJISAKI!!
SAKUMA-SAN WAS PREYING ON SHUICHI'S DULL WIT.
ALTHOUGH THEY'RE BOTH LEADERS OF THEIR RESPECTIVE BANDS, THEY'RE ALSO BOTH A BIT OFF THEIR ROCKERS. I'M SURE MANAGEMENT AND THE LABEL WILL PUT A STOP TO THIS.
WHADDAYAMEAN "OFF THEIR ROCKERS"?! SINCE WHEN?!
UH... YOU'RE PROBABLY RIGHT! HA HA HA HA HA!
SO, THEN... HOW ARE WE GOING TO APPROACH GETTING REIJI TO SHOOT THIS IDEA DOWN...?
I DUNNO. SHOULDN'T OUR MANAGER HAVE BEEN HERE ALREADY?
OH! COME TO THINK OF IT...

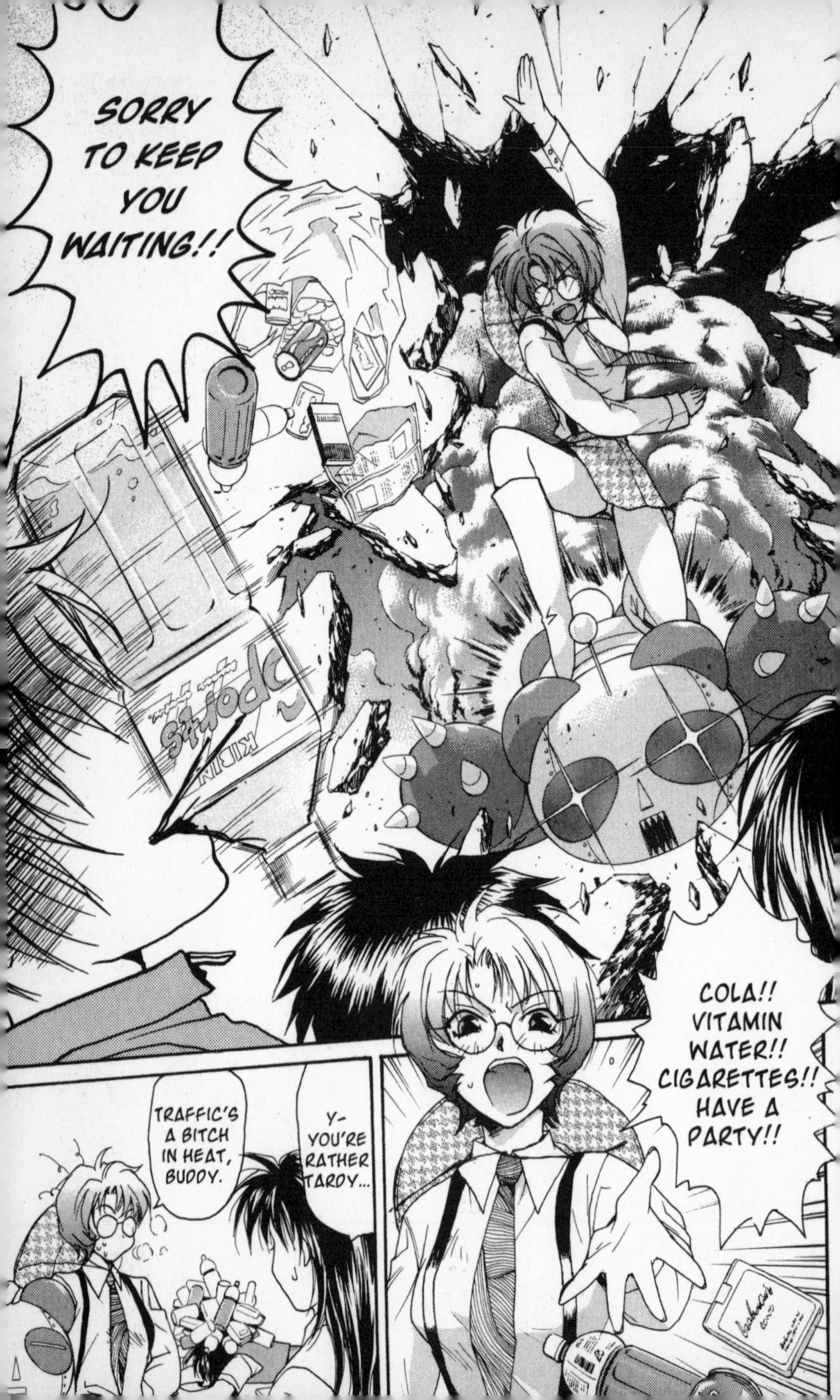
SORRY TO KEEP YOU WAITING!!
COLA!! VITAMIN WATER!! CIGARETTES!! HAVE A PARTY!!
Y- YOU'RE RATHER TARDY...
TRAFFIC'S A BITCH IN HEAT, BUDDY.

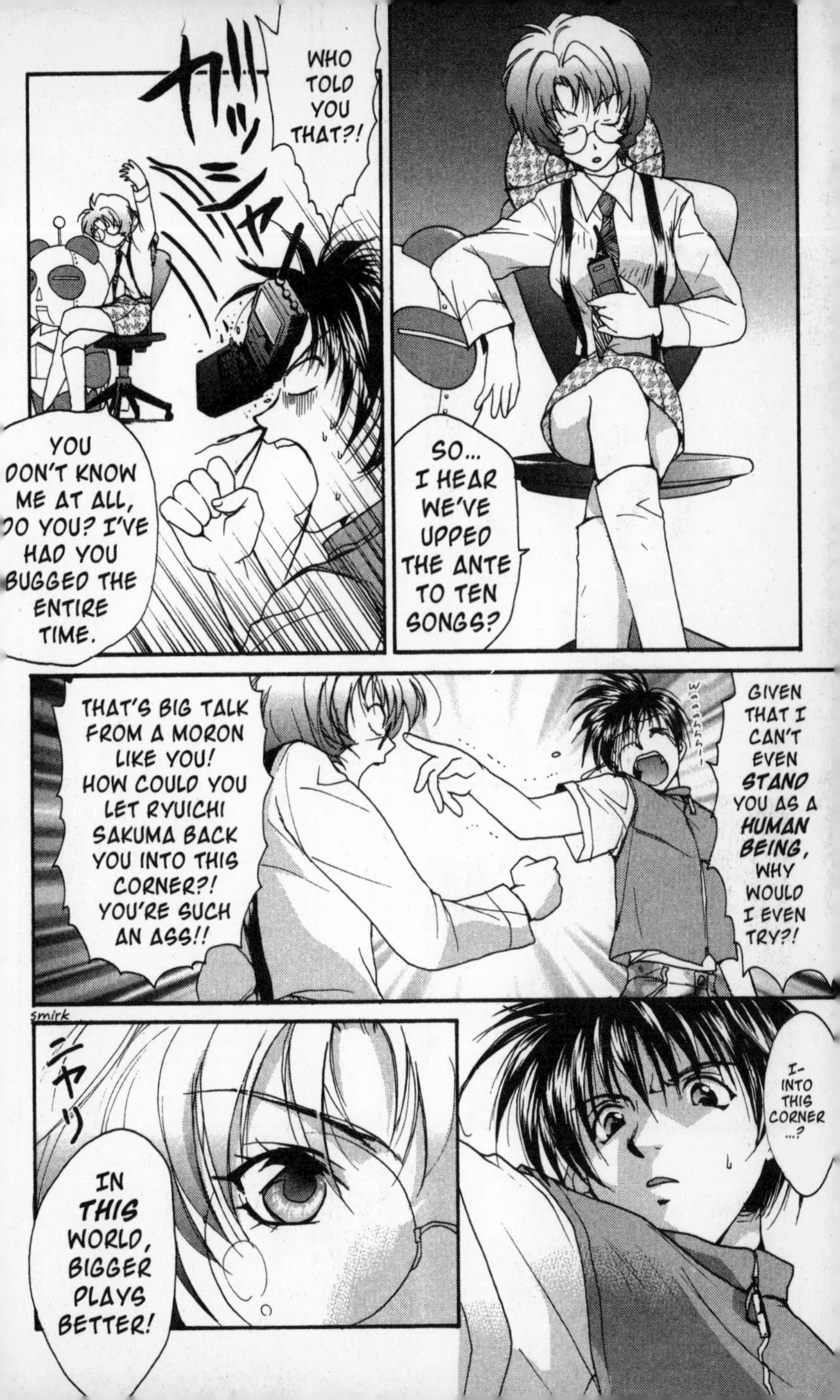
SO... I HEAR WE'VE UPPED THE ANTE TO TEN SONGS?
WHO TOLD YOU THAT?!
YOU DON'T KNOW ME AT ALL, DO YOU? I'VE HAD YOU BUGGED THE ENTIRE TIME.
GIVEN THAT I CAN'T EVEN **STAND** YOU AS A **HUMAN BEING**, WHY WOULD I EVEN TRY?!
THAT'S BIG TALK FROM A MORON LIKE YOU! HOW COULD YOU LET RYUICHI SAKUMA BACK YOU INTO THIS CORNER?! YOU'RE SUCH AN ASS!!
I- INTO THIS CORNER ...?
smirk
ニヤリ
IN **THIS** WORLD, BIGGER PLAYS BETTER!

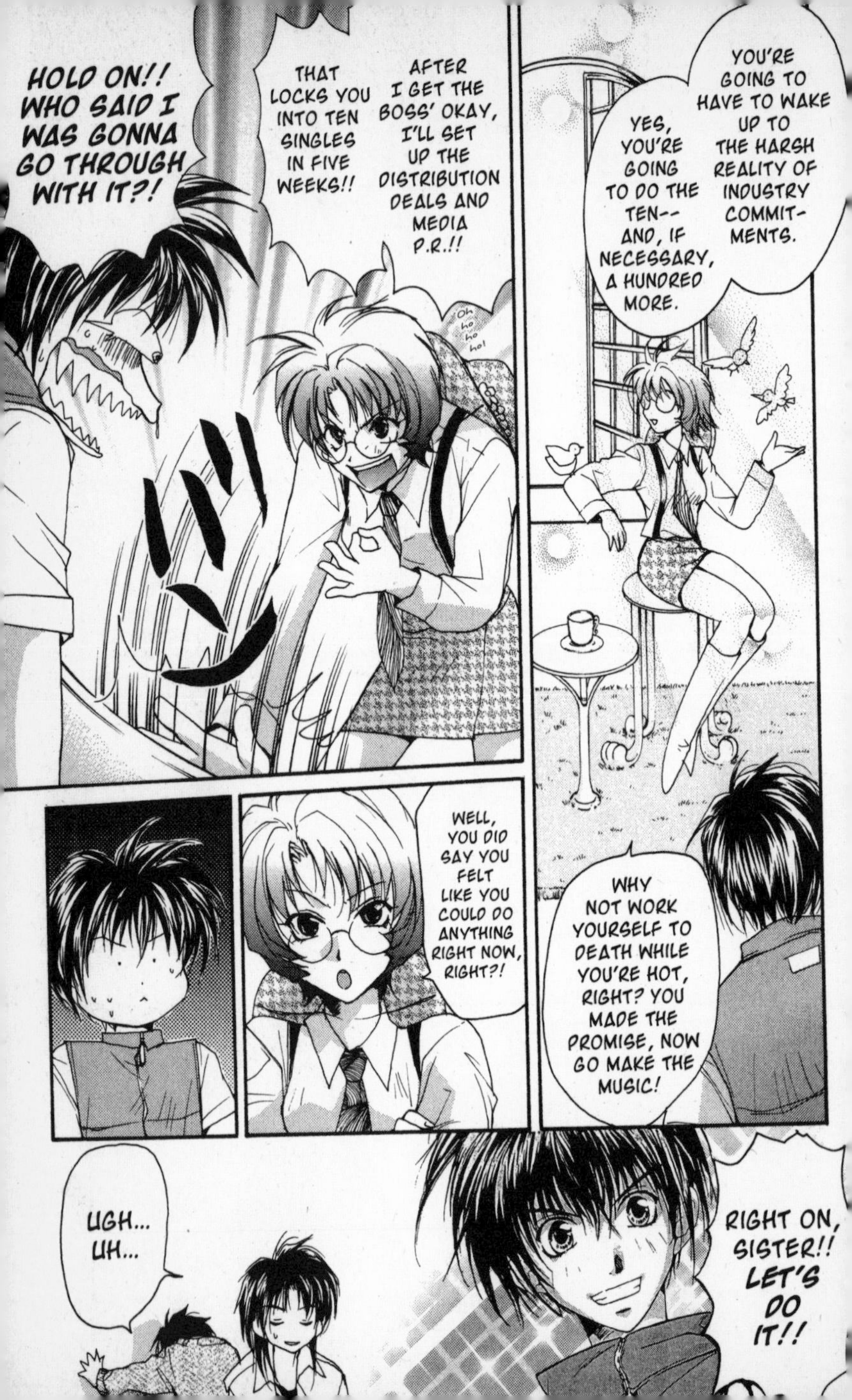
YOU'RE GOING TO HAVE TO WAKE UP TO THE HARSH REALITY OF INDUSTRY COMMIT-MENTS.
YES, YOU'RE GOING TO DO THE TEN-- AND, IF NECESSARY, A HUNDRED MORE.
WHY NOT WORK YOURSELF TO DEATH WHILE YOU'RE HOT, RIGHT? YOU MADE THE PROMISE, NOW GO MAKE THE MUSIC!
AFTER I GET THE BOSS' OKAY, I'LL SET UP THE DISTRIBUTION DEALS AND MEDIA P.R.!!
THAT LOCKS YOU INTO TEN SINGLES IN FIVE WEEKS!!
Oh ho ho ho!
HOLD ON!! WHO SAID I WAS GONNA GO THROUGH WITH IT?!
WELL, YOU DID SAY YOU FELT LIKE YOU COULD DO ANYTHING RIGHT NOW, RIGHT?!
RIGHT ON, SISTER!! LET'S DO IT!!
UGH... UH...

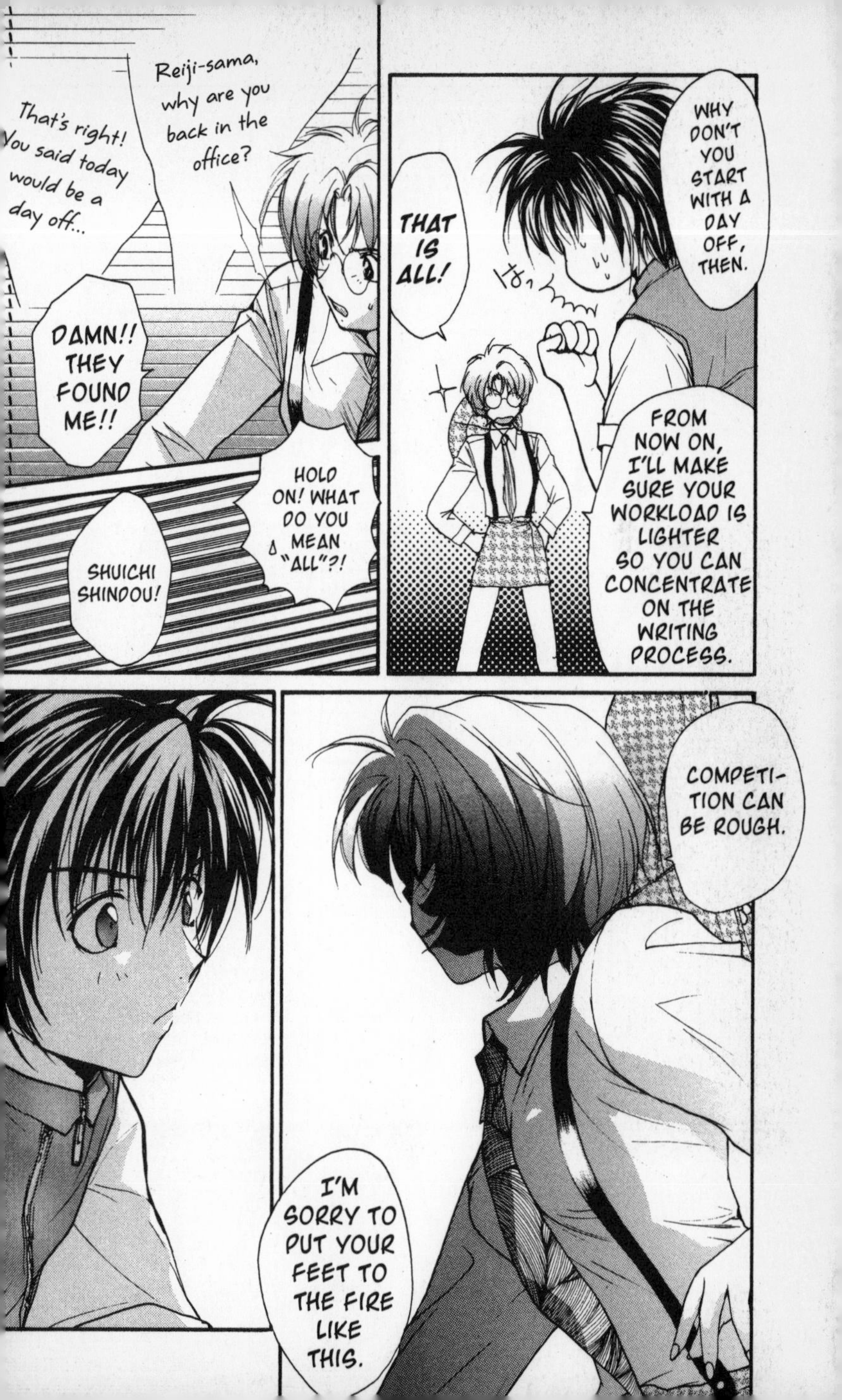
WHY DON'T YOU START WITH A DAY OFF, THEN.
THAT IS ALL!
はっ
FROM NOW ON, I'LL MAKE SURE YOUR WORKLOAD IS LIGHTER SO YOU CAN CONCENTRATE ON THE WRITING PROCESS.
Reiji-sama, why are you back in the office?
That's right! You said today would be a day off...
DAMN!! THEY FOUND ME!!
HOLD ON! WHAT DO YOU MEAN "ALL"?!
SHUICHI SHINDOU!
COMPETITION CAN BE ROUGH.
I'M SORRY TO PUT YOUR FEET TO THE FIRE LIKE THIS.

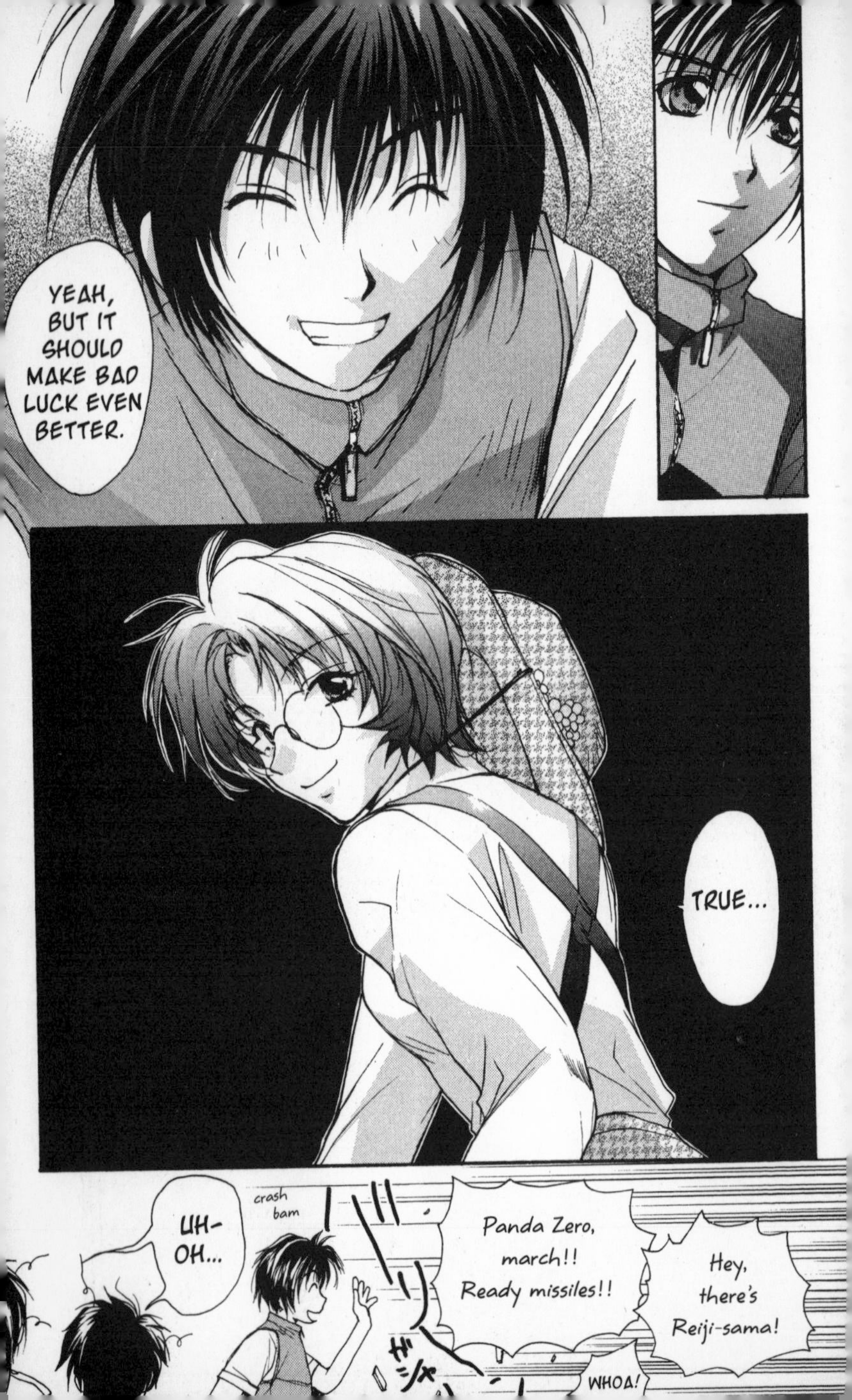
YEAH, BUT IT SHOULD MAKE BAD LUCK EVEN BETTER.
TRUE...
Hey, there's Reiji-sama!
Panda Zero, march!! Ready missiles!!
WHOA!
ガシャ
crash bam
UH-OH...

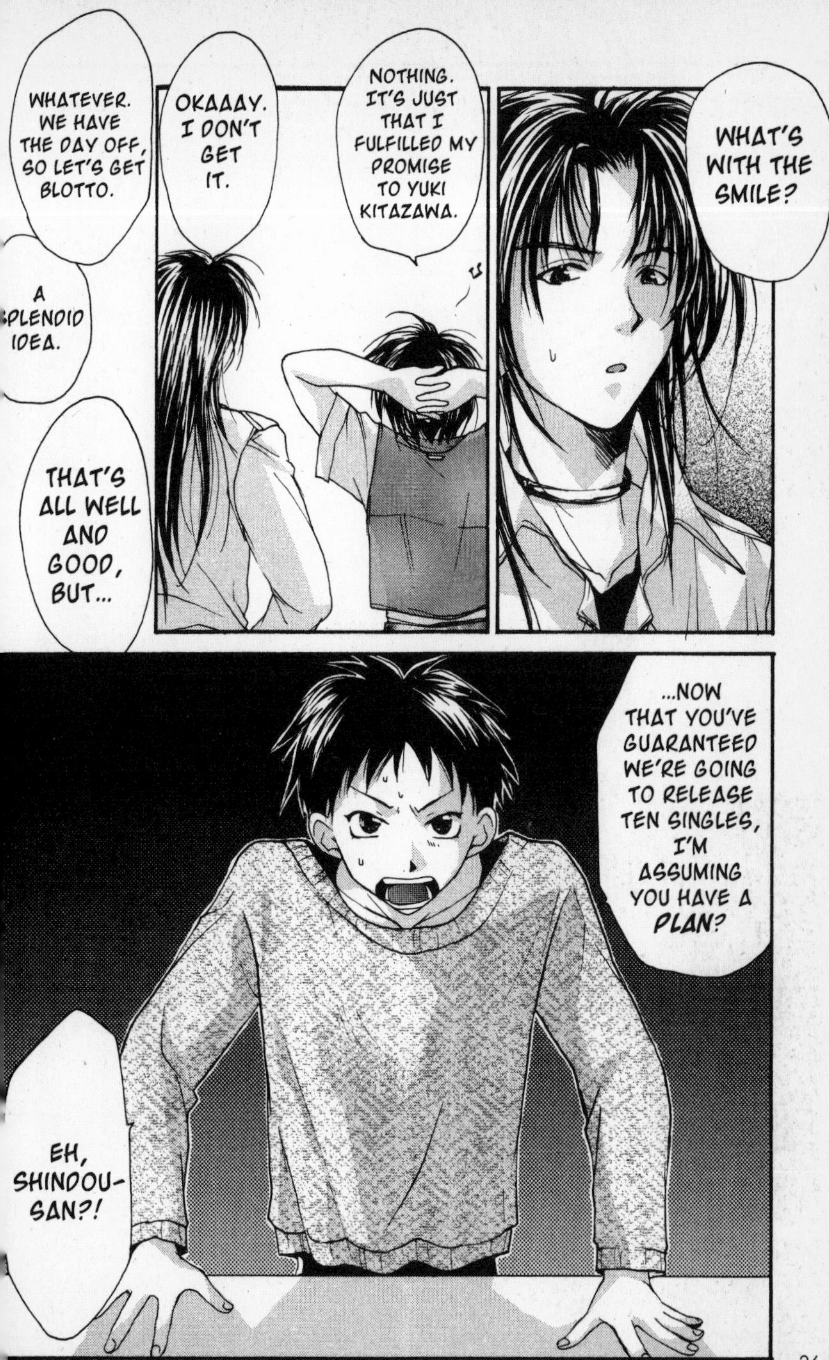
WHAT'S WITH THE SMILE?
NOTHING. IT'S JUST THAT I FULFILLED MY PROMISE TO YUKI KITAZAWA.
OKAAAY. I DON'T GET IT.
WHATEVER. WE HAVE THE DAY OFF, SO LET'S GET BLOTTO.
A SPLENDID IDEA.
THAT'S ALL WELL AND GOOD, BUT...
...NOW THAT YOU'VE GUARANTEED WE'RE GOING TO RELEASE TEN SINGLES, I'M ASSUMING YOU HAVE A *PLAN*?
EH, SHINDOU-SAN?!

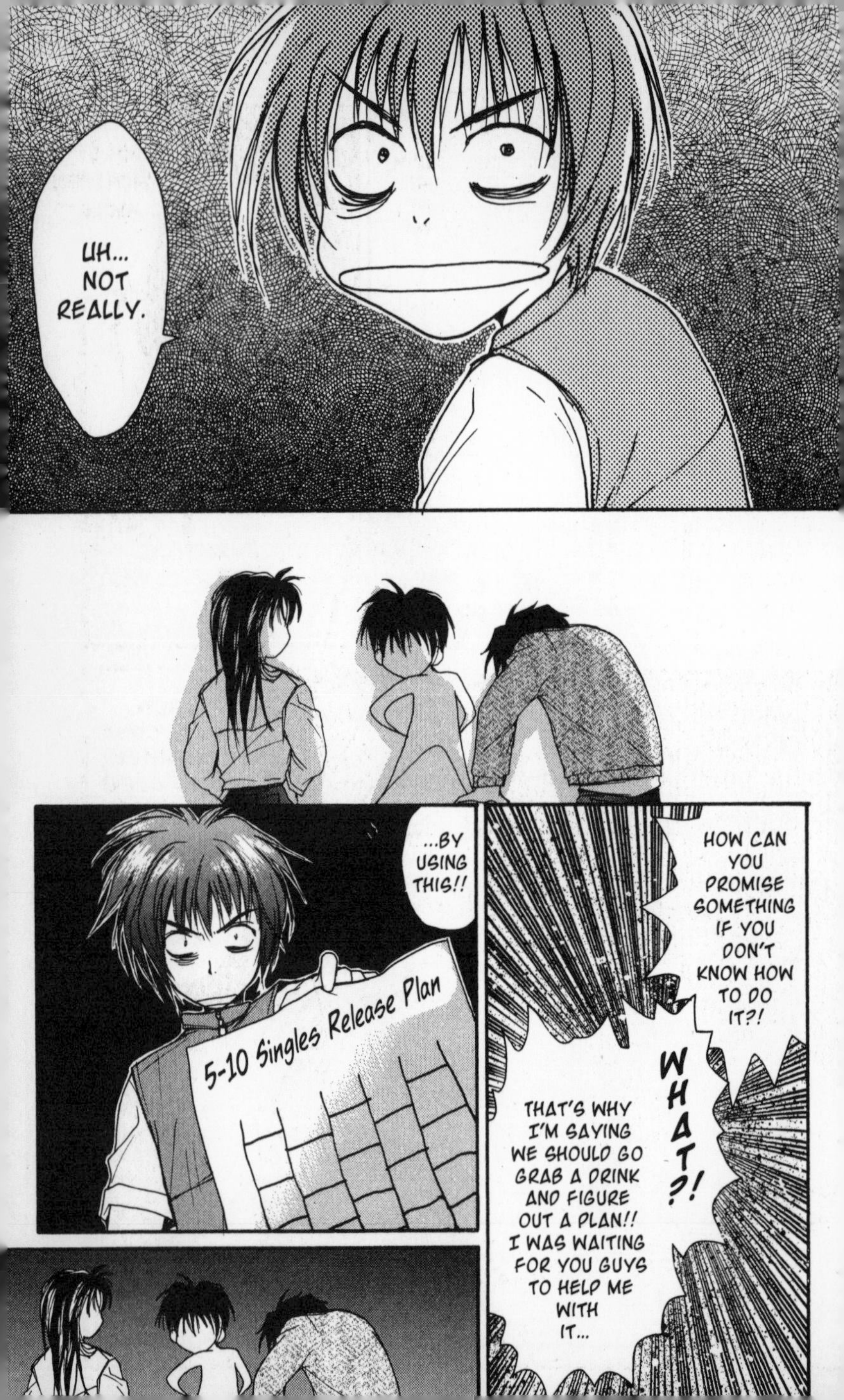
UH... NOT REALLY.
HOW CAN YOU PROMISE SOMETHING IF YOU DON'T KNOW HOW TO DO IT?!
WHAT?!
THAT'S WHY I'M SAYING WE SHOULD GO GRAB A DRINK AND FIGURE OUT A PLAN!! I WAS WAITING FOR YOU GUYS TO HELP ME WITH IT...
...BY USING THIS!!
5-10 Singles Release Plan

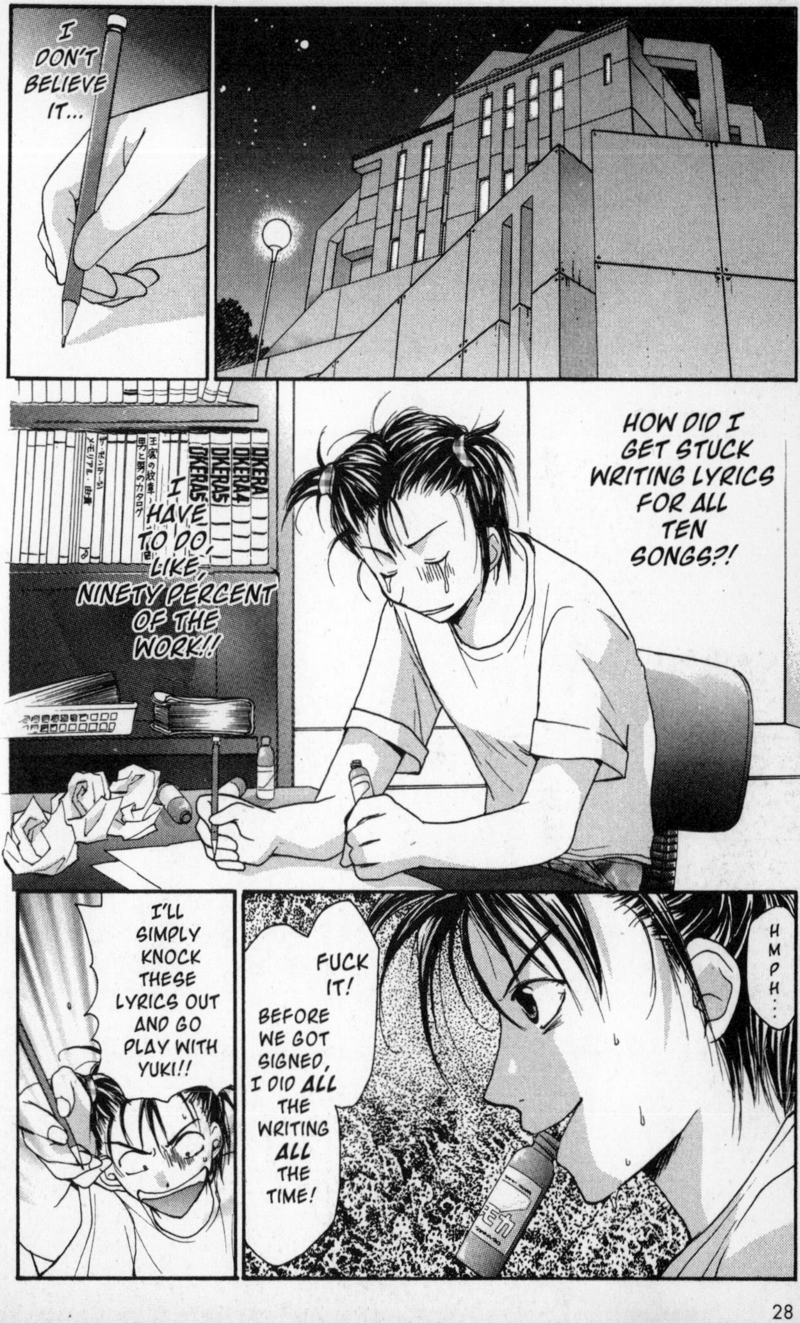
I DON'T BELIEVE IT...
HOW DID I GET STUCK WRITING LYRICS FOR ALL TEN SONGS?!
I HAVE TO DO, LIKE, NINETY PERCENT OF THE WORK!!
HMPH...
FUCK IT!
BEFORE WE GOT SIGNED, I DID **ALL** THE WRITING **ALL** THE TIME!
I'LL SIMPLY KNOCK THESE LYRICS OUT AND GO PLAY WITH YUKI!!

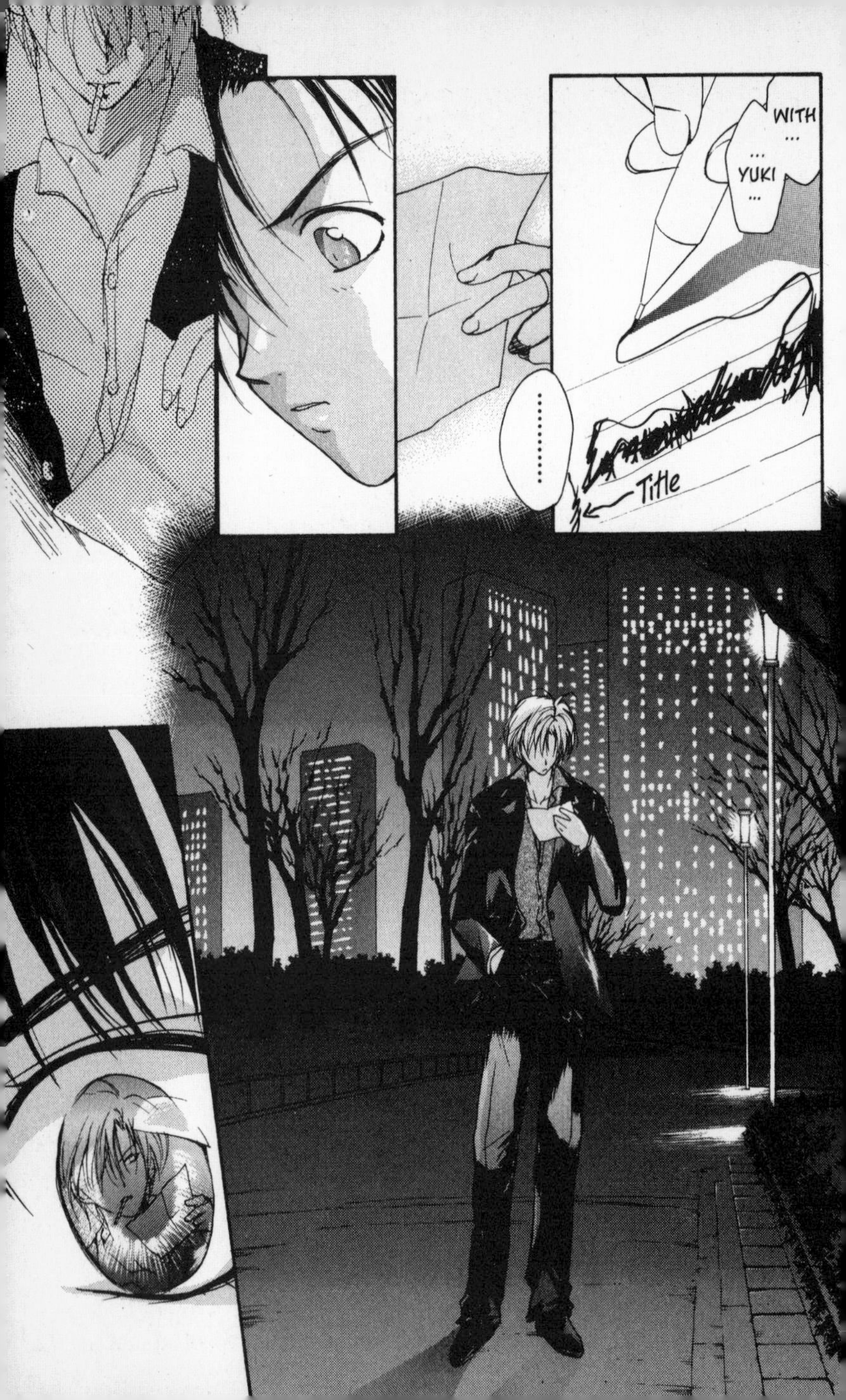
WITH ...
... YUKI ...
....
Title

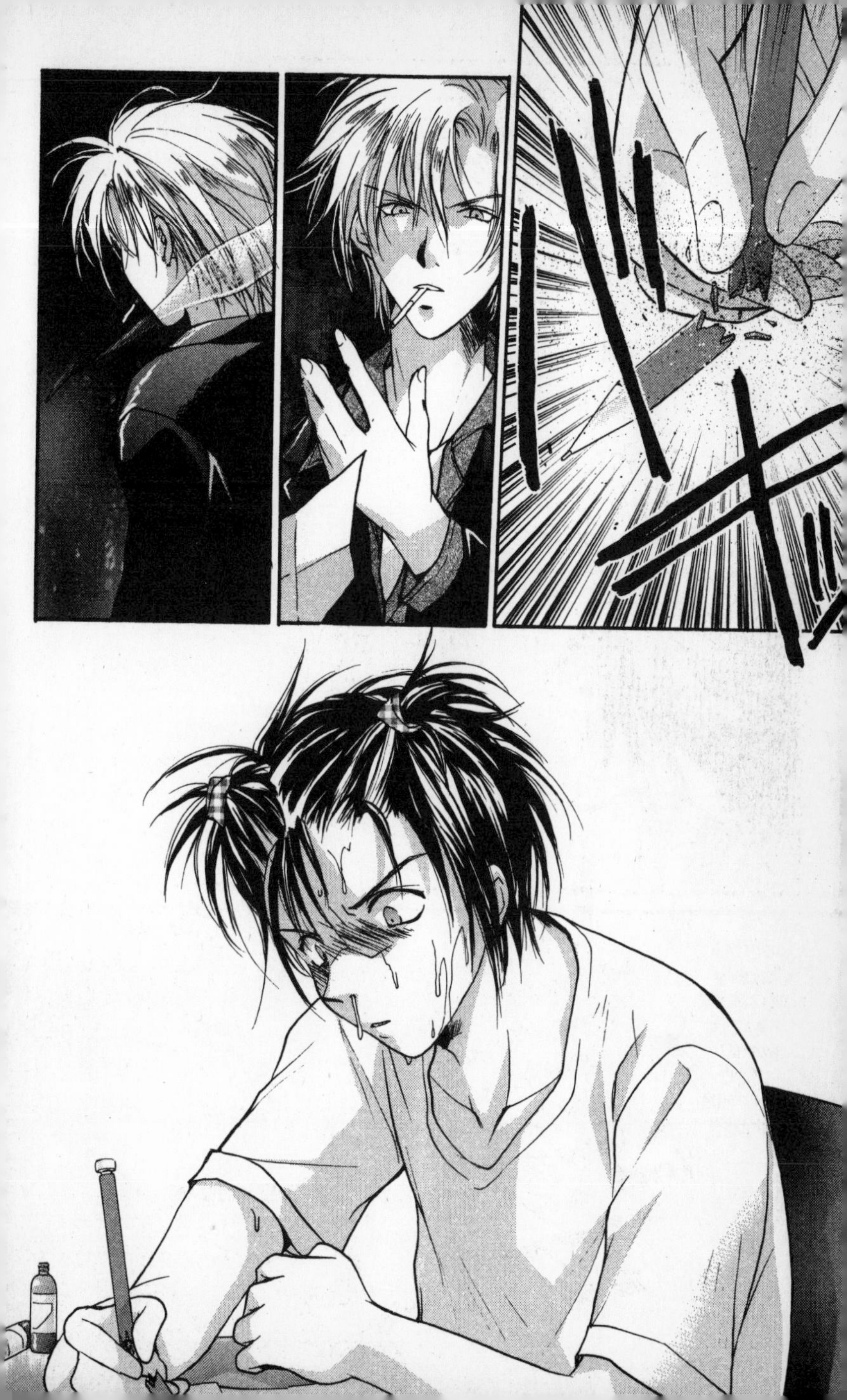

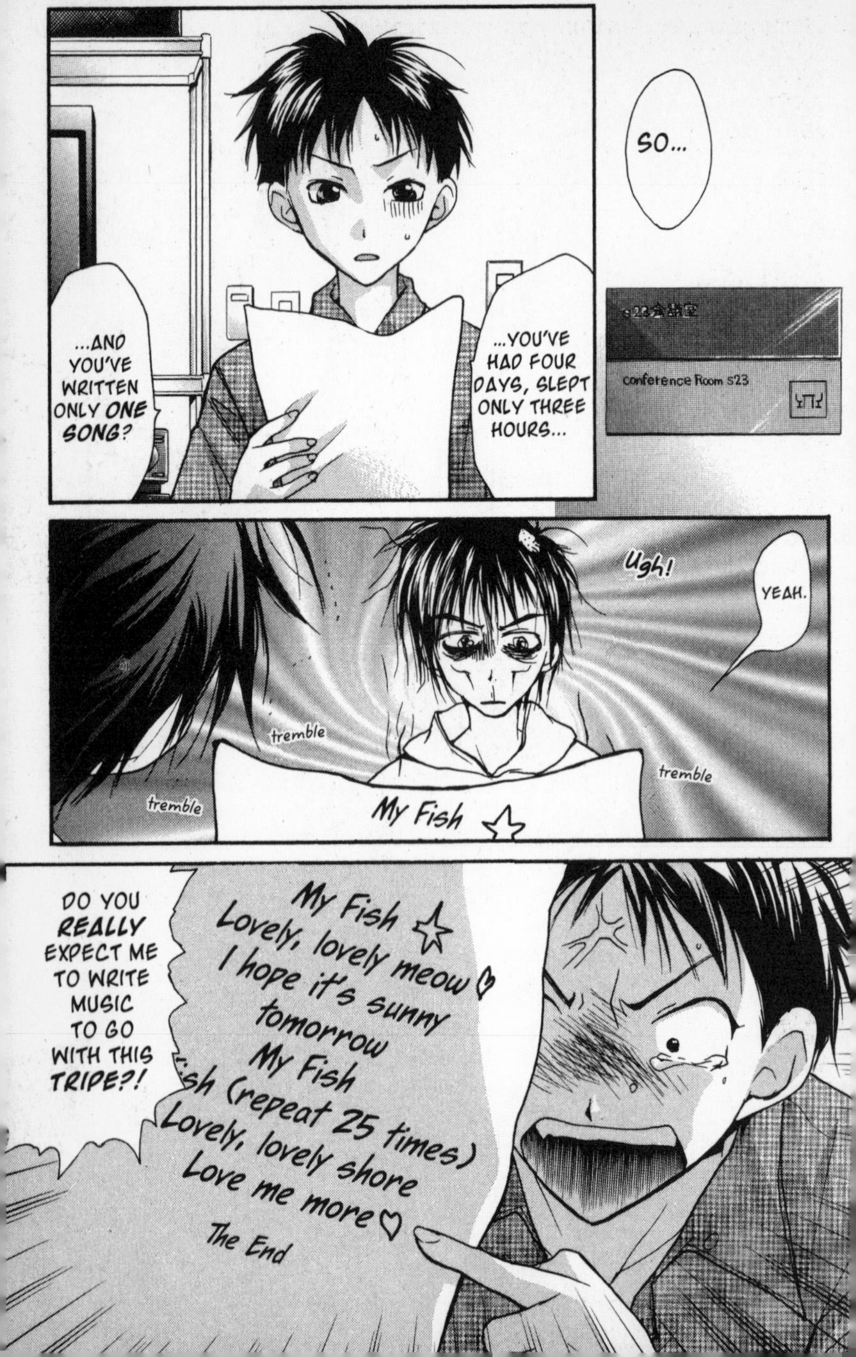
SO...
conference Room s23
...YOU'VE HAD FOUR DAYS, SLEPT ONLY THREE HOURS...
...AND YOU'VE WRITTEN ONLY ONE SONG?
YEAH.
Ugh!
tremble
tremble
tremble
My Fish
My Fish
Lovely, lovely meow
I hope it's sunny tomorrow
My Fish
Fish (repeat 25 times)
Lovely, lovely shore
Love me more
The End
DO YOU REALLY EXPECT ME TO WRITE MUSIC TO GO WITH THIS TRIPE?!

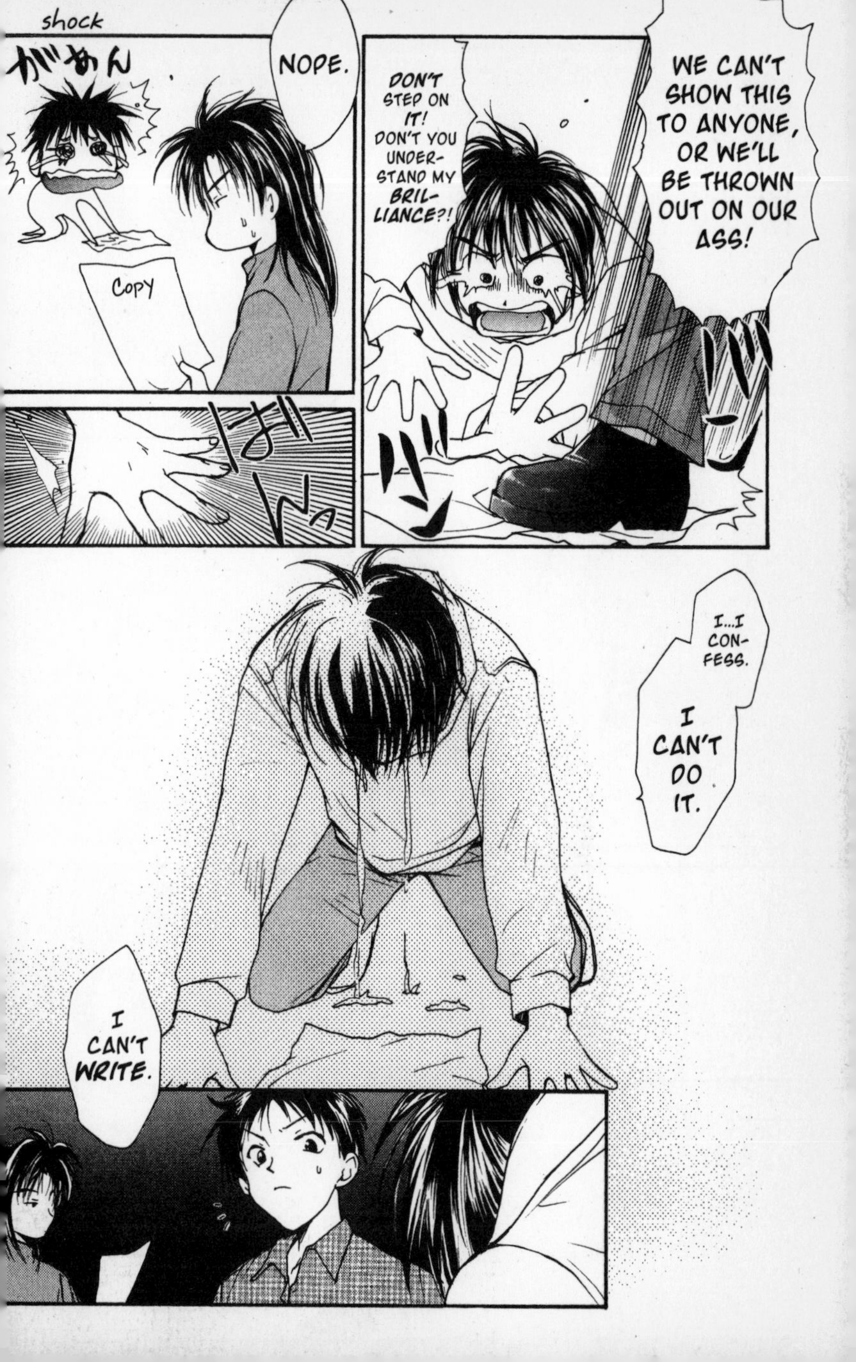
WE CAN'T SHOW THIS TO ANYONE, OR WE'LL BE THROWN OUT ON OUR ASS!
DON'T STEP ON IT! DON'T YOU UNDERSTAND MY BRILLIANCE?!
NOPE.
shock
Copy
I...I CONFESS.
I CAN'T DO IT.
I CAN'T WRITE.

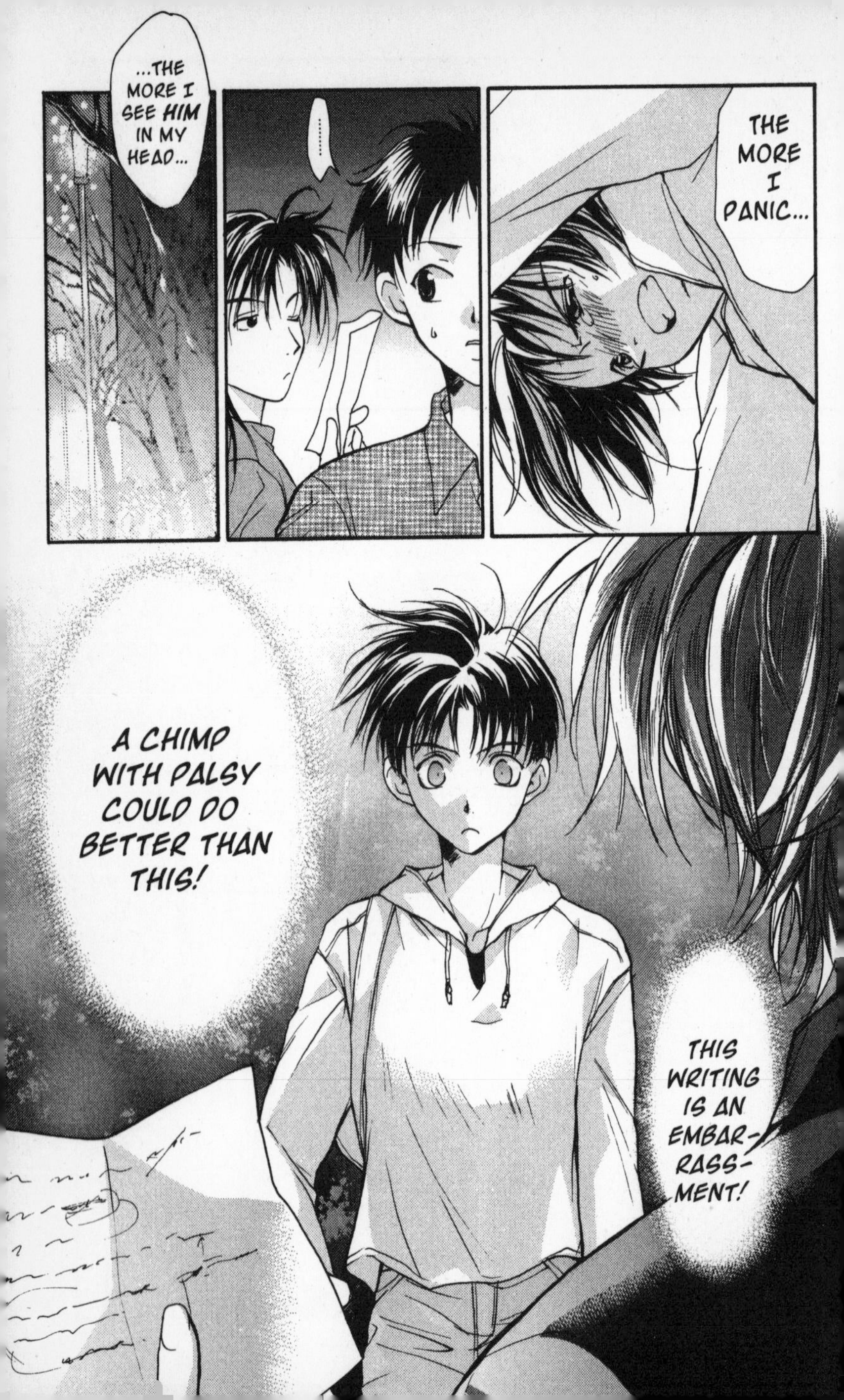
THE MORE I PANIC...
......
...THE MORE I SEE HIM IN MY HEAD...
THIS WRITING IS AN EMBARRASSMENT!
A CHIMP WITH PALSY COULD DO BETTER THAN THIS!

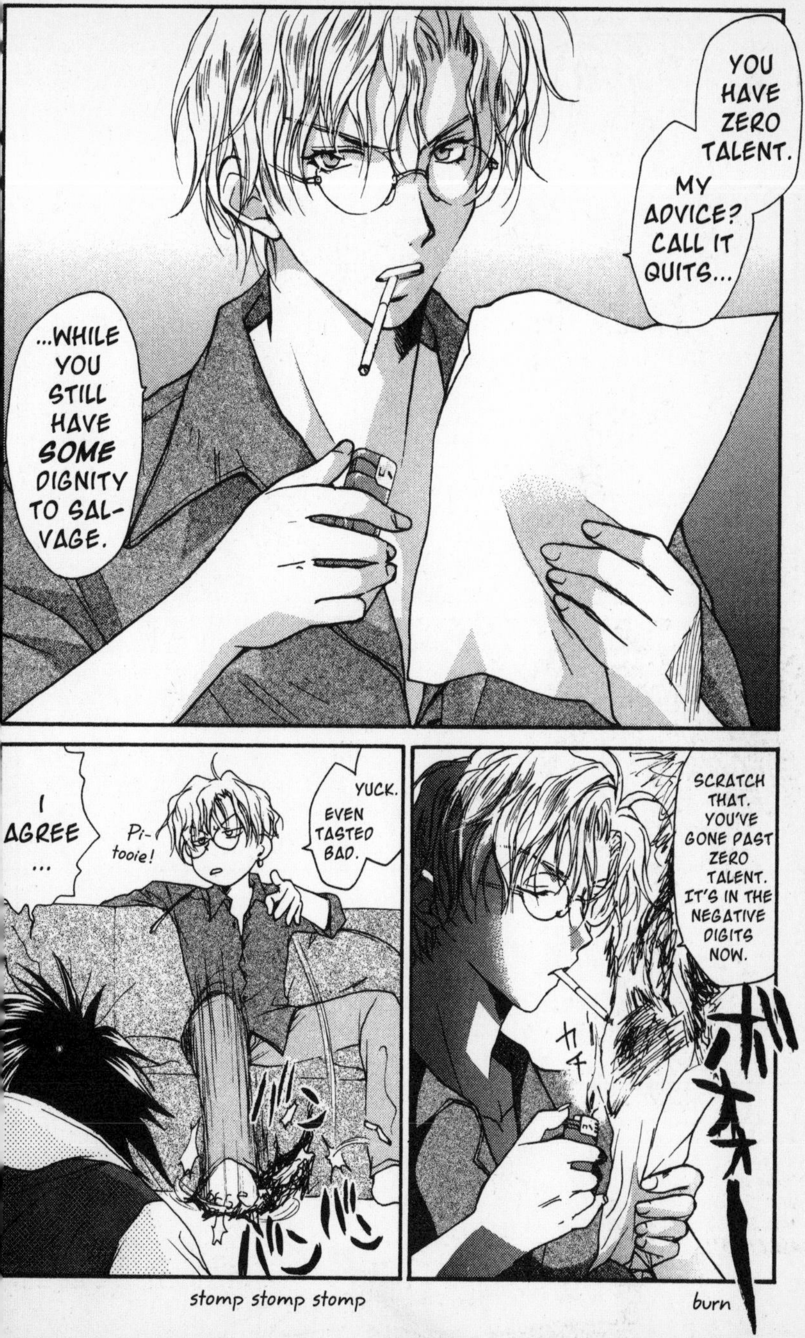
YOU HAVE ZERO TALENT.
MY ADVICE? CALL IT QUITS...
...WHILE YOU STILL HAVE SOME DIGNITY TO SAL-VAGE.
SCRATCH THAT. YOU'VE GONE PAST ZERO TALENT. IT'S IN THE NEGATIVE DIGITS NOW.
burn
YUCK.
EVEN TASTED BAD.
Pi-tooie!
I AGREE ...
stomp stomp stomp

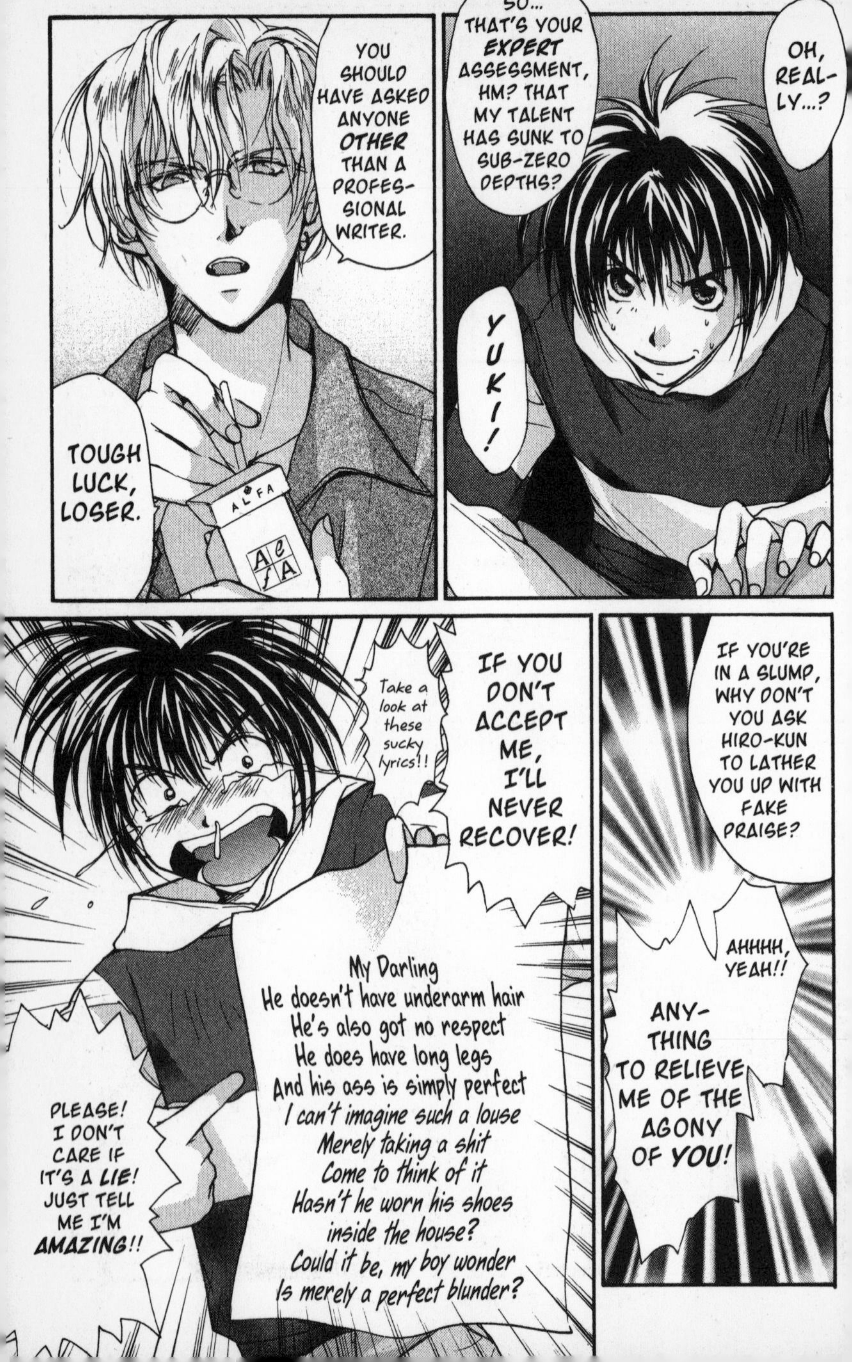
OH, REALLY...?
SO... THAT'S YOUR EXPERT ASSESSMENT, HM? THAT MY TALENT HAS SUNK TO SUB-ZERO DEPTHS?
YUKI!!
YOU SHOULD HAVE ASKED ANYONE OTHER THAN A PROFESSIONAL WRITER.
TOUGH LUCK, LOSER.
ALFA
IF YOU'RE IN A SLUMP, WHY DON'T YOU ASK HIRO-KUN TO LATHER YOU UP WITH FAKE PRAISE?
AHHHH, YEAH!!
ANYTHING TO RELIEVE ME OF THE AGONY OF YOU!
IF YOU DON'T ACCEPT ME, I'LL NEVER RECOVER!
Take a look at these sucky lyrics!!
My Darling
He doesn't have underarm hair
He's also got no respect
He does have long legs
And his ass is simply perfect
I can't imagine such a louse
Merely taking a shit
Come to think of it
Hasn't he worn his shoes
inside the house?
Could it be, my boy wonder
Is merely a perfect blunder?
PLEASE! I DON'T CARE IF IT'S A LIE! JUST TELL ME I'M AMAZING!!

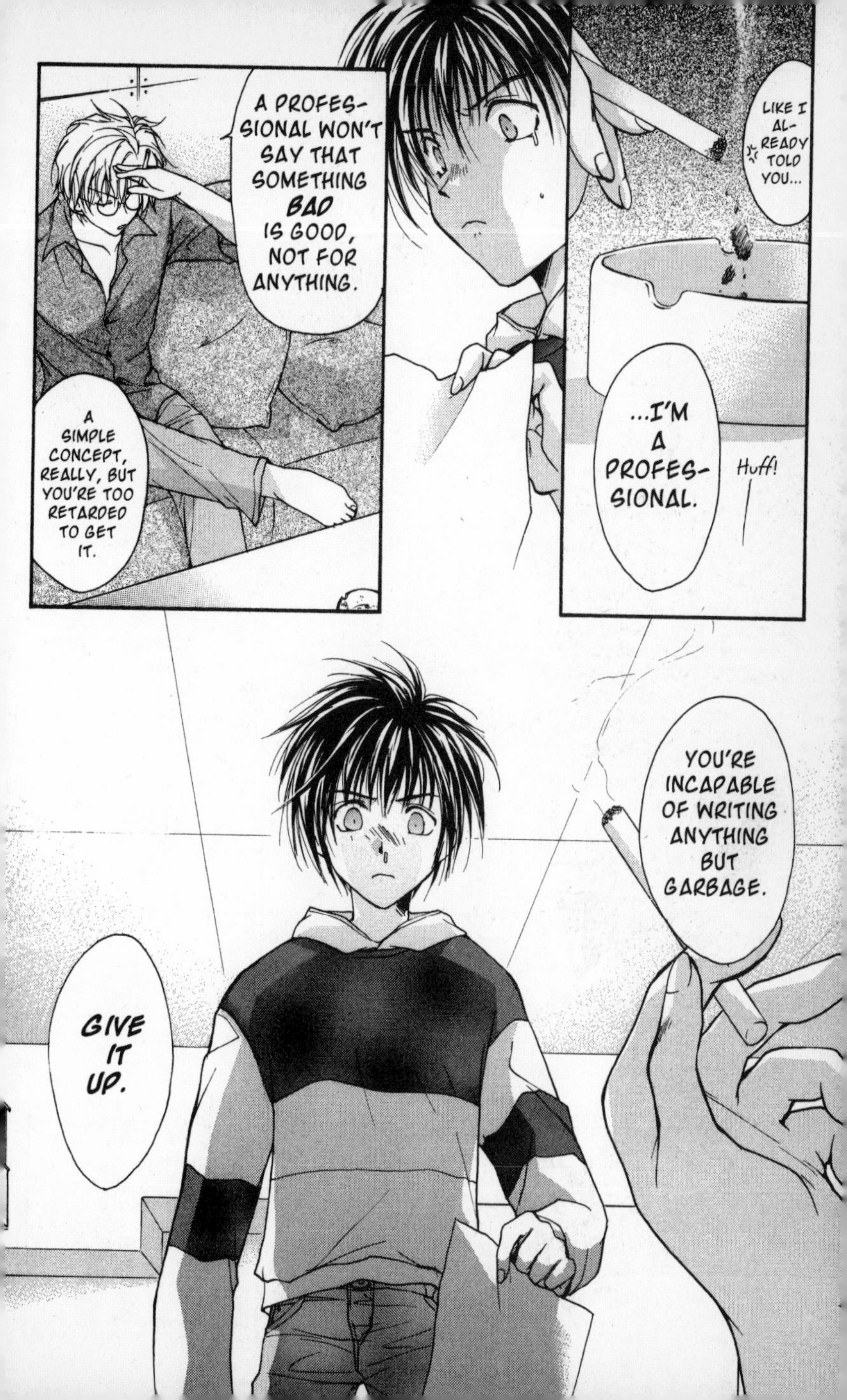
LIKE I AL-READY TOLD YOU...
...I'M A PROFES-SIONAL.
Huff!
A PROFES-SIONAL WON'T SAY THAT SOMETHING BAD IS GOOD, NOT FOR ANYTHING.
A SIMPLE CONCEPT, REALLY, BUT YOU'RE TOO RETARDED TO GET IT.
YOU'RE INCAPABLE OF WRITING ANYTHING BUT GARBAGE.
GIVE IT UP.

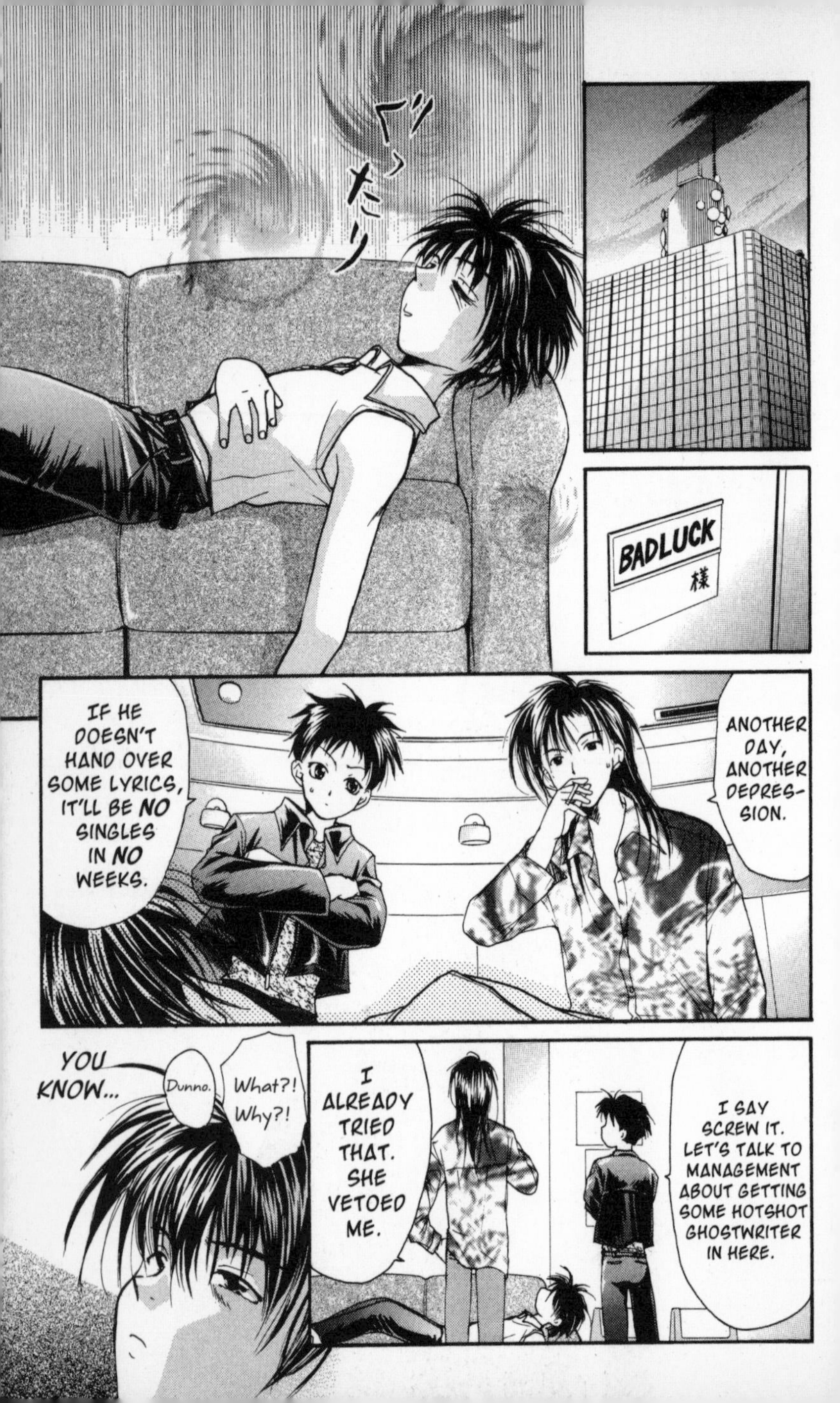

BADLUCK
様
ぐったり
ANOTHER DAY, ANOTHER DEPRES-SION.
IF HE DOESN'T HAND OVER SOME LYRICS, IT'LL BE **NO** SINGLES IN **NO** WEEKS.
I SAY SCREW IT. LET'S TALK TO MANAGEMENT ABOUT GETTING SOME HOTSHOT GHOSTWRITER IN HERE.
I ALREADY TRIED THAT. SHE VETOED ME.
What?! Why?!
Dunno.
YOU KNOW...

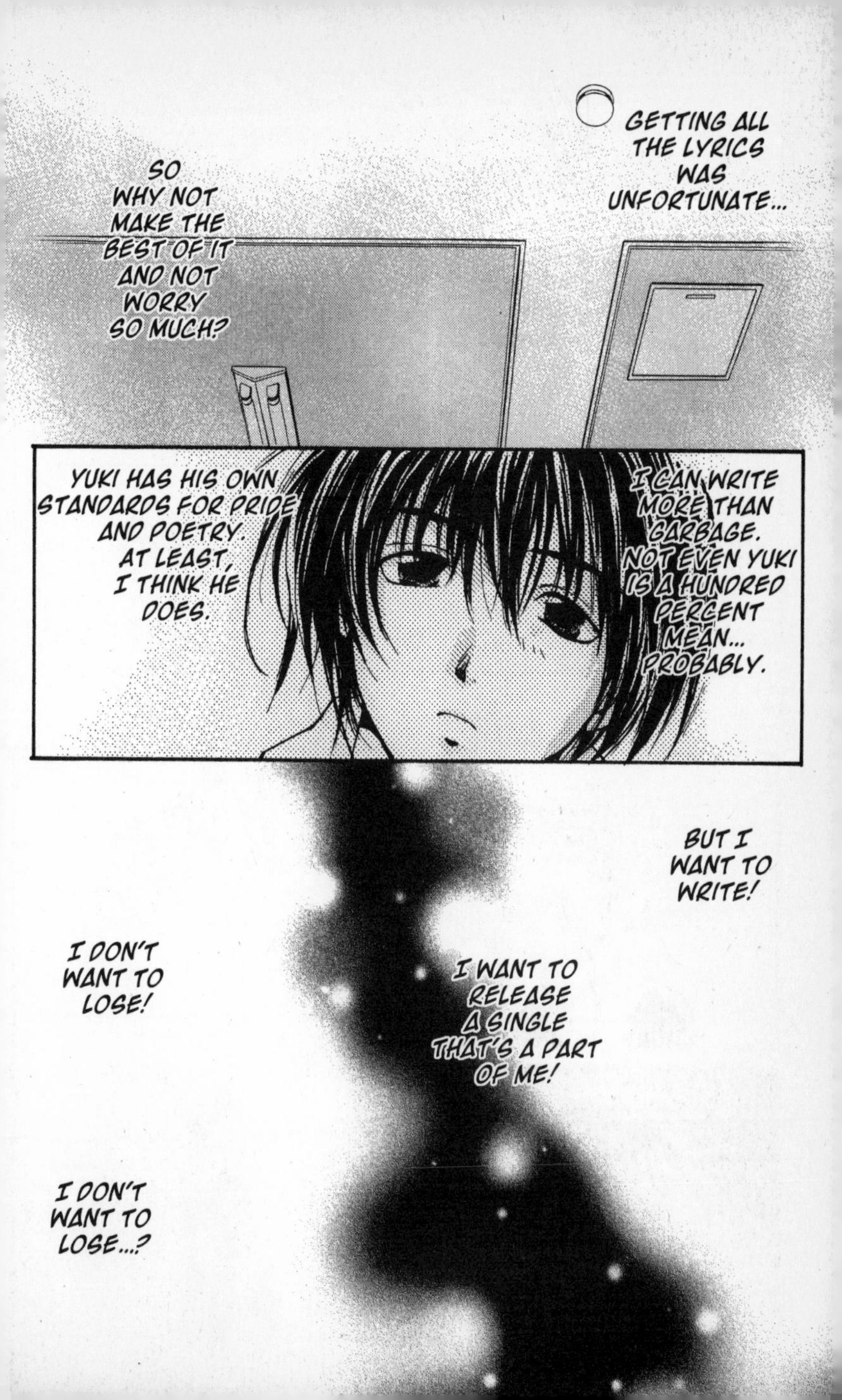
GETTING ALL THE LYRICS WAS UNFORTUNATE...
SO WHY NOT MAKE THE BEST OF IT AND NOT WORRY SO MUCH?
I CAN WRITE MORE THAN GARBAGE. NOT EVEN YUKI IS A HUNDRED PERCENT MEAN... PROBABLY.
YUKI HAS HIS OWN STANDARDS FOR PRIDE AND POETRY. AT LEAST, I THINK HE DOES.
BUT I WANT TO WRITE!
I WANT TO RELEASE A SINGLE THAT'S A PART OF ME!
I DON'T WANT TO LOSE!
I DON'T WANT TO LOSE...?

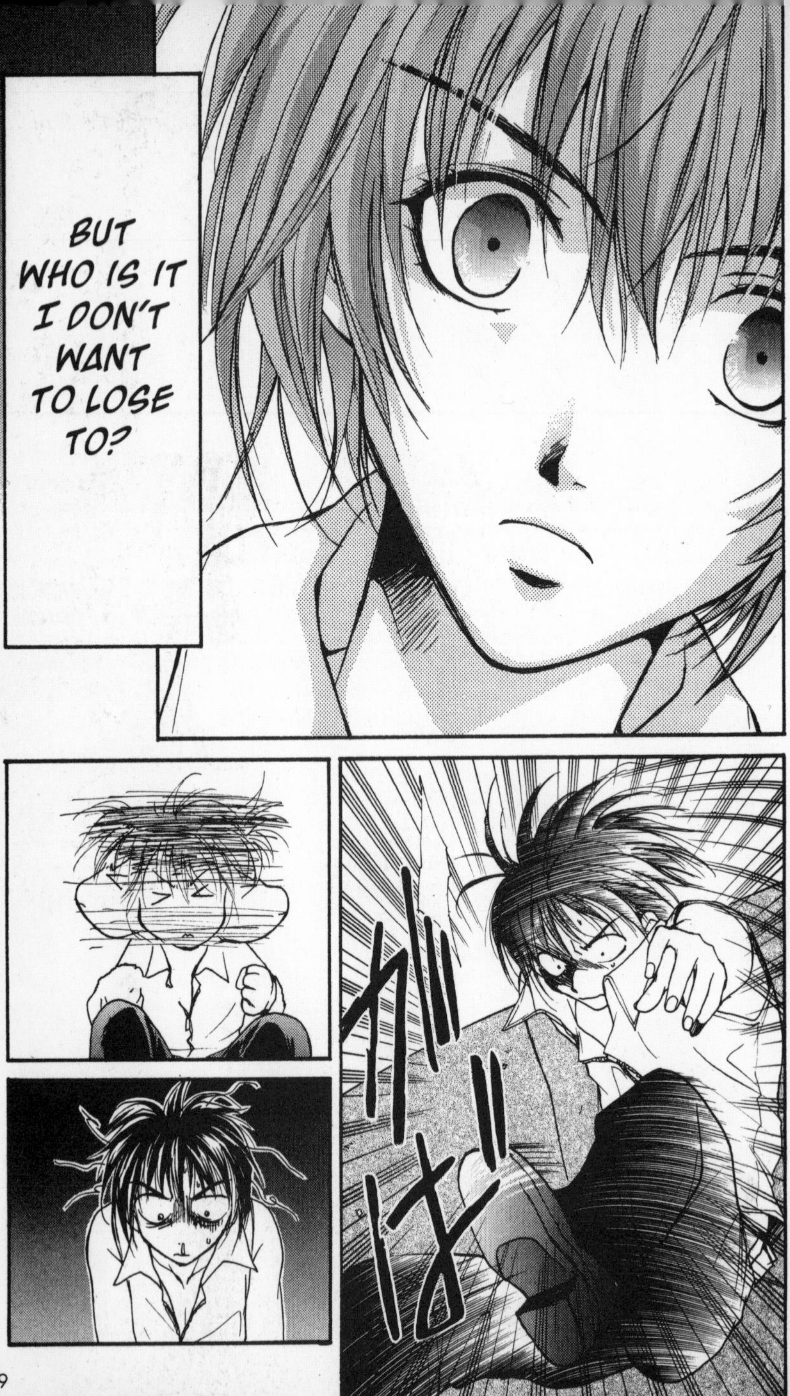
BUT WHO IS IT I DON'T WANT TO LOSE TO?

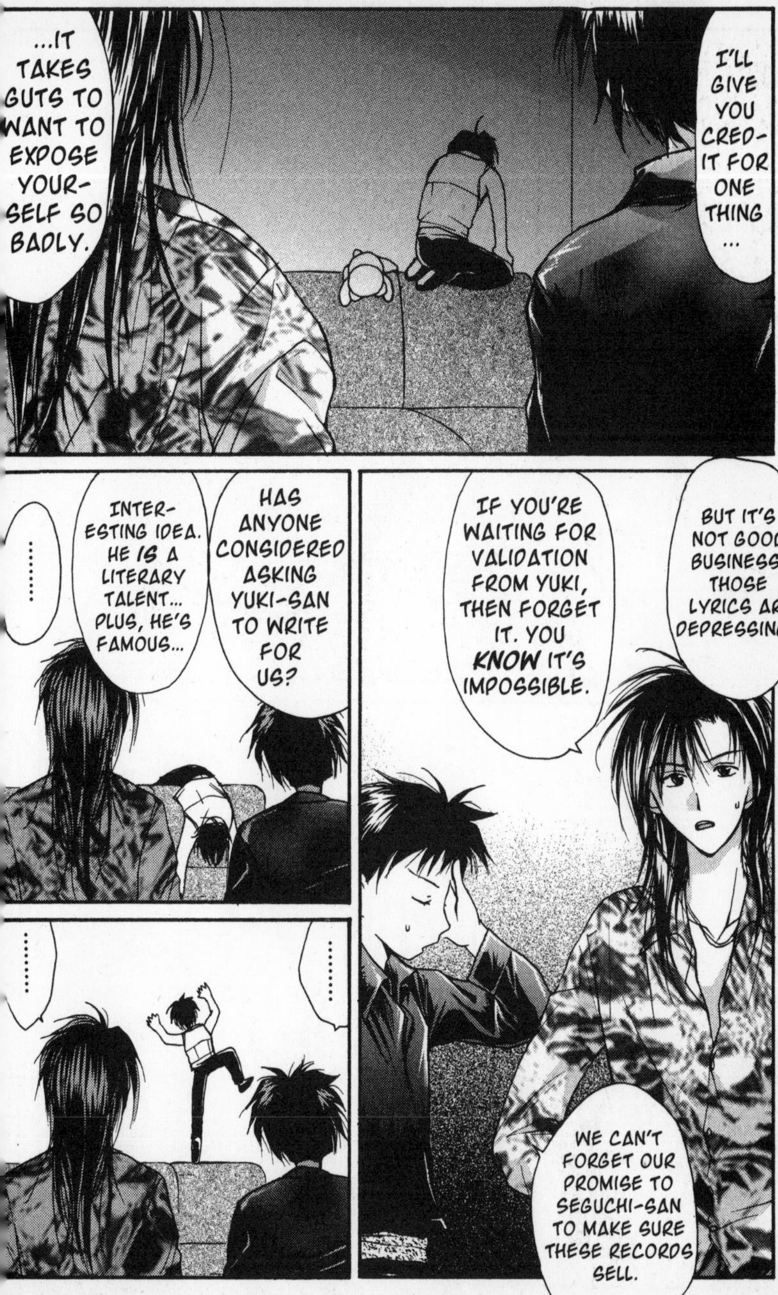
I'LL GIVE YOU CRED-IT FOR ONE THING ...
...IT TAKES GUTS TO WANT TO EXPOSE YOUR-SELF SO BADLY.
BUT IT'S NOT GOOD BUSINESS. THOSE LYRICS ARE DEPRESSING.
IF YOU'RE WAITING FOR VALIDATION FROM YUKI, THEN FORGET IT. YOU KNOW IT'S IMPOSSIBLE.
WE CAN'T FORGET OUR PROMISE TO SEGUCHI-SAN TO MAKE SURE THESE RECORDS SELL.
HAS ANYONE CONSIDERED ASKING YUKI-SAN TO WRITE FOR US?
INTER-ESTING IDEA. HE IS A LITERARY TALENT... PLUS, HE'S FAMOUS...
....
....
....

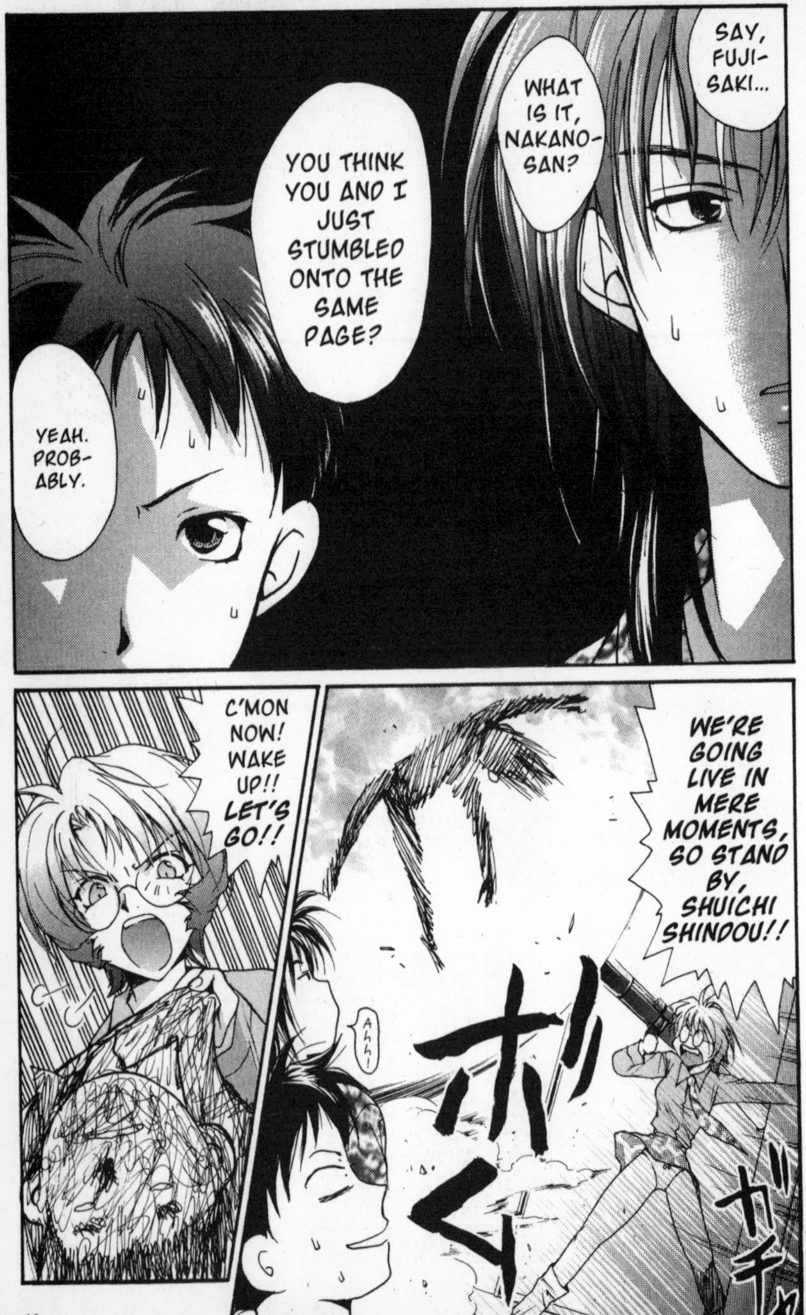
SAY, FUJI-SAKI...
WHAT IS IT, NAKANO-SAN?
YOU THINK YOU AND I JUST STUMBLED ONTO THE SAME PAGE?
YEAH. PROBABLY.
WE'RE GOING LIVE IN MERE MOMENTS, SO STAND BY, SHUICHI SHINDOU!!
Ahh!
C'MON NOW! WAKE UP!! LET'S GO!!

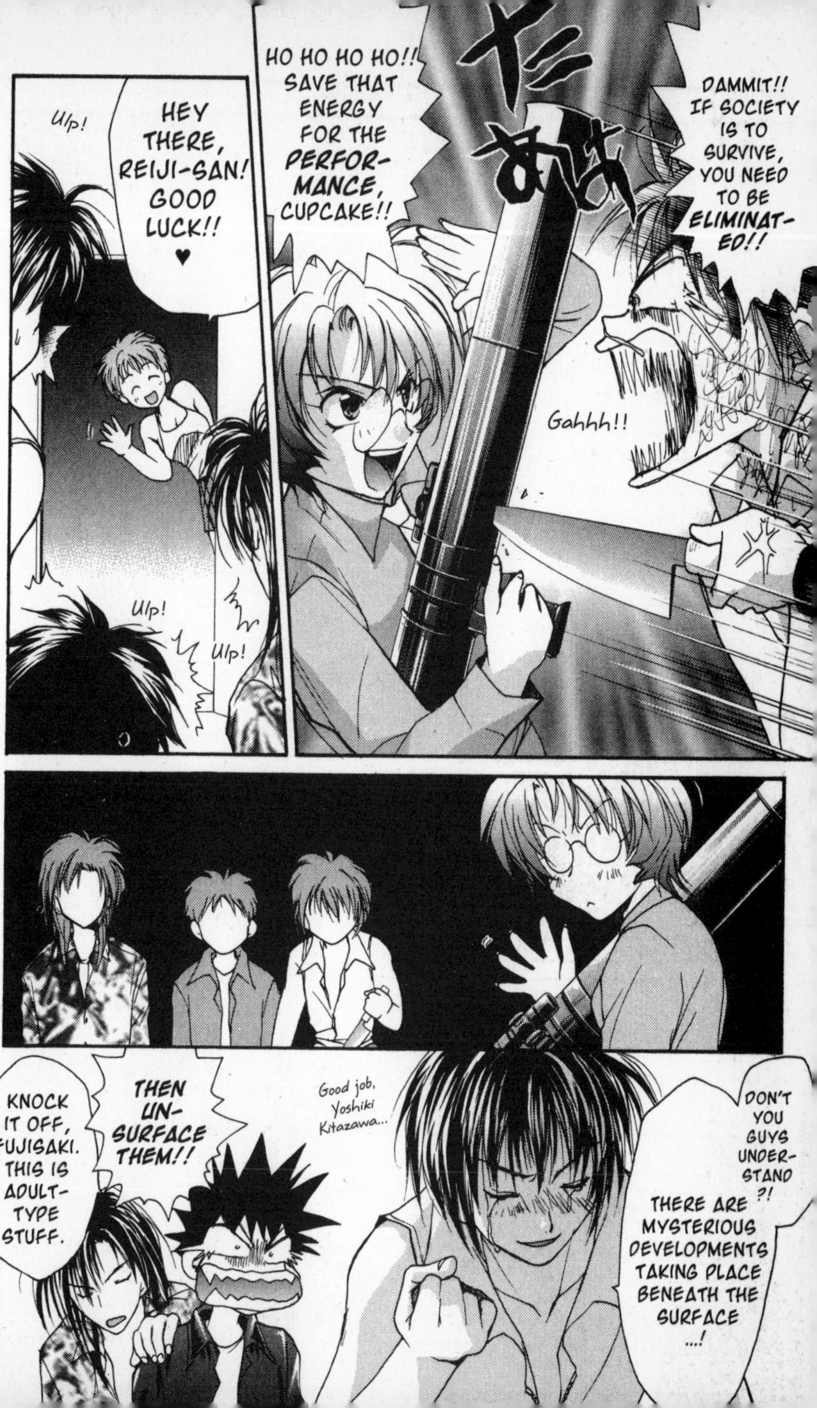
DAMMIT!! IF SOCIETY IS TO SURVIVE, YOU NEED TO BE ELIMINATED!!
HO HO HO HO!! SAVE THAT ENERGY FOR THE PERFORMANCE, CUPCAKE!!
Gahhh!!
HEY THERE, REIJI-SAN! GOOD LUCK!! ♥
Ulp!
Ulp!
Ulp!
DON'T YOU GUYS UNDERSTAND?!
THERE ARE MYSTERIOUS DEVELOPMENTS TAKING PLACE BENEATH THE SURFACE ...!
Good job, Yoshiki Kitazawa...
THEN UNSURFACE THEM!!
KNOCK IT OFF, FUJISAKI. THIS IS ADULT-TYPE STUFF.

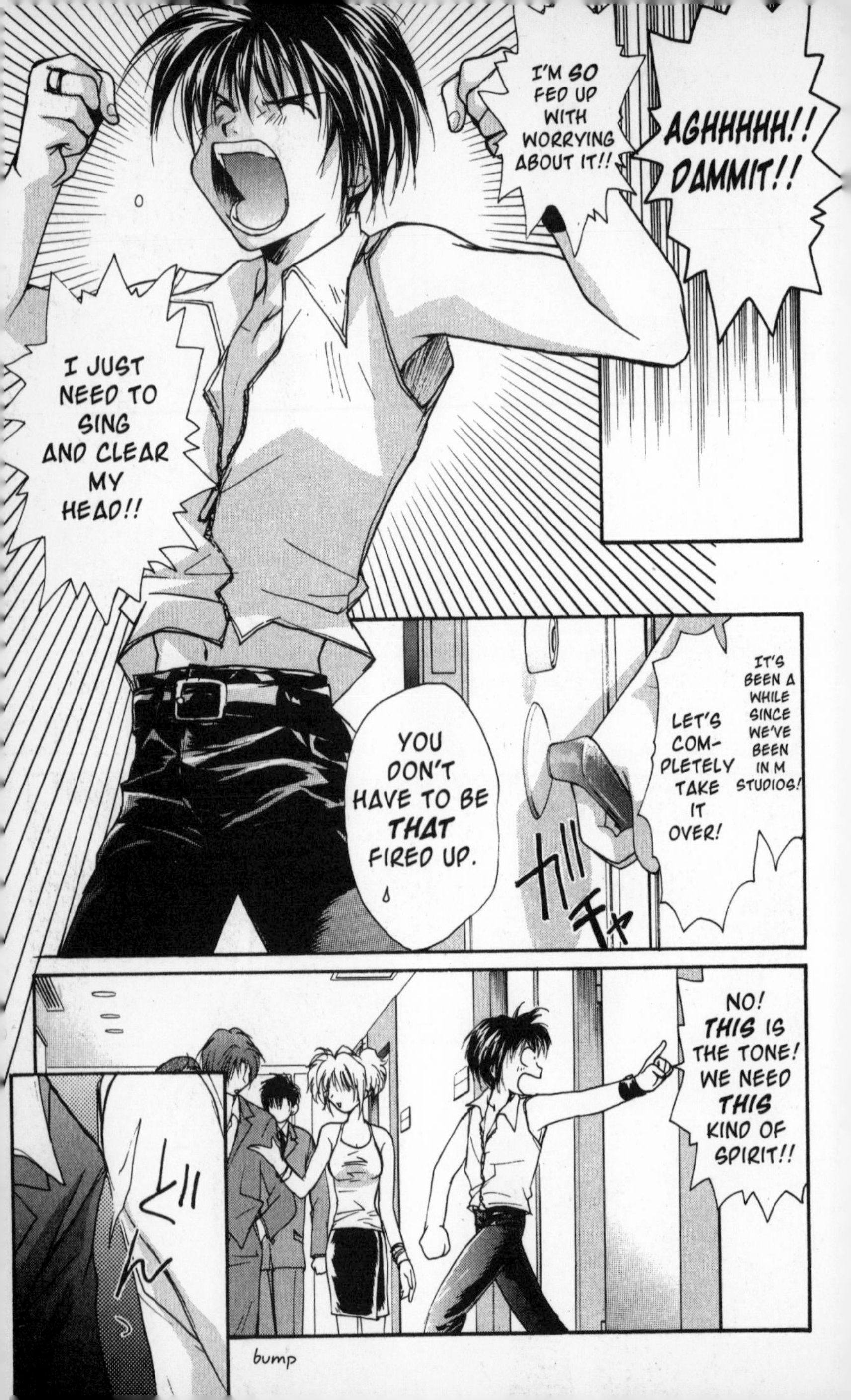
AGHHHHH!! DAMMIT!!
I'M SO FED UP WITH WORRYING ABOUT IT!!
I JUST NEED TO SING AND CLEAR MY HEAD!!
IT'S BEEN A WHILE SINCE WE'VE BEEN IN M STUDIOS!
LET'S COMPLETELY TAKE IT OVER!
ガチャ
YOU DON'T HAVE TO BE THAT FIRED UP.
NO! THIS IS THE TONE! WE NEED THIS KIND OF SPIRIT!!
どん
bump

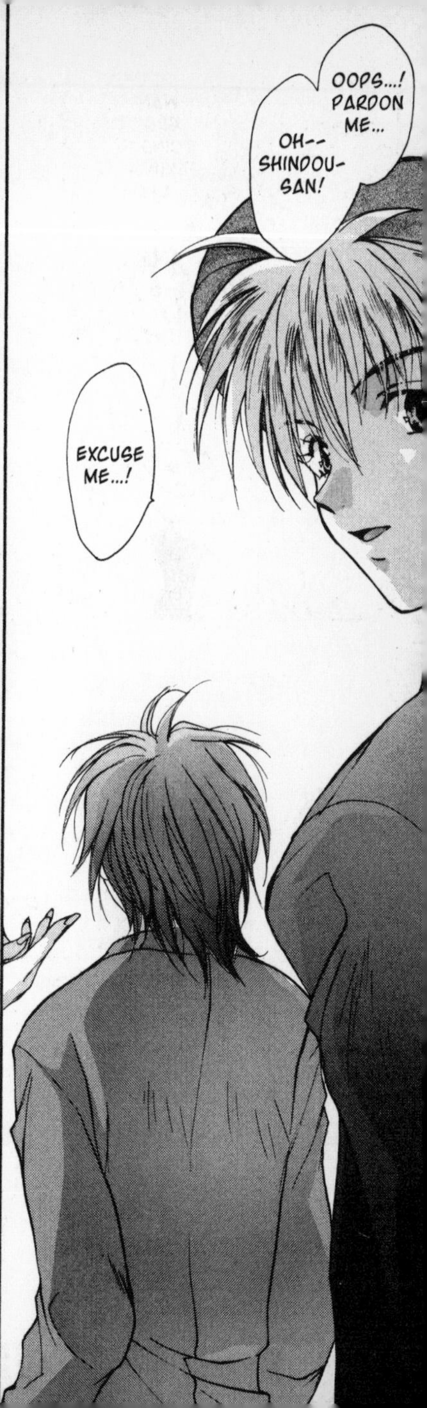
OOPS...! PARDON ME...
OH-- SHINDOU-SAN!
EXCUSE ME...!
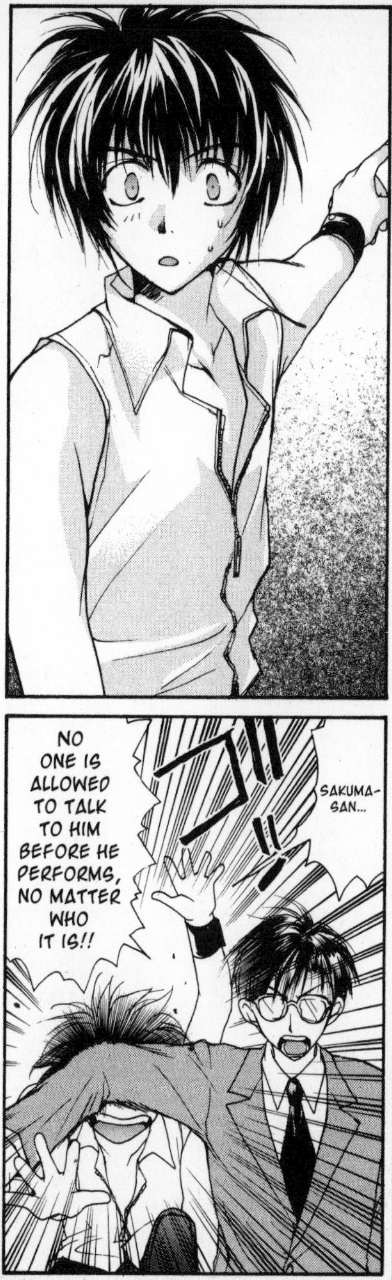
SAKUMA-SAN...
NO ONE IS ALLOWED TO TALK TO HIM BEFORE HE PERFORMS, NO MATTER WHO IT IS!!

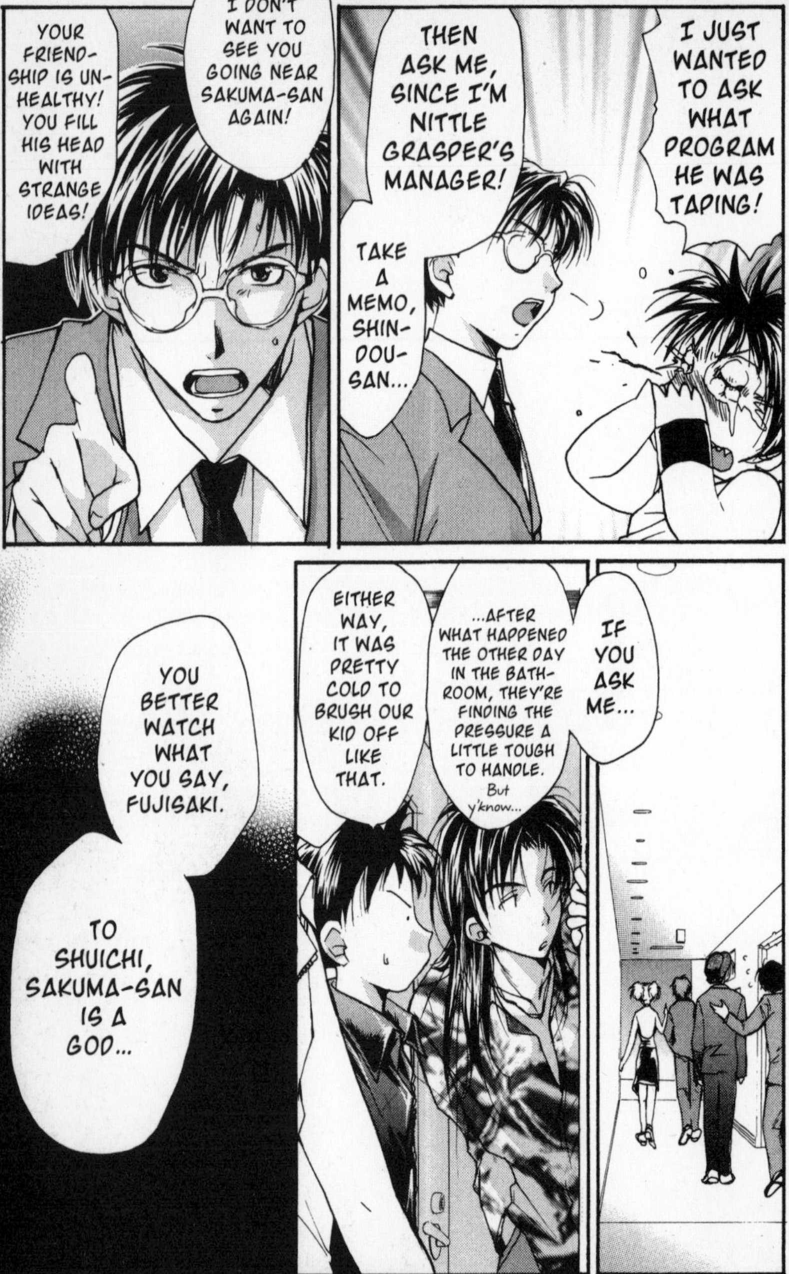
I JUST WANTED TO ASK WHAT PROGRAM HE WAS TAPING!
THEN ASK ME, SINCE I'M NITTLE GRASPER'S MANAGER!
TAKE A MEMO, SHINDOU-SAN...
I DON'T WANT TO SEE YOU GOING NEAR SAKUMA-SAN AGAIN!
YOUR FRIENDSHIP IS UNHEALTHY! YOU FILL HIS HEAD WITH STRANGE IDEAS!
IF YOU ASK ME...
...AFTER WHAT HAPPENED THE OTHER DAY IN THE BATHROOM, THEY'RE FINDING THE PRESSURE A LITTLE TOUGH TO HANDLE.
But y'know...
EITHER WAY, IT WAS PRETTY COLD TO BRUSH OUR KID OFF LIKE THAT.
YOU BETTER WATCH WHAT YOU SAY, FUJISAKI.
TO SHUICHI, SAKUMA-SAN IS A GOD...

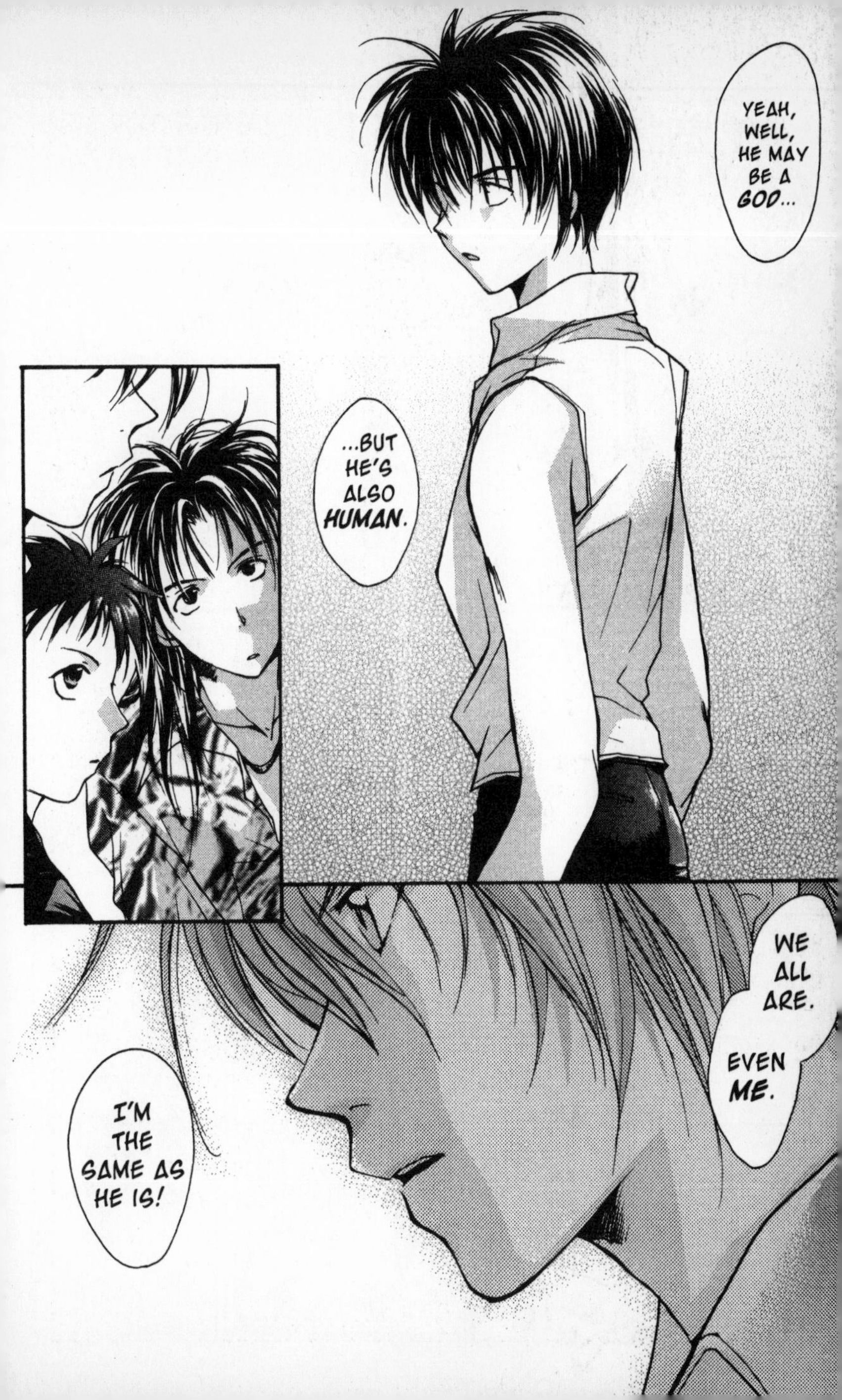
YEAH, WELL, HE MAY BE A GOD...
...BUT HE'S ALSO HUMAN.
WE ALL ARE.
EVEN ME.
I'M THE SAME AS HE IS!

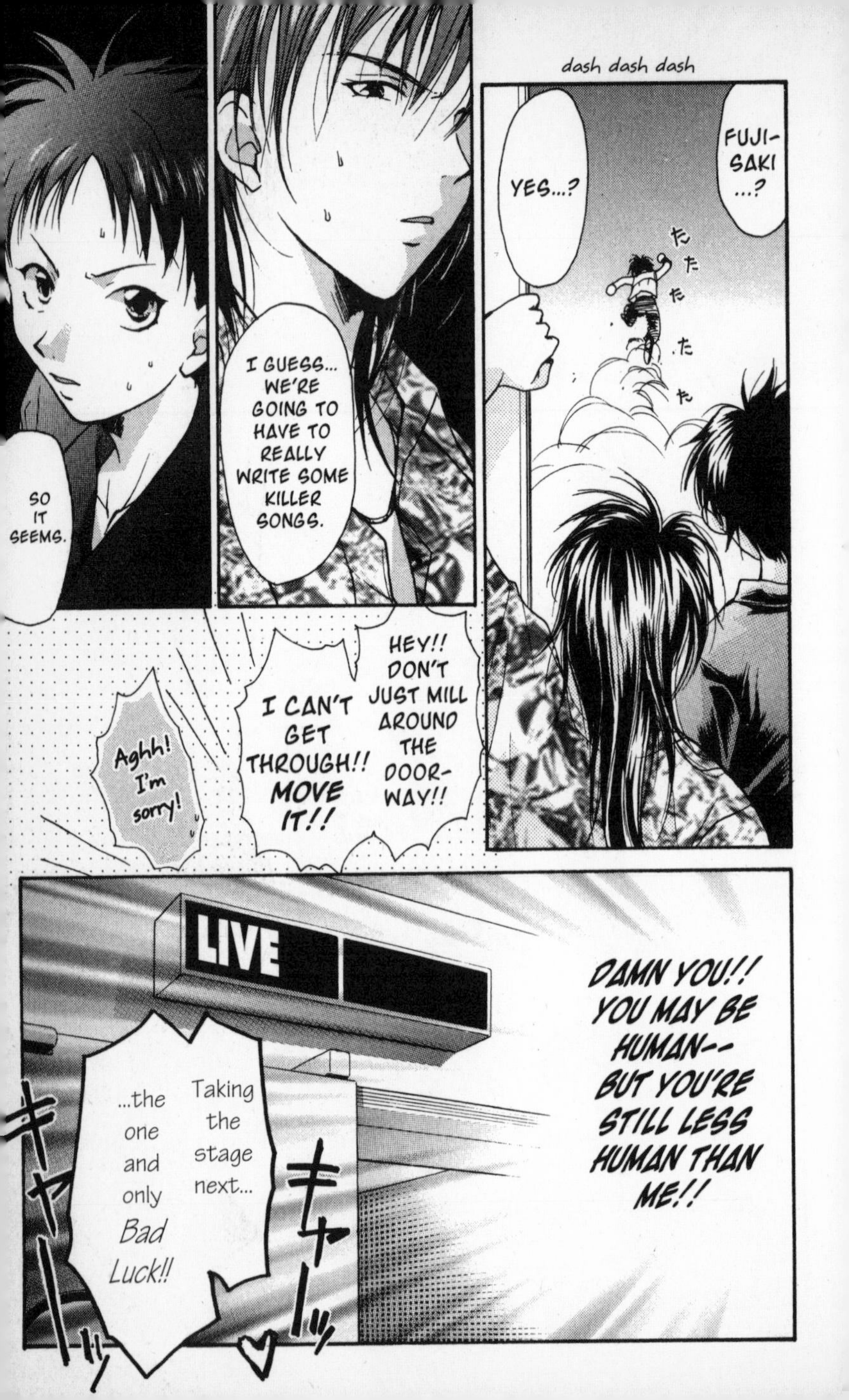
dash dash dash
FUJI-SAKI ...?
YES...?
たたたたた
I GUESS... WE'RE GOING TO HAVE TO REALLY WRITE SOME KILLER SONGS.
SO IT SEEMS.
HEY!! DON'T JUST MILL AROUND THE DOOR-WAY!!
I CAN'T GET THROUGH!! MOVE IT!!
Aghh! I'm sorry!
LIVE
DAMN YOU!! YOU MAY BE HUMAN-- BUT YOU'RE STILL LESS HUMAN THAN ME!!
Taking the stage next...
...the one and only Bad Luck!!
キャー
キャー

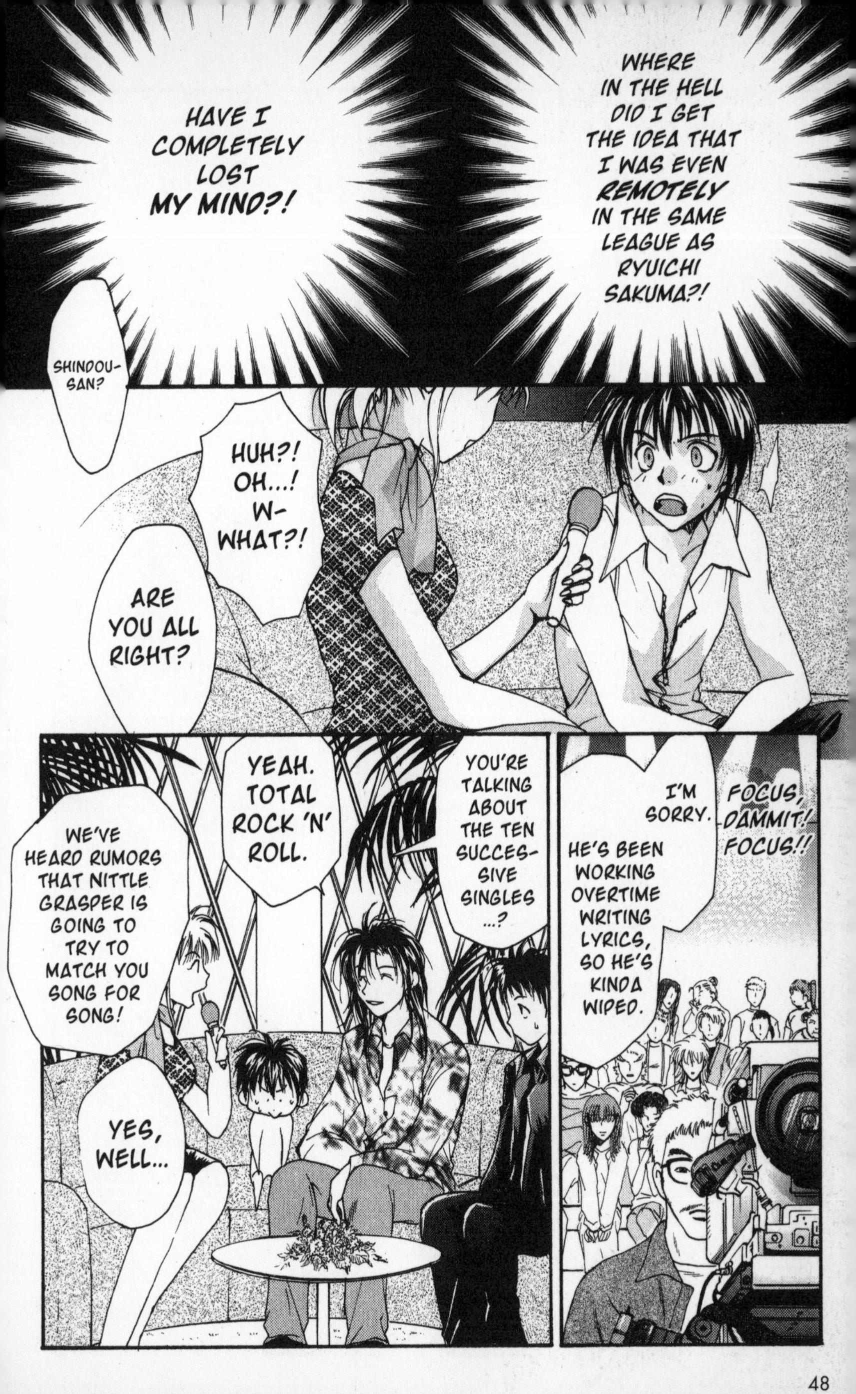
WHERE IN THE HELL DID I GET THE IDEA THAT I WAS EVEN REMOTELY IN THE SAME LEAGUE AS RYUICHI SAKUMA?!
HAVE I COMPLETELY LOST MY MIND?!
SHINDOU-SAN?
HUH?! OH...! W-WHAT?!
ARE YOU ALL RIGHT?
FOCUS, DAMMIT! FOCUS!!
I'M SORRY.
HE'S BEEN WORKING OVERTIME WRITING LYRICS, SO HE'S KINDA WIPED.
YOU'RE TALKING ABOUT THE TEN SUCCES-SIVE SINGLES ...?
YEAH. TOTAL ROCK 'N' ROLL.
WE'VE HEARD RUMORS THAT NITTLE GRASPER IS GOING TO TRY TO MATCH YOU SONG FOR SONG!
YES, WELL...

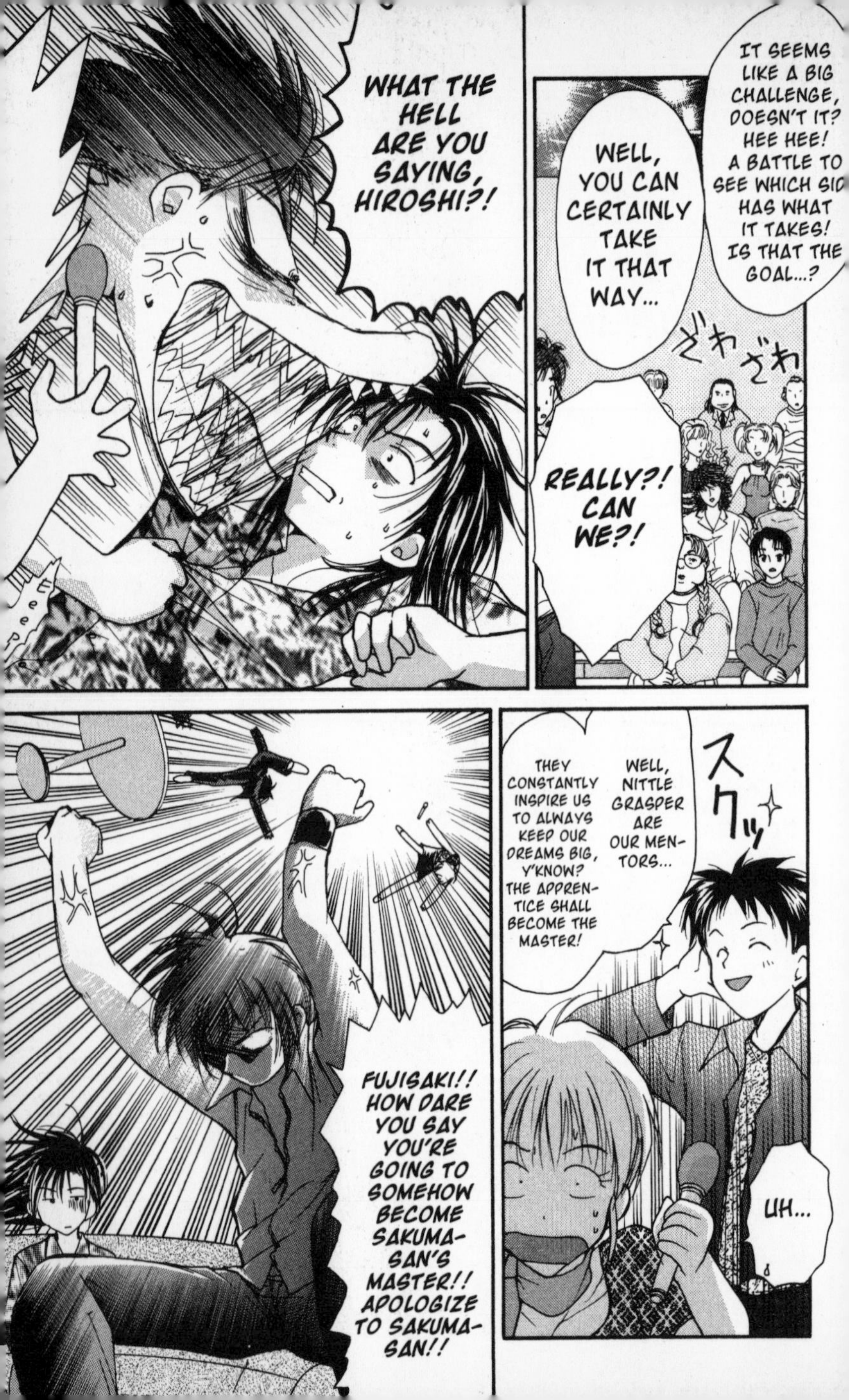
IT SEEMS LIKE A BIG CHALLENGE, DOESN'T IT? HEE HEE! A BATTLE TO SEE WHICH SID HAS WHAT IT TAKES! IS THAT THE GOAL...?
WELL, YOU CAN CERTAINLY TAKE IT THAT WAY...
ざわざわ
REALLY?! CAN WE?!
WHAT THE HELL ARE YOU SAYING, HIROSHI?!
スクッ
WELL, NITTLE GRASPER ARE OUR MEN-TORS...
THEY CONSTANTLY INSPIRE US TO ALWAYS KEEP OUR DREAMS BIG, Y'KNOW? THE APPREN-TICE SHALL BECOME THE MASTER!
UH...
FUJISAKI!! HOW DARE YOU SAY YOU'RE GOING TO SOMEHOW BECOME SAKUMA-SAN'S MASTER!! APOLOGIZE TO SAKUMA-SAN!!

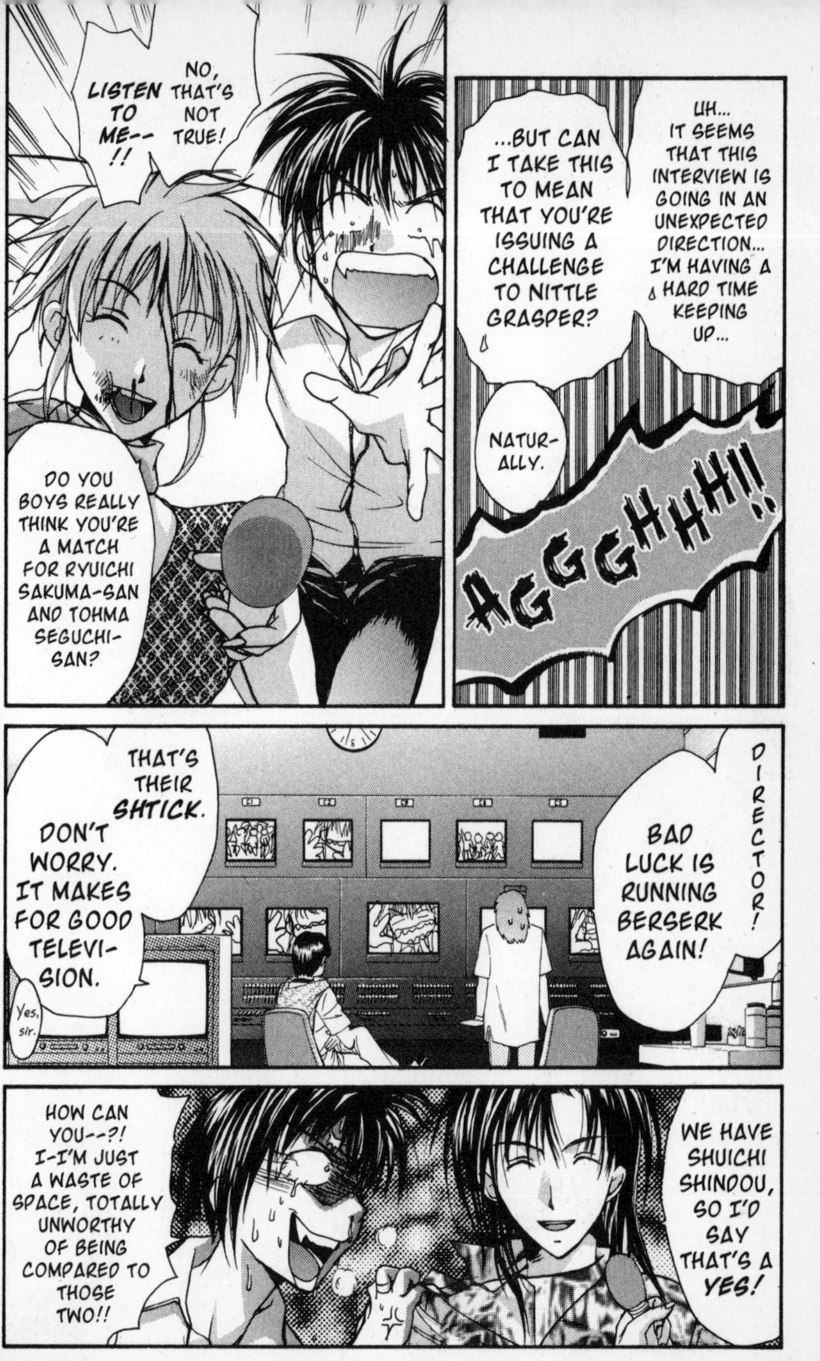
UH... IT SEEMS THAT THIS INTERVIEW IS GOING IN AN UNEXPECTED DIRECTION... I'M HAVING A HARD TIME KEEPING UP...
...BUT CAN I TAKE THIS TO MEAN THAT YOU'RE ISSUING A CHALLENGE TO NITTLE GRASPER?
NATURALLY.
AGGGHHH!!
NO, THAT'S NOT TRUE!
LISTEN TO ME--!!
DO YOU BOYS REALLY THINK YOU'RE A MATCH FOR RYUICHI SAKUMA-SAN AND TOHMA SEGUCHI-SAN?
DIRECTOR!
BAD LUCK IS RUNNING BERSERK AGAIN!
THAT'S THEIR SHTICK.
DON'T WORRY. IT MAKES FOR GOOD TELEVISION.
Yes, sir.
WE HAVE SHUICHI SHINDOU, SO I'D SAY THAT'S A YES!
HOW CAN YOU--?! I-I'M JUST A WASTE OF SPACE, TOTALLY UNWORTHY OF BEING COMPARED TO THOSE TWO!!

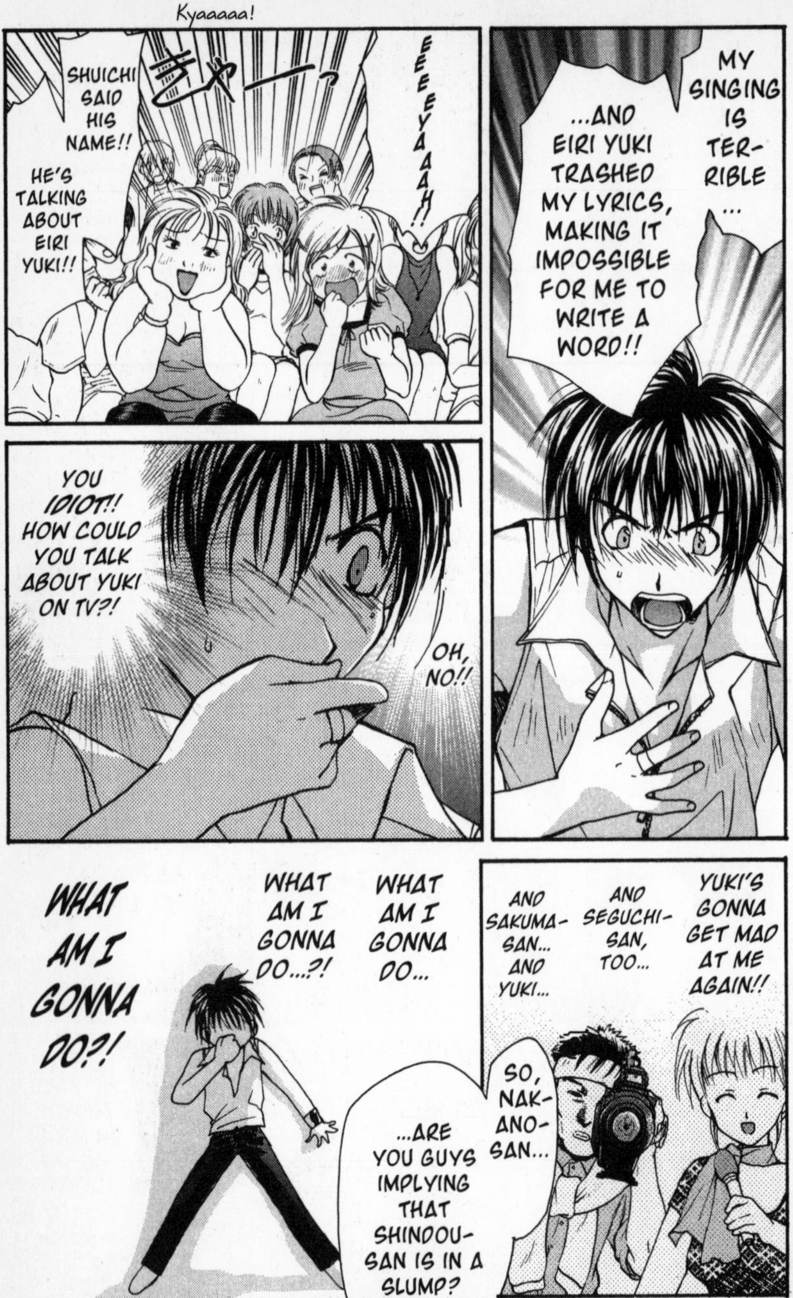
MY SINGING IS TERRIBLE...
...AND EIRI YUKI TRASHED MY LYRICS, MAKING IT IMPOSSIBLE FOR ME TO WRITE A WORD!!
EEEEEYAAAAH!!
Kyaaaaa!
SHUICHI SAID HIS NAME!!
HE'S TALKING ABOUT EIRI YUKI!!
OH, NO!!
YOU IDIOT!! HOW COULD YOU TALK ABOUT YUKI ON TV?!
YUKI'S GONNA GET MAD AT ME AGAIN!!
AND SEGUCHI-SAN, TOO...
AND SAKUMA-SAN... AND YUKI...
SO, NAKANO-SAN...
...ARE YOU GUYS IMPLYING THAT SHINDOU-SAN IS IN A SLUMP?
WHAT AM I GONNA DO...
WHAT AM I GONNA DO...?!
WHAT AM I GONNA DO?!

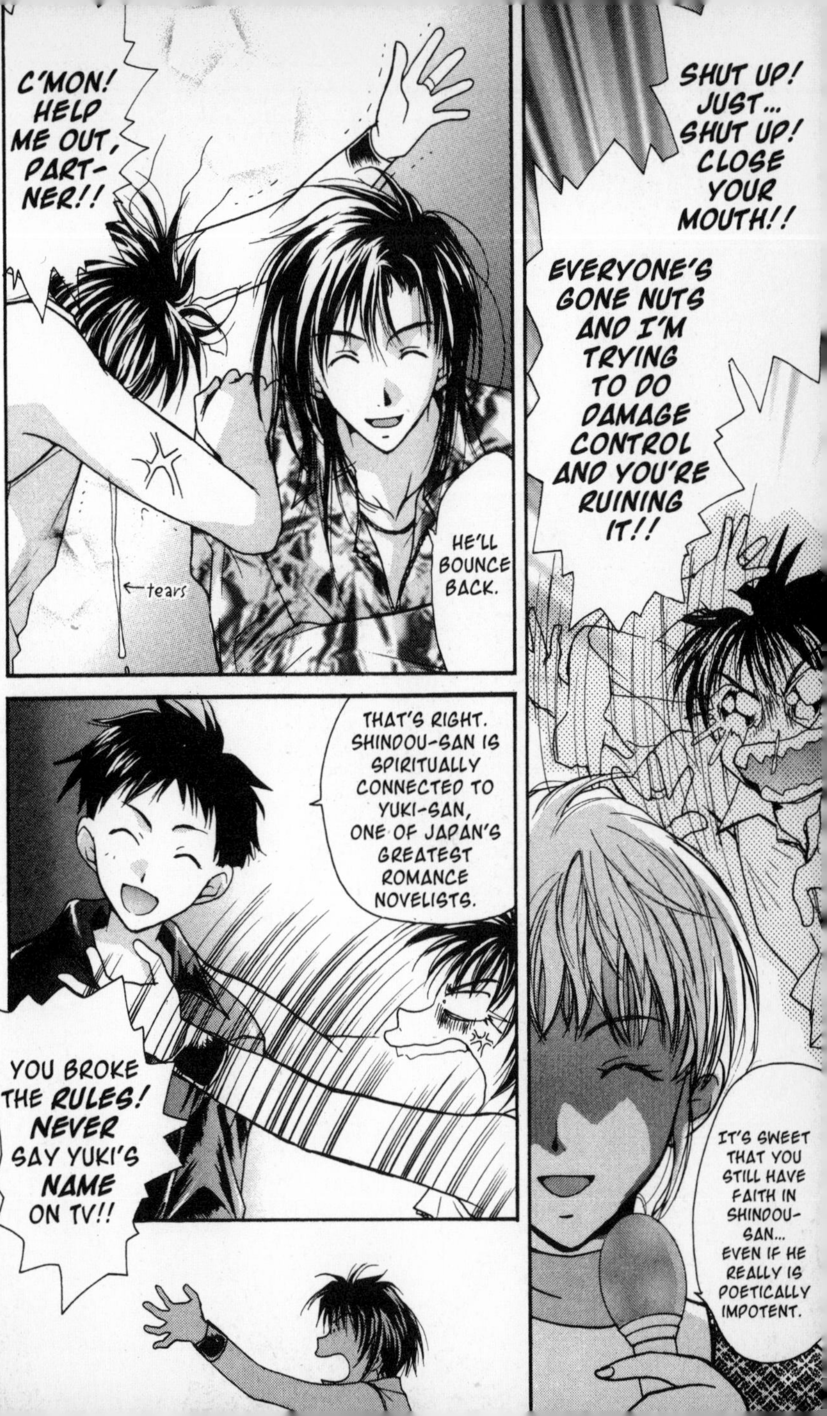
SHUT UP! JUST... SHUT UP! CLOSE YOUR MOUTH!!
EVERYONE'S GONE NUTS AND I'M TRYING TO DO DAMAGE CONTROL AND YOU'RE RUINING IT!!
IT'S SWEET THAT YOU STILL HAVE FAITH IN SHINDOU-SAN... EVEN IF HE REALLY IS POETICALLY IMPOTENT.
C'MON! HELP ME OUT, PARTNER!!
HE'LL BOUNCE BACK.
←tears
THAT'S RIGHT. SHINDOU-SAN IS SPIRITUALLY CONNECTED TO YUKI-SAN, ONE OF JAPAN'S GREATEST ROMANCE NOVELISTS.
YOU BROKE THE RULES! NEVER SAY YUKI'S NAME ON TV!!

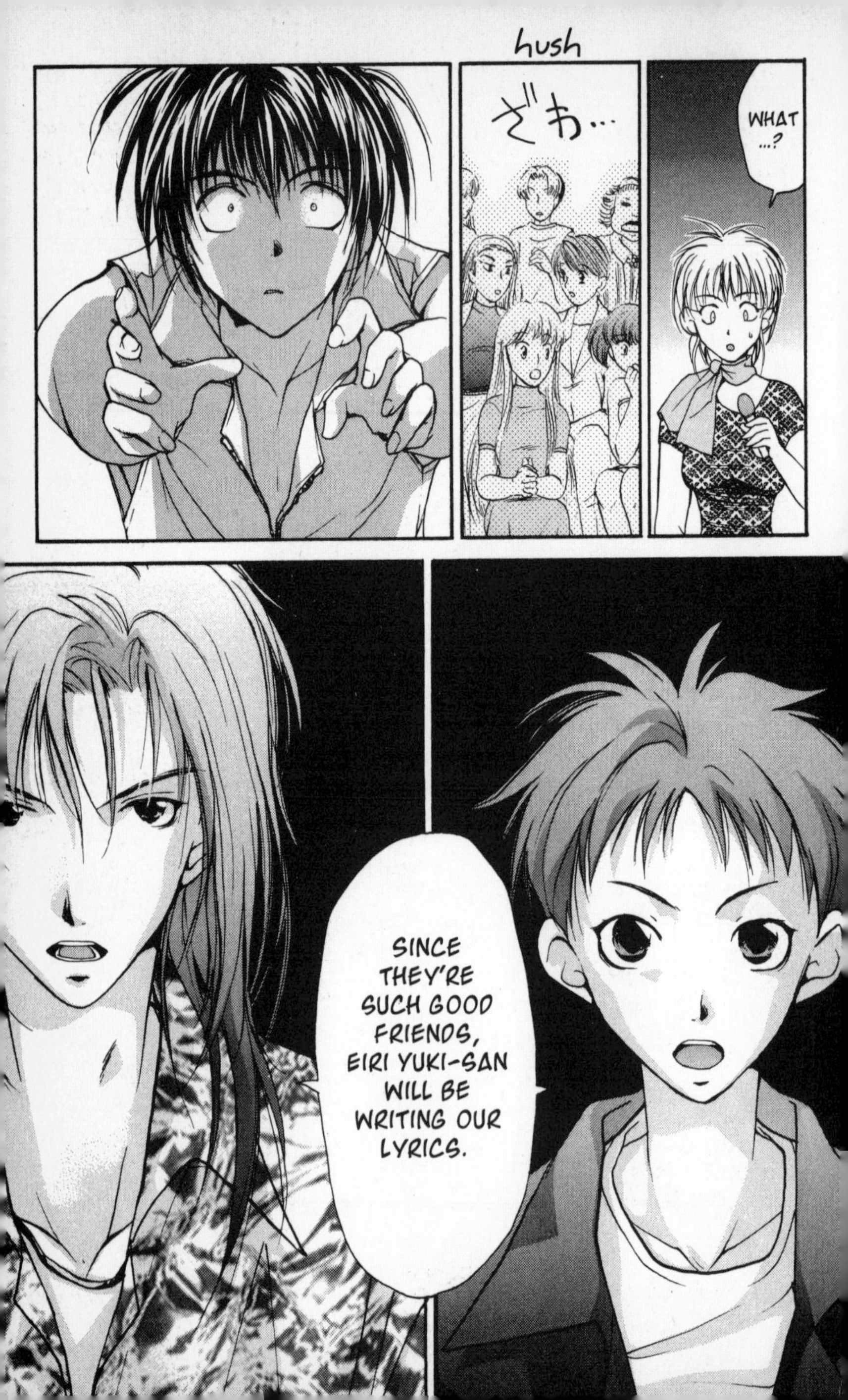
WHAT ...?
ざわ…
hush
SINCE THEY'RE SUCH GOOD FRIENDS, EIRI YUKI-SAN WILL BE WRITING OUR LYRICS.

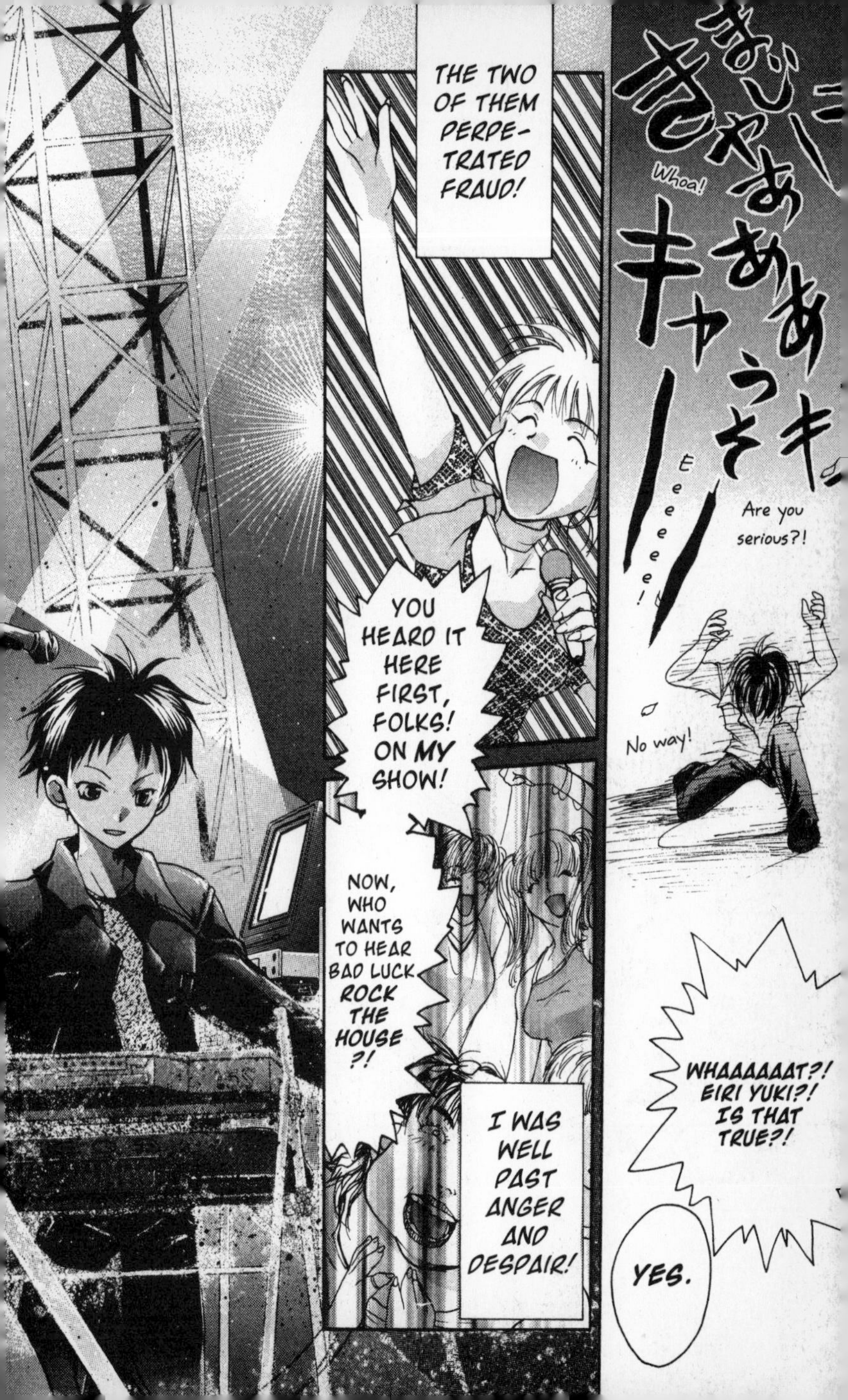

Whoa!
Eeeeee!
Are you serious?!
No way!
WHAAAAAAT?! EIRI YUKI?! IS THAT TRUE?!
YES.
THE TWO OF THEM PERPE-TRATED FRAUD!
YOU HEARD IT HERE FIRST, FOLKS! ON MY SHOW!
NOW, WHO WANTS TO HEAR BAD LUCK ROCK THE HOUSE?!
I WAS WELL PAST ANGER AND DESPAIR!

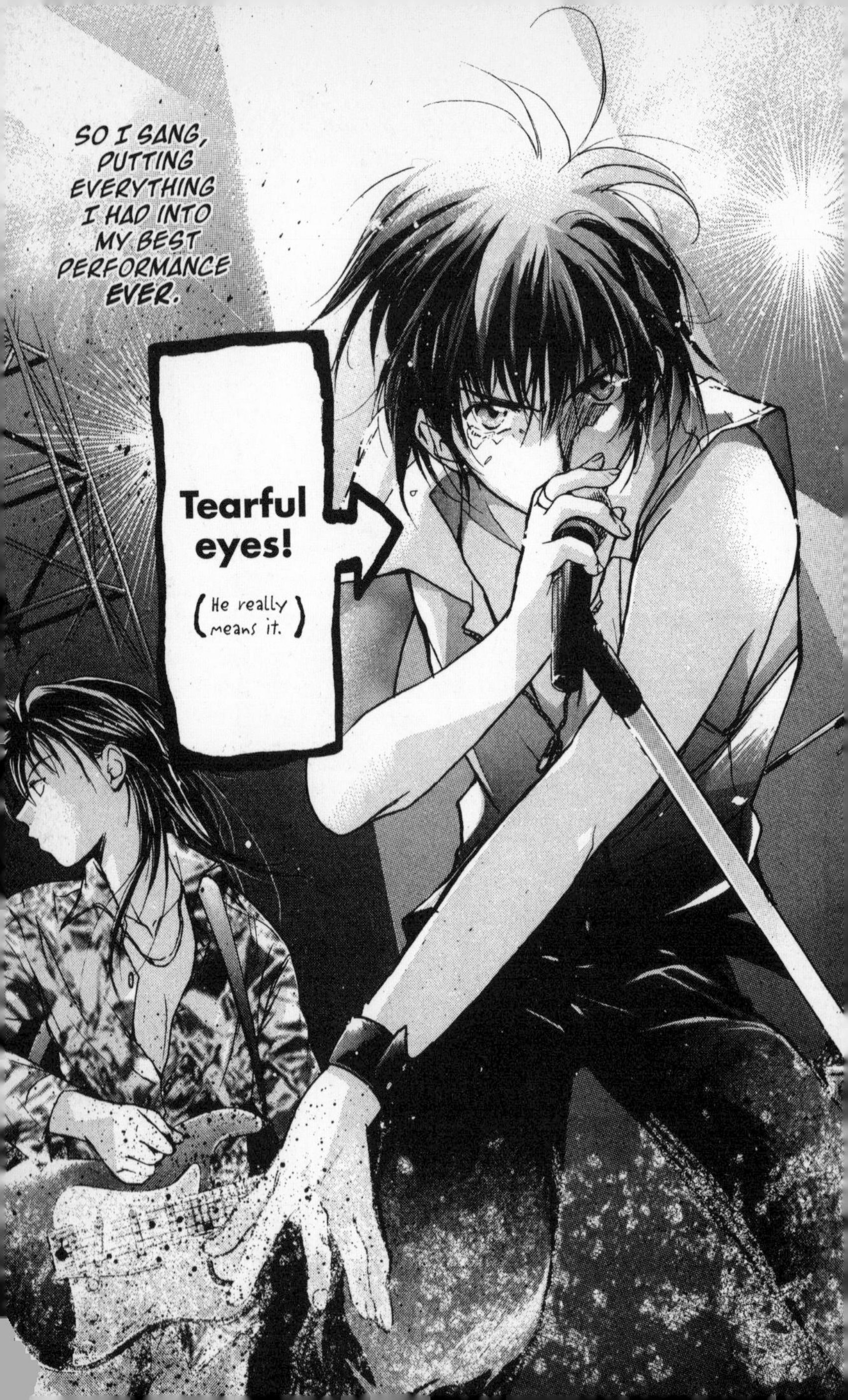
SO I SANG, PUTTING EVERYTHING I HAD INTO MY BEST PERFORMANCE EVER.
Tearful eyes!
(He really means it.)

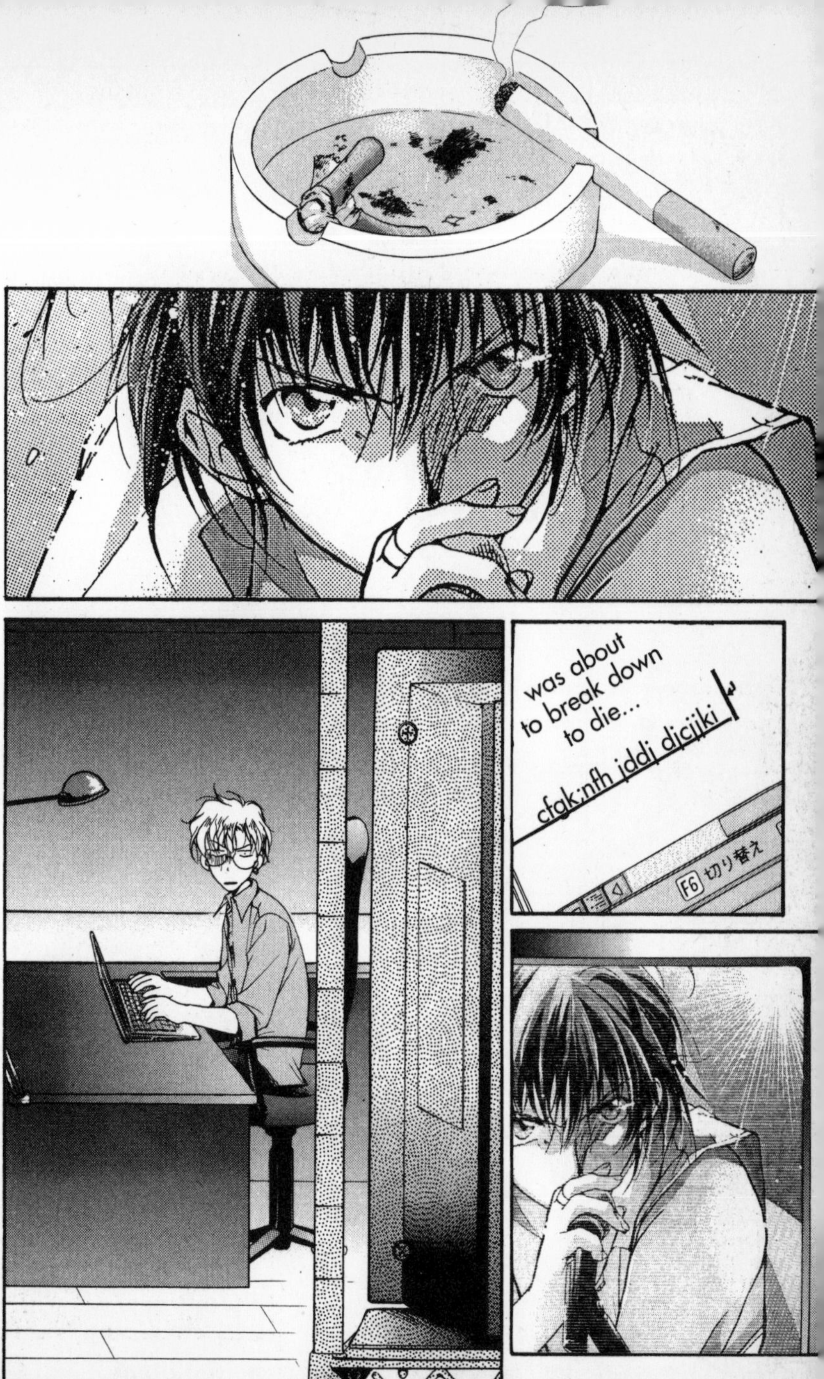
was about
to break down
to die...
cfqk;nfh iddi dicijki
F6 切り替え

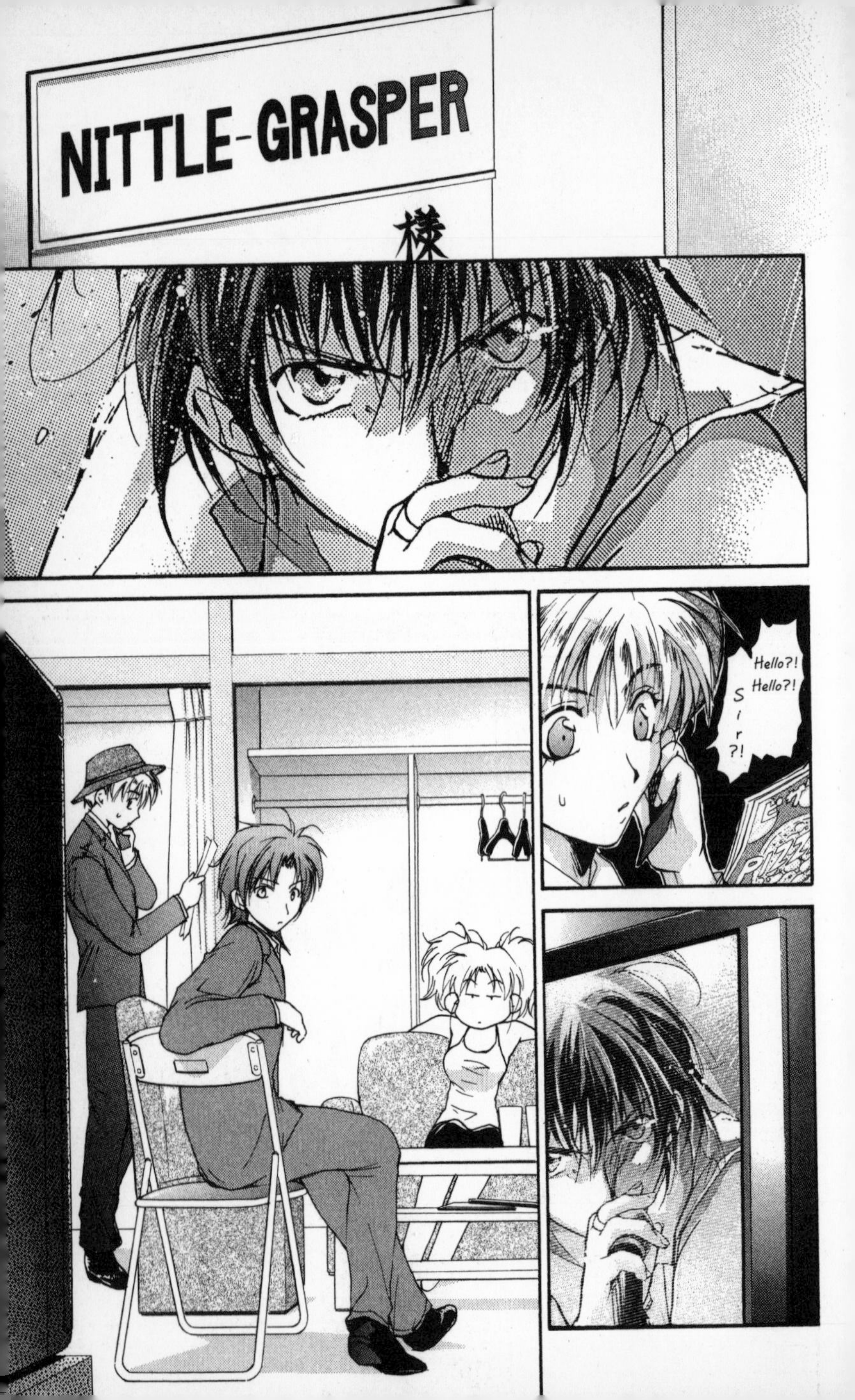
NITTLE-GRASPER
様
Hello?! Hello?! Sir?!

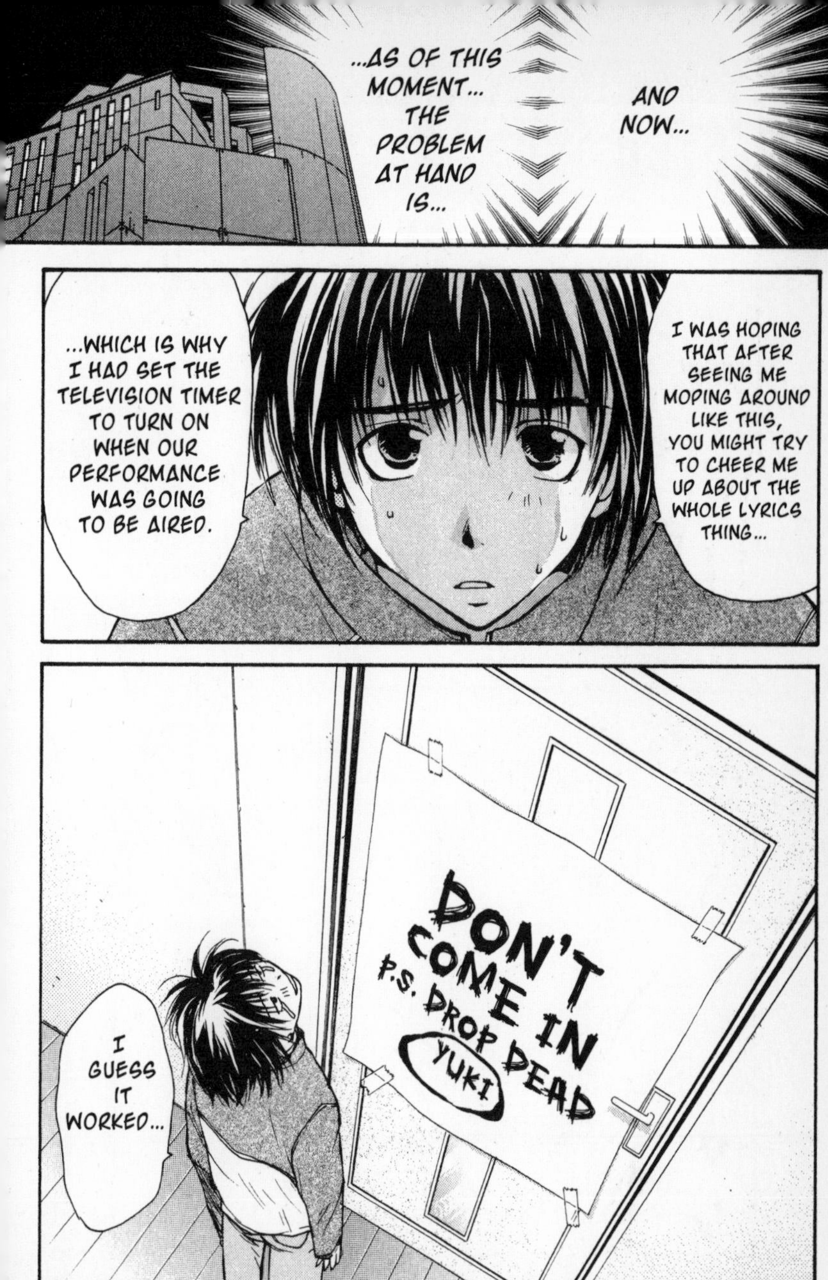
AND NOW...
...AS OF THIS MOMENT... THE PROBLEM AT HAND IS...
I WAS HOPING THAT AFTER SEEING ME MOPING AROUND LIKE THIS, YOU MIGHT TRY TO CHEER ME UP ABOUT THE WHOLE LYRICS THING...
...WHICH IS WHY I HAD SET THE TELEVISION TIMER TO TURN ON WHEN OUR PERFORMANCE WAS GOING TO BE AIRED.
DON'T COME IN
P.S. DROP DEAD
YUKI
I GUESS IT WORKED...

track46▶END

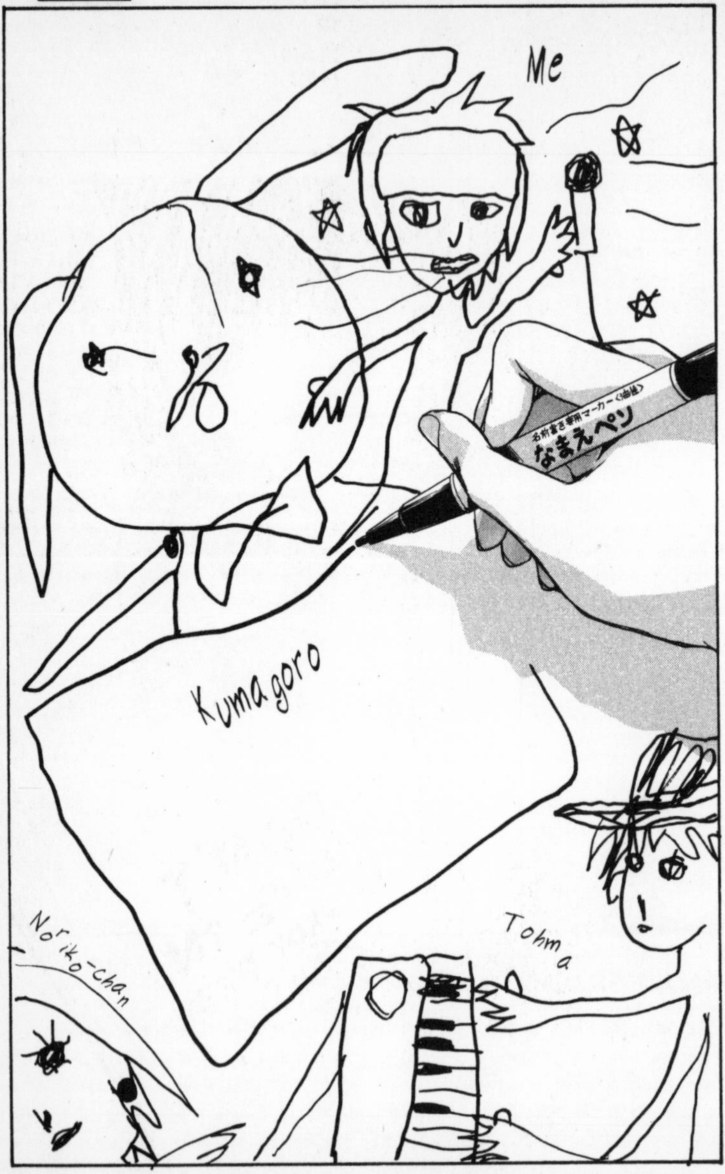
Me
名前書き専用マーカー〈油性〉
なまえペン
Kumagoro
Tohma
Noriko-chan

track47

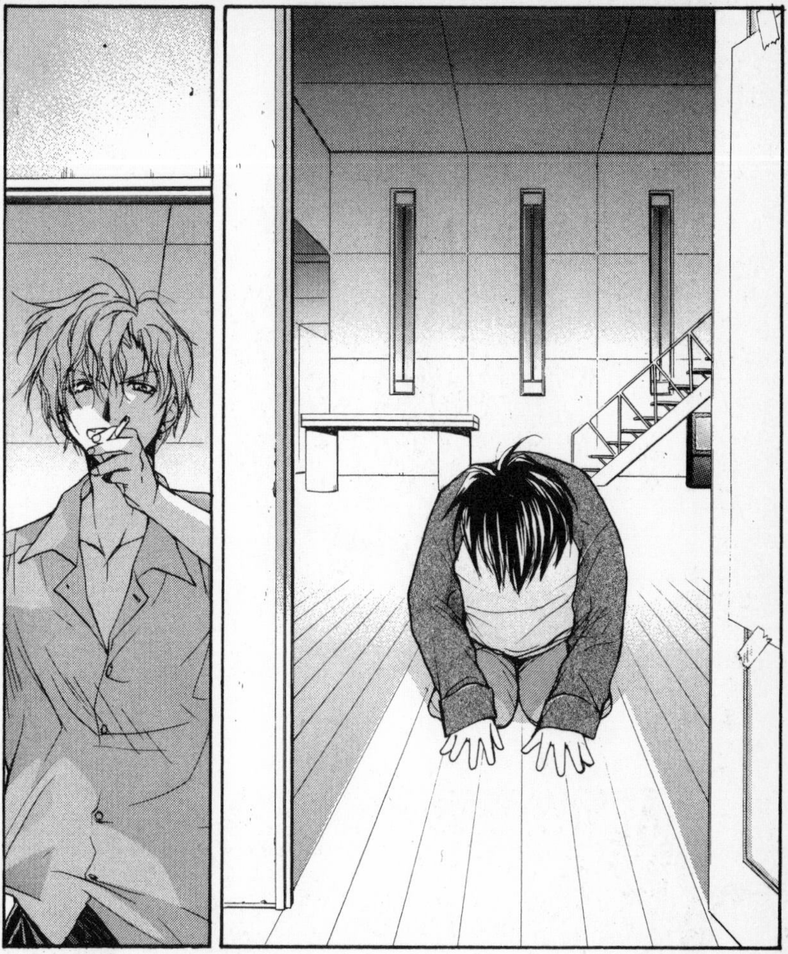

ABOUT GRAVITATION TRACK 47

This is episode 47, which simply reeks of misery. Not just the characters', but mine. The whole thing looks like it was drawn in a panic. It's pathetic! I hate feeling like I could have done more. But it'll make me happy if you can look past that and read it for what it is. I won't blame you if you get discouraged, though. It's gotten really chilly these days. Please be careful not to catch cold. And if it's not chilly where you are...I'm sorry if things are too hot. What's good to eat over there during this kind of season? Let's go have a drink someday. But I'm not a heavy drinker. But people used to say they thought I looked like I could hold my liquor...I dunno. They also said that I looked like I could operate a combine...but I don't have a license.

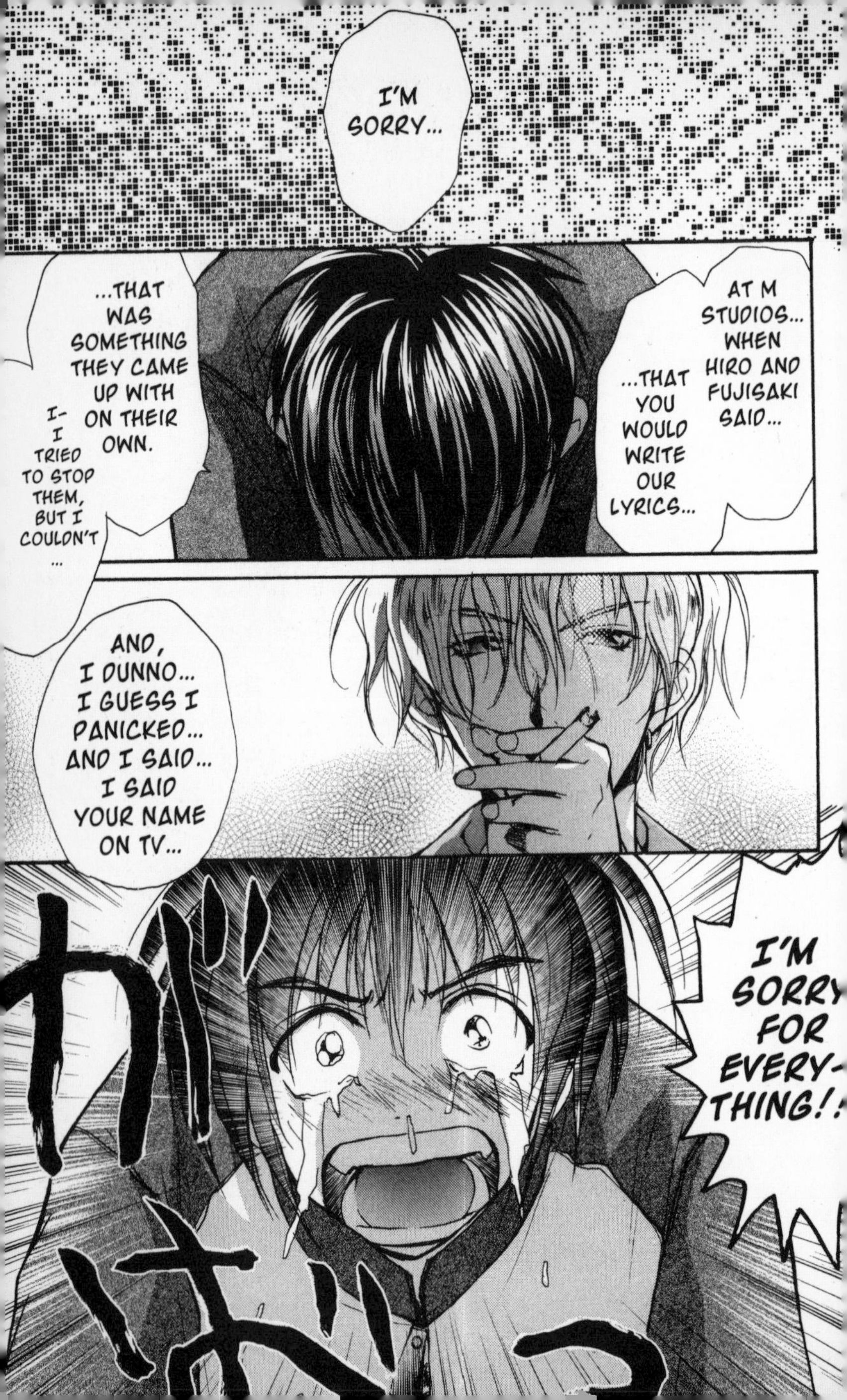
I'M SORRY...
AT M STUDIOS... WHEN HIRO AND FUJISAKI SAID...
...THAT YOU WOULD WRITE OUR LYRICS...
...THAT WAS SOMETHING THEY CAME UP WITH ON THEIR OWN.
I-I TRIED TO STOP THEM, BUT I COULDN'T ...
AND, I DUNNO... I GUESS I PANICKED... AND I SAID... I SAID YOUR NAME ON TV...
I'M SORRY FOR EVERY-THING!!

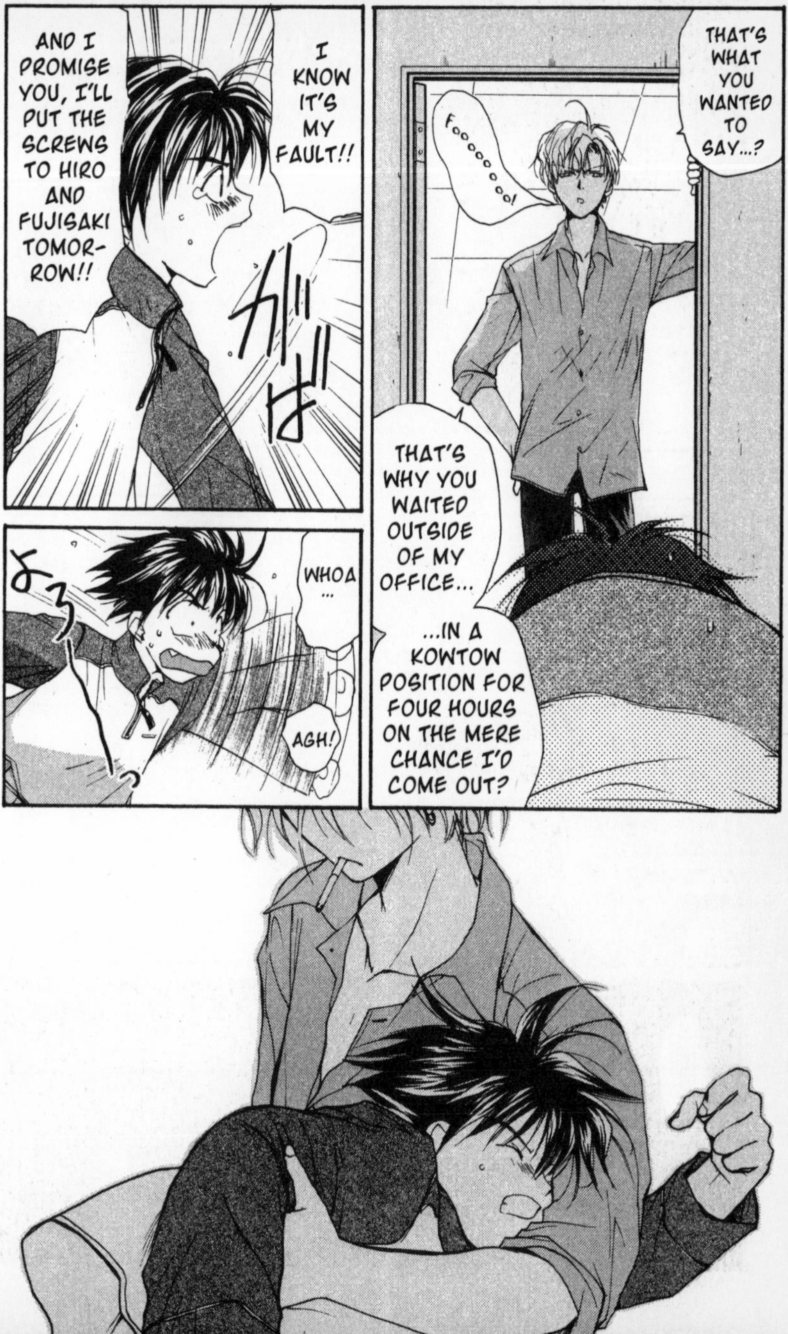
THAT'S WHAT YOU WANTED TO SAY...?
Fooooooooo!
THAT'S WHY YOU WAITED OUTSIDE OF MY OFFICE...
...IN A KOWTOW POSITION FOR FOUR HOURS ON THE MERE CHANCE I'D COME OUT?
I KNOW IT'S MY FAULT!!
AND I PROMISE YOU, I'LL PUT THE SCREWS TO HIRO AND FUJISAKI TOMORROW!!
WHOA...
AGH!

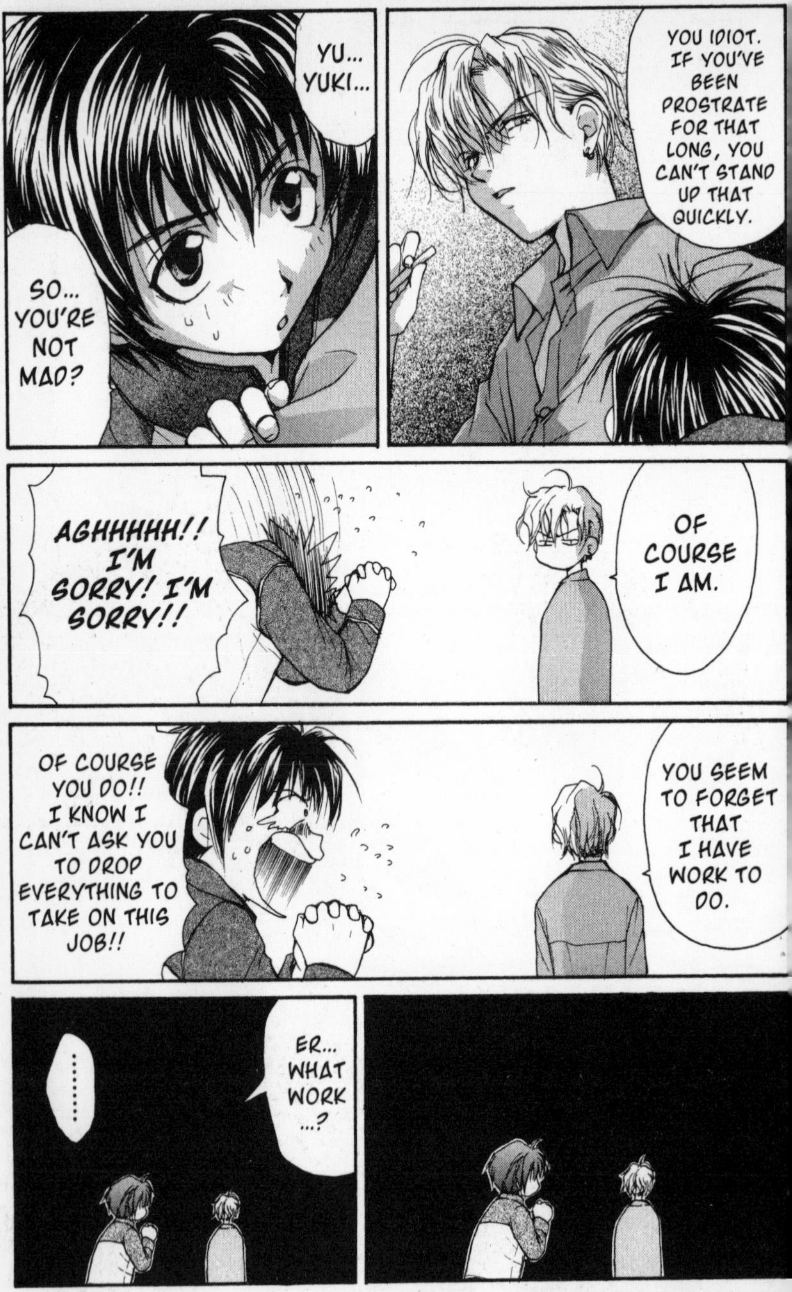
YOU IDIOT. IF YOU'VE BEEN PROSTRATE FOR THAT LONG, YOU CAN'T STAND UP THAT QUICKLY.
YU... YUKI...
SO... YOU'RE NOT MAD?
OF COURSE I AM.
AGHHHHH!! I'M SORRY! I'M SORRY!!
YOU SEEM TO FORGET THAT I HAVE WORK TO DO.
OF COURSE YOU DO!! I KNOW I CAN'T ASK YOU TO DROP EVERYTHING TO TAKE ON THIS JOB!!
ER... WHAT WORK ...?
....

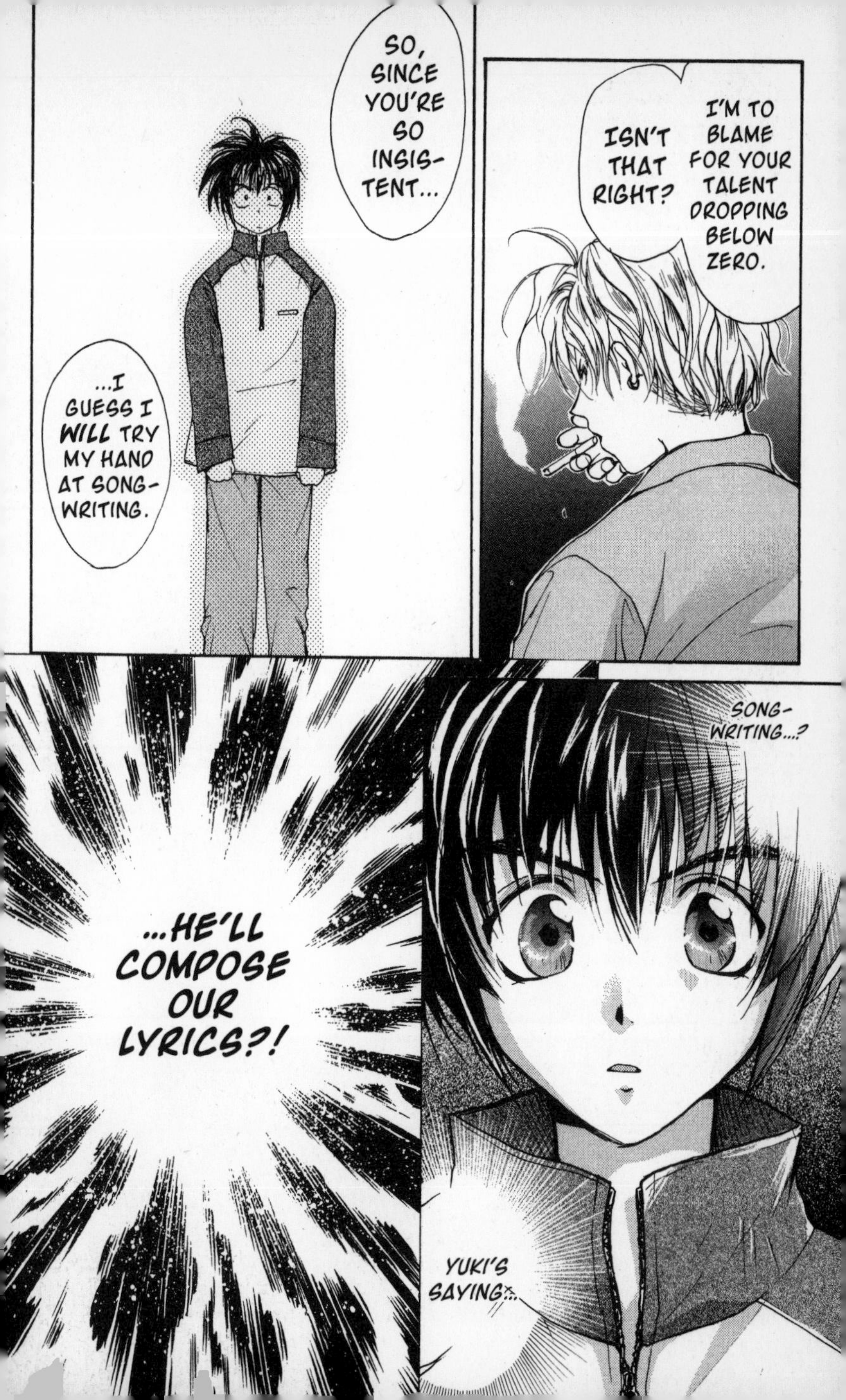
I'M TO BLAME FOR YOUR TALENT DROPPING BELOW ZERO.
ISN'T THAT RIGHT?
SO, SINCE YOU'RE SO INSIS-TENT...
...I GUESS I **WILL** TRY MY HAND AT SONG-WRITING.
SONG-WRITING...?
YUKI'S SAYING...
...HE'LL COMPOSE OUR LYRICS?!

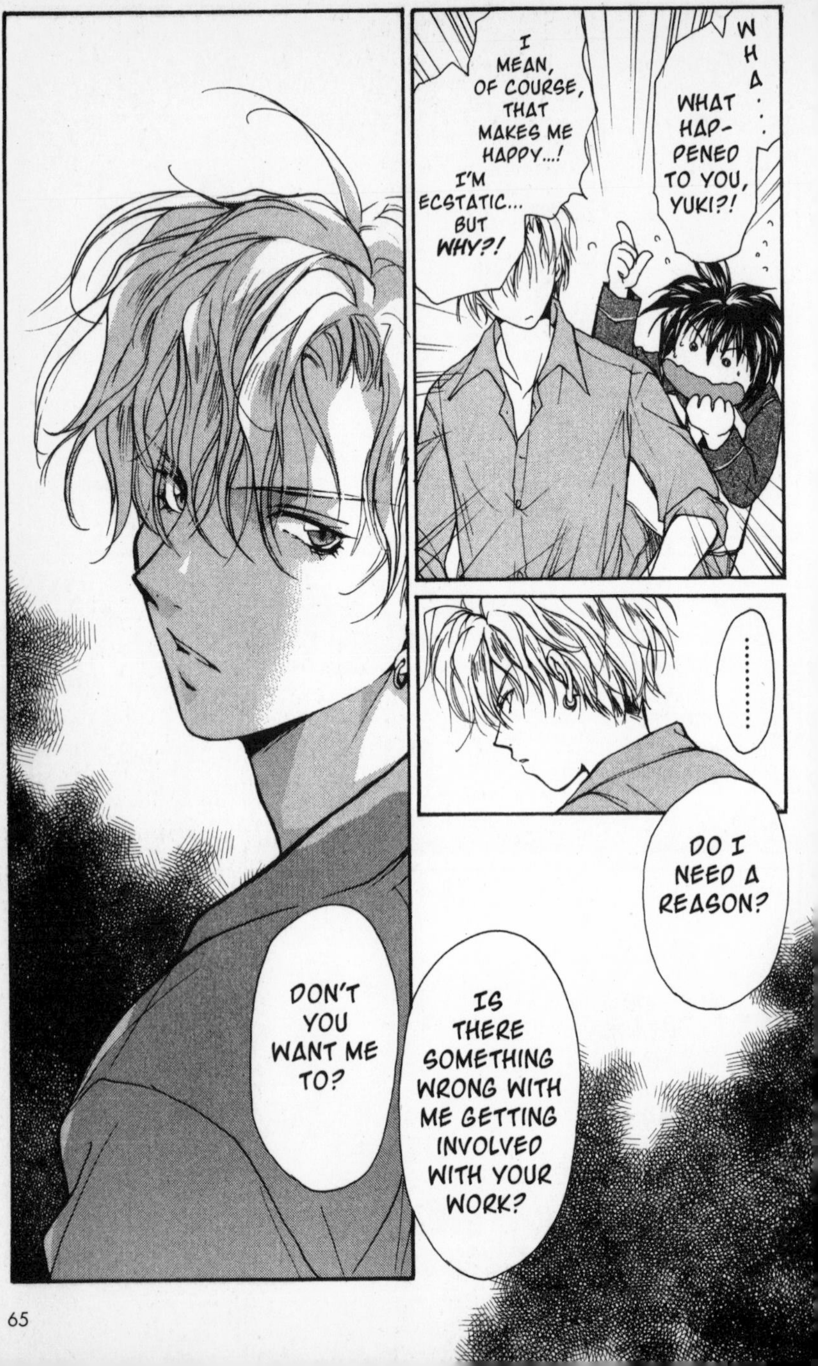
WHA...
WHAT HAP-PENED TO YOU, YUKI?!
I MEAN, OF COURSE, THAT MAKES ME HAPPY...! I'M ECSTATIC... BUT WHY?!
......
DO I NEED A REASON?
IS THERE SOMETHING WRONG WITH ME GETTING INVOLVED WITH YOUR WORK?
DON'T YOU WANT ME TO?

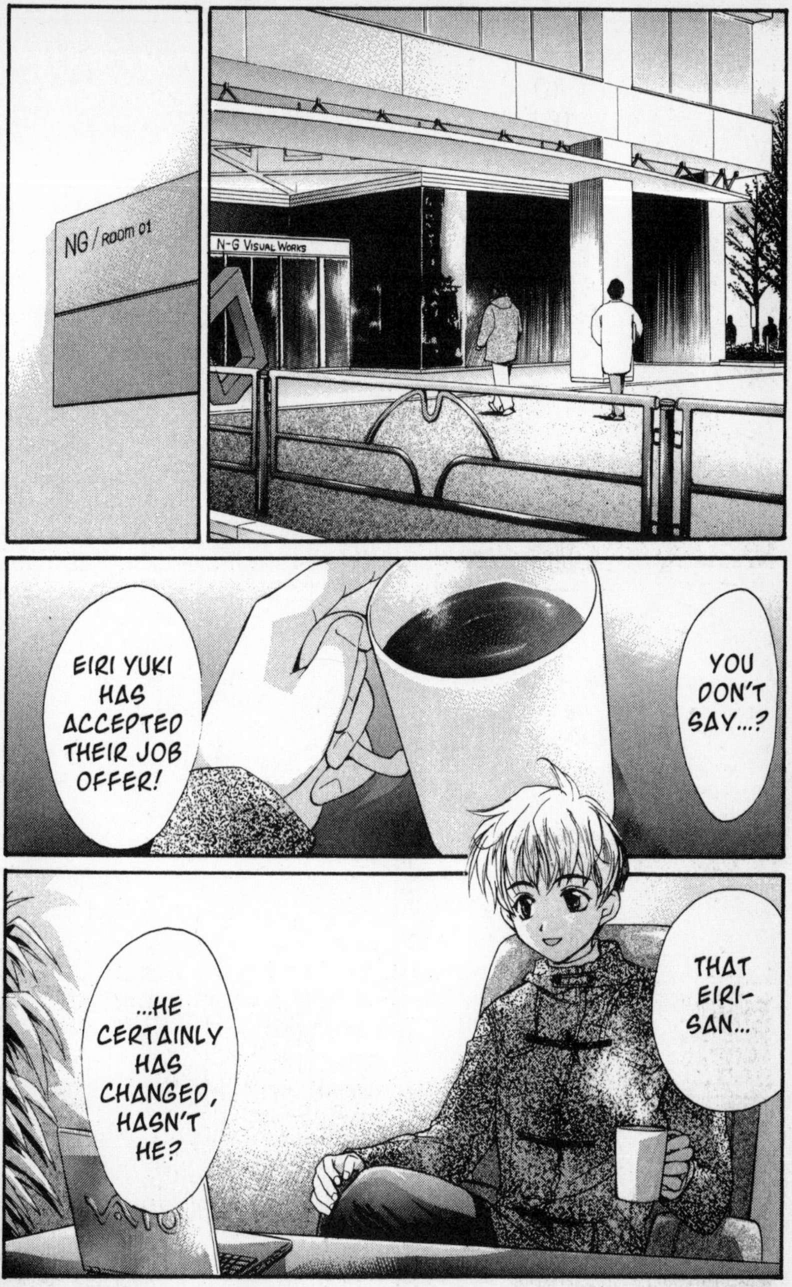
N-G VISUAL WORKS
NG / ROOM 01
YOU DON'T SAY...?
EIRI YUKI HAS ACCEPTED THEIR JOB OFFER!
THAT EIRI-SAN...
...HE CERTAINLY HAS CHANGED, HASN'T HE?

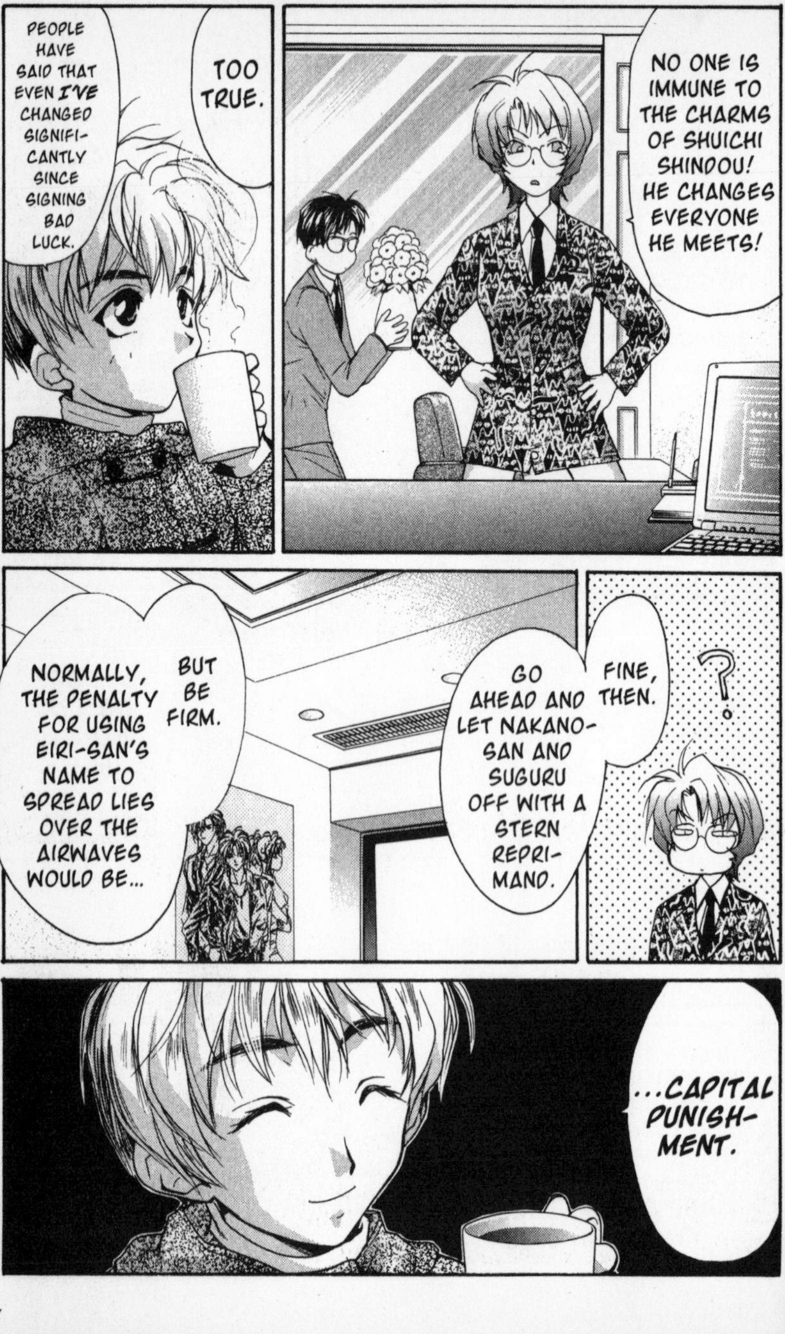
NO ONE IS IMMUNE TO THE CHARMS OF SHUICHI SHINDOU! HE CHANGES EVERYONE HE MEETS!
TOO TRUE.
PEOPLE HAVE SAID THAT EVEN *I'VE* CHANGED SIGNIFICANTLY SINCE SIGNING BAD LUCK.
?
FINE, THEN.
GO AHEAD AND LET NAKANO-SAN AND SUGURU OFF WITH A STERN REPRIMAND.
BUT BE FIRM.
NORMALLY, THE PENALTY FOR USING EIRI-SAN'S NAME TO SPREAD LIES OVER THE AIRWAVES WOULD BE...
...CAPITAL PUNISHMENT.

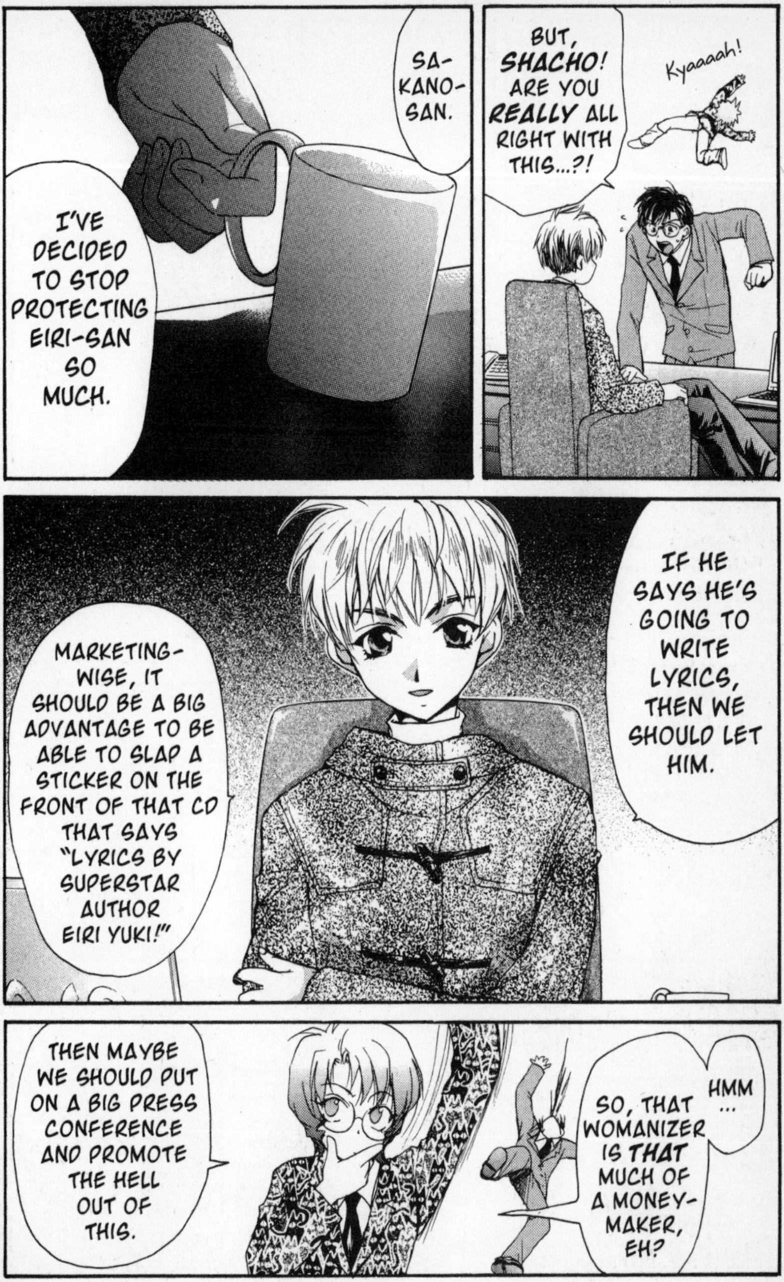
BUT, SHACHO! ARE YOU REALLY ALL RIGHT WITH THIS...?!
Kyaaaah!
SA-KANO-SAN.
I'VE DECIDED TO STOP PROTECTING EIRI-SAN SO MUCH.
IF HE SAYS HE'S GOING TO WRITE LYRICS, THEN WE SHOULD LET HIM.
MARKETING-WISE, IT SHOULD BE A BIG ADVANTAGE TO BE ABLE TO SLAP A STICKER ON THE FRONT OF THAT CD THAT SAYS "LYRICS BY SUPERSTAR AUTHOR EIRI YUKI!"
HMM ...
SO, THAT WOMANIZER IS THAT MUCH OF A MONEY-MAKER, EH?
THEN MAYBE WE SHOULD PUT ON A BIG PRESS CONFERENCE AND PROMOTE THE HELL OUT OF THIS.

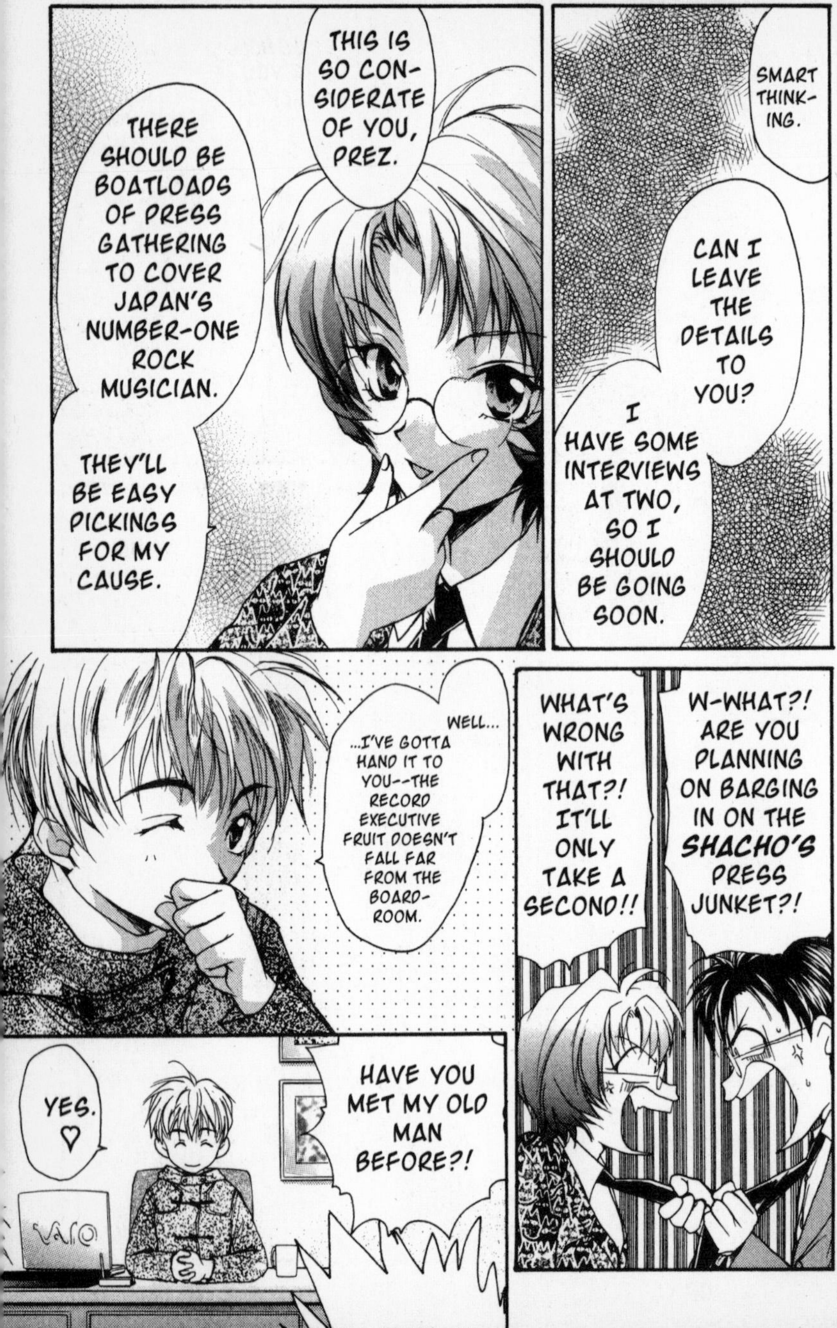
SMART THINKING.
CAN I LEAVE THE DETAILS TO YOU?
I HAVE SOME INTERVIEWS AT TWO, SO I SHOULD BE GOING SOON.
THIS IS SO CONSIDERATE OF YOU, PREZ.
THERE SHOULD BE BOATLOADS OF PRESS GATHERING TO COVER JAPAN'S NUMBER-ONE ROCK MUSICIAN.
THEY'LL BE EASY PICKINGS FOR MY CAUSE.
W-WHAT?! ARE YOU PLANNING ON BARGING IN ON THE ***SHACHO'S*** PRESS JUNKET?!
WHAT'S WRONG WITH THAT?! IT'LL ONLY TAKE A SECOND!!
WELL...
...I'VE GOTTA HAND IT TO YOU--THE RECORD EXECUTIVE FRUIT DOESN'T FALL FAR FROM THE BOARD-ROOM.
HAVE YOU MET MY OLD MAN BEFORE?!
YES. ♡

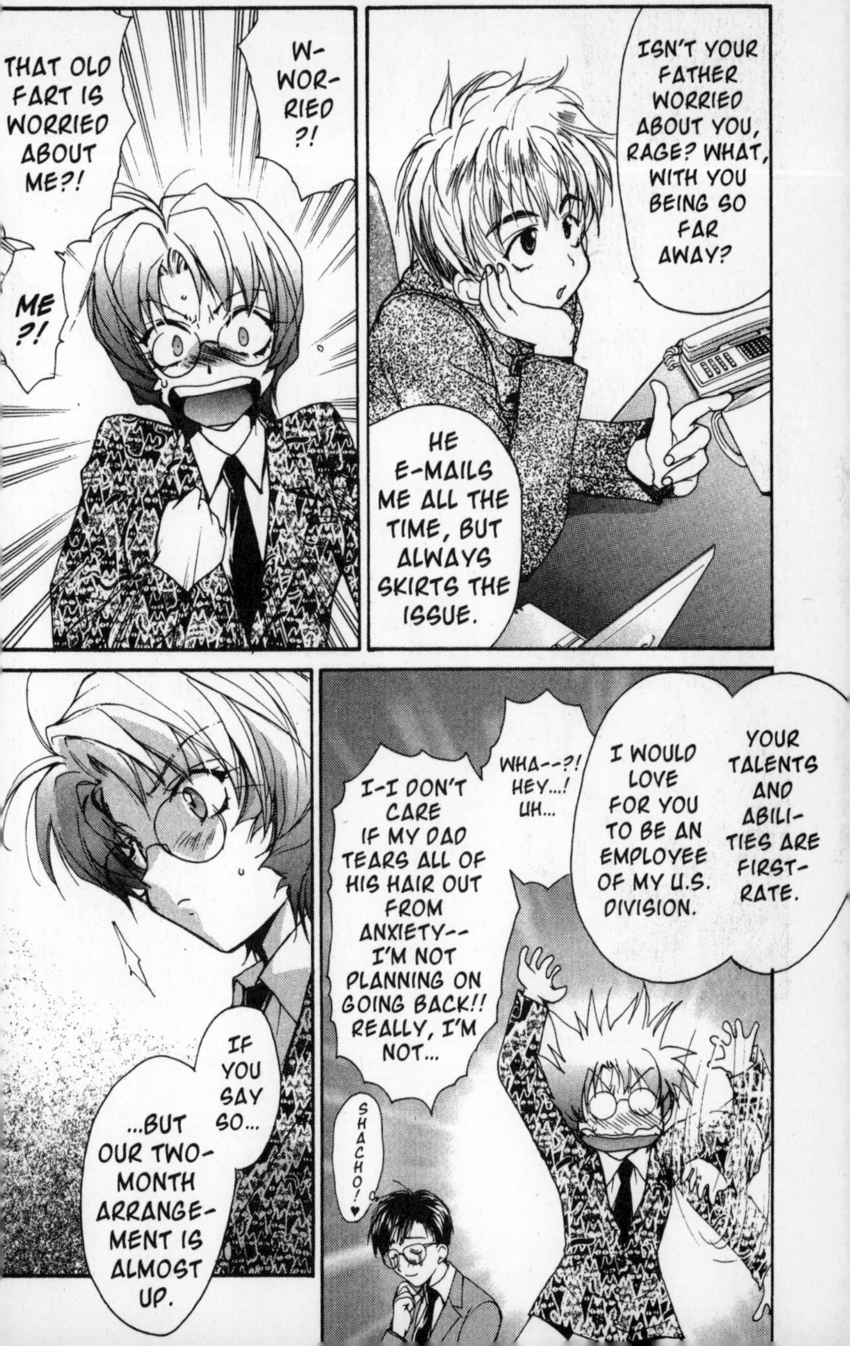
ISN'T YOUR FATHER WORRIED ABOUT YOU, RAGE? WHAT, WITH YOU BEING SO FAR AWAY?
HE E-MAILS ME ALL THE TIME, BUT ALWAYS SKIRTS THE ISSUE.
W-WOR-RIED ?!
THAT OLD FART IS WORRIED ABOUT ME?!
ME ?!
YOUR TALENTS AND ABILI-TIES ARE FIRST-RATE.
I WOULD LOVE FOR YOU TO BE AN EMPLOYEE OF MY U.S. DIVISION.
WHA--?! HEY...! UH...
I-I DON'T CARE IF MY DAD TEARS ALL OF HIS HAIR OUT FROM ANXIETY-- I'M NOT PLANNING ON GOING BACK!! REALLY, I'M NOT...
SHACHO!♥
IF YOU SAY SO...
...BUT OUR TWO-MONTH ARRANGE-MENT IS ALMOST UP.

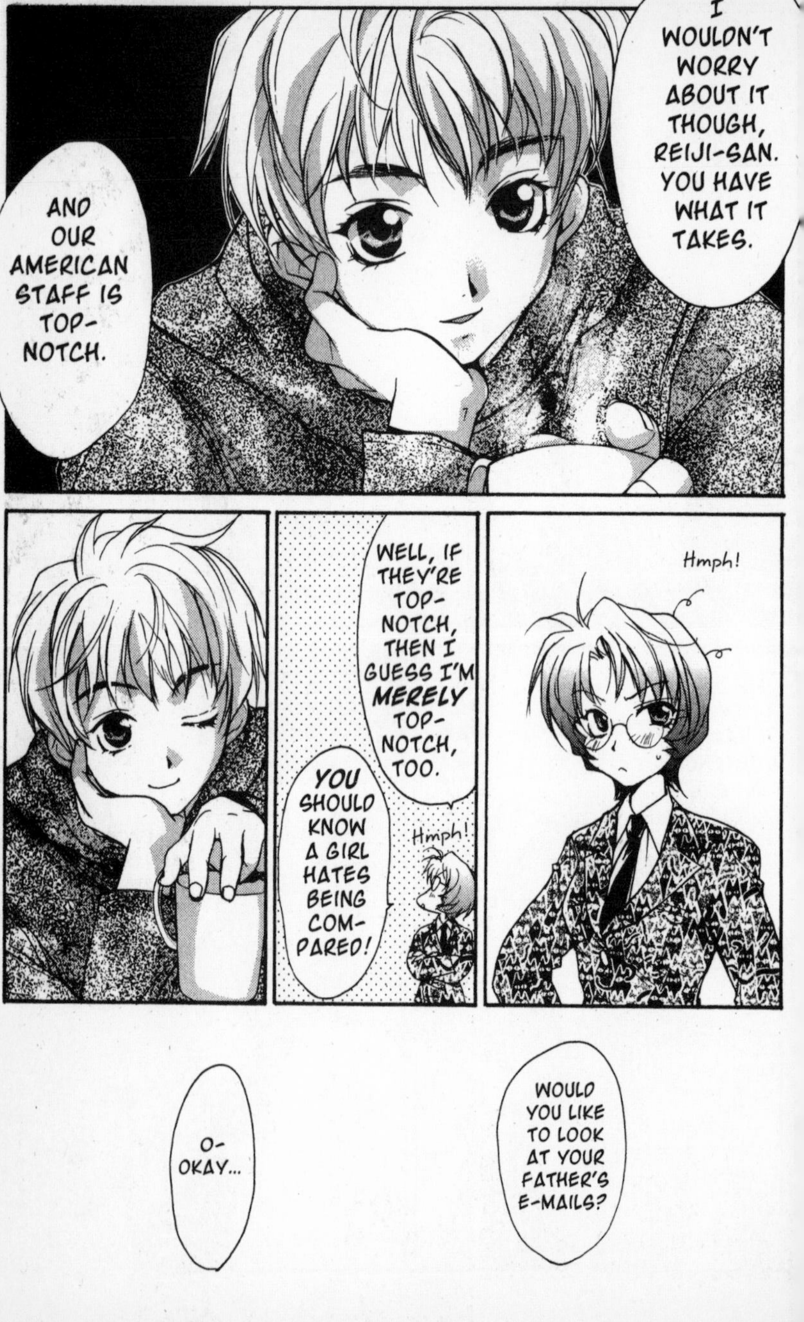
I WOULDN'T WORRY ABOUT IT THOUGH, REIJI-SAN. YOU HAVE WHAT IT TAKES.
AND OUR AMERICAN STAFF IS TOP-NOTCH.
Hmph!
WELL, IF THEY'RE TOP-NOTCH, THEN I GUESS I'M ***MERELY*** TOP-NOTCH, TOO.
Hmph!
YOU SHOULD KNOW A GIRL HATES BEING COMPARED!
WOULD YOU LIKE TO LOOK AT YOUR FATHER'S E-MAILS?
O-OKAY...

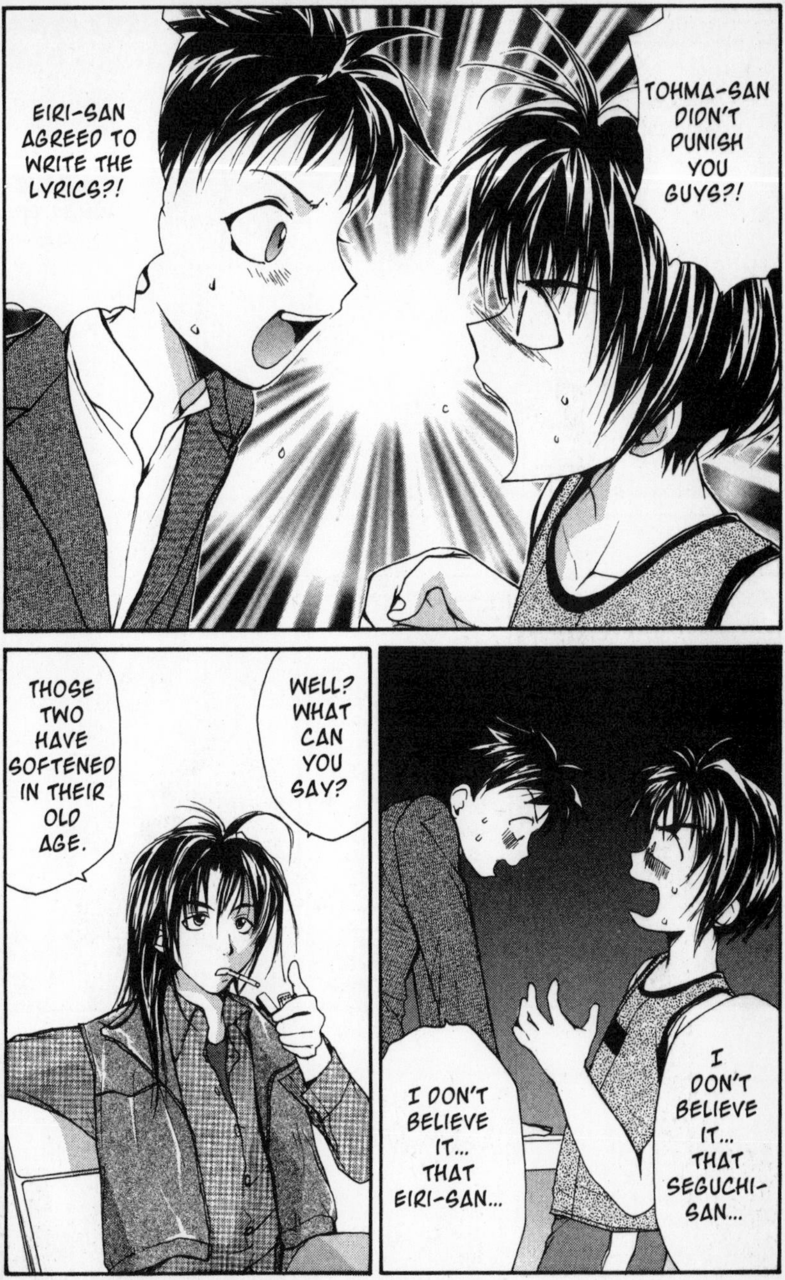
TOHMA-SAN DIDN'T PUNISH YOU GUYS?!
EIRI-SAN AGREED TO WRITE THE LYRICS?!
I DON'T BELIEVE IT... THAT SEGUCHI-SAN...
I DON'T BELIEVE IT... THAT EIRI-SAN...
WELL? WHAT CAN YOU SAY?
THOSE TWO HAVE SOFTENED IN THEIR OLD AGE.

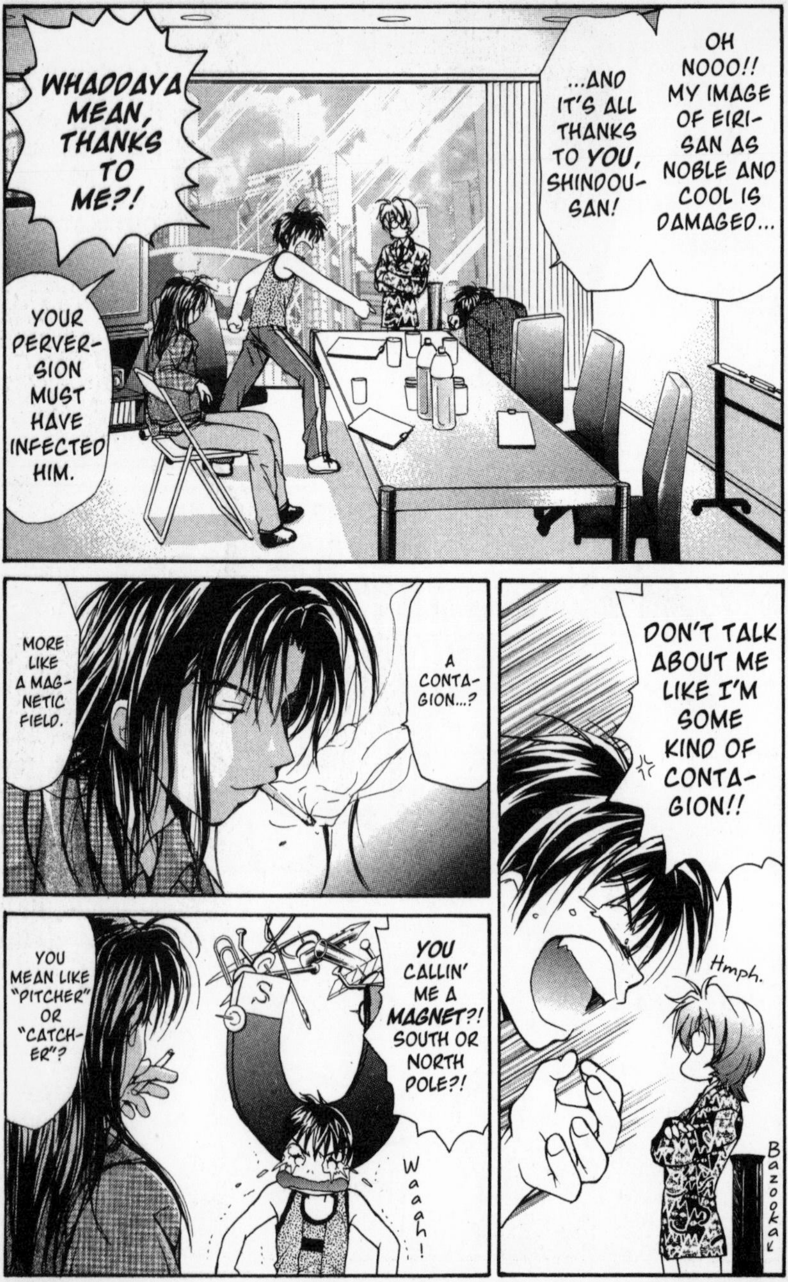
OH NOOO!! MY IMAGE OF EIRI-SAN AS NOBLE AND COOL IS DAMAGED...
...AND IT'S ALL THANKS TO YOU, SHINDOU-SAN!
WHADDAYA MEAN, THANKS TO ME?!
YOUR PERVERSION MUST HAVE INFECTED HIM.
DON'T TALK ABOUT ME LIKE I'M SOME KIND OF CONTAGION!!
Hmph.
Bazookak
A CONTAGION...?
MORE LIKE A MAGNETIC FIELD.
YOU CALLIN' ME A MAGNET?! SOUTH OR NORTH POLE?!
S
Waaah!
YOU MEAN LIKE "PITCHER" OR "CATCHER"?

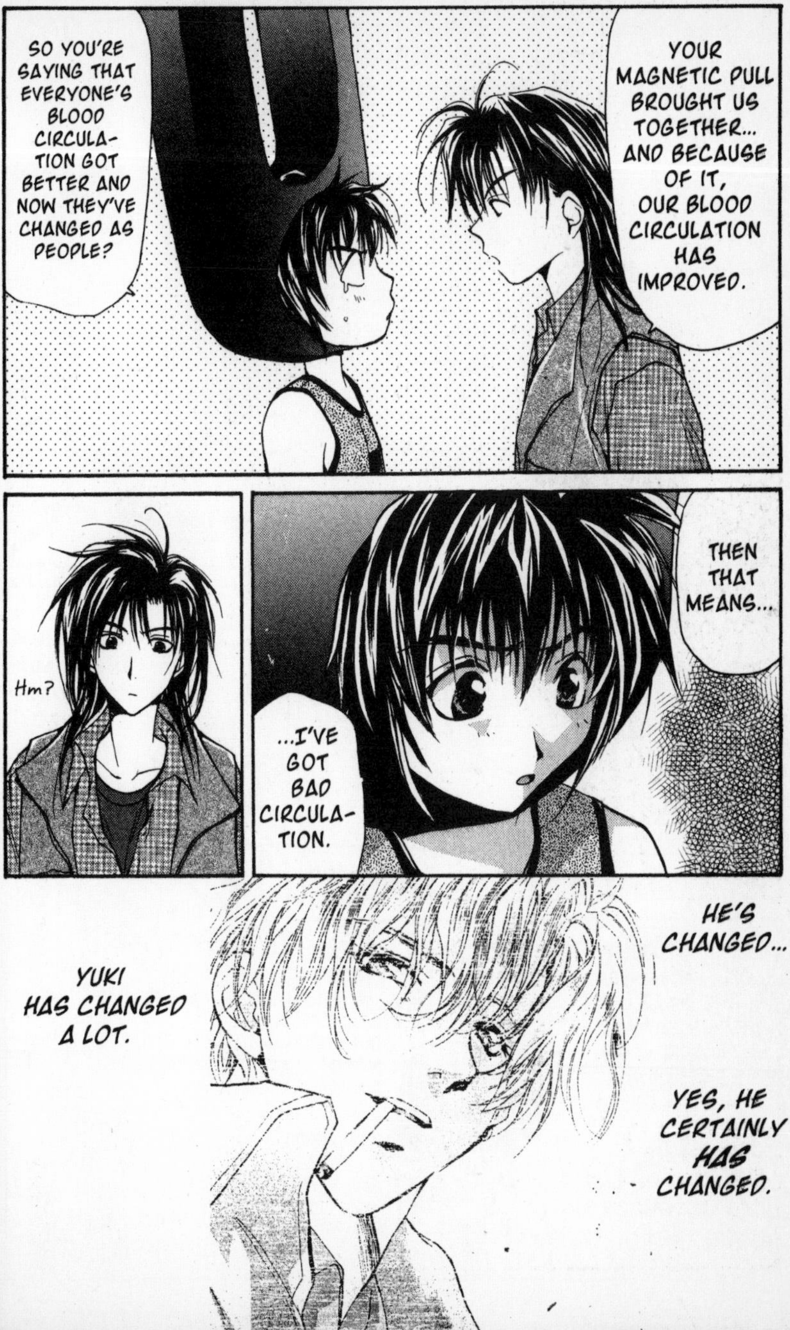
YOUR MAGNETIC PULL BROUGHT US TOGETHER... AND BECAUSE OF IT, OUR BLOOD CIRCULATION HAS IMPROVED.
SO YOU'RE SAYING THAT EVERYONE'S BLOOD CIRCULATION GOT BETTER AND NOW THEY'VE CHANGED AS PEOPLE?
THEN THAT MEANS...
...I'VE GOT BAD CIRCULATION.
Hm?
HE'S CHANGED...
YUKI HAS CHANGED A LOT.
YES, HE CERTAINLY HAS CHANGED.

BUT NOT ME...

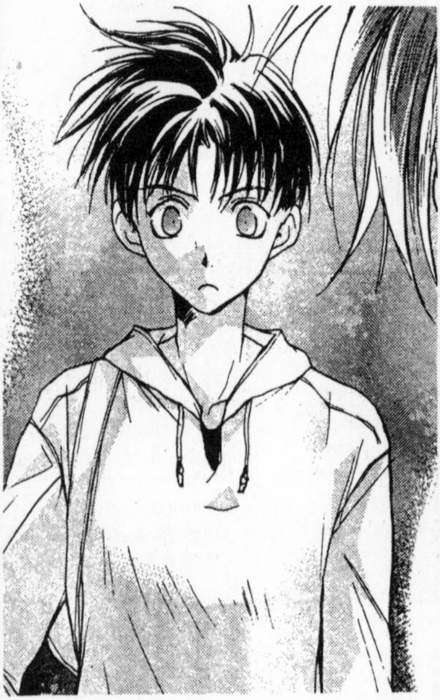

I'M STILL THE SAME...

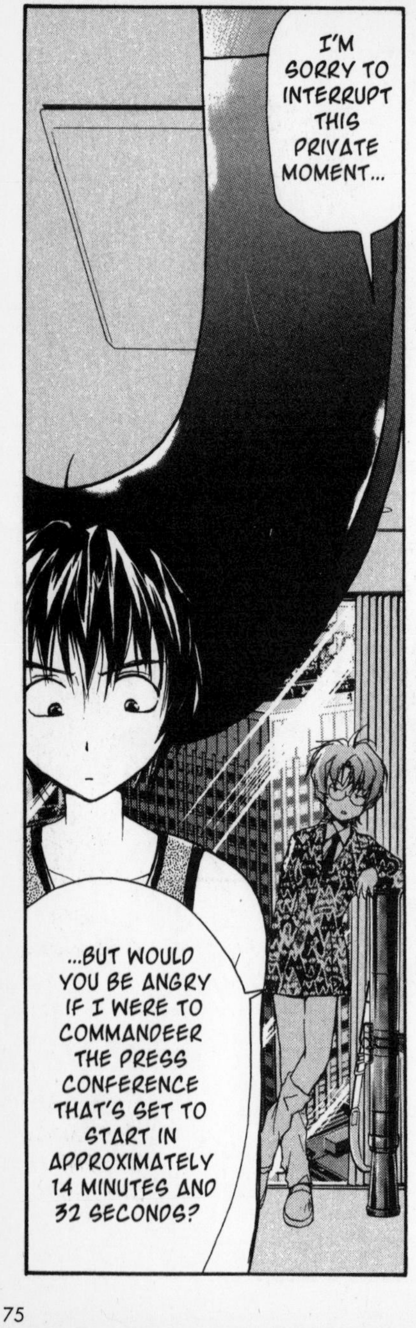
I'M SORRY TO INTERRUPT THIS PRIVATE MOMENT...
...BUT WOULD YOU BE ANGRY IF I WERE TO COMMANDEER THE PRESS CONFERENCE THAT'S SET TO START IN APPROXIMATELY 14 MINUTES AND 32 SECONDS?

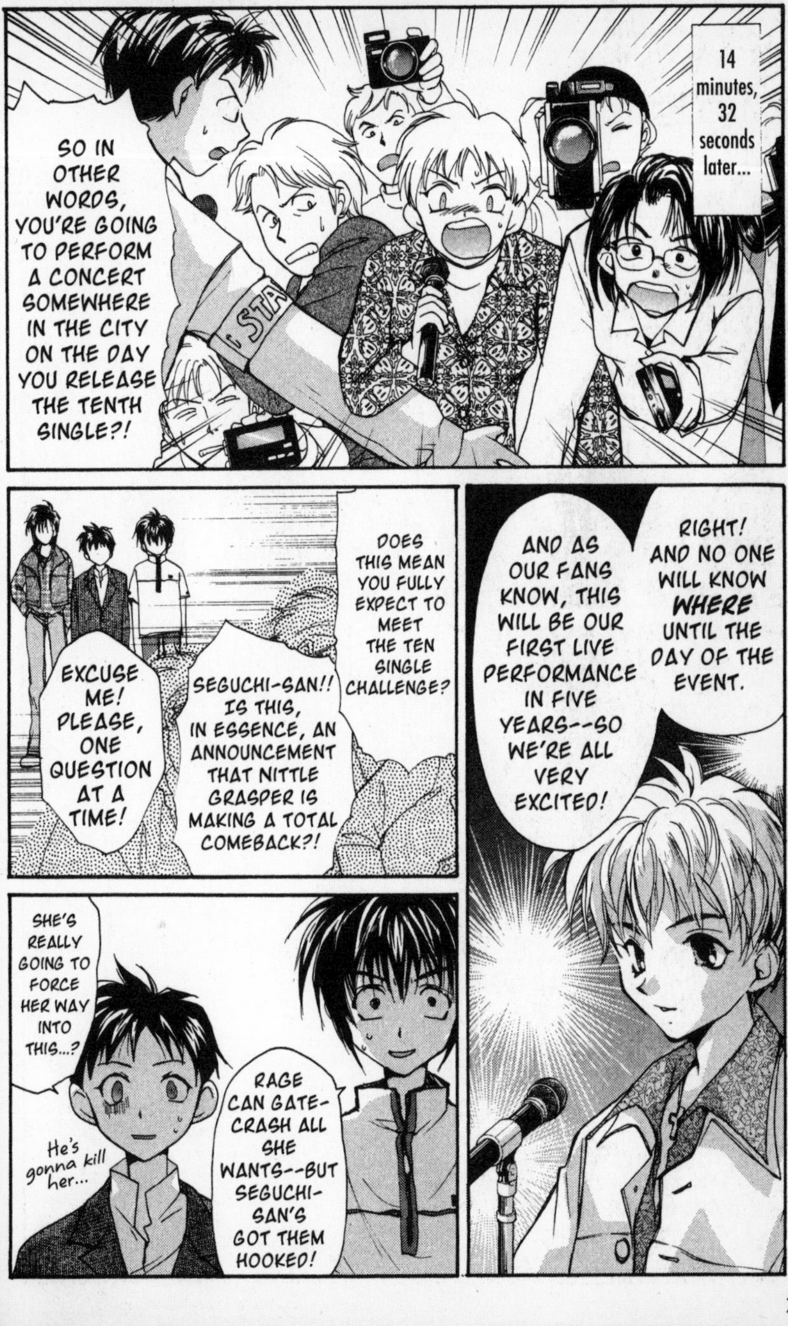
14 minutes, 32 seconds later...
SO IN OTHER WORDS, YOU'RE GOING TO PERFORM A CONCERT SOMEWHERE IN THE CITY ON THE DAY YOU RELEASE THE TENTH SINGLE?!
RIGHT! AND NO ONE WILL KNOW ***WHERE*** UNTIL THE DAY OF THE EVENT.
AND AS OUR FANS KNOW, THIS WILL BE OUR FIRST LIVE PERFORMANCE IN FIVE YEARS--SO WE'RE ALL VERY EXCITED!
DOES THIS MEAN YOU FULLY EXPECT TO MEET THE TEN SINGLE CHALLENGE?
SEGUCHI-SAN!! IS THIS, IN ESSENCE, AN ANNOUNCEMENT THAT NITTLE GRASPER IS MAKING A TOTAL COMEBACK?!
EXCUSE ME! PLEASE, ONE QUESTION AT A TIME!
SHE'S REALLY GOING TO FORCE HER WAY INTO THIS...?
RAGE CAN GATE-CRASH ALL SHE WANTS--BUT SEGUCHI-SAN'S GOT THEM HOOKED!
He's gonna kill her...

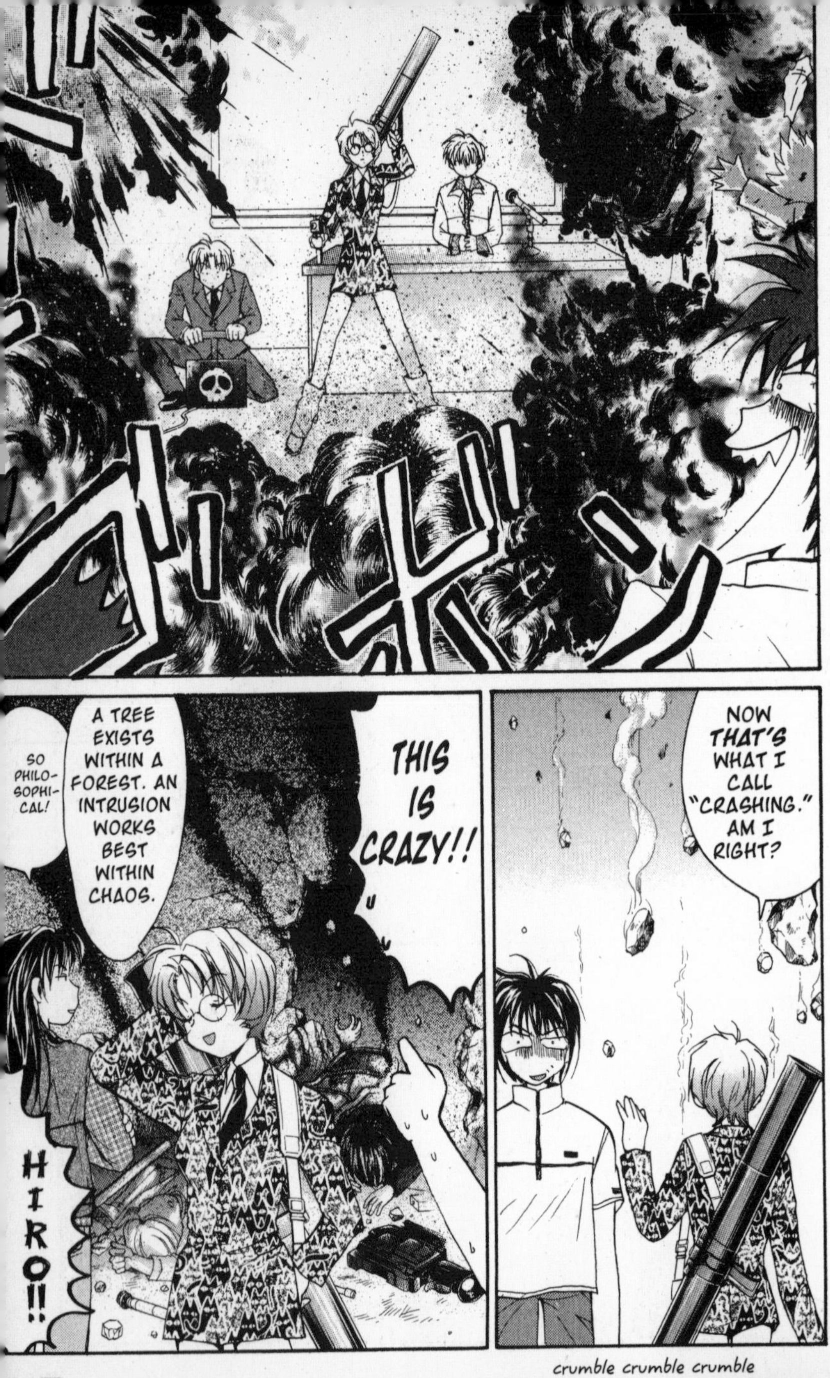
NOW THAT'S WHAT I CALL "CRASHING." AM I RIGHT?
THIS IS CRAZY!!
A TREE EXISTS WITHIN A FOREST. AN INTRUSION WORKS BEST WITHIN CHAOS.
SO PHILOSOPHICAL!
HIRO!!

crumble crumble crumble

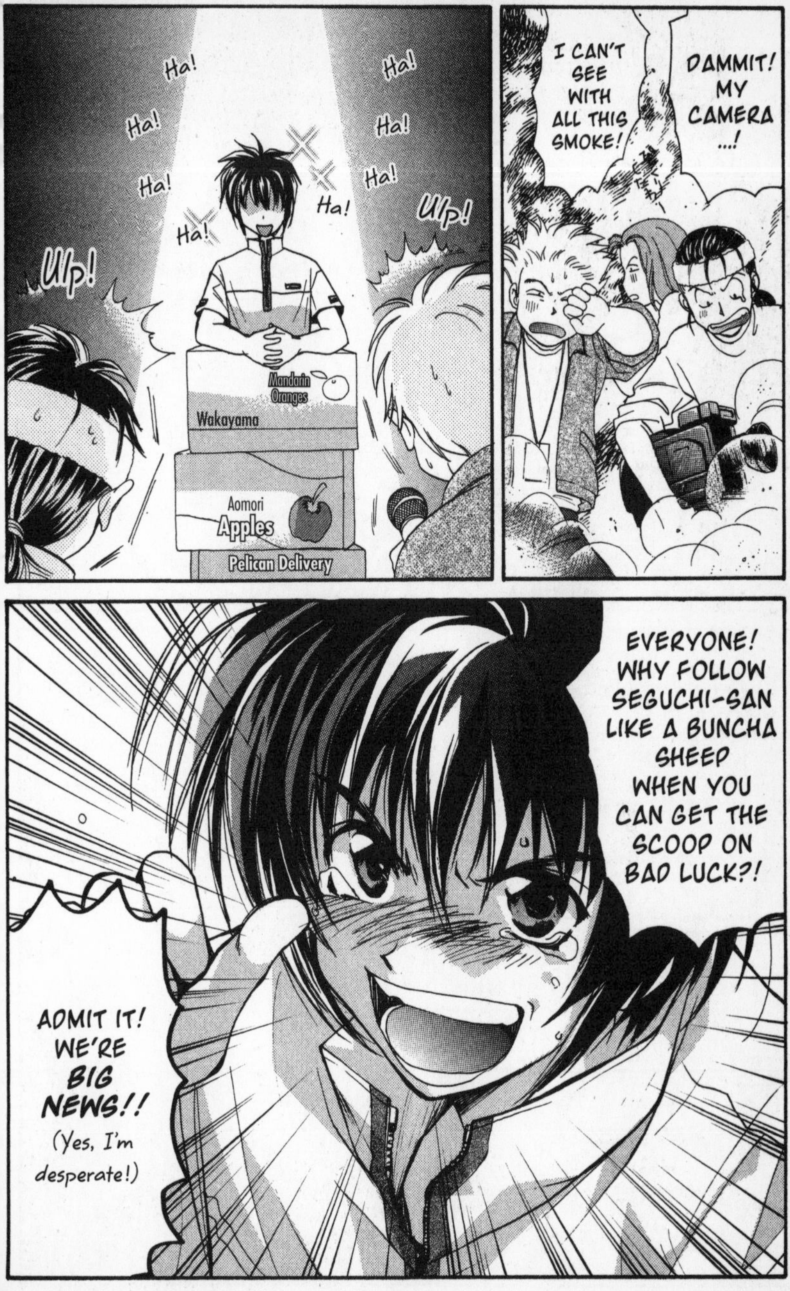
DAMMIT! MY CAMERA ...!
I CAN'T SEE WITH ALL THIS SMOKE!
Ha!
Ha!
Ha!
Ha!
Ulp!
Ha!
Ha!
Ha!
Ha!
Ulp!
Mandarin Oranges
Wakayama
Aomori Apples
Pelican Delivery
EVERYONE! WHY FOLLOW SEGUCHI-SAN LIKE A BUNCHA SHEEP WHEN YOU CAN GET THE SCOOP ON BAD LUCK?!
ADMIT IT! WE'RE BIG NEWS!!
(Yes, I'm desperate!)

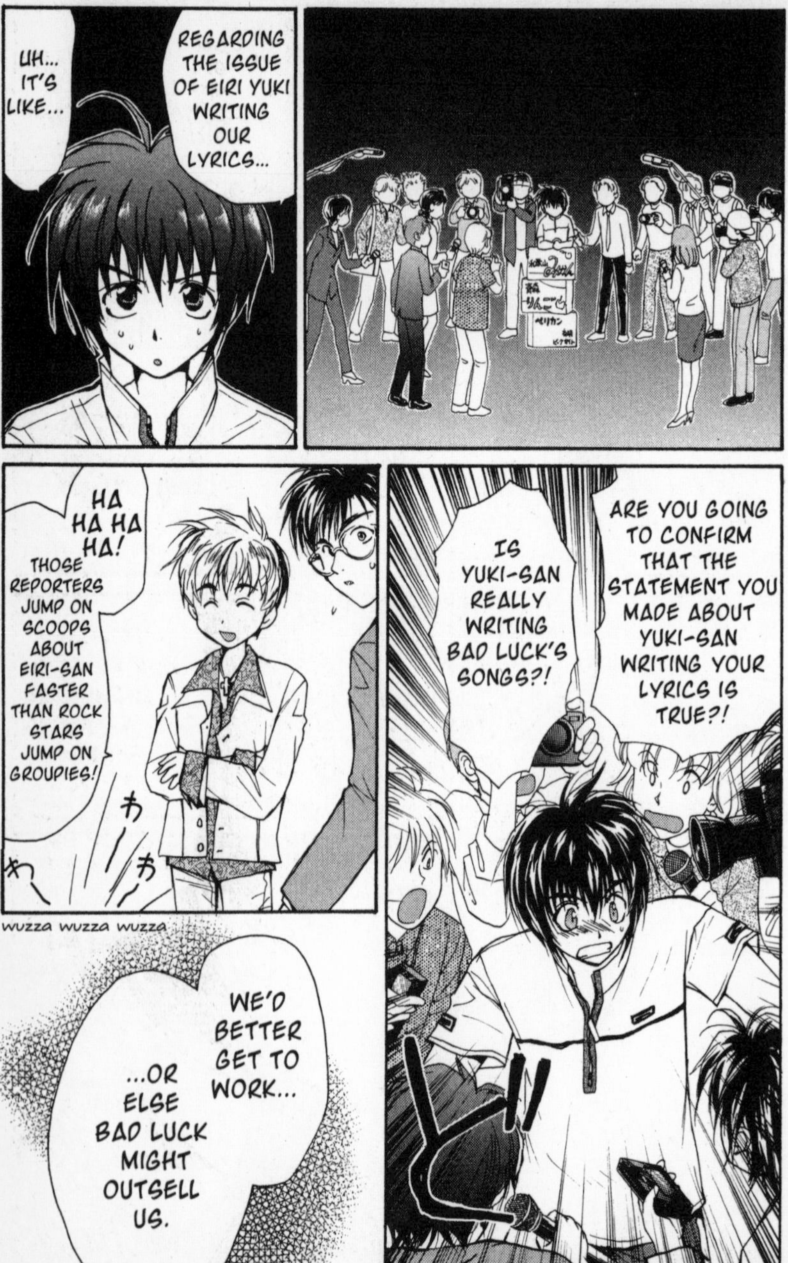
REGARDING THE ISSUE OF EIRI YUKI WRITING OUR LYRICS...
UH... IT'S LIKE...
ARE YOU GOING TO CONFIRM THAT THE STATEMENT YOU MADE ABOUT YUKI-SAN WRITING YOUR LYRICS IS TRUE?!
IS YUKI-SAN REALLY WRITING BAD LUCK'S SONGS?!
HA HA HA HA! THOSE REPORTERS JUMP ON SCOOPS ABOUT EIRI-SAN FASTER THAN ROCK STARS JUMP ON GROUPIES!
わ～ わ～ わ～
wuzza wuzza wuzza
WE'D BETTER GET TO WORK...
...OR ELSE BAD LUCK MIGHT OUTSELL US.

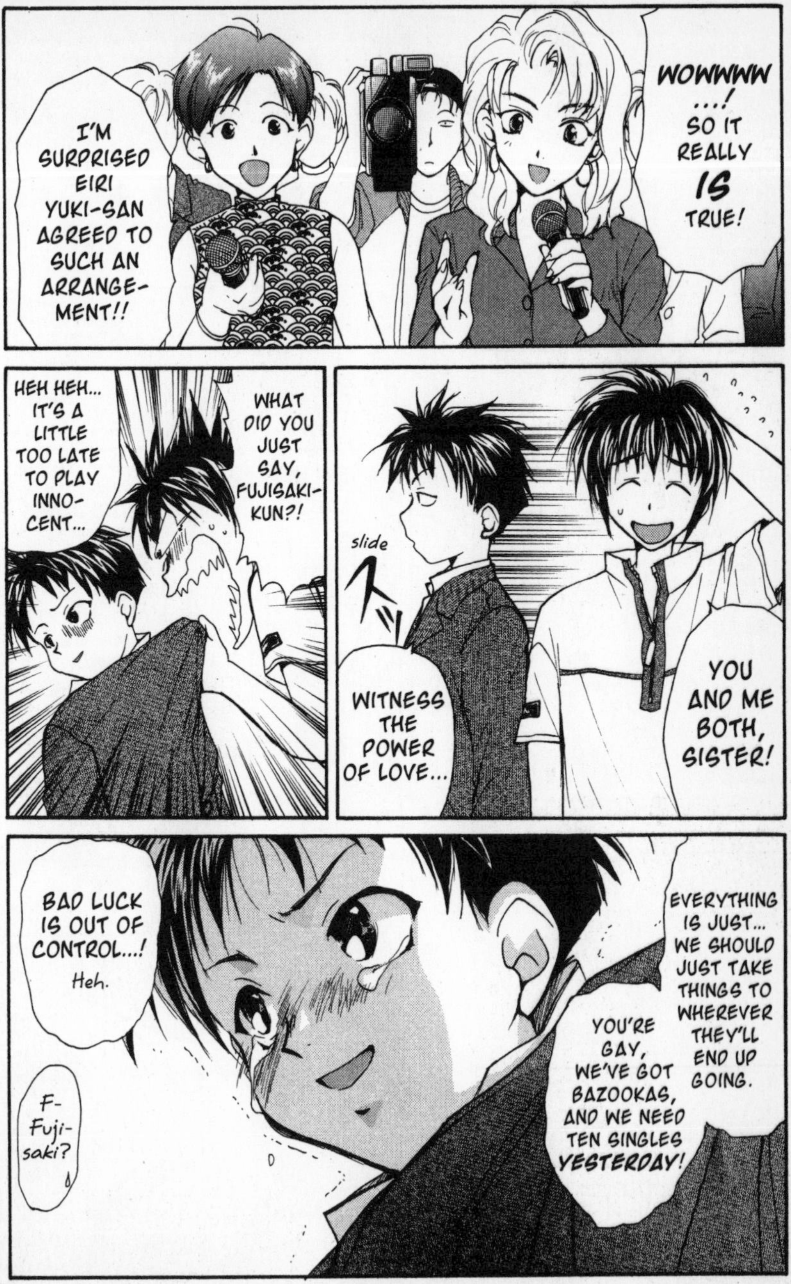
WOWWWW...! SO IT REALLY IS TRUE!
I'M SURPRISED EIRI YUKI-SAN AGREED TO SUCH AN ARRANGE-MENT!!
YOU AND ME BOTH, SISTER!
slide
WITNESS THE POWER OF LOVE...
WHAT DID YOU JUST SAY, FUJISAKI-KUN?!
HEH HEH... IT'S A LITTLE TOO LATE TO PLAY INNO-CENT...
EVERYTHING IS JUST... WE SHOULD JUST TAKE THINGS TO WHEREVER THEY'LL END UP GOING.
YOU'RE GAY, WE'VE GOT BAZOOKAS, AND WE NEED TEN SINGLES YESTERDAY!
BAD LUCK IS OUT OF CONTROL...!
Heh.
F-Fuji-saki?

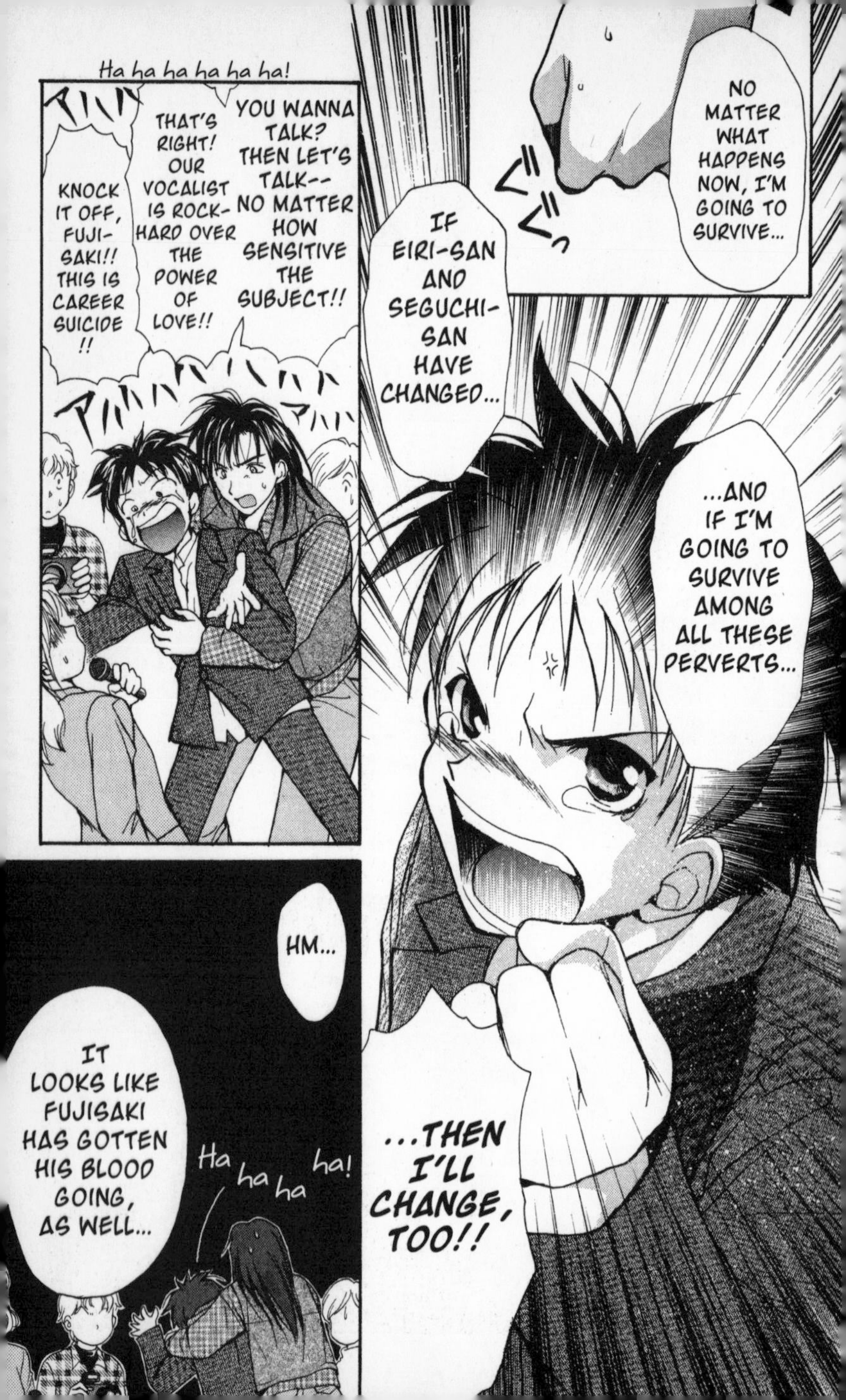
NO MATTER WHAT HAPPENS NOW, I'M GOING TO SURVIVE...
IF EIRI-SAN AND SEGUCHI-SAN HAVE CHANGED...
...AND IF I'M GOING TO SURVIVE AMONG ALL THESE PERVERTS...
...THEN I'LL CHANGE, TOO!!
Ha ha ha ha ha ha ha!
YOU WANNA TALK? THEN LET'S TALK-- NO MATTER HOW SENSITIVE THE SUBJECT!!
THAT'S RIGHT! OUR VOCALIST IS ROCK-HARD OVER THE POWER OF LOVE!!
KNOCK IT OFF, FUJI-SAKI!! THIS IS CAREER SUICIDE!!
HM...
IT LOOKS LIKE FUJISAKI HAS GOTTEN HIS BLOOD GOING, AS WELL...
Ha ha ha ha!

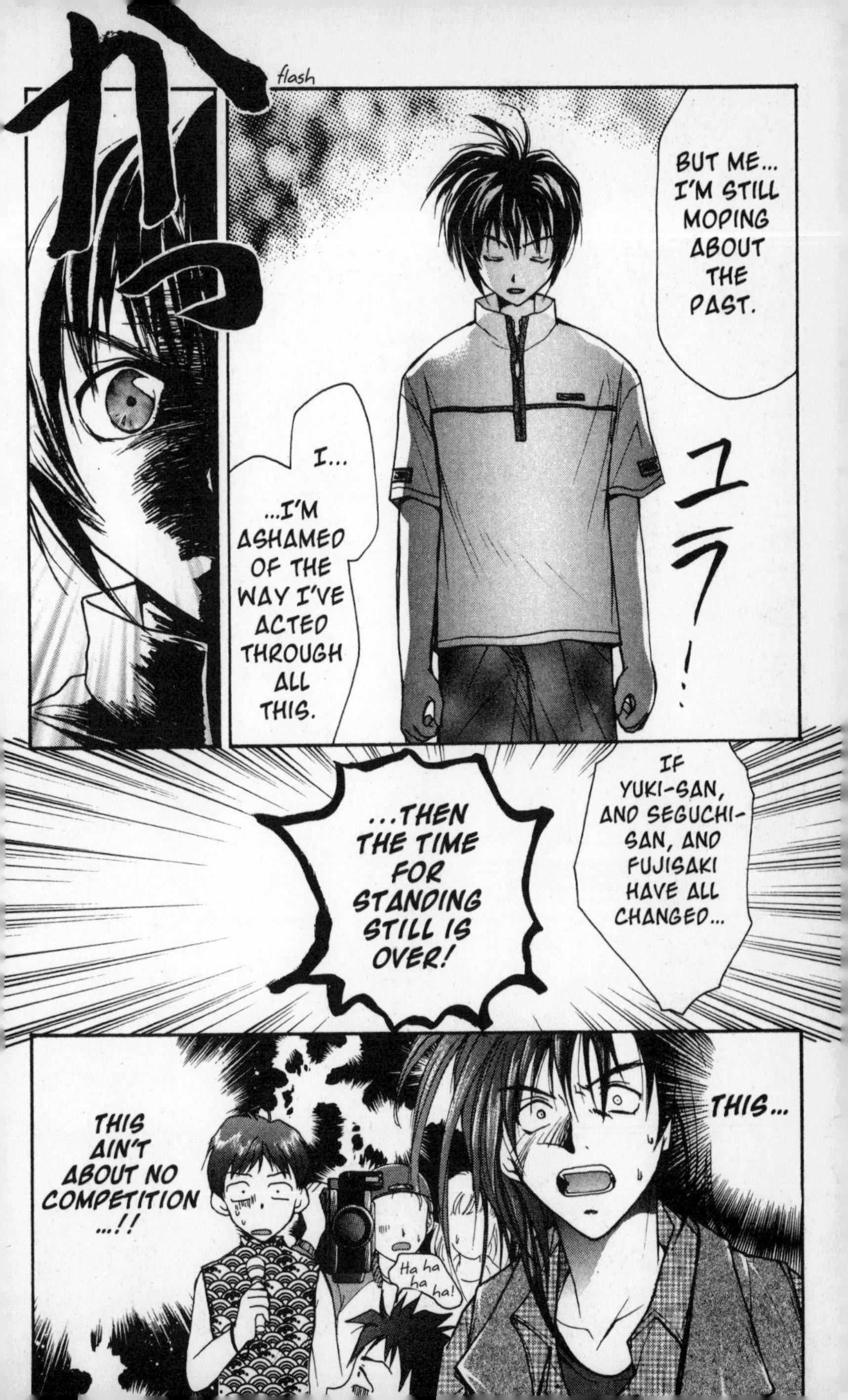
BUT ME... I'M STILL MOPING ABOUT THE PAST.
ユラ
I...
...I'M ASHAMED OF THE WAY I'VE ACTED THROUGH ALL THIS.
かっ
flash
IF YUKI-SAN, AND SEGUCHI-SAN, AND FUJISAKI HAVE ALL CHANGED...
...THEN THE TIME FOR STANDING STILL IS OVER!
THIS...
Ha ha ha ha ha!
THIS AIN'T ABOUT NO COMPETITION ...!!

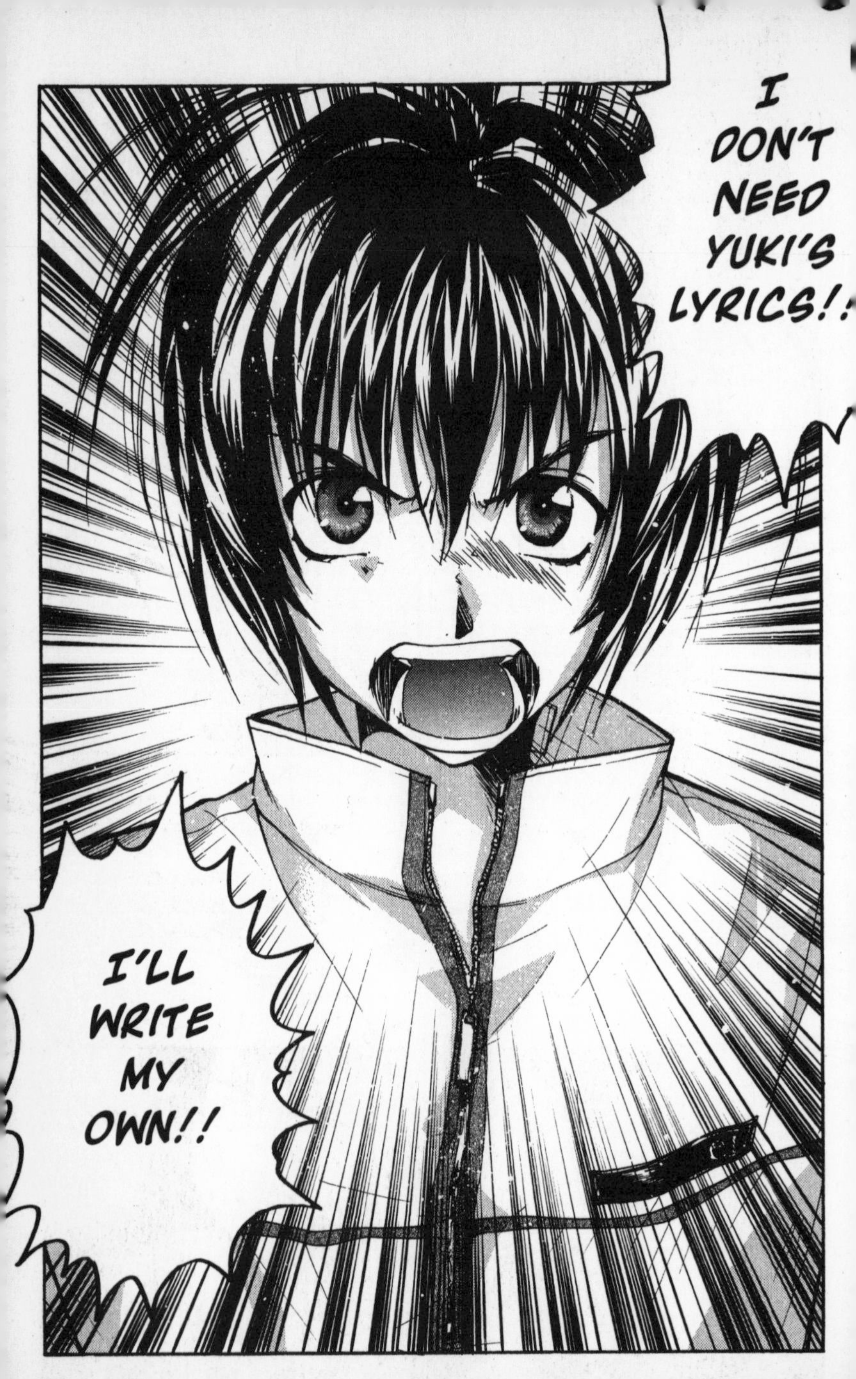
I DON'T NEED YUKI'S LYRICS!!
I'LL WRITE MY OWN!!

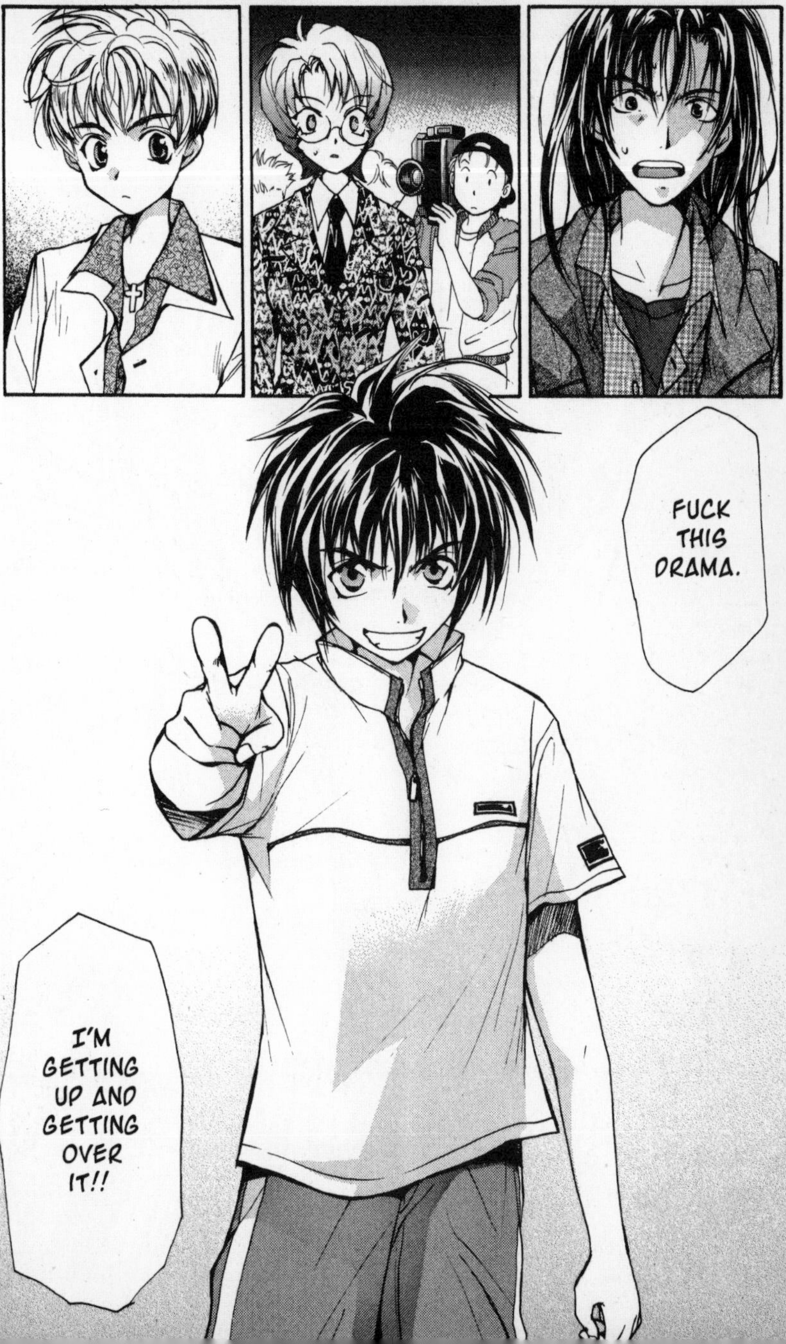
FUCK THIS DRAMA.
I'M GETTING UP AND GETTING OVER IT!!

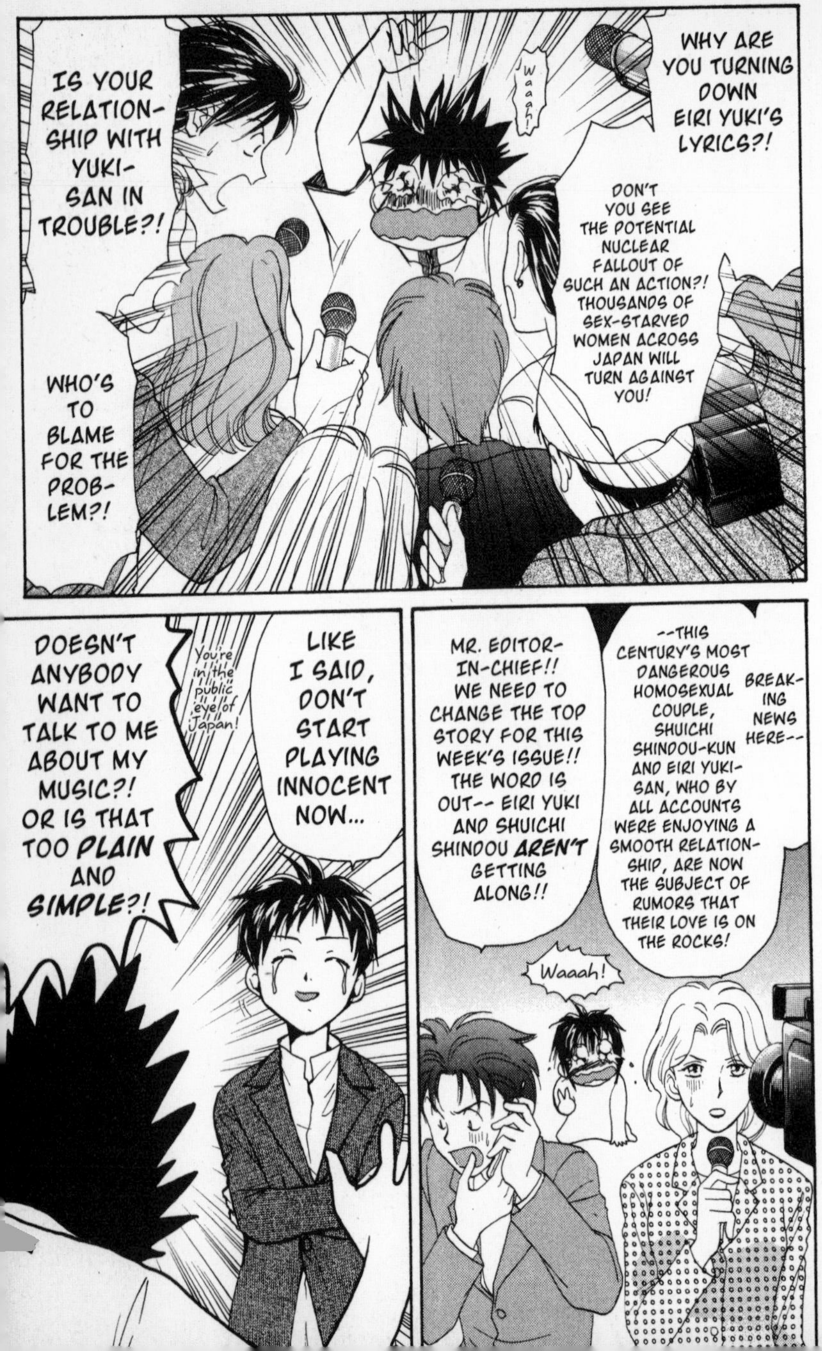
WHY ARE YOU TURNING DOWN EIRI YUKI'S LYRICS?!
Waaah!
IS YOUR RELATION-SHIP WITH YUKI-SAN IN TROUBLE?!
DON'T YOU SEE THE POTENTIAL NUCLEAR FALLOUT OF SUCH AN ACTION?! THOUSANDS OF SEX-STARVED WOMEN ACROSS JAPAN WILL TURN AGAINST YOU!
WHO'S TO BLAME FOR THE PROB-LEM?!
BREAK-ING NEWS HERE--
--THIS CENTURY'S MOST DANGEROUS HOMOSEXUAL COUPLE, SHUICHI SHINDOU-KUN AND EIRI YUKI-SAN, WHO BY ALL ACCOUNTS WERE ENJOYING A SMOOTH RELATION-SHIP, ARE NOW THE SUBJECT OF RUMORS THAT THEIR LOVE IS ON THE ROCKS!
MR. EDITOR-IN-CHIEF!! WE NEED TO CHANGE THE TOP STORY FOR THIS WEEK'S ISSUE!! THE WORD IS OUT-- EIRI YUKI AND SHUICHI SHINDOU AREN'T GETTING ALONG!!
Waaah!
LIKE I SAID, DON'T START PLAYING INNOCENT NOW...
You're in the public eye of Japan!
DOESN'T ANYBODY WANT TO TALK TO ME ABOUT MY MUSIC?! OR IS THAT TOO PLAIN AND SIMPLE?!

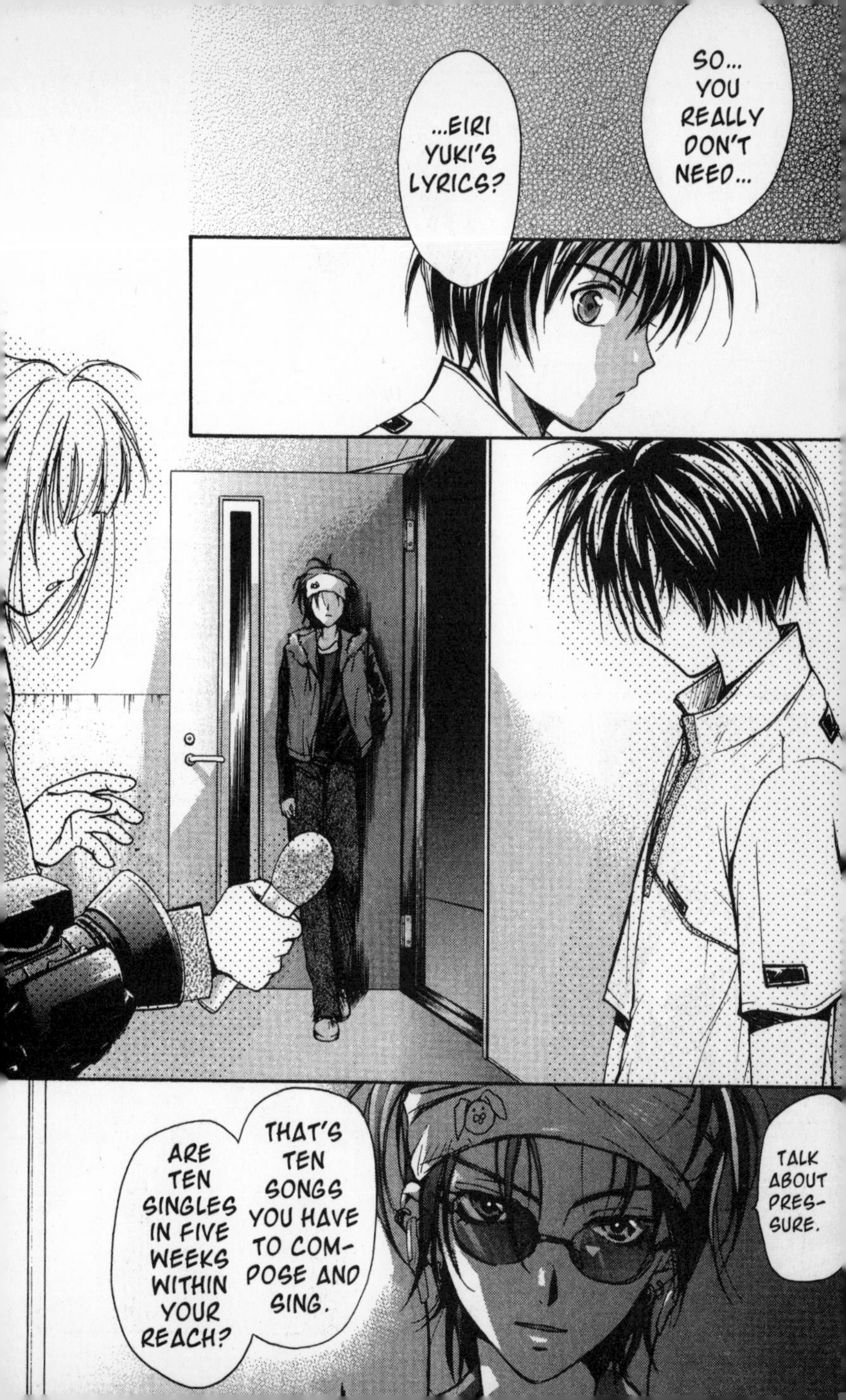
SO... YOU REALLY DON'T NEED...
...EIRI YUKI'S LYRICS?
TALK ABOUT PRES-SURE.
THAT'S TEN SONGS YOU HAVE TO COM-POSE AND SING.
ARE TEN SINGLES IN FIVE WEEKS WITHIN YOUR REACH?

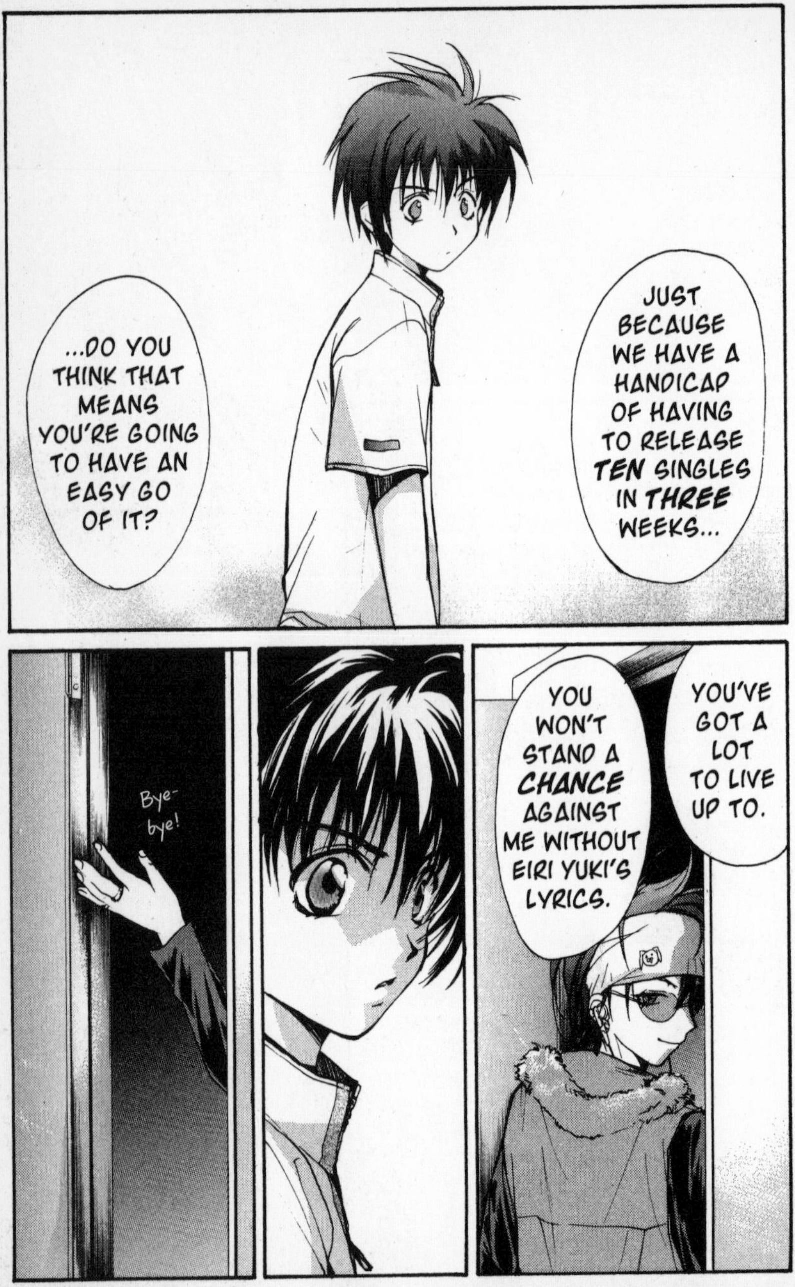
JUST BECAUSE WE HAVE A HANDICAP OF HAVING TO RELEASE TEN SINGLES IN THREE WEEKS...
...DO YOU THINK THAT MEANS YOU'RE GOING TO HAVE AN EASY GO OF IT?
YOU'VE GOT A LOT TO LIVE UP TO.
YOU WON'T STAND A CHANCE AGAINST ME WITHOUT EIRI YUKI'S LYRICS.
Bye-bye!

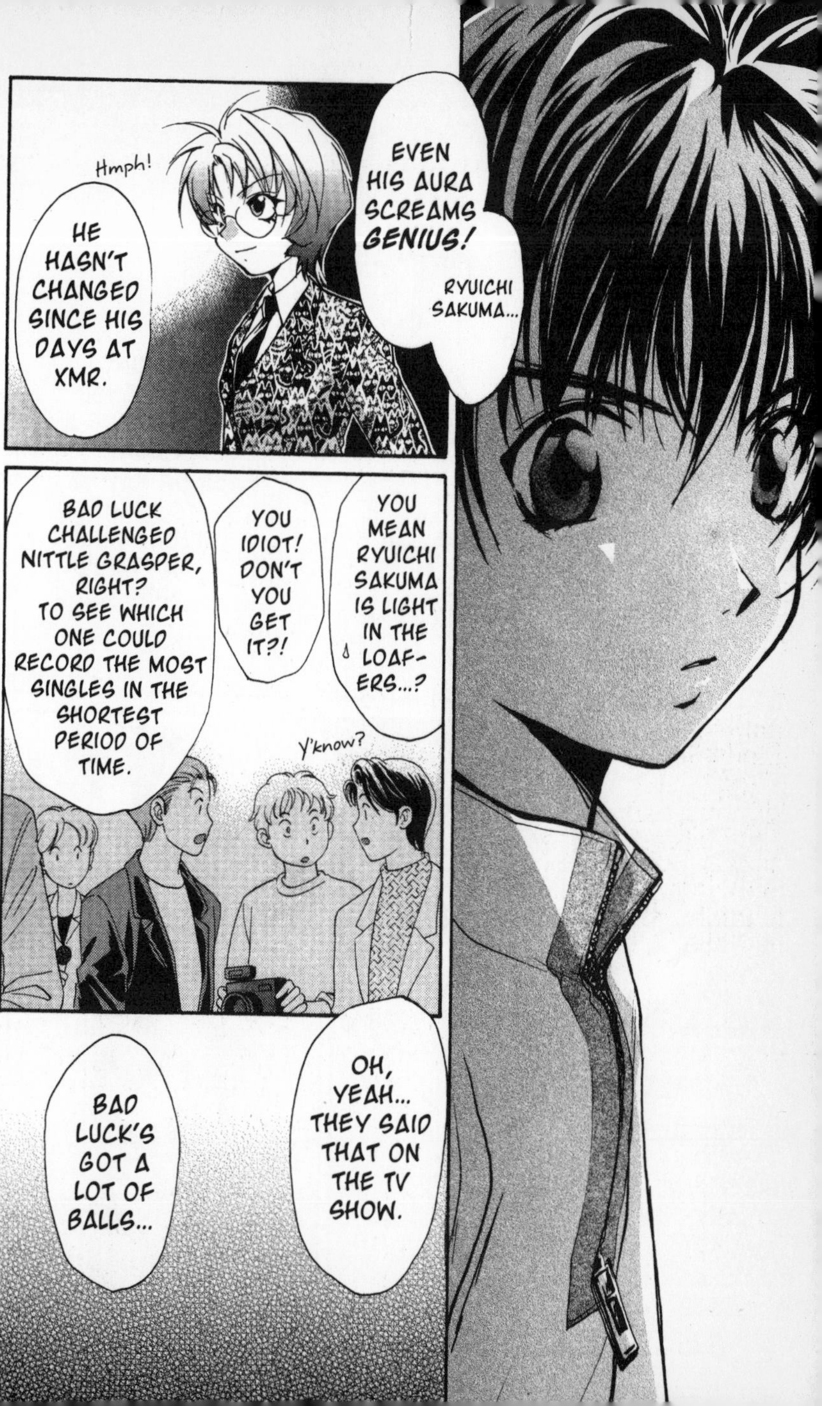
EVEN HIS AURA SCREAMS GENIUS!
RYUICHI SAKUMA...
Hmph!
HE HASN'T CHANGED SINCE HIS DAYS AT XMR.
YOU MEAN RYUICHI SAKUMA IS LIGHT IN THE LOAF-ERS...?
YOU IDIOT! DON'T YOU GET IT?!
Y'know?
BAD LUCK CHALLENGED NITTLE GRASPER, RIGHT? TO SEE WHICH ONE COULD RECORD THE MOST SINGLES IN THE SHORTEST PERIOD OF TIME.
OH, YEAH... THEY SAID THAT ON THE TV SHOW.
BAD LUCK'S GOT A LOT OF BALLS...

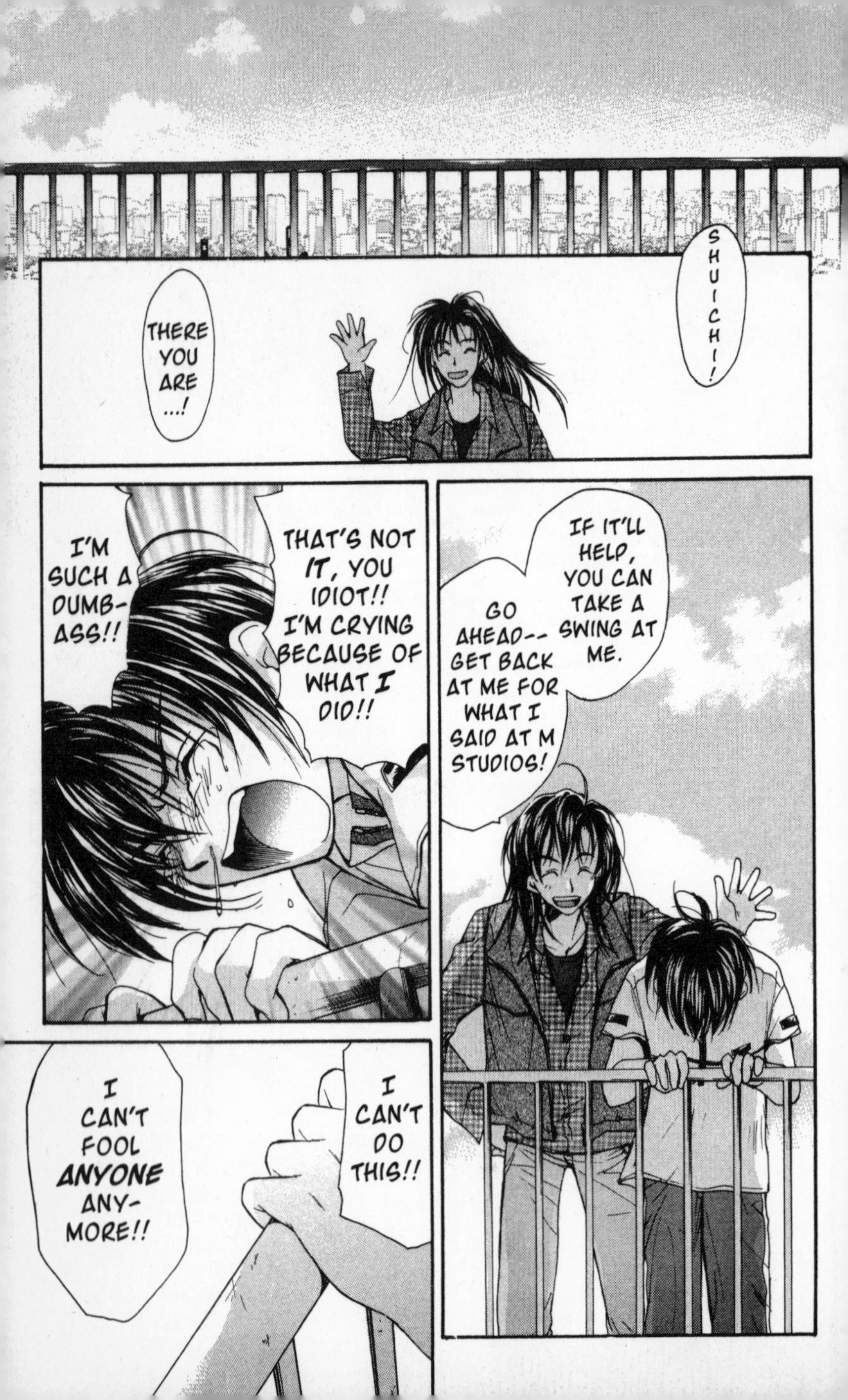
SHUICHI!
THERE YOU ARE...!
IF IT'LL HELP, YOU CAN TAKE A SWING AT ME.
GO AHEAD-- GET BACK AT ME FOR WHAT I SAID AT M STUDIOS!
THAT'S NOT IT, YOU IDIOT!! I'M CRYING BECAUSE OF WHAT I DID!!
I'M SUCH A DUMB-ASS!!
I CAN'T DO THIS!!
I CAN'T FOOL ANYONE ANY-MORE!!

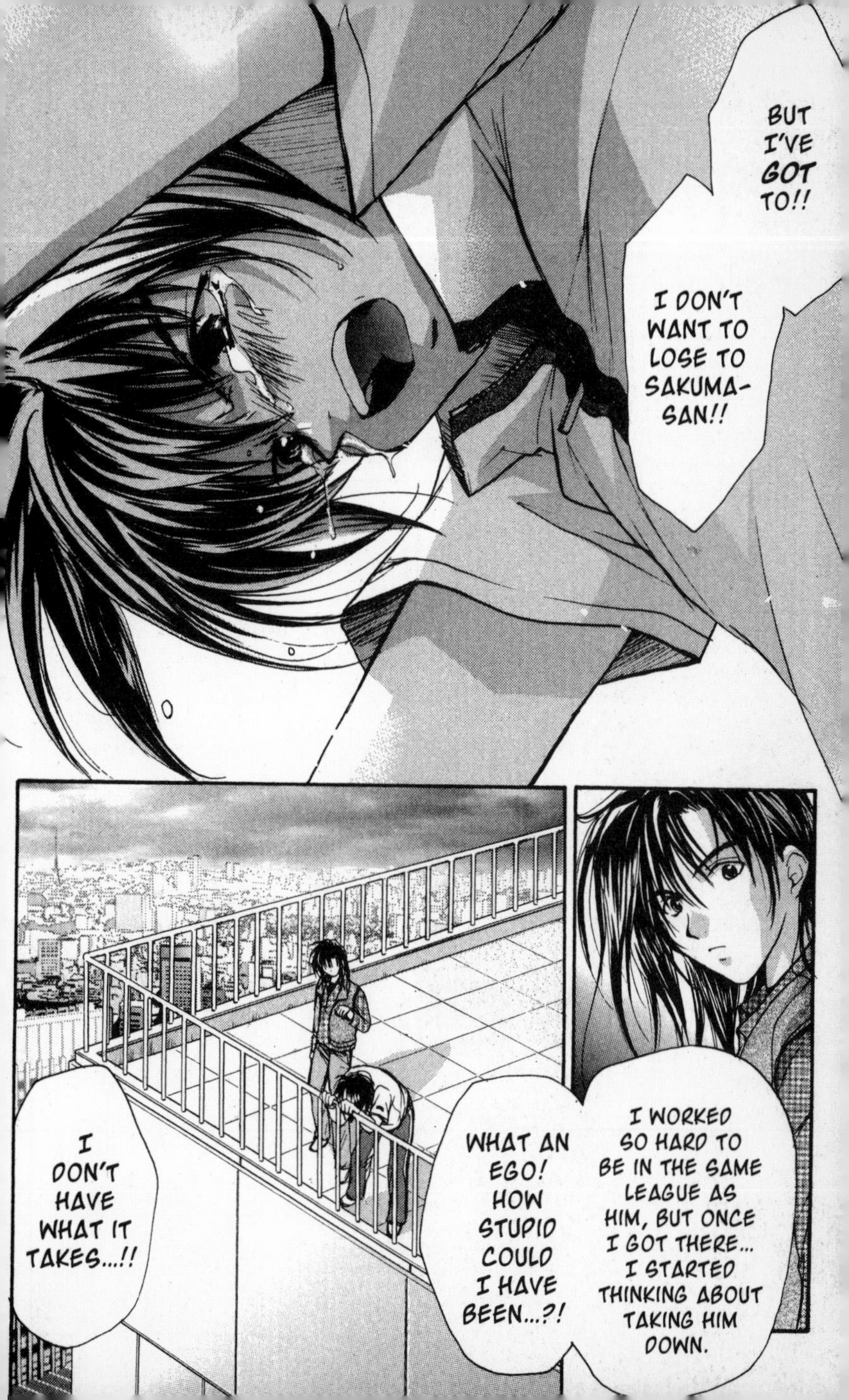
BUT I'VE GOT TO!!
I DON'T WANT TO LOSE TO SAKUMA-SAN!!
I WORKED SO HARD TO BE IN THE SAME LEAGUE AS HIM, BUT ONCE I GOT THERE... I STARTED THINKING ABOUT TAKING HIM DOWN.
WHAT AN EGO! HOW STUPID COULD I HAVE BEEN...?!
I DON'T HAVE WHAT IT TAKES...!!

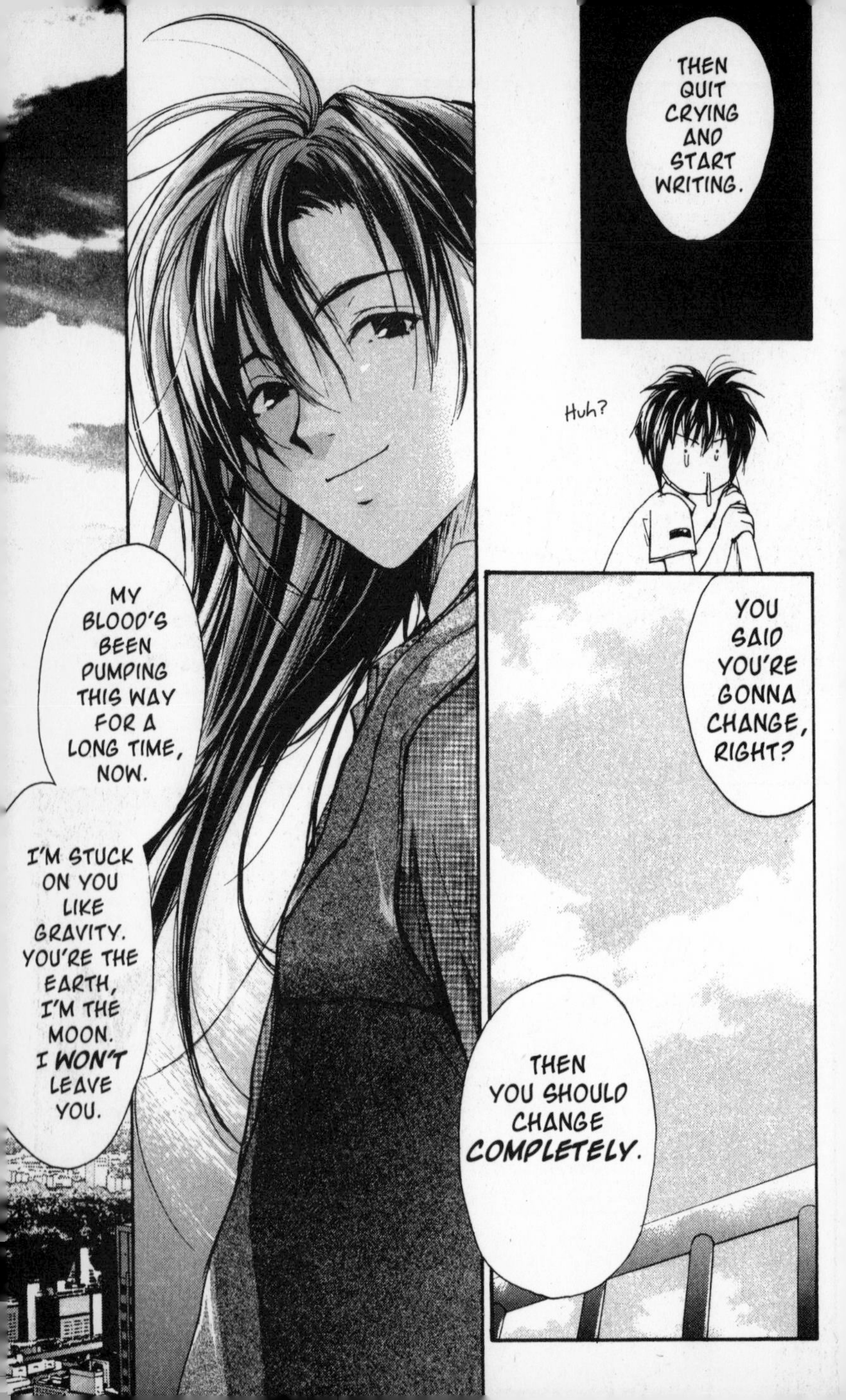
THEN QUIT CRYING AND START WRITING.
Huh?
YOU SAID YOU'RE GONNA CHANGE, RIGHT?
THEN YOU SHOULD CHANGE **COMPLETELY.**
MY BLOOD'S BEEN PUMPING THIS WAY FOR A LONG TIME, NOW.
I'M STUCK ON YOU LIKE GRAVITY. YOU'RE THE EARTH, I'M THE MOON. I **WON'T** LEAVE YOU.

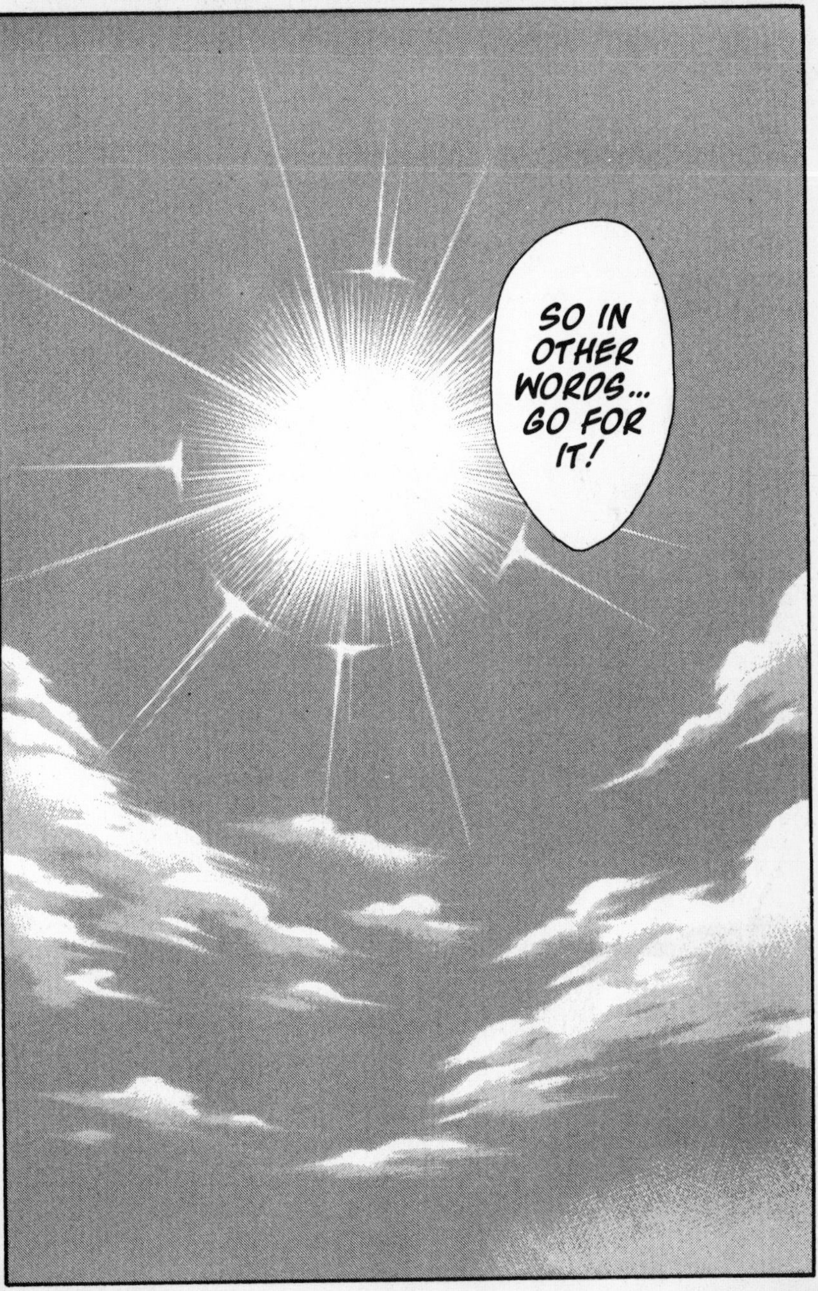
SO IN OTHER WORDS... GO FOR IT!

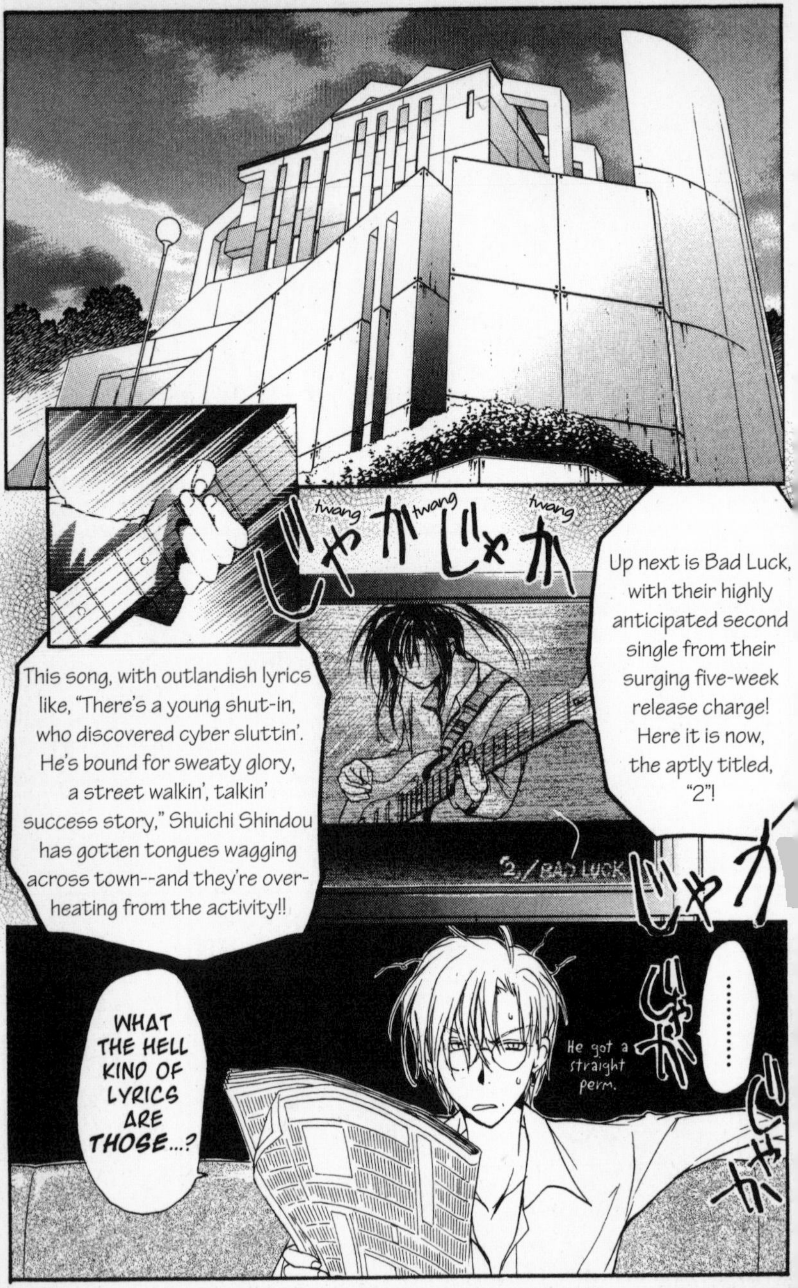
Up next is Bad Luck, with their highly anticipated second single from their surging five-week release charge! Here it is now, the aptly titled, "2"!
twang twang twang
This song, with outlandish lyrics like, "There's a young shut-in, who discovered cyber sluttin'. He's bound for sweaty glory, a street walkin', talkin' success story," Shuichi Shindou has gotten tongues wagging across town--and they're over-heating from the activity!!
2 / BAD LUCK
......
He got a straight perm.
WHAT THE HELL KIND OF LYRICS ARE THOSE...?

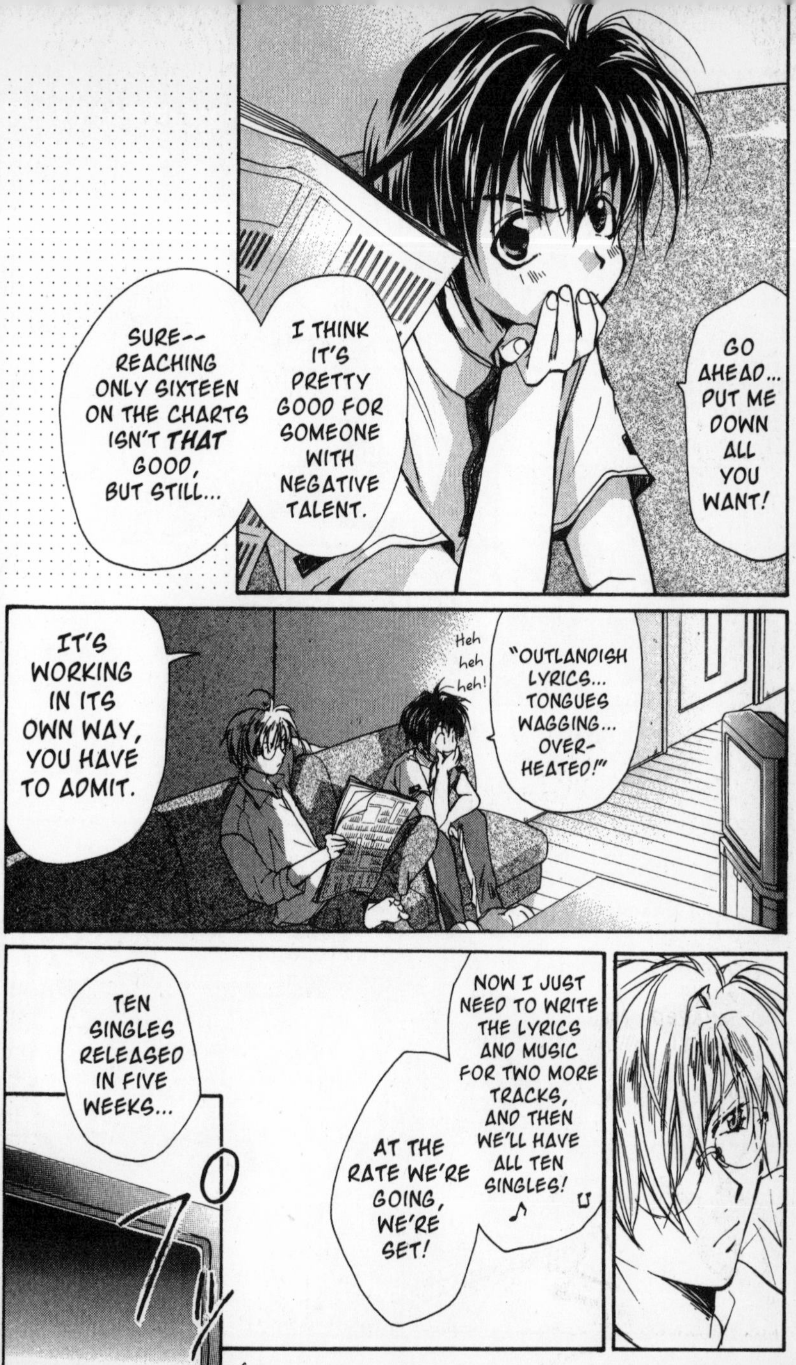
GO AHEAD... PUT ME DOWN ALL YOU WANT!
I THINK IT'S PRETTY GOOD FOR SOMEONE WITH NEGATIVE TALENT.
SURE-- REACHING ONLY SIXTEEN ON THE CHARTS ISN'T **THAT** GOOD, BUT STILL...
"OUTLANDISH LYRICS... TONGUES WAGGING... OVER-HEATED!"
Heh heh heh!
IT'S WORKING IN ITS OWN WAY, YOU HAVE TO ADMIT.
NOW I JUST NEED TO WRITE THE LYRICS AND MUSIC FOR TWO MORE TRACKS, AND THEN WE'LL HAVE ALL TEN SINGLES!
AT THE RATE WE'RE GOING, WE'RE SET!
TEN SINGLES RELEASED IN FIVE WEEKS...
flick

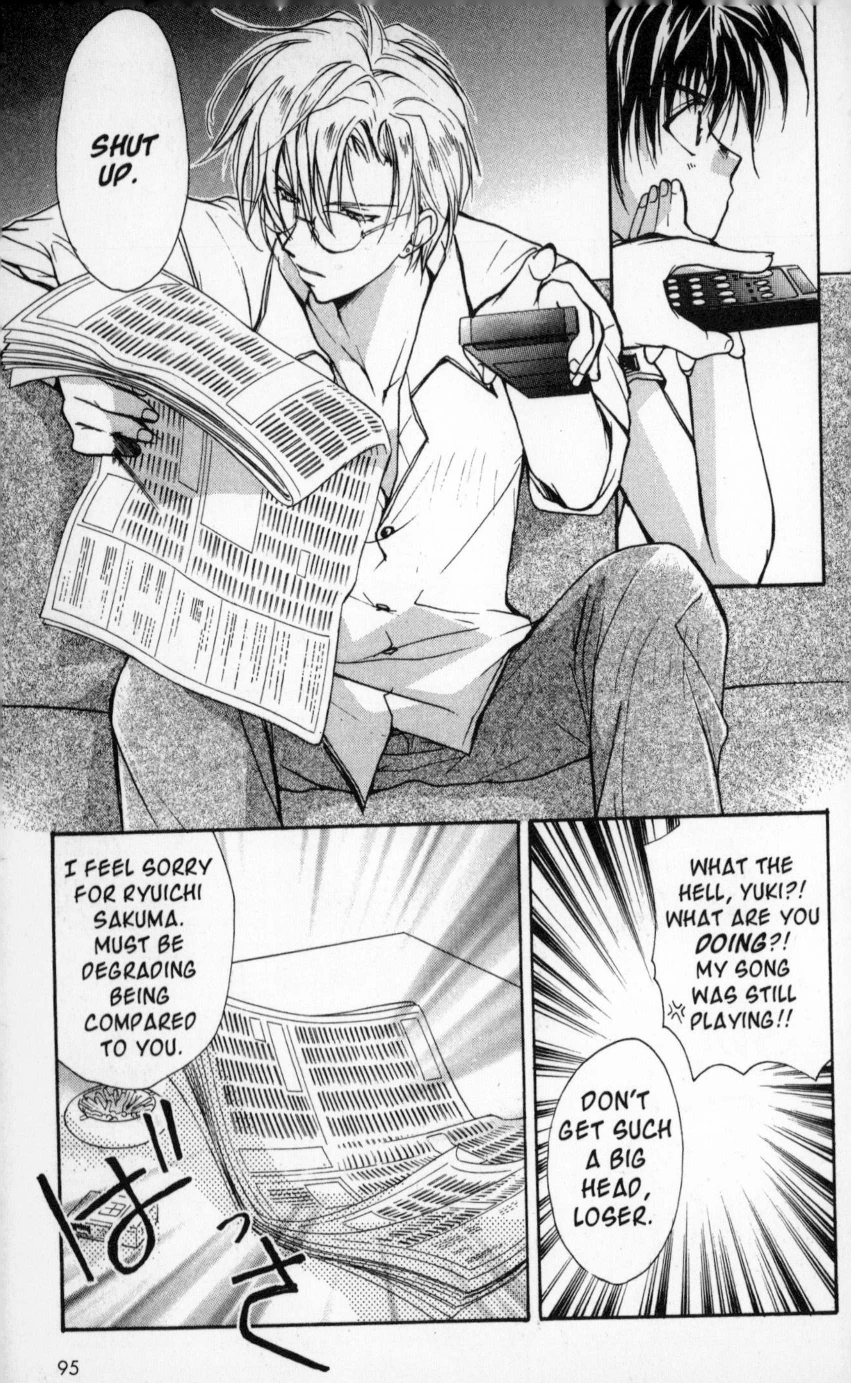
SHUT UP.
WHAT THE HELL, YUKI?! WHAT ARE YOU DOING?! MY SONG WAS STILL PLAYING!!
DON'T GET SUCH A BIG HEAD, LOSER.
I FEEL SORRY FOR RYUICHI SAKUMA. MUST BE DEGRADING BEING COMPARED TO YOU.
ばっさ

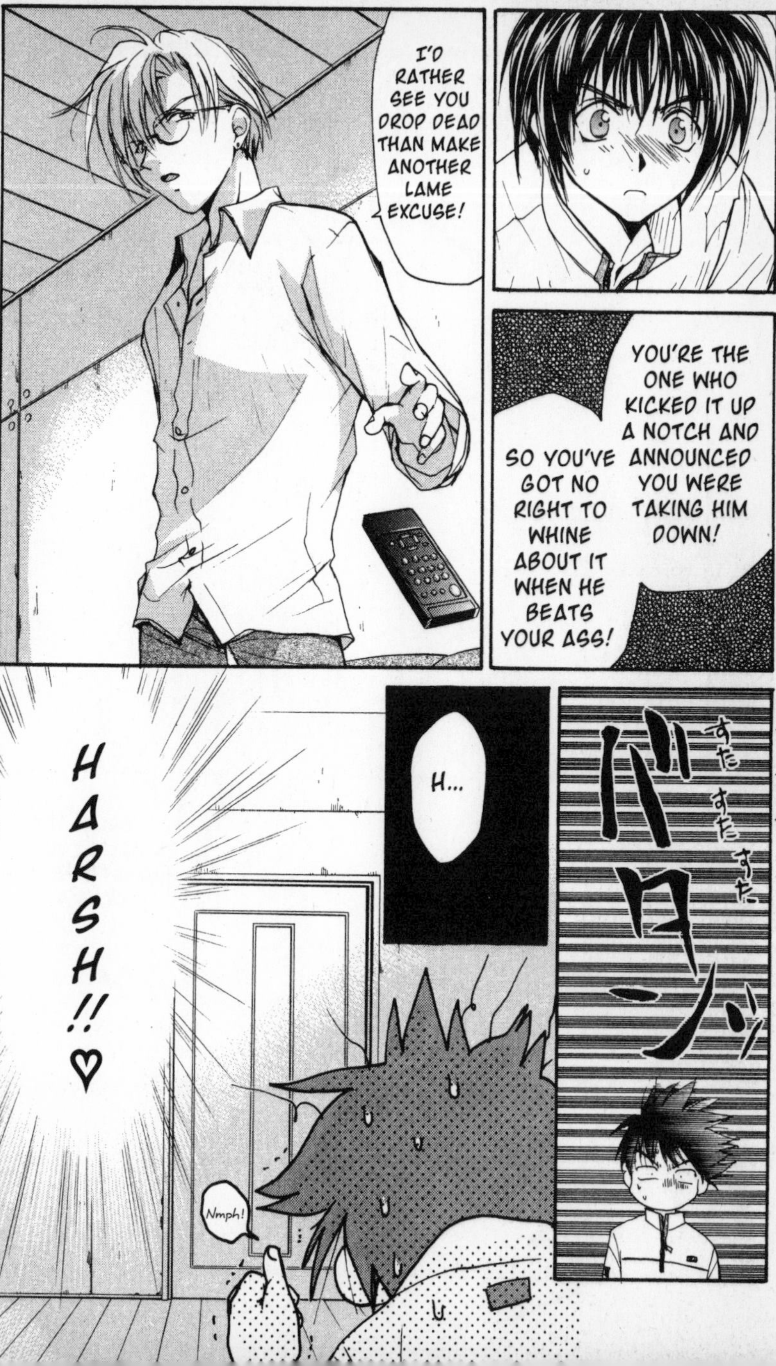
YOU'RE THE ONE WHO KICKED IT UP A NOTCH AND ANNOUNCED YOU WERE TAKING HIM DOWN!
SO YOU'VE GOT NO RIGHT TO WHINE ABOUT IT WHEN HE BEATS YOUR ASS!
I'D RATHER SEE YOU DROP DEAD THAN MAKE ANOTHER LAME EXCUSE!
stomp stomp stomp slam
すた すた すた
バタン
H...
HARSH!!♡
Nmph!

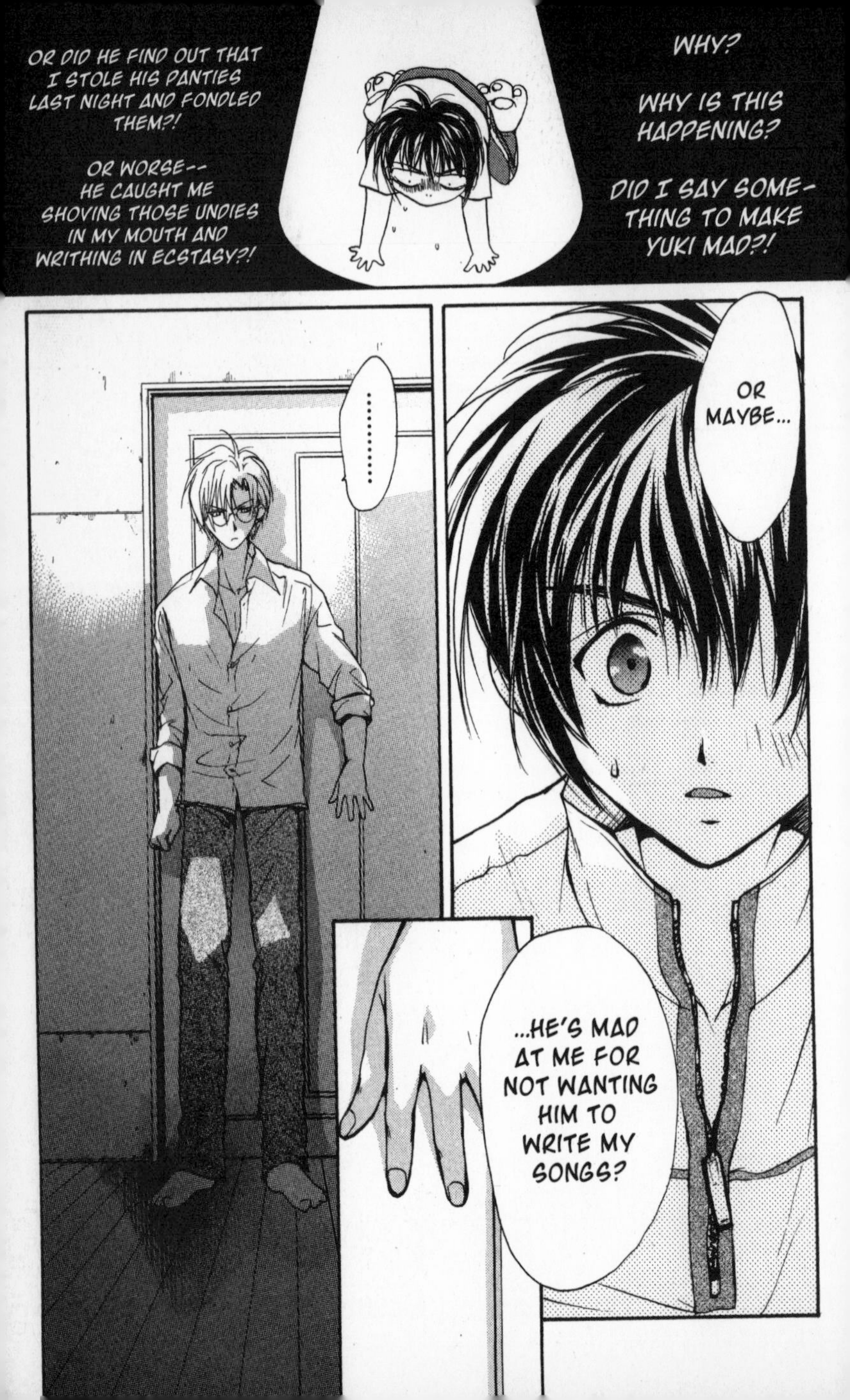
WHY?
WHY IS THIS HAPPENING?
DID I SAY SOME-THING TO MAKE YUKI MAD?!
OR DID HE FIND OUT THAT I STOLE HIS PANTIES LAST NIGHT AND FONDLED THEM?!
OR WORSE-- HE CAUGHT ME SHOVING THOSE UNDIES IN MY MOUTH AND WRITHING IN ECSTASY?!
OR MAYBE...
...HE'S MAD AT ME FOR NOT WANTING HIM TO WRITE MY SONGS?
....

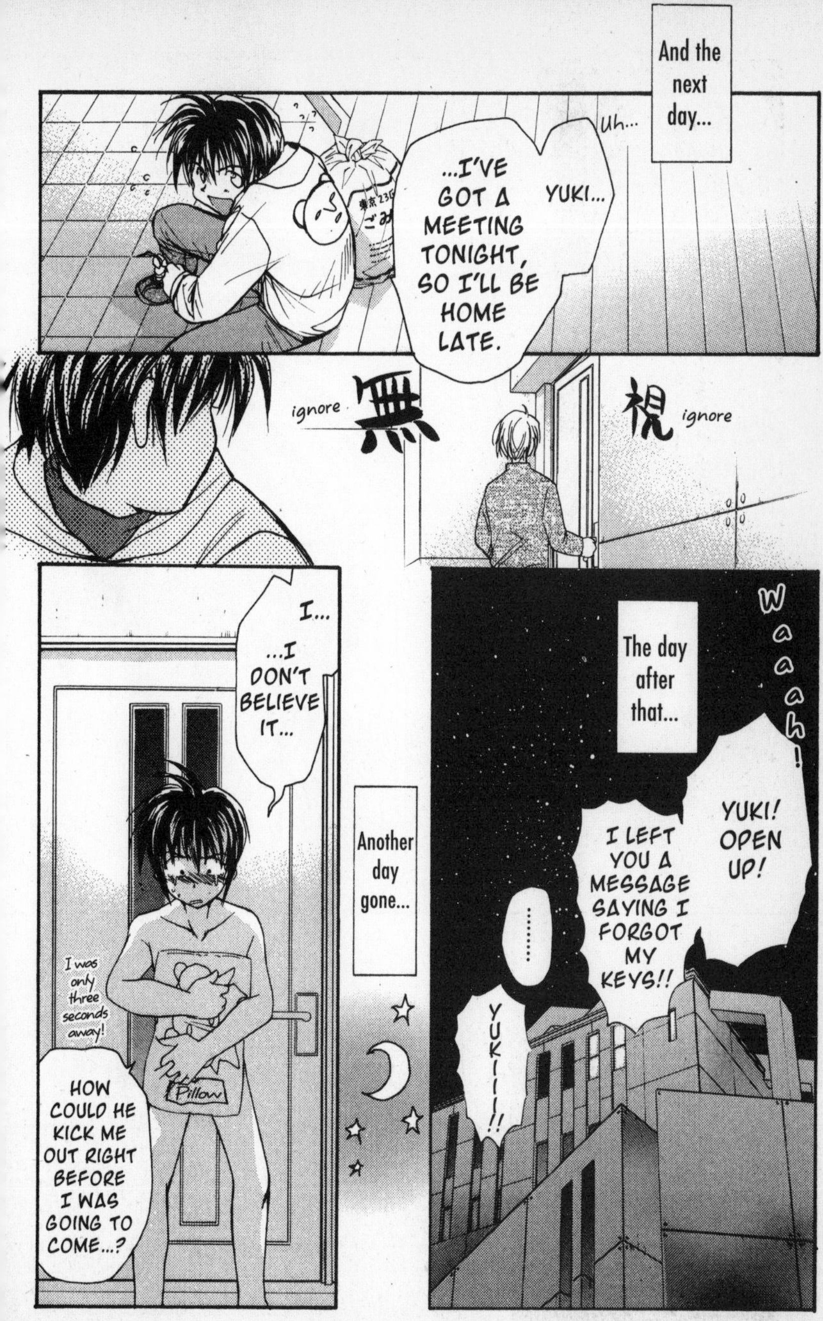
And the next day...
Uh...
YUKI...
...I'VE GOT A MEETING TONIGHT, SO I'LL BE HOME LATE.
ignore 無 視 ignore
The day after that...
Waaaah!
YUKI! OPEN UP!
I LEFT YOU A MESSAGE SAYING I FORGOT MY KEYS!!
......
YUKIIII!!
Another day gone...
I...
...I DON'T BELIEVE IT...
I was only three seconds away!
Pillow
HOW COULD HE KICK ME OUT RIGHT BEFORE I WAS GOING TO COME...?

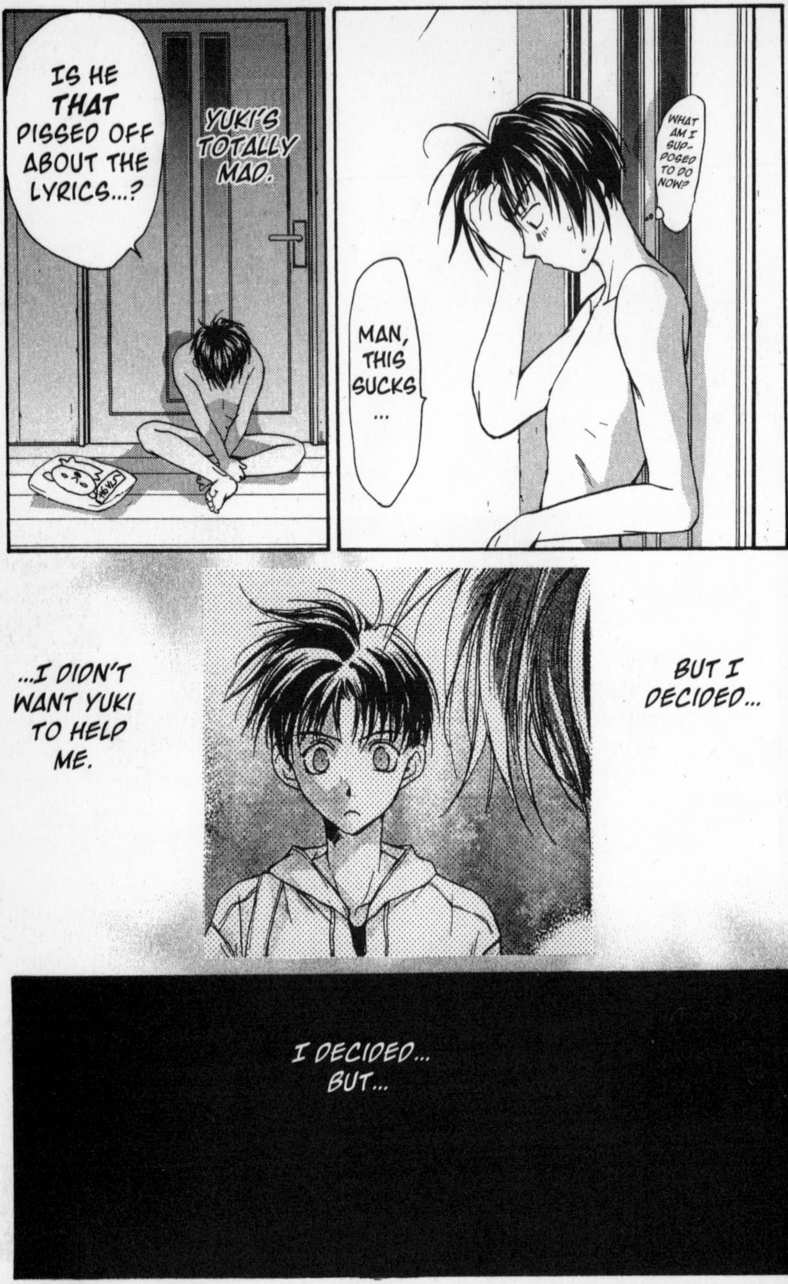

WHAT AM I SUP-POSED TO DO NOW?
MAN, THIS SUCKS ...
IS HE THAT PISSED OFF ABOUT THE LYRICS...?
YUKI'S TOTALLY MAD.
BUT I DECIDED...
...I DIDN'T WANT YUKI TO HELP ME.
I DECIDED... BUT...

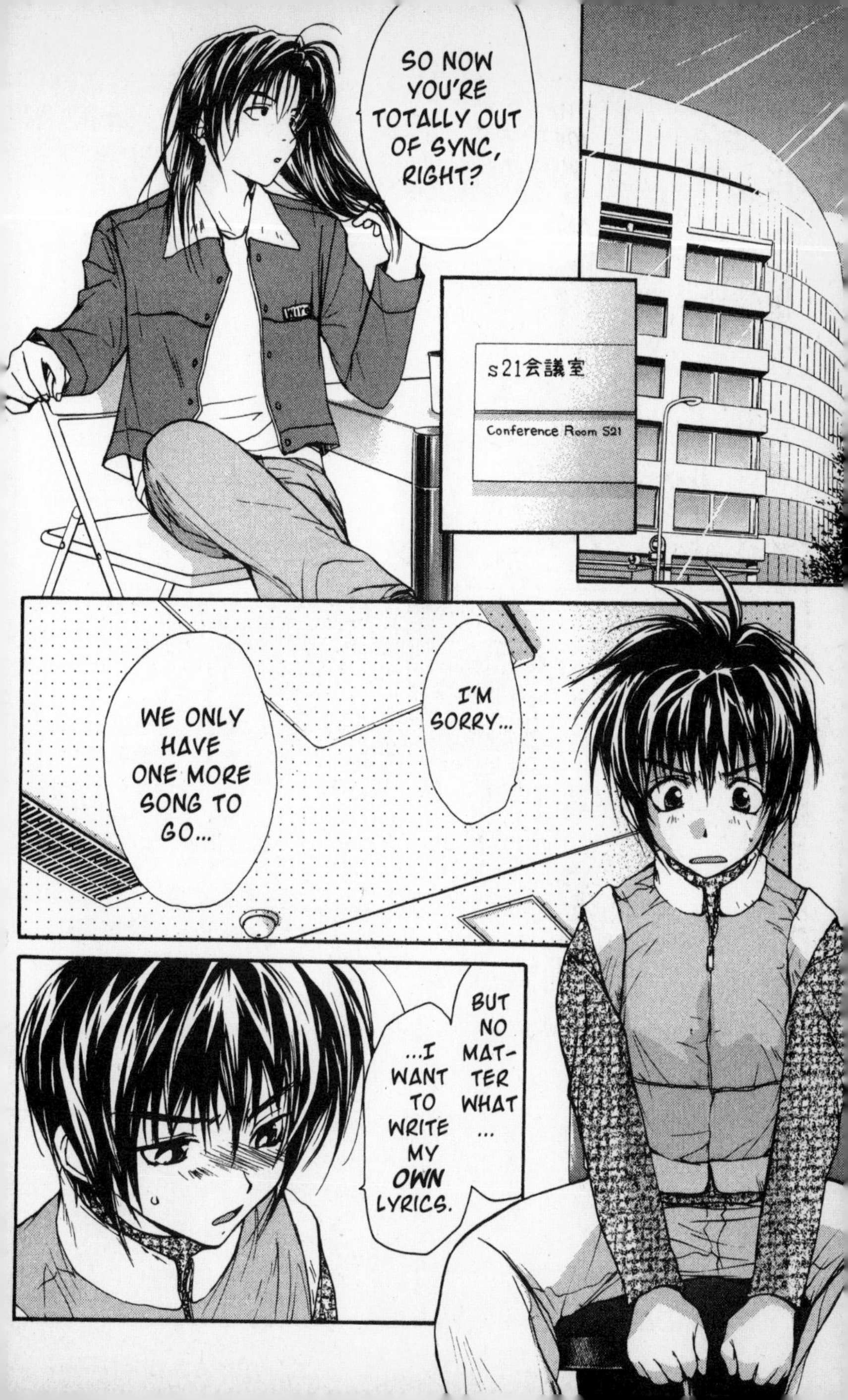
SO NOW YOU'RE TOTALLY OUT OF SYNC, RIGHT?
s21会議室
Conference Room S21
I'M SORRY...
WE ONLY HAVE ONE MORE SONG TO GO...
BUT NO MATTER WHAT...
...I WANT TO WRITE MY OWN LYRICS.

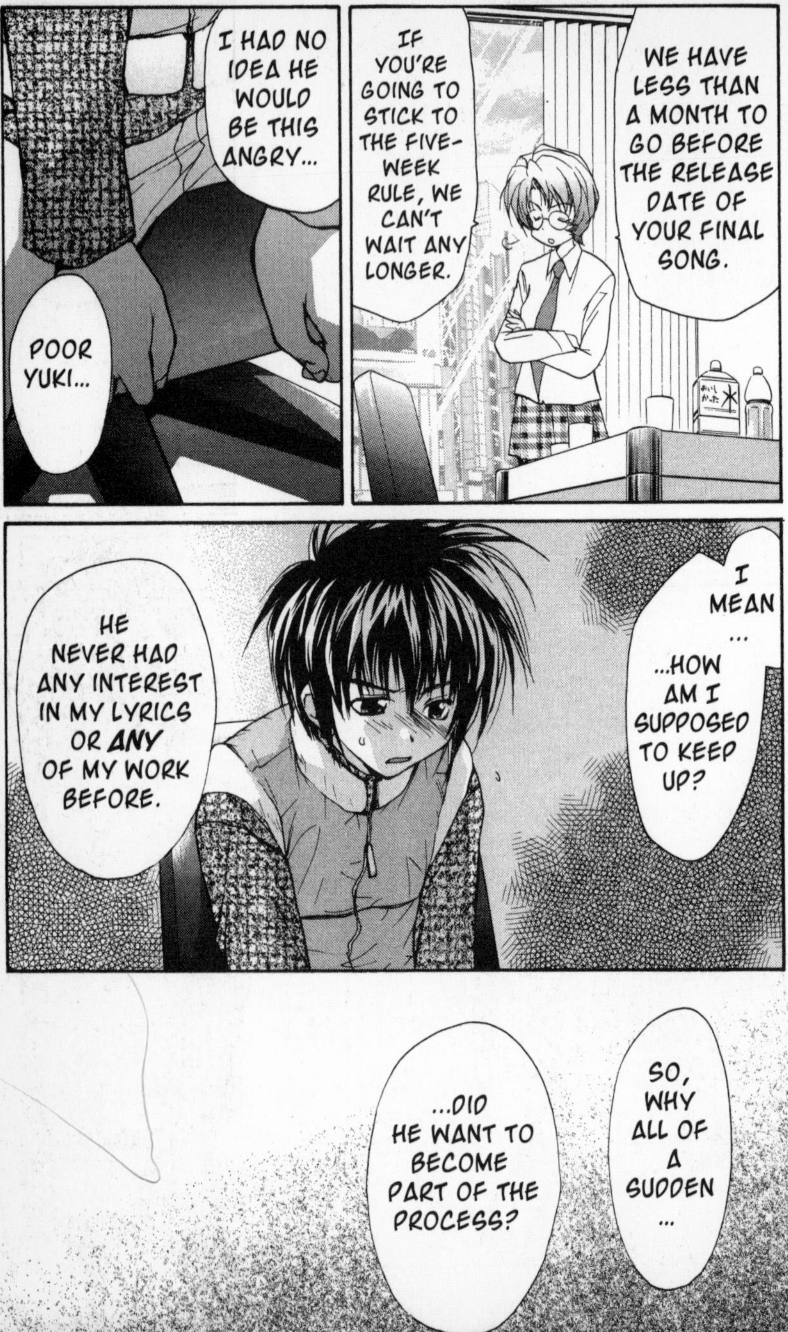
WE HAVE LESS THAN A MONTH TO GO BEFORE THE RELEASE DATE OF YOUR FINAL SONG.
IF YOU'RE GOING TO STICK TO THE FIVE-WEEK RULE, WE CAN'T WAIT ANY LONGER.
I HAD NO IDEA HE WOULD BE THIS ANGRY...
POOR YUKI...
I MEAN... ...HOW AM I SUPPOSED TO KEEP UP?
HE NEVER HAD ANY INTEREST IN MY LYRICS OR ANY OF MY WORK BEFORE.
SO, WHY ALL OF A SUDDEN...
...DID HE WANT TO BECOME PART OF THE PROCESS?

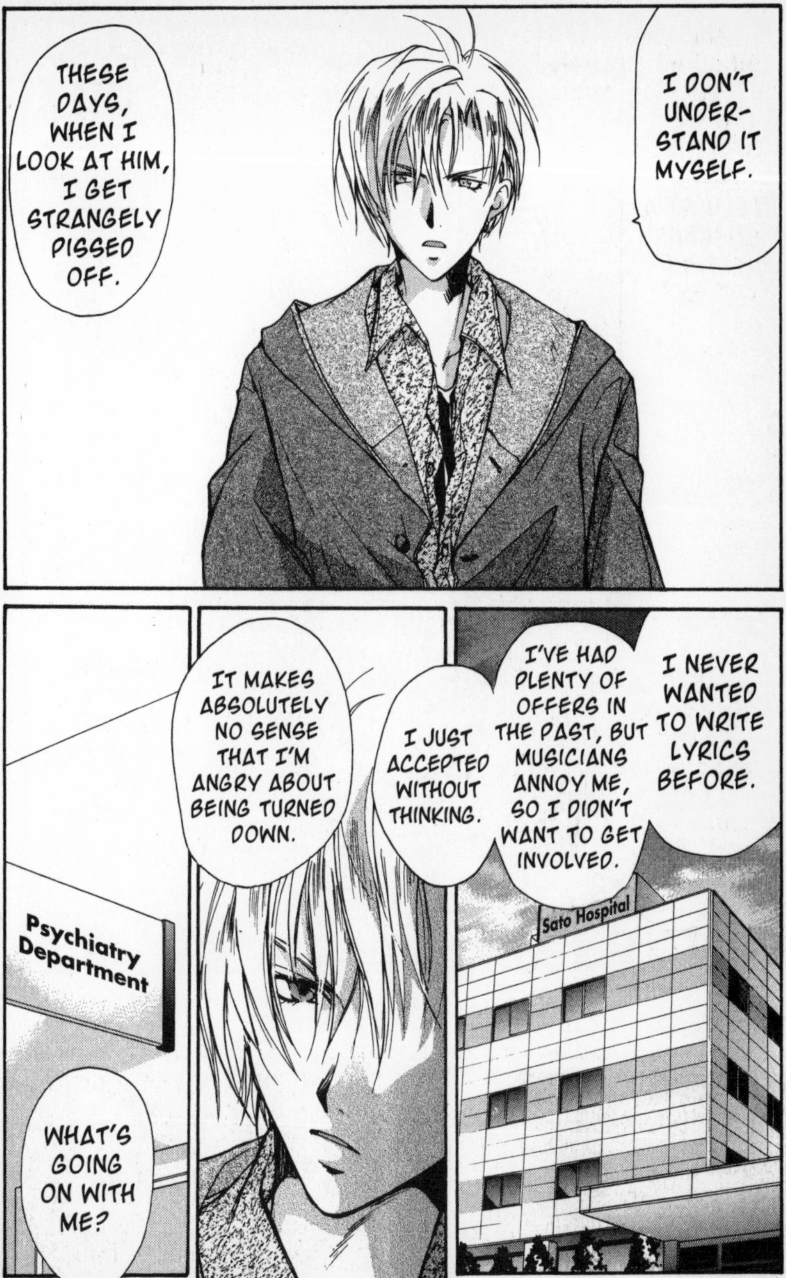
I DON'T UNDER-STAND IT MYSELF.
THESE DAYS, WHEN I LOOK AT HIM, I GET STRANGELY PISSED OFF.
I NEVER WANTED TO WRITE LYRICS BEFORE.
I'VE HAD PLENTY OF OFFERS IN THE PAST, BUT MUSICIANS ANNOY ME, SO I DIDN'T WANT TO GET INVOLVED.
Sato Hospital
I JUST ACCEPTED WITHOUT THINKING.
IT MAKES ABSOLUTELY NO SENSE THAT I'M ANGRY ABOUT BEING TURNED DOWN.
Psychiatry Department
WHAT'S GOING ON WITH ME?

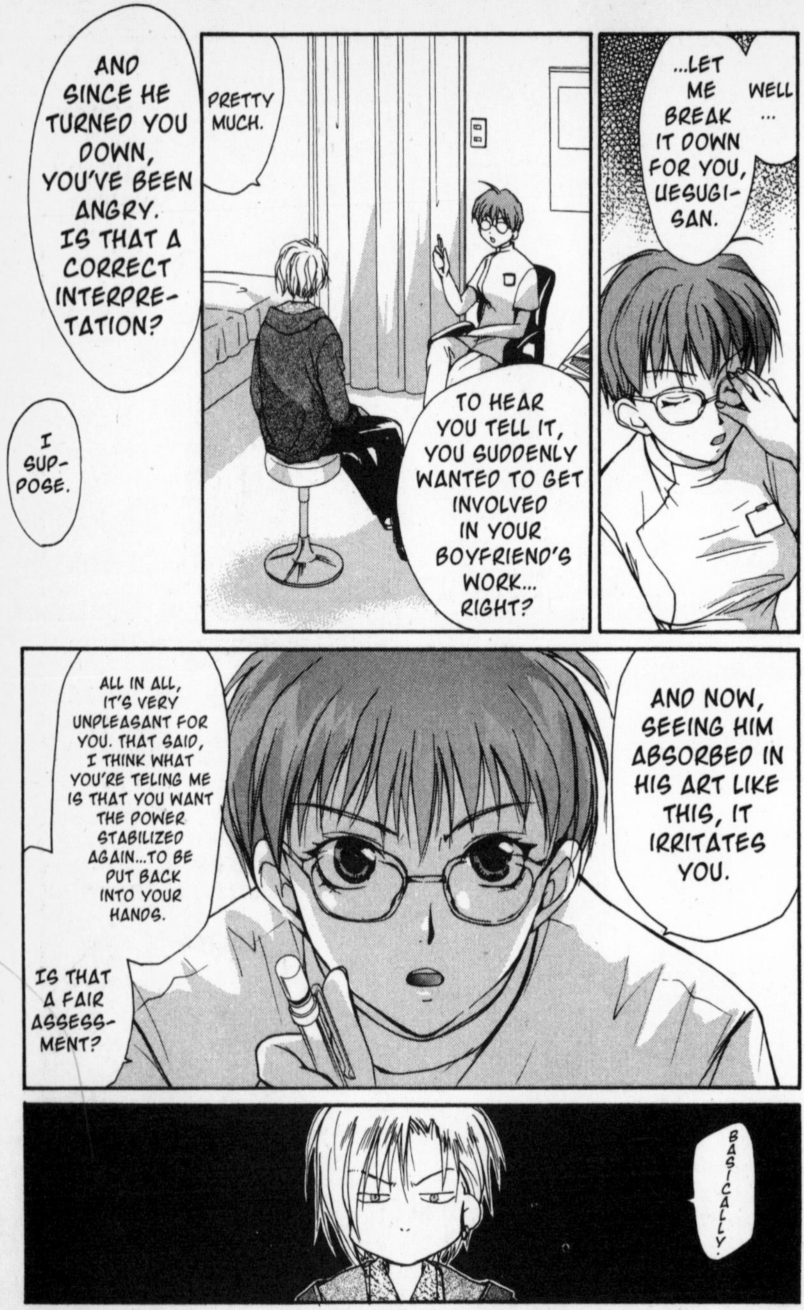
WELL...
...LET ME BREAK IT DOWN FOR YOU, UESUGI-SAN.
TO HEAR YOU TELL IT, YOU SUDDENLY WANTED TO GET INVOLVED IN YOUR BOYFRIEND'S WORK... RIGHT?
PRETTY MUCH.
AND SINCE HE TURNED YOU DOWN, YOU'VE BEEN ANGRY. IS THAT A CORRECT INTERPRE-TATION?
I SUP-POSE.
AND NOW, SEEING HIM ABSORBED IN HIS ART LIKE THIS, IT IRRITATES YOU.
ALL IN ALL, IT'S VERY UNPLEASANT FOR YOU. THAT SAID, I THINK WHAT YOU'RE TELING ME IS THAT YOU WANT THE POWER STABILIZED AGAIN...TO BE PUT BACK INTO YOUR HANDS.
IS THAT A FAIR ASSESS-MENT?
BASICALLY.

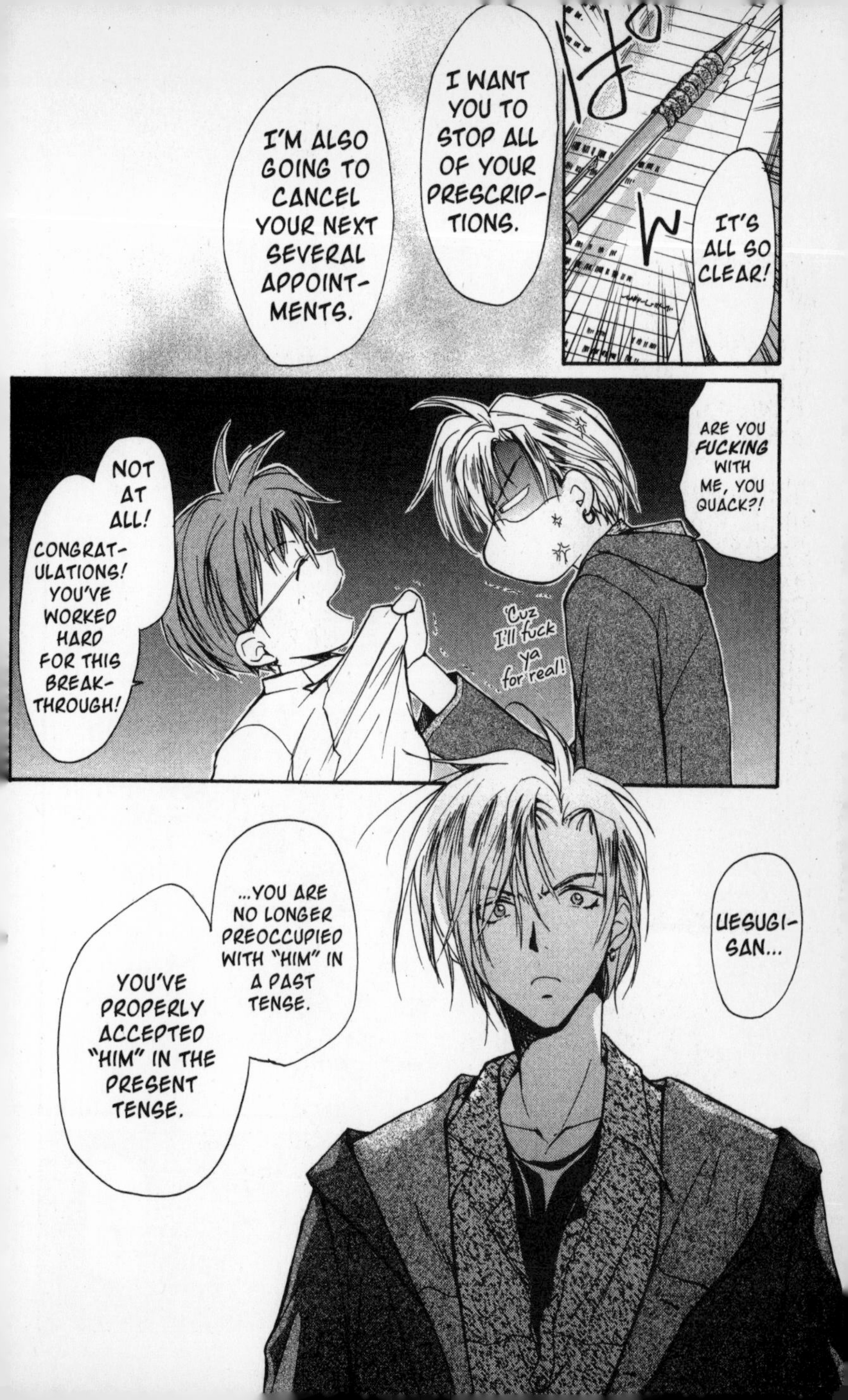
IT'S ALL SO CLEAR!
I WANT YOU TO STOP ALL OF YOUR PRESCRIPTIONS.
I'M ALSO GOING TO CANCEL YOUR NEXT SEVERAL APPOINTMENTS.
ARE YOU FUCKING WITH ME, YOU QUACK?!
'Cuz I'll fuck ya for real!
NOT AT ALL!
CONGRATULATIONS! YOU'VE WORKED HARD FOR THIS BREAKTHROUGH!
UESUGI-SAN...
...YOU ARE NO LONGER PREOCCUPIED WITH "HIM" IN A PAST TENSE.
YOU'VE PROPERLY ACCEPTED "HIM" IN THE PRESENT TENSE.

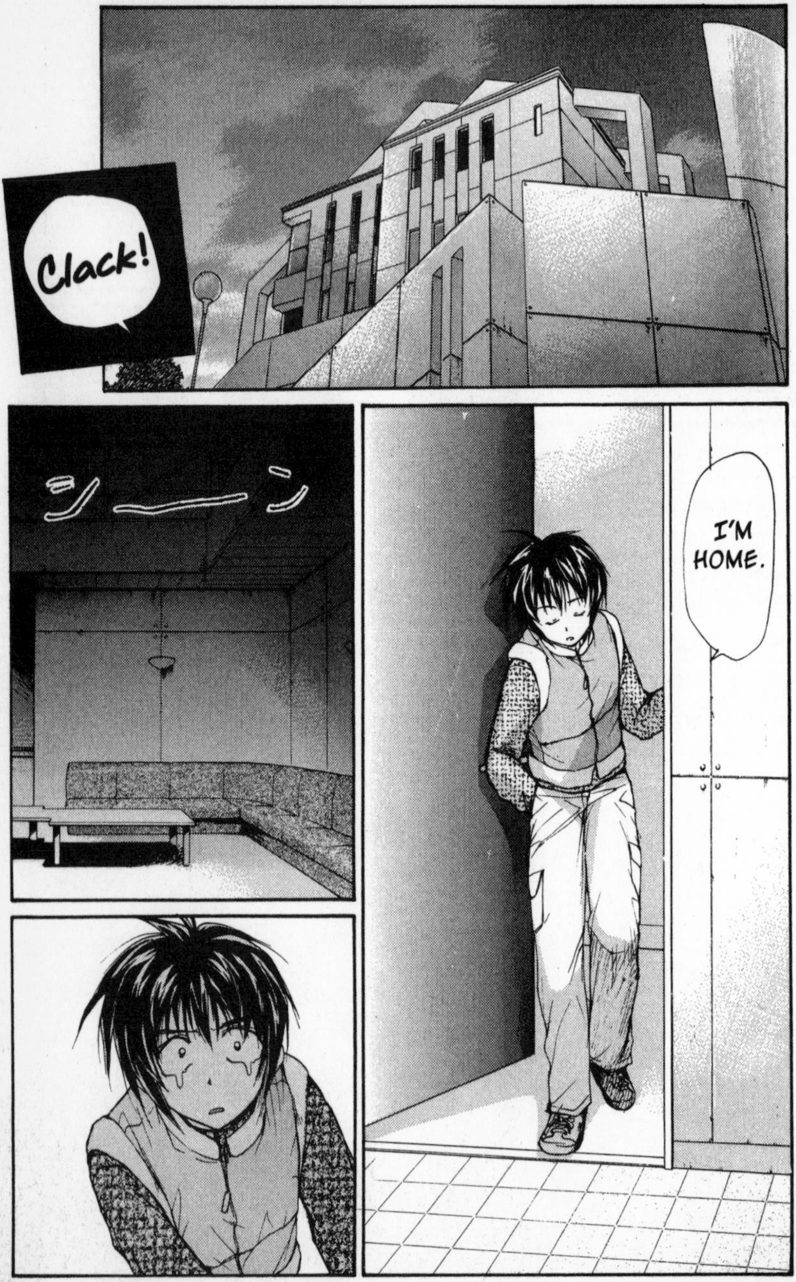
Clack!
I'M HOME.
シーーン

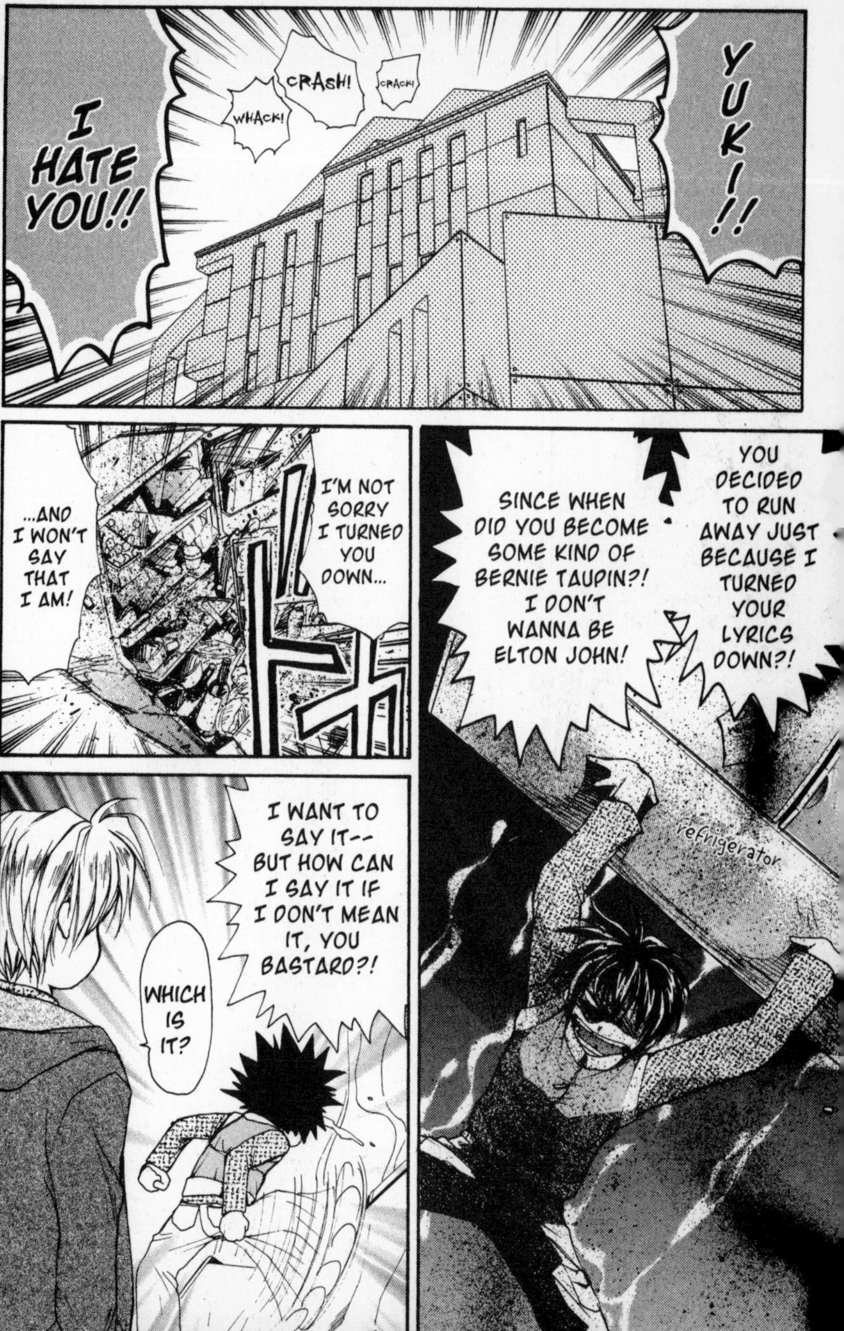
YUKI!!
CRACK!
CRASH!
WHACK!
I HATE YOU!!
YOU DECIDED TO RUN AWAY JUST BECAUSE I TURNED YOUR LYRICS DOWN?!
SINCE WHEN DID YOU BECOME SOME KIND OF BERNIE TAUPIN?! I DON'T WANNA BE ELTON JOHN!
refrigerator
I'M NOT SORRY I TURNED YOU DOWN...
...AND I WON'T SAY THAT I AM!
I WANT TO SAY IT-- BUT HOW CAN I SAY IT IF I DON'T MEAN IT, YOU BASTARD?!
WHICH IS IT?

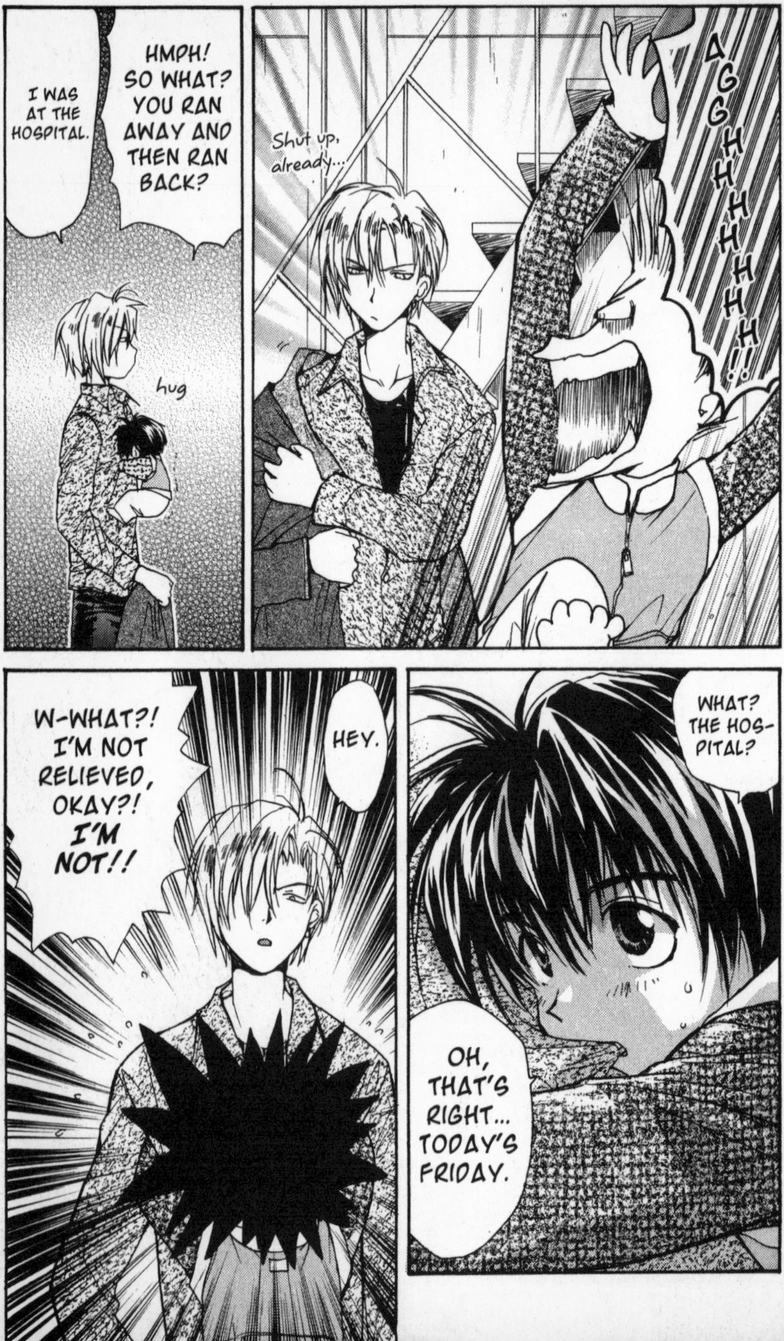
AGGHHHHHHH!!
Shut up, already...
HMPH! SO WHAT? YOU RAN AWAY AND THEN RAN BACK?
I WAS AT THE HOSPITAL.
hug
WHAT? THE HOS-PITAL?
OH, THAT'S RIGHT... TODAY'S FRIDAY.
HEY.
W-WHAT?! I'M NOT RELIEVED, OKAY?! I'M NOT!!

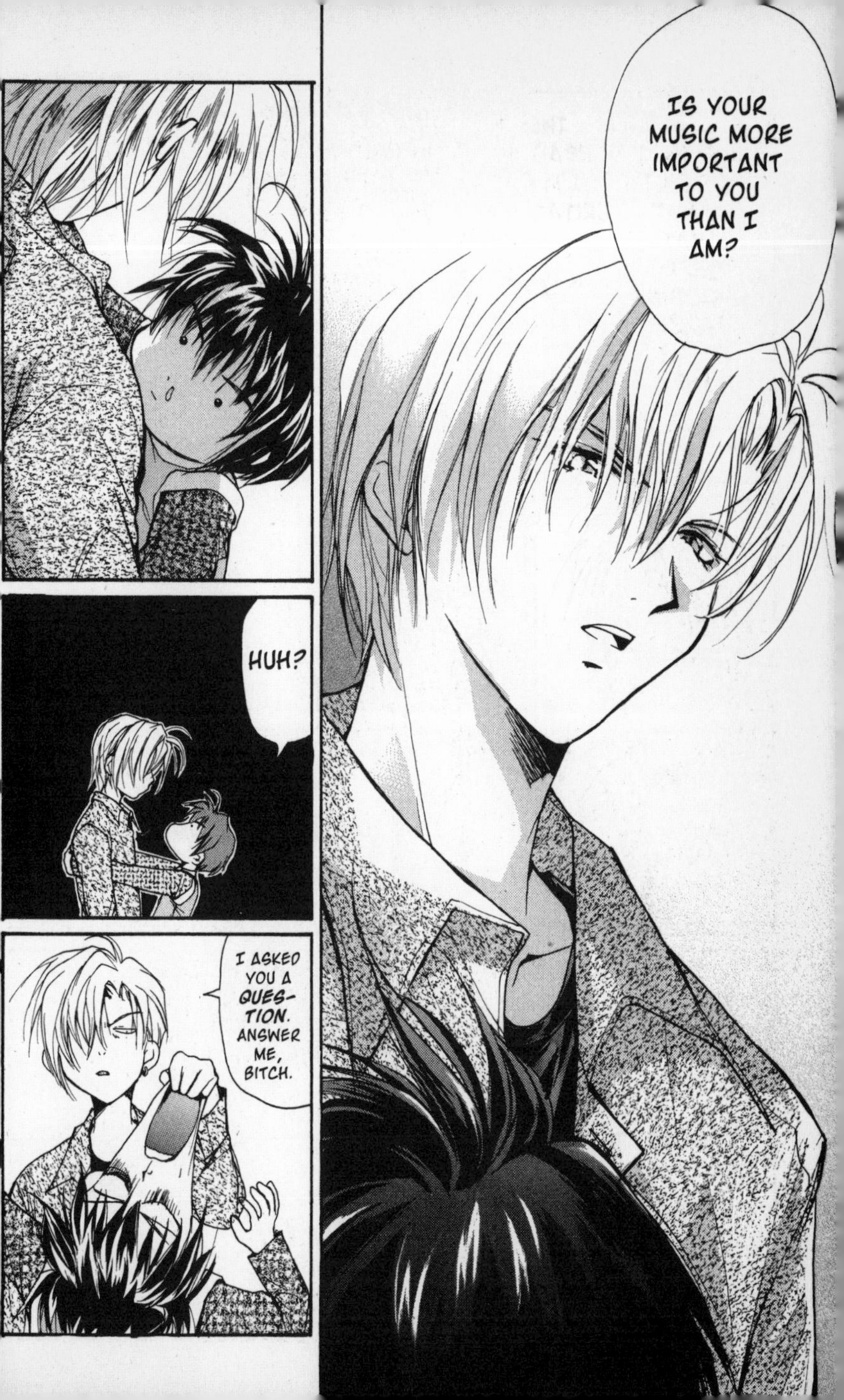
IS YOUR MUSIC MORE IMPORTANT TO YOU THAN I AM?
HUH?
I ASKED YOU A QUESTION. ANSWER ME, BITCH.

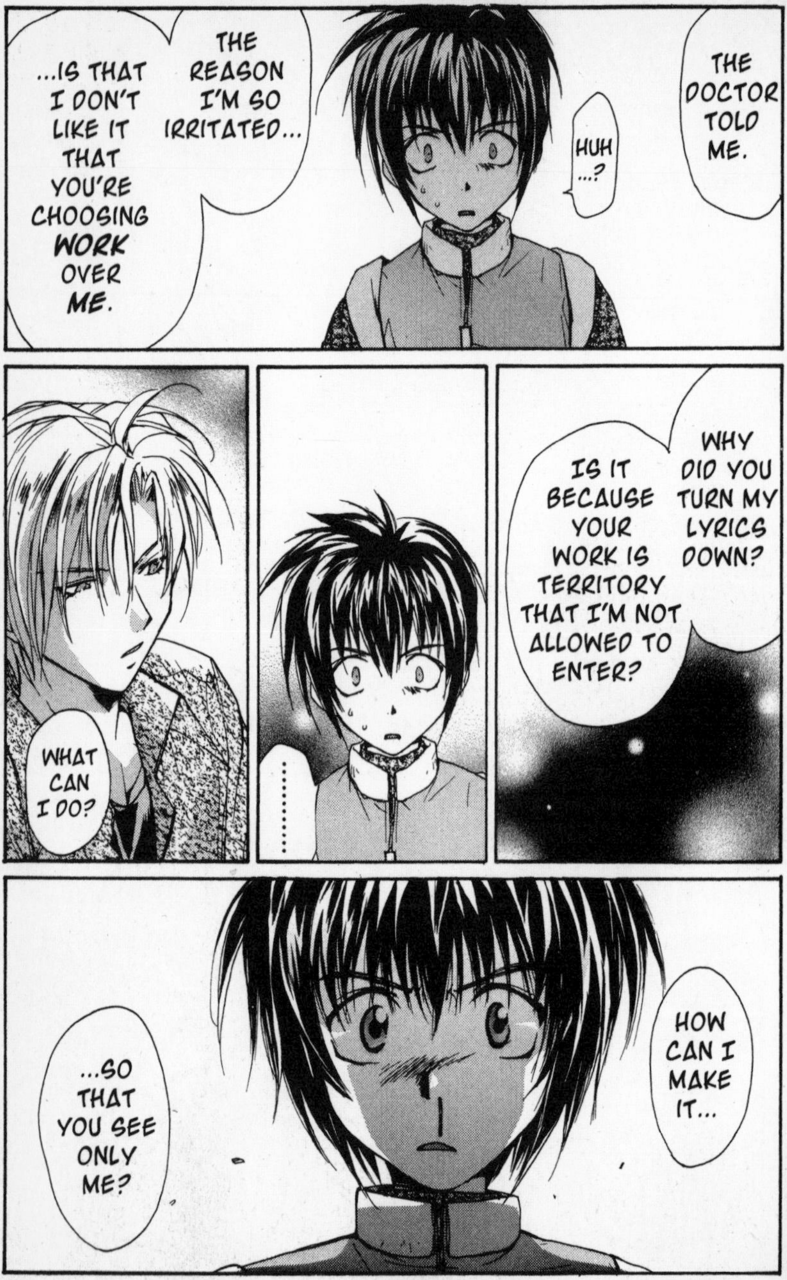
THE DOCTOR TOLD ME.
HUH ...?
THE REASON I'M SO IRRITATED...
...IS THAT I DON'T LIKE IT THAT YOU'RE CHOOSING WORK OVER ME.
WHY DID YOU TURN MY LYRICS DOWN?
IS IT BECAUSE YOUR WORK IS TERRITORY THAT I'M NOT ALLOWED TO ENTER?
....
WHAT CAN I DO?
HOW CAN I MAKE IT...
...SO THAT YOU SEE ONLY ME?

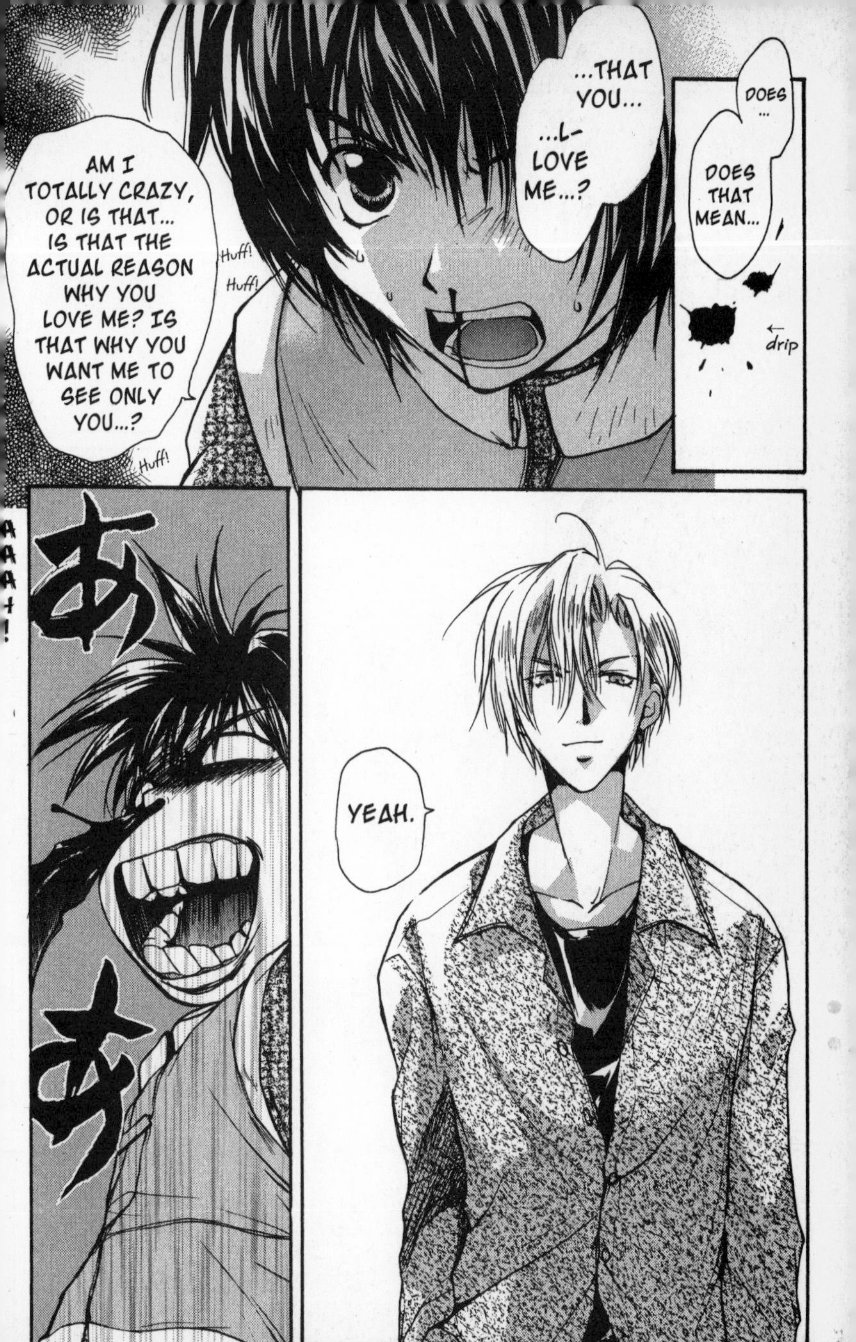
DOES...
DOES THAT MEAN...
...THAT YOU...
...L-LOVE ME...?
drip
Huff!
Huff!
AM I TOTALLY CRAZY, OR IS THAT... IS THAT THE ACTUAL REASON WHY YOU LOVE ME? IS THAT WHY YOU WANT ME TO SEE ONLY YOU...?
Huff!
YEAH.
あ
あ
AAAH!

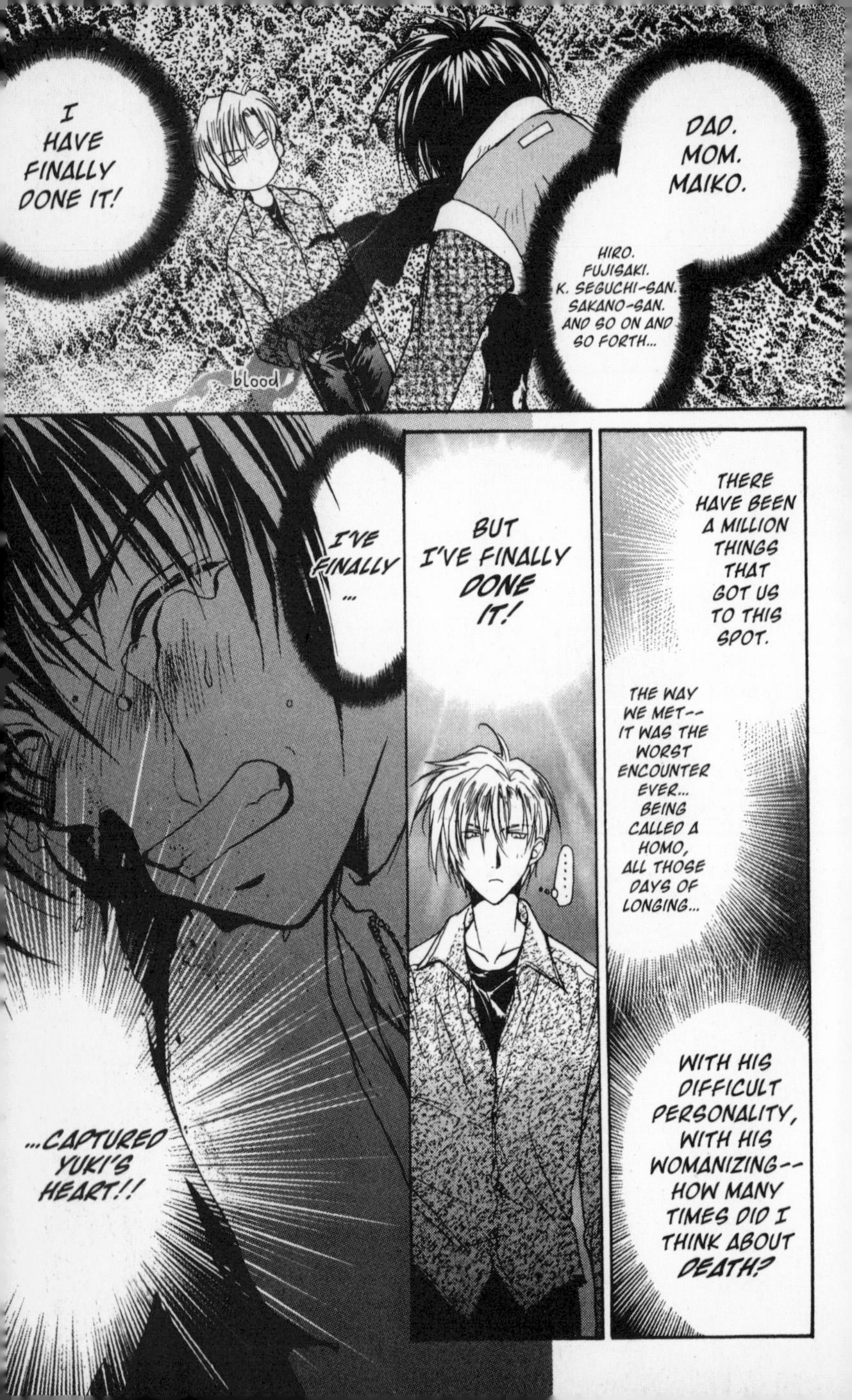
DAD. MOM. MAIKO.
HIRO. FUJISAKI. K. SEGUCHI-SAN. SAKANO-SAN. AND SO ON AND SO FORTH...
I HAVE FINALLY DONE IT!
blood
THERE HAVE BEEN A MILLION THINGS THAT GOT US TO THIS SPOT.
THE WAY WE MET--IT WAS THE WORST ENCOUNTER EVER... BEING CALLED A HOMO, ALL THOSE DAYS OF LONGING...
WITH HIS DIFFICULT PERSONALITY, WITH HIS WOMANIZING--HOW MANY TIMES DID I THINK ABOUT DEATH?
BUT I'VE FINALLY DONE IT!
......
I'VE FINALLY ...
...CAPTURED YUKI'S HEART!!

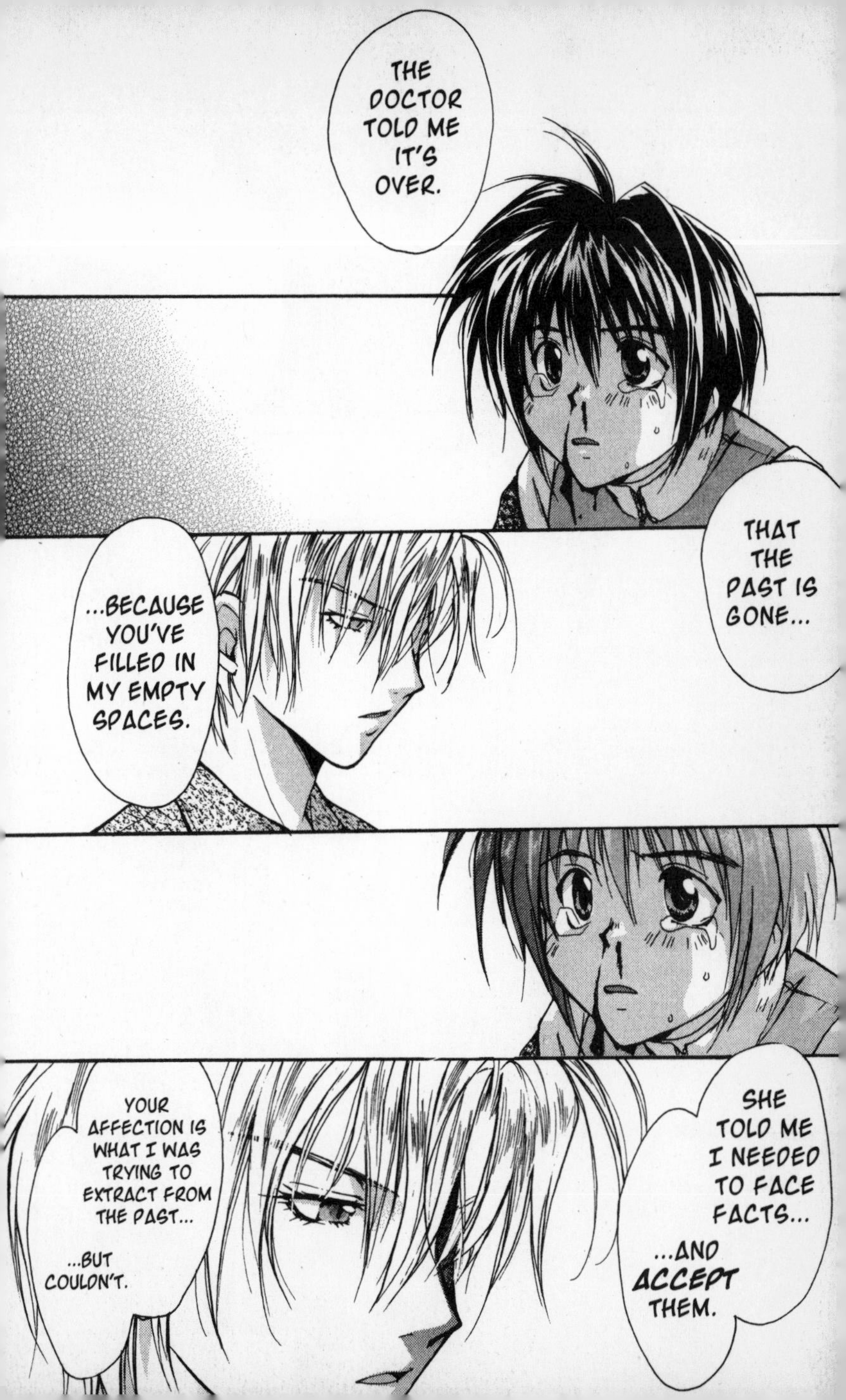
THE DOCTOR TOLD ME IT'S OVER.
THAT THE PAST IS GONE...
...BECAUSE YOU'VE FILLED IN MY EMPTY SPACES.
SHE TOLD ME I NEEDED TO FACE FACTS...
...AND **ACCEPT** THEM.
YOUR AFFECTION IS WHAT I WAS TRYING TO EXTRACT FROM THE PAST...
...BUT COULDN'T.

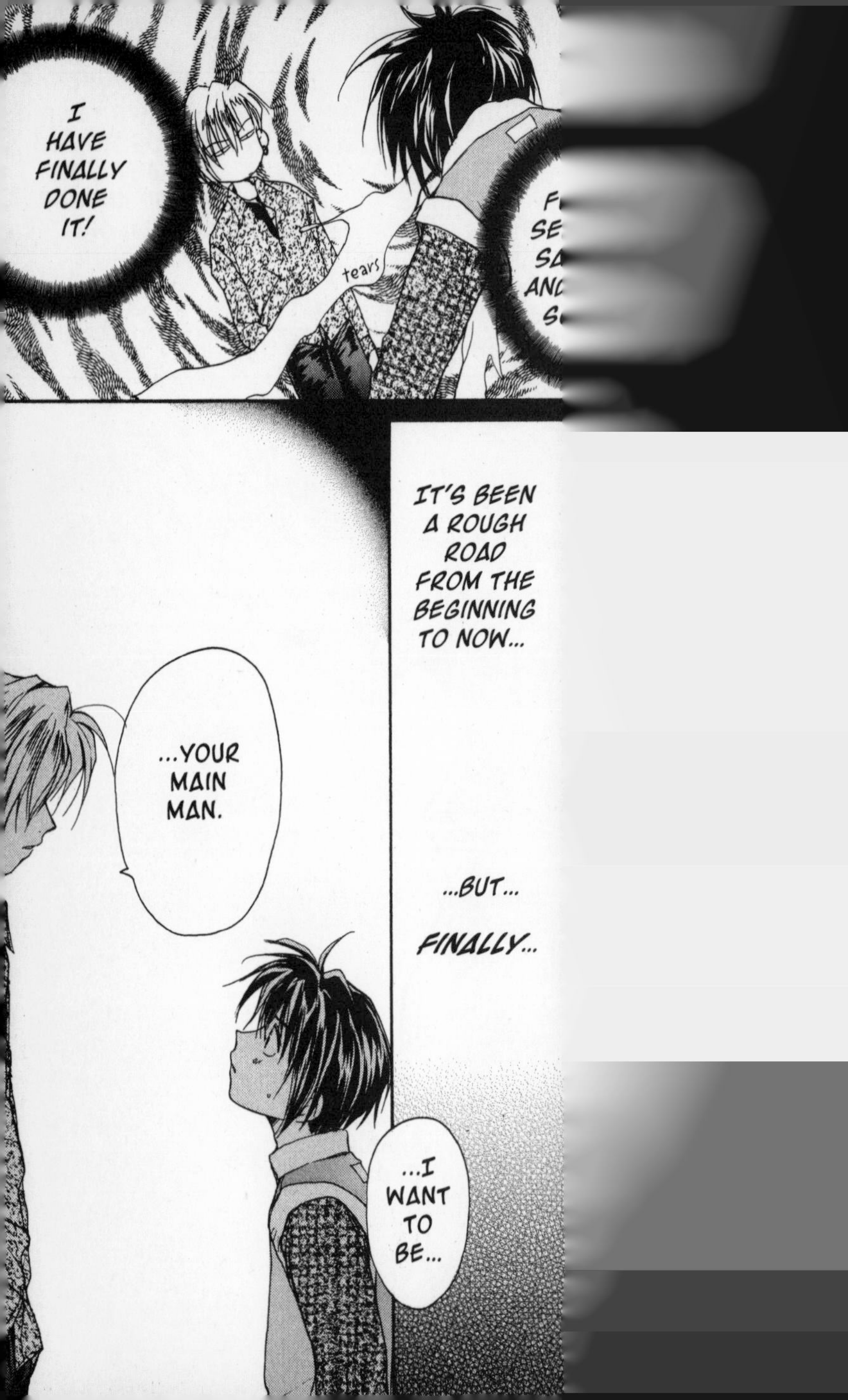
tears
I HAVE FINALLY DONE IT!
IT'S BEEN A ROUGH ROAD FROM THE BEGINNING TO NOW...
...BUT...
FINALLY...
...I WANT TO BE...
...YOUR MAIN MAN.

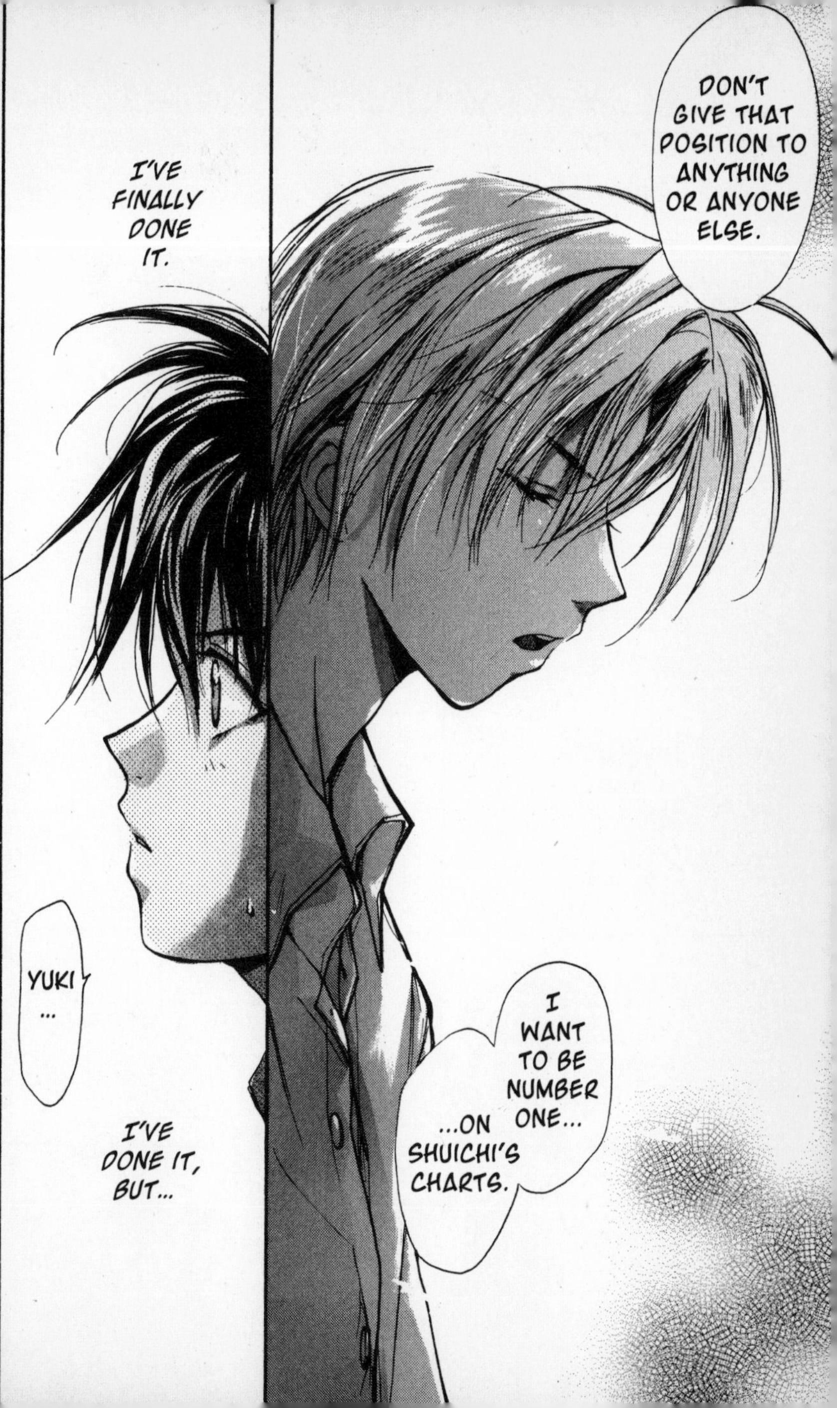
DON'T GIVE THAT POSITION TO ANYTHING OR ANYONE ELSE.
I WANT TO BE NUMBER ONE...
...ON SHUICHI'S CHARTS.
I'VE FINALLY DONE IT.
YUKI ...
I'VE DONE IT, BUT...

...WHY CAN'T I STOP THINKING THAT THERE'S SOMETHING WRONG WITH ALL THIS?

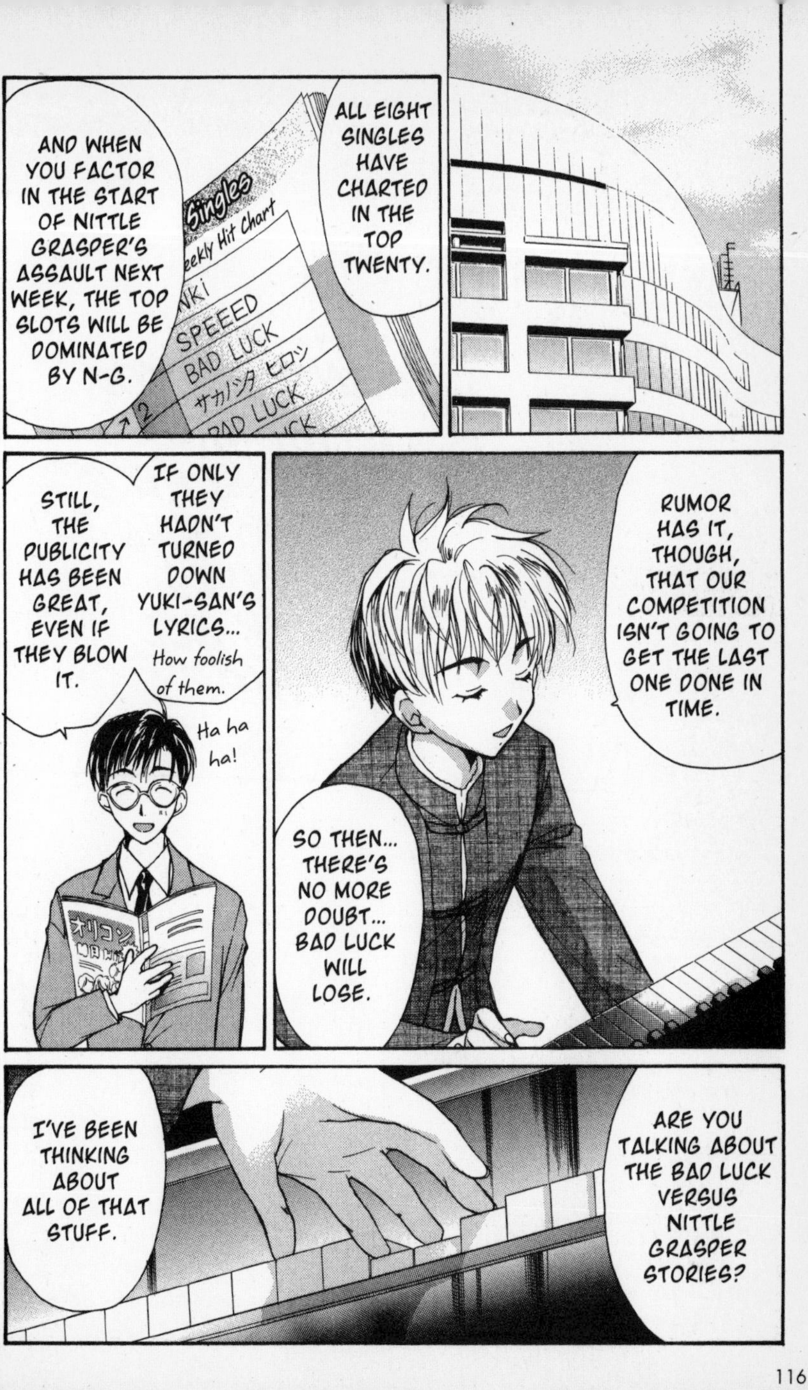
ALL EIGHT SINGLES HAVE CHARTED IN THE TOP TWENTY.
AND WHEN YOU FACTOR IN THE START OF NITTLE GRASPER'S ASSAULT NEXT WEEK, THE TOP SLOTS WILL BE DOMINATED BY N-G.
Singles
eekly Hit Chart
SPEEED
BAD LUCK
サカノシタ ヒロシ
BAD LUCK
RUMOR HAS IT, THOUGH, THAT OUR COMPETITION ISN'T GOING TO GET THE LAST ONE DONE IN TIME.
SO THEN... THERE'S NO MORE DOUBT... BAD LUCK WILL LOSE.
IF ONLY THEY HADN'T TURNED DOWN YUKI-SAN'S LYRICS...
STILL, THE PUBLICITY HAS BEEN GREAT, EVEN IF THEY BLOW IT.
How foolish of them.
Ha ha ha!
オリコン
ARE YOU TALKING ABOUT THE BAD LUCK VERSUS NITTLE GRASPER STORIES?
I'VE BEEN THINKING ABOUT ALL OF THAT STUFF.

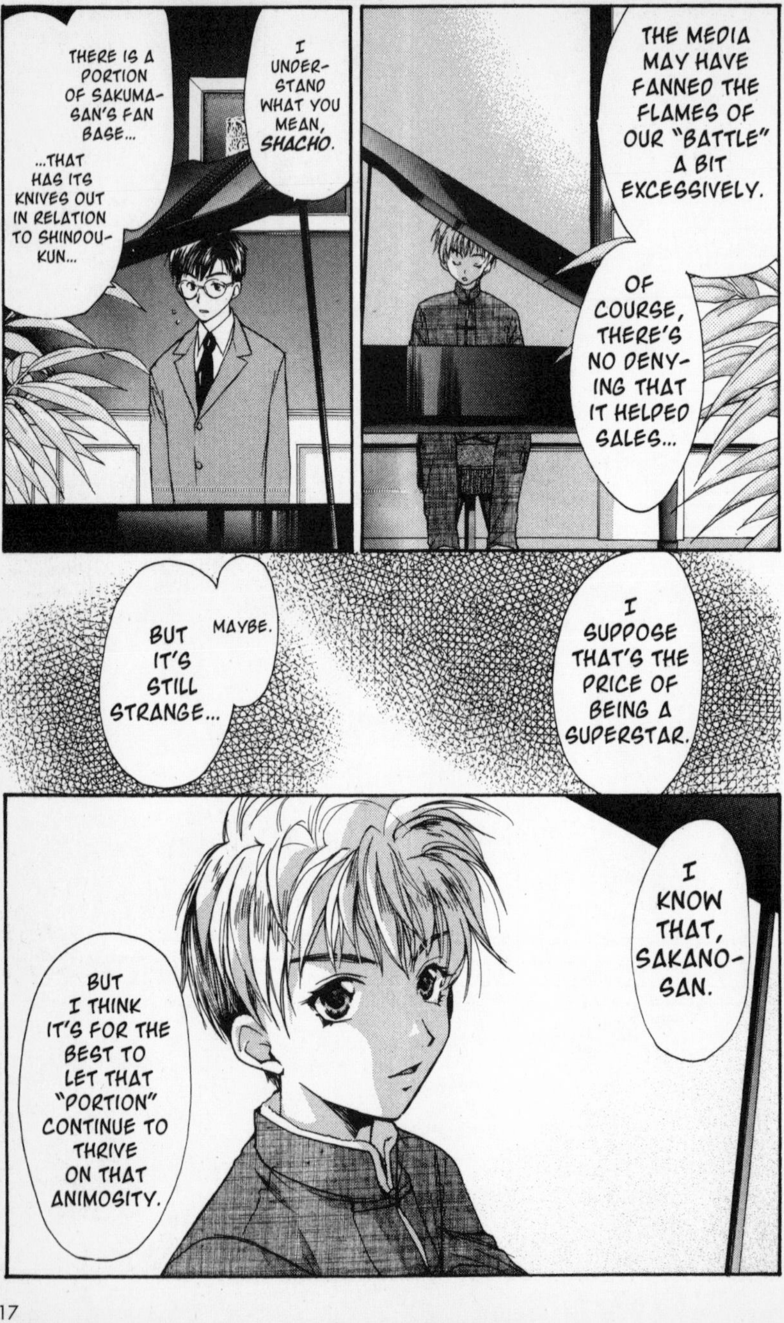
THE MEDIA MAY HAVE FANNED THE FLAMES OF OUR "BATTLE" A BIT EXCESSIVELY.
OF COURSE, THERE'S NO DENYING THAT IT HELPED SALES...
I UNDERSTAND WHAT YOU MEAN, *SHACHO*.
THERE IS A PORTION OF SAKUMA-SAN'S FAN BASE...
...THAT HAS ITS KNIVES OUT IN RELATION TO SHINDOU-KUN...
I SUPPOSE THAT'S THE PRICE OF BEING A SUPERSTAR.
MAYBE.
BUT IT'S STILL STRANGE...
I KNOW THAT, SAKANO-SAN.
BUT I THINK IT'S FOR THE BEST TO LET THAT "PORTION" CONTINUE TO THRIVE ON THAT ANIMOSITY.

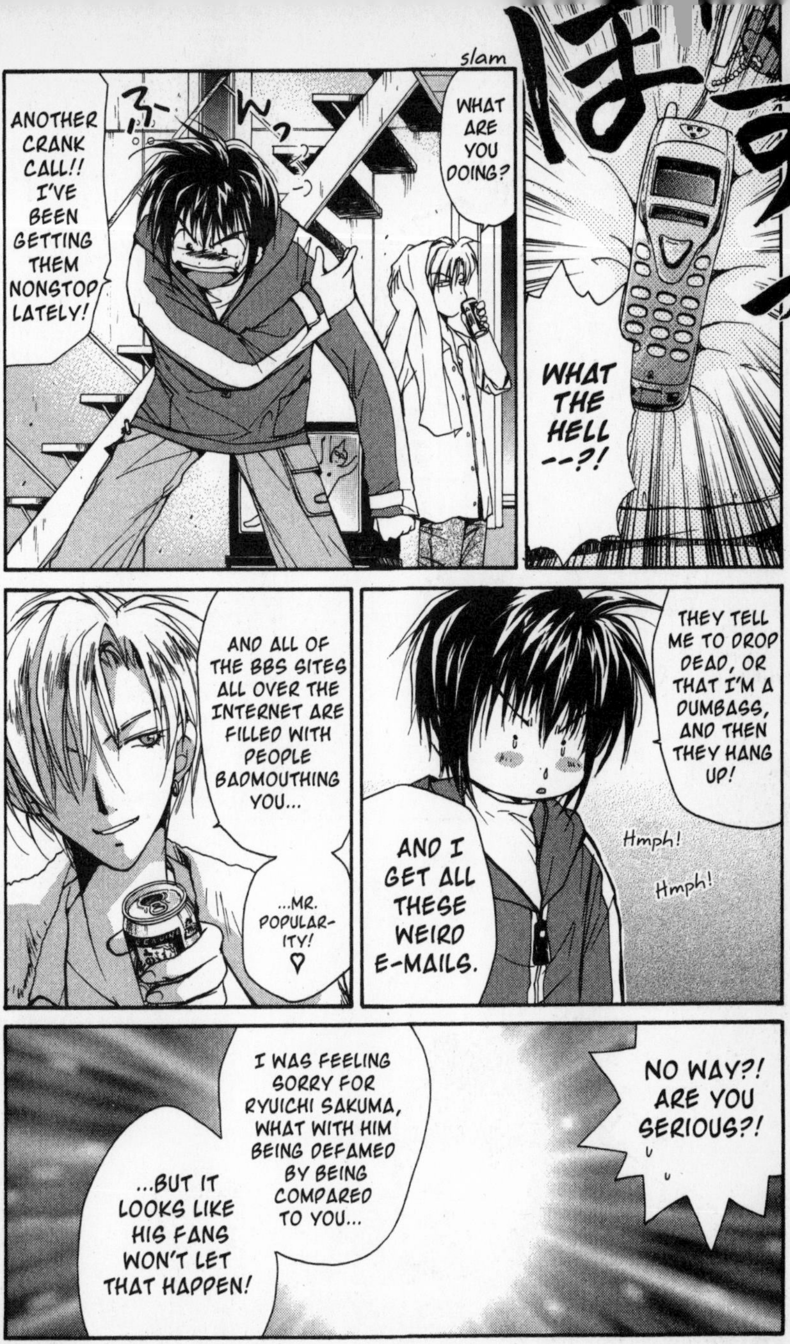
slam
WHAT THE HELL --?!
WHAT ARE YOU DOING?
ANOTHER CRANK CALL!! I'VE BEEN GETTING THEM NONSTOP LATELY!
THEY TELL ME TO DROP DEAD, OR THAT I'M A DUMBASS, AND THEN THEY HANG UP!
Hmph!
Hmph!
AND I GET ALL THESE WEIRD E-MAILS.
AND ALL OF THE BBS SITES ALL OVER THE INTERNET ARE FILLED WITH PEOPLE BADMOUTHING YOU...
...MR. POPULARITY! ♡
NO WAY?! ARE YOU SERIOUS?!
I WAS FEELING SORRY FOR RYUICHI SAKUMA, WHAT WITH HIM BEING DEFAMED BY BEING COMPARED TO YOU...
...BUT IT LOOKS LIKE HIS FANS WON'T LET THAT HAPPEN!

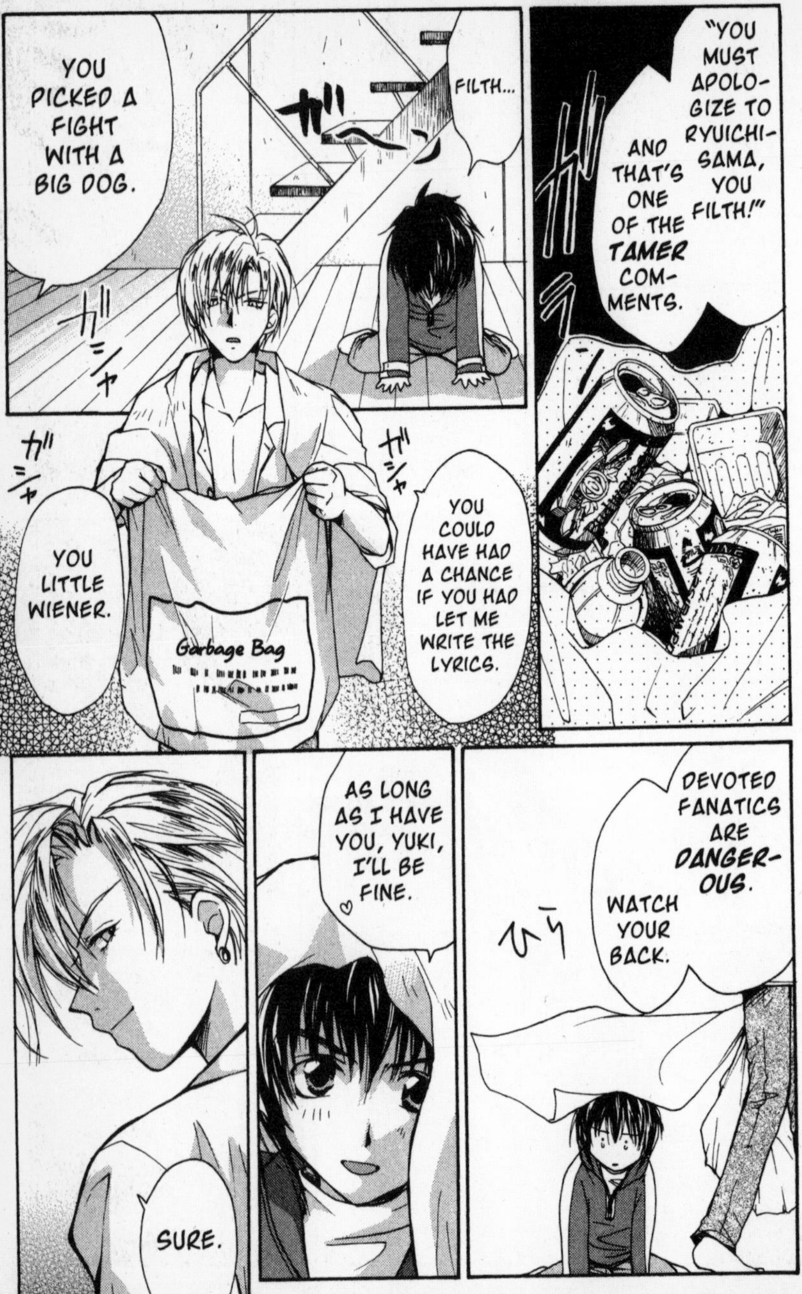
"YOU MUST APOLOGIZE TO RYUICHI-SAMA, YOU FILTH!"
AND THAT'S ONE OF THE TAMER COMMENTS.
FILTH...
YOU PICKED A FIGHT WITH A BIG DOG.
YOU COULD HAVE HAD A CHANCE IF YOU HAD LET ME WRITE THE LYRICS.
YOU LITTLE WIENER.
Garbage Bag
DEVOTED FANATICS ARE DANGEROUS.
WATCH YOUR BACK.
AS LONG AS I HAVE YOU, YUKI, I'LL BE FINE.
SURE.

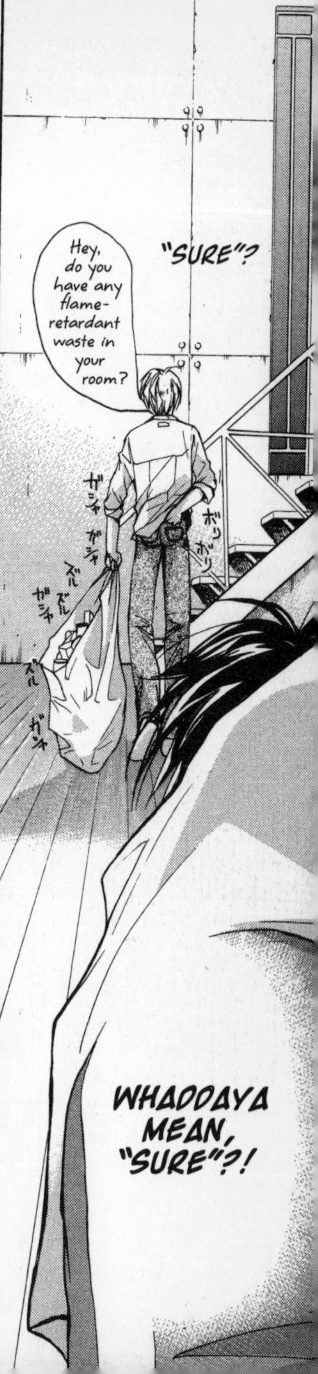

"SURE"?
Hey, do you have any flame-retardant waste in your room?
ガシャ ガシャ
ボリ ボリ
ズル ズル
ガシャ
ズル
ガシャ
WHADDAYA MEAN, "SURE"?!

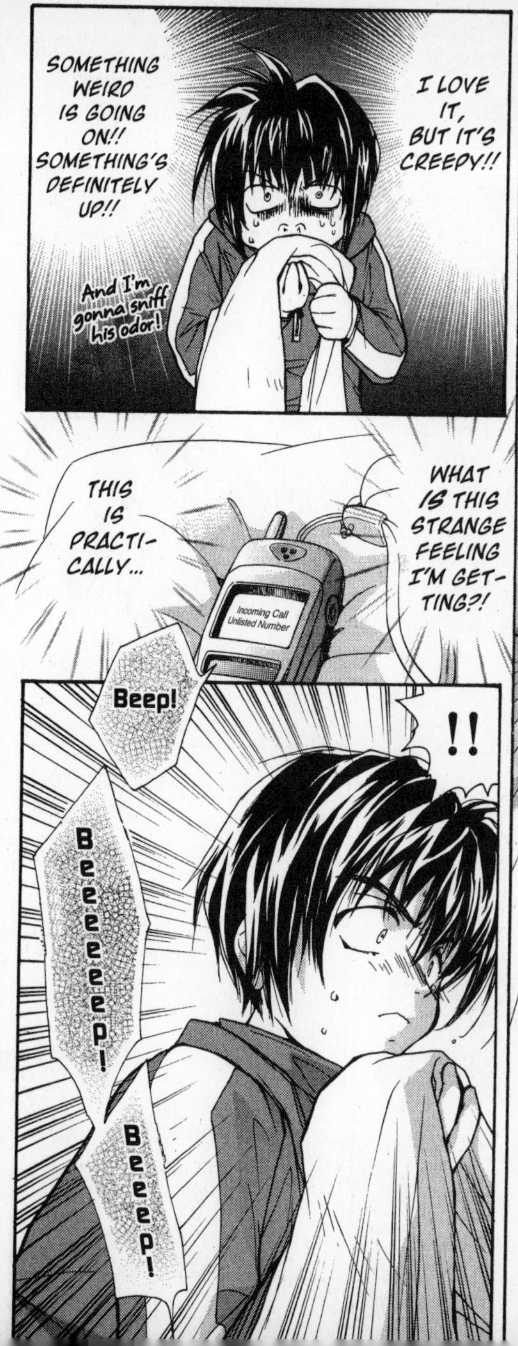

I LOVE IT, BUT IT'S CREEPY!!
SOMETHING WEIRD IS GOING ON!! SOMETHING'S DEFINITELY UP!!
And I'm gonna sniff his odor!
WHAT IS THIS STRANGE FEELING I'M GETTING?!
THIS IS PRACTICALLY...
Incoming Call Unlisted Number
Beep!
!!
Beeeeeeep!
Beeep!

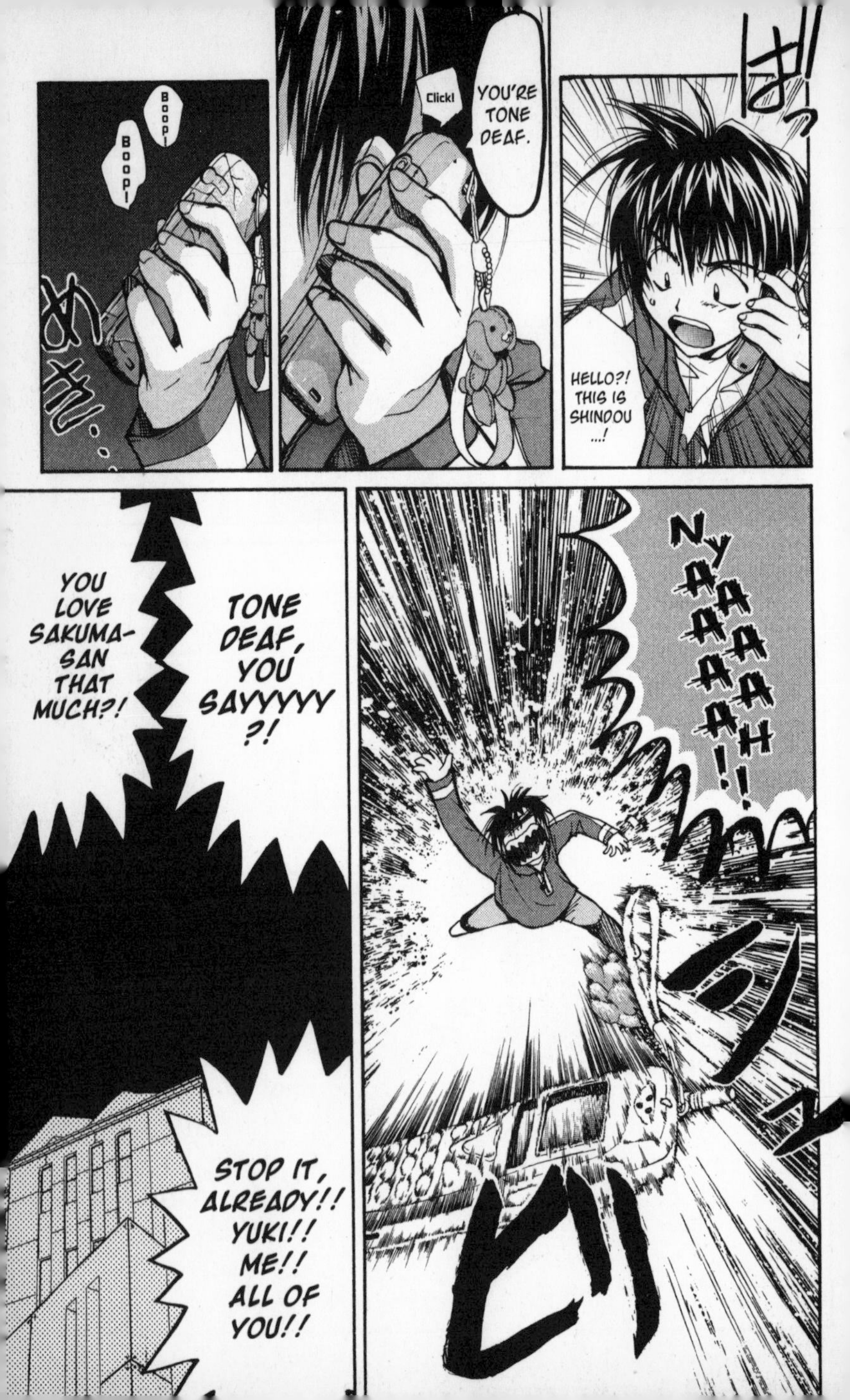
HELLO?! THIS IS SHINDOU ...!
Click!
YOU'RE TONE DEAF.
Boop!
Boop!
NyAAAAAAAH!!
TONE DEAF, YOU SAYYYYY?!
YOU LOVE SAKUMA-SAN THAT MUCH?!
STOP IT, ALREADY!! YUKI!! ME!! ALL OF YOU!!

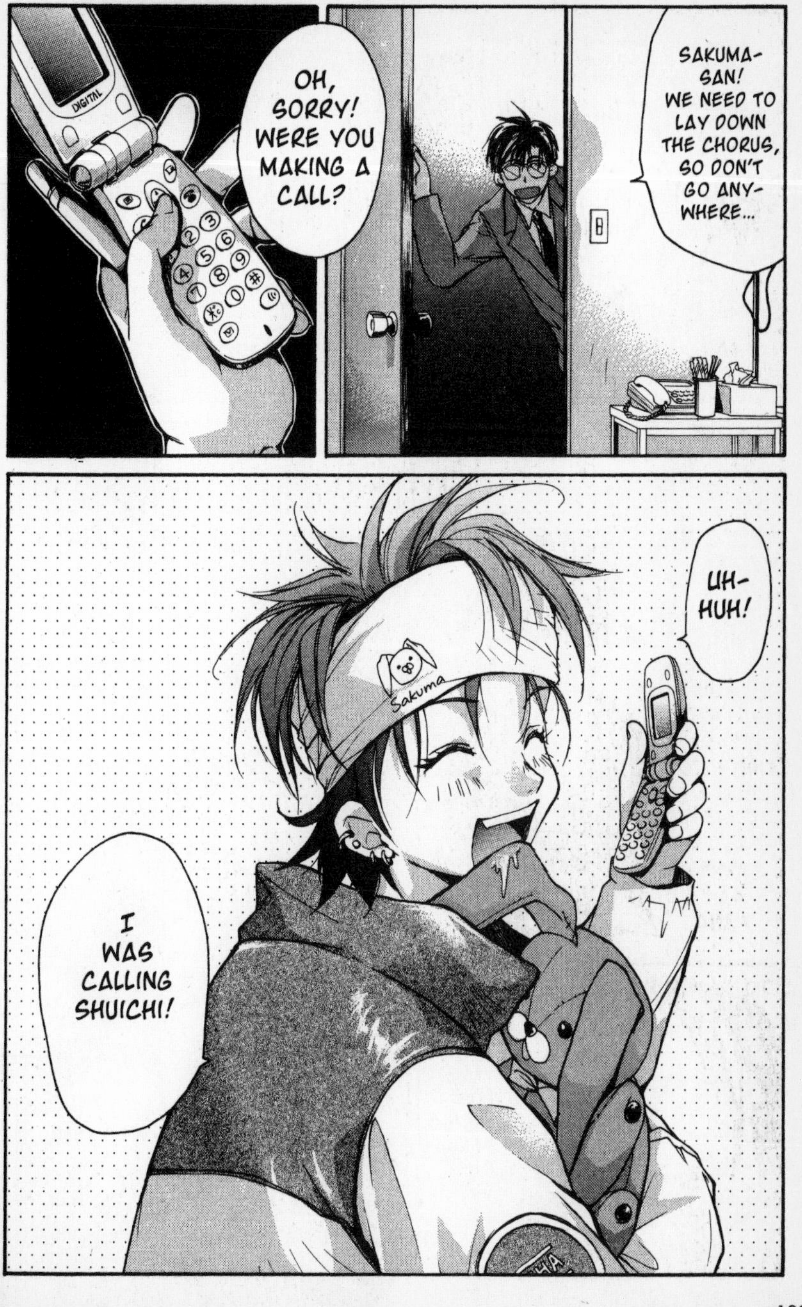
SAKUMA-SAN! WE NEED TO LAY DOWN THE CHORUS, SO DON'T GO ANY-WHERE...
OH, SORRY! WERE YOU MAKING A CALL?
DIGITAL
UH-HUH!
Sakuma
I WAS CALLING SHUICHI!

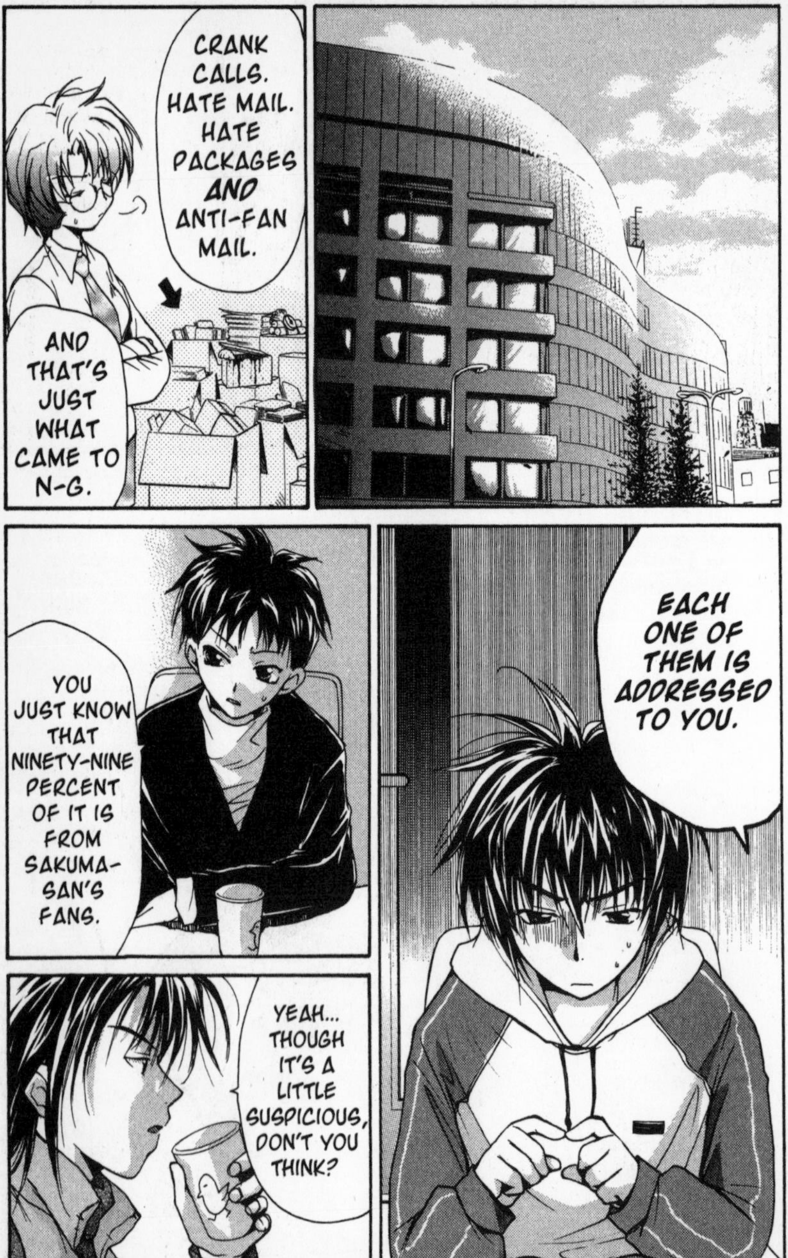
CRANK CALLS. HATE MAIL. HATE PACKAGES AND ANTI-FAN MAIL.
AND THAT'S JUST WHAT CAME TO N-G.
EACH ONE OF THEM IS ADDRESSED TO YOU.
YOU JUST KNOW THAT NINETY-NINE PERCENT OF IT IS FROM SAKUMA-SAN'S FANS.
YEAH... THOUGH IT'S A LITTLE SUSPICIOUS, DON'T YOU THINK?

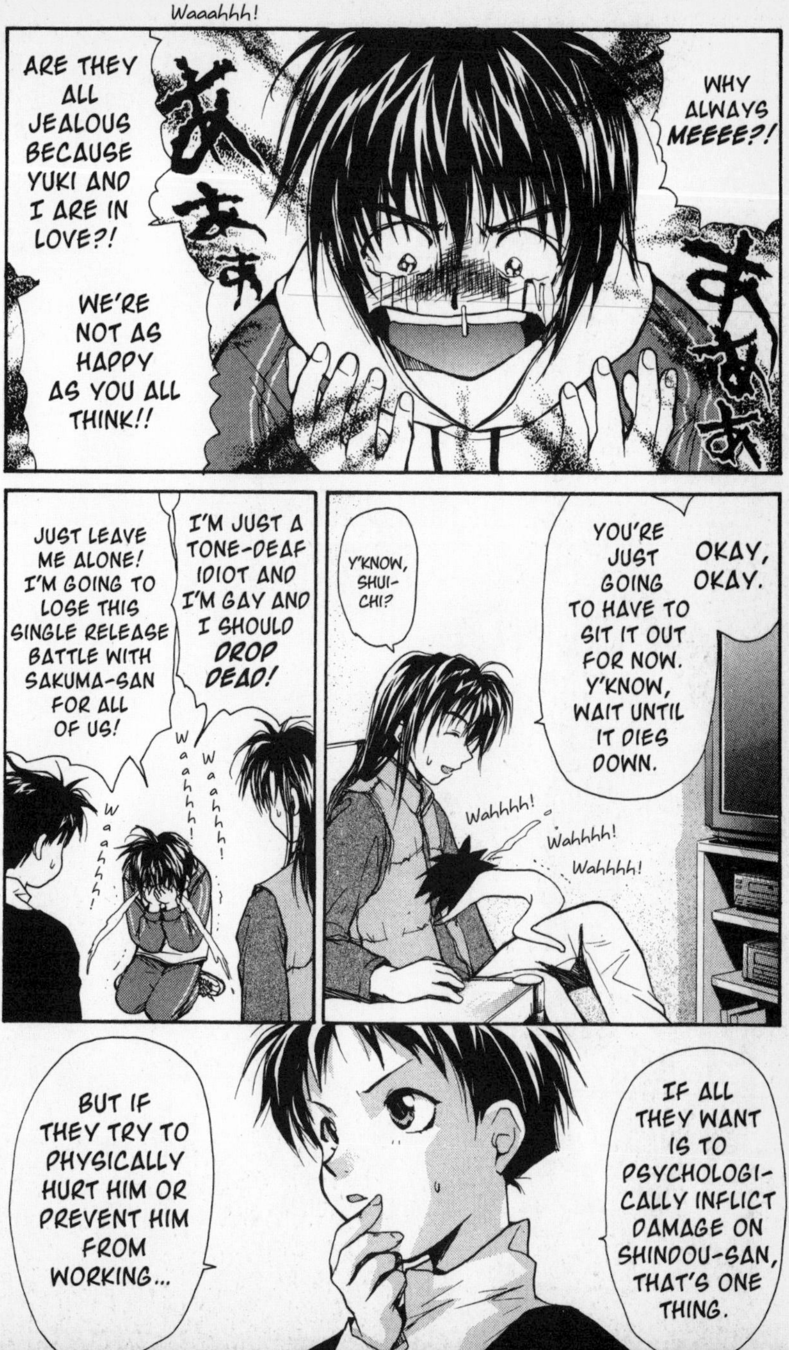
Waaahhh!
WHY ALWAYS MEEEE?!
ARE THEY ALL JEALOUS BECAUSE YUKI AND I ARE IN LOVE?!
WE'RE NOT AS HAPPY AS YOU ALL THINK!!
OKAY, OKAY.
YOU'RE JUST GOING TO HAVE TO SIT IT OUT FOR NOW. Y'KNOW, WAIT UNTIL IT DIES DOWN.
Y'KNOW, SHUI-CHI?
Wahhhh!
Wahhhh!
Wahhhh!
I'M JUST A TONE-DEAF IDIOT AND I'M GAY AND I SHOULD DROP DEAD!
JUST LEAVE ME ALONE! I'M GOING TO LOSE THIS SINGLE RELEASE BATTLE WITH SAKUMA-SAN FOR ALL OF US!
Waahhh!
Waahhh!
Waahhh!
IF ALL THEY WANT IS TO PSYCHOLOGI-CALLY INFLICT DAMAGE ON SHINDOU-SAN, THAT'S ONE THING.
BUT IF THEY TRY TO PHYSICALLY HURT HIM OR PREVENT HIM FROM WORKING...

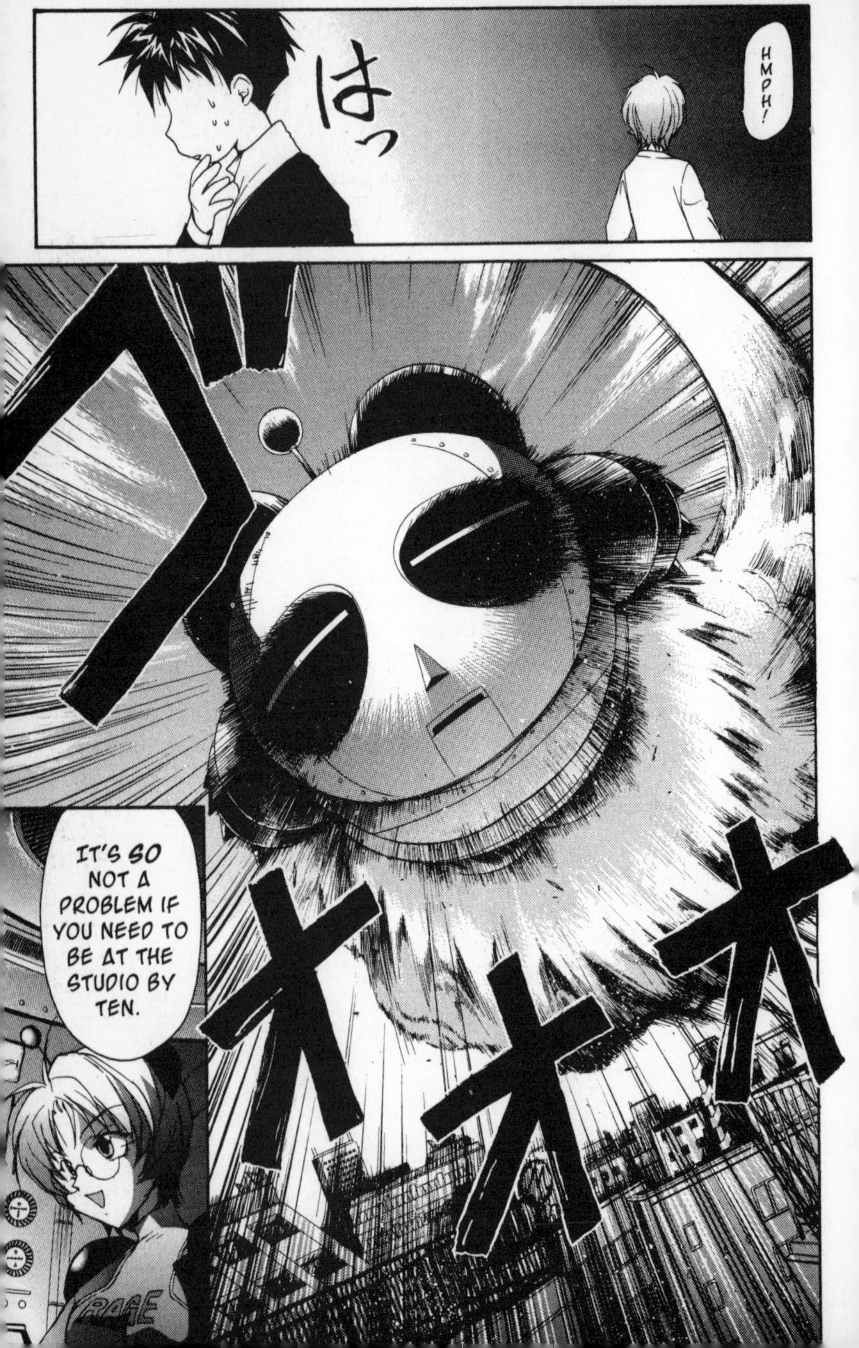
HMPH!
はっ
IT'S SO NOT A PROBLEM IF YOU NEED TO BE AT THE STUDIO BY TEN.

Ho ho ho ho ho ho ho!

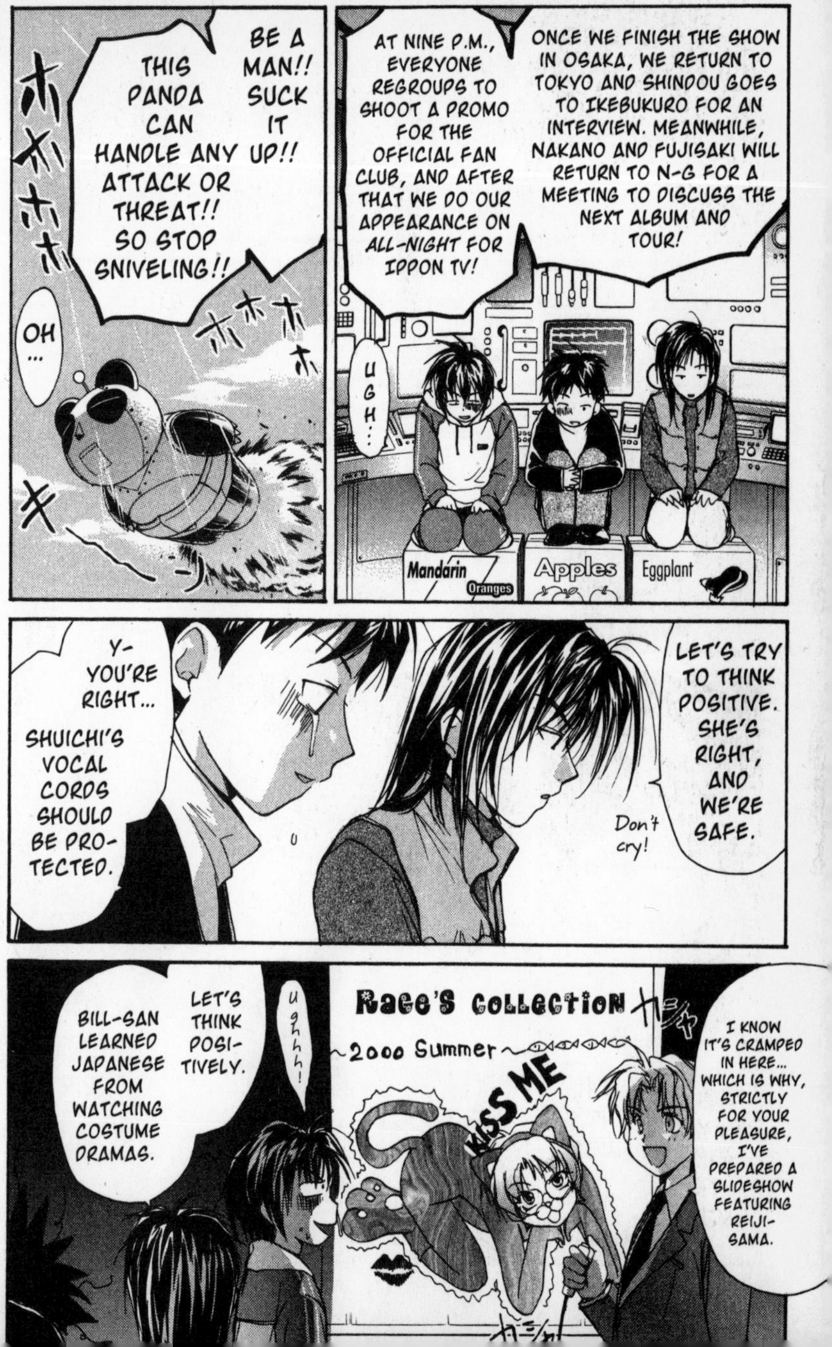
ONCE WE FINISH THE SHOW IN OSAKA, WE RETURN TO TOKYO AND SHINDOU GOES TO IKEBUKURO FOR AN INTERVIEW. MEANWHILE, NAKANO AND FUJISAKI WILL RETURN TO N-G FOR A MEETING TO DISCUSS THE NEXT ALBUM AND TOUR!
AT NINE P.M., EVERYONE REGROUPS TO SHOOT A PROMO FOR THE OFFICIAL FAN CLUB, AND AFTER THAT WE DO OUR APPEARANCE ON ALL-NIGHT FOR IPPON TV!
UGH...
Eggplant
Apples
Mandarin Oranges
BE A MAN!! SUCK IT UP!!
THIS PANDA CAN HANDLE ANY ATTACK OR THREAT!! SO STOP SNIVELING!!
OH...
LET'S TRY TO THINK POSITIVE. SHE'S RIGHT, AND WE'RE SAFE.
Don't cry!
Y-YOU'RE RIGHT...
SHUICHI'S VOCAL CORDS SHOULD BE PRO-TECTED.
I KNOW IT'S CRAMPED IN HERE... WHICH IS WHY, STRICTLY FOR YOUR PLEASURE, I'VE PREPARED A SLIDESHOW FEATURING REIJI-SAMA.
Rage's Collection
~2000 Summer~
KISS ME
Ughhh!
LET'S THINK POSI-TIVELY.
BILL-SAN LEARNED JAPANESE FROM WATCHING COSTUME DRAMAS.

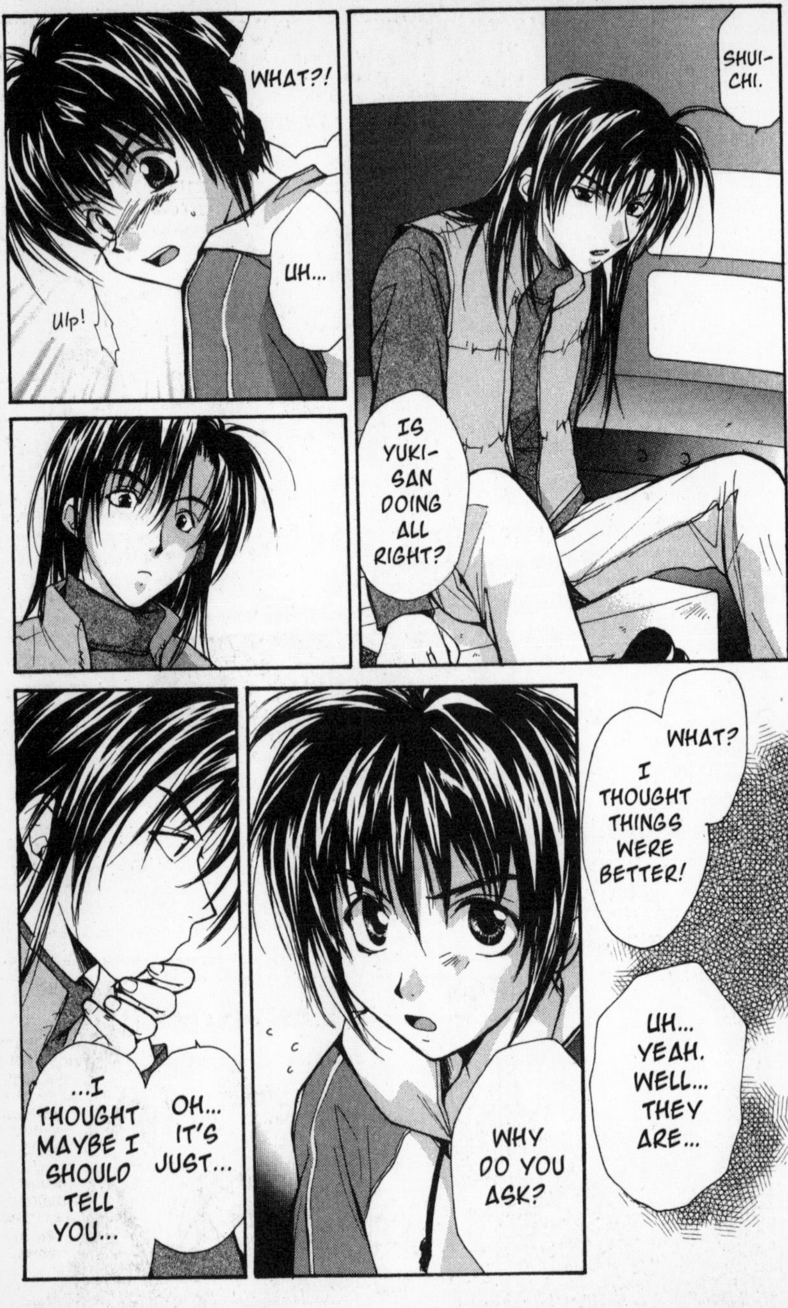
SHUI-CHI.
IS YUKI-SAN DOING ALL RIGHT?
WHAT?!
UH...
Ulp!
WHAT? I THOUGHT THINGS WERE BETTER!
UH... YEAH. WELL... THEY ARE...
WHY DO YOU ASK?
OH... IT'S JUST...
...I THOUGHT MAYBE I SHOULD TELL YOU...

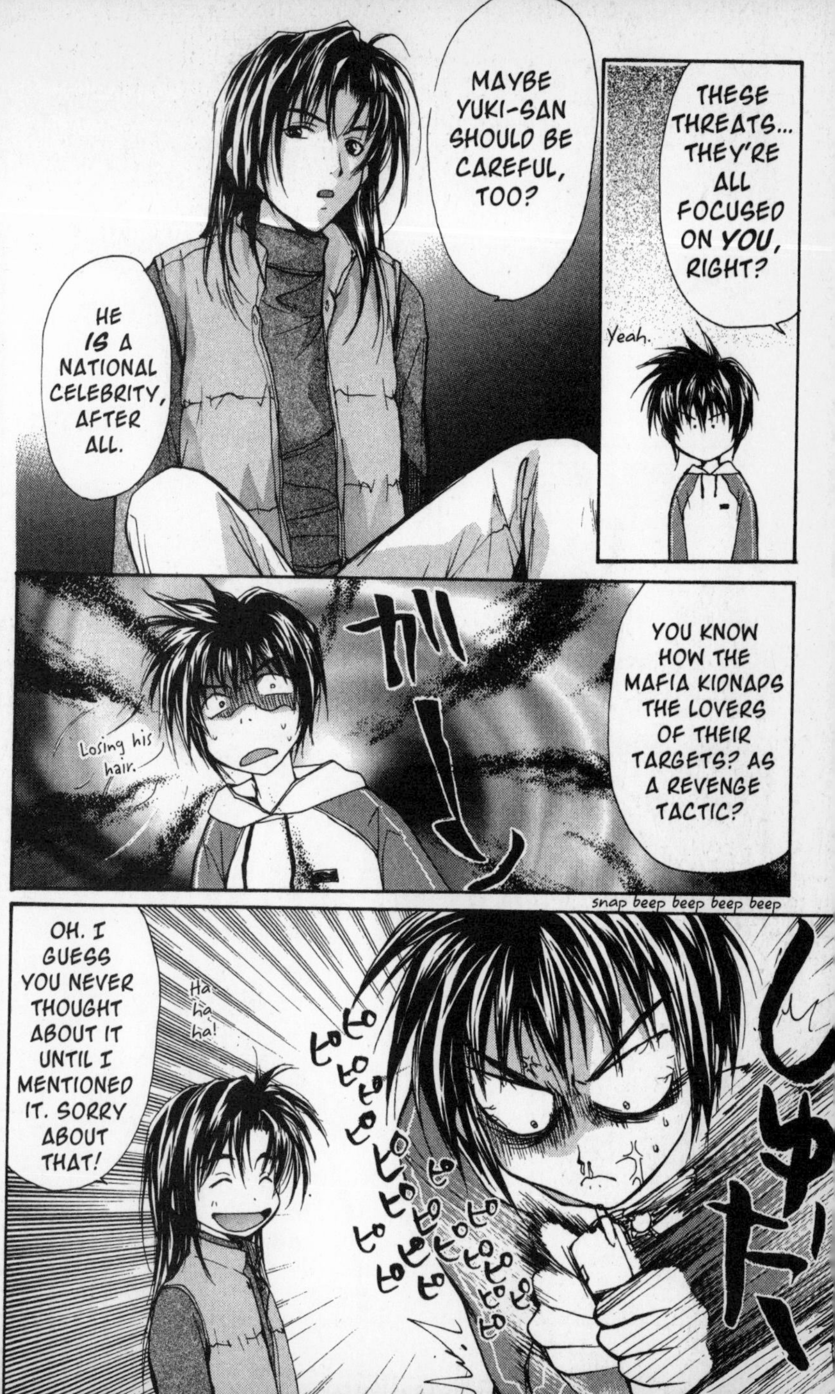
THESE THREATS... THEY'RE ALL FOCUSED ON YOU, RIGHT?
Yeah.
MAYBE YUKI-SAN SHOULD BE CAREFUL, TOO?
HE IS A NATIONAL CELEBRITY, AFTER ALL.
YOU KNOW HOW THE MAFIA KIDNAPS THE LOVERS OF THEIR TARGETS? AS A REVENGE TACTIC?
Losing his hair.
snap beep beep beep beep
OH. I GUESS YOU NEVER THOUGHT ABOUT IT UNTIL I MENTIONED IT. SORRY ABOUT THAT!
Ha ha ha!

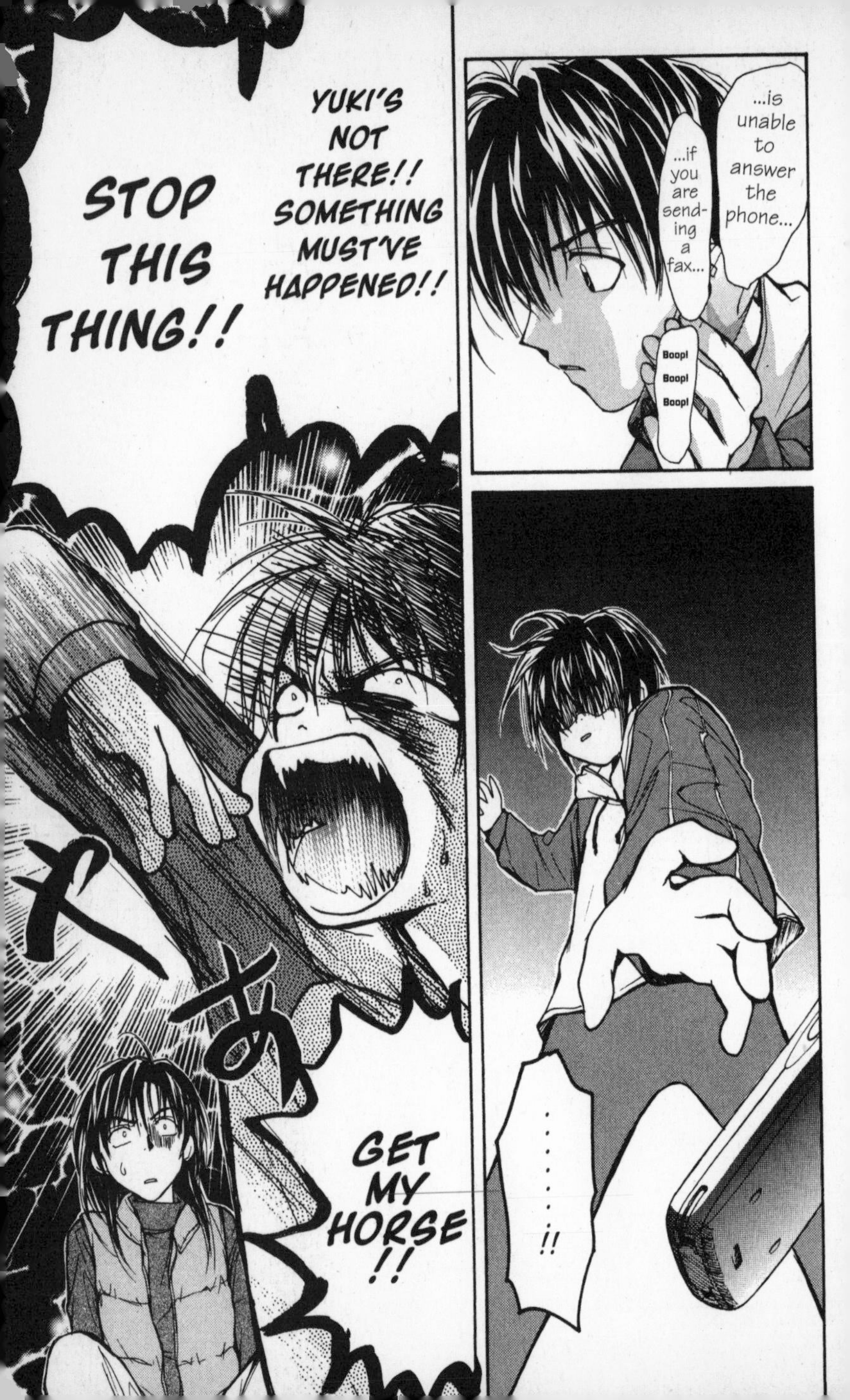
...is unable to answer the phone...
...if you are sending a fax...
Boop! Boop! Boop!
........!!
YUKI'S NOT THERE!! SOMETHING MUST'VE HAPPENED!!
STOP THIS THING!!
GET MY HORSE!!

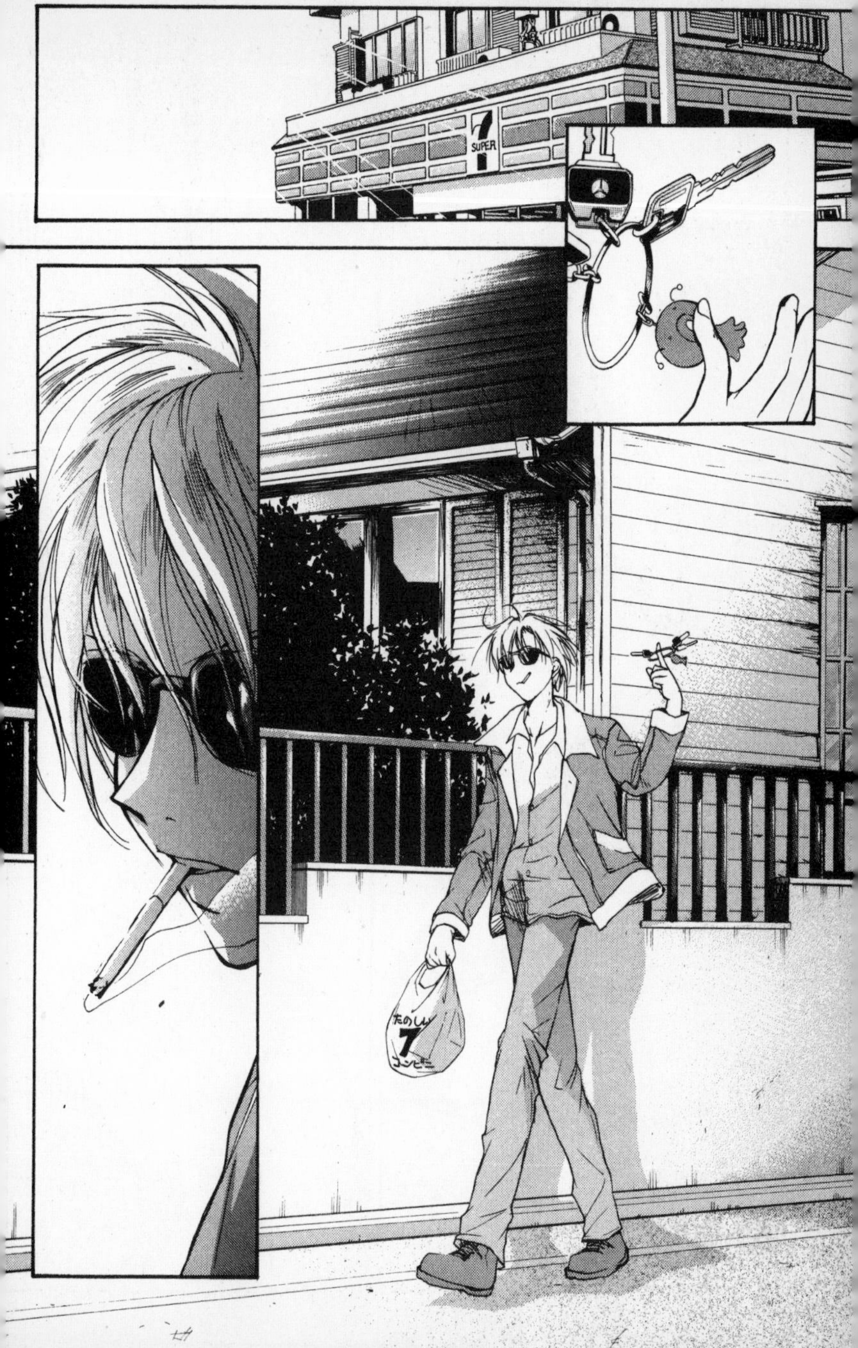
SUPER
コンビニ

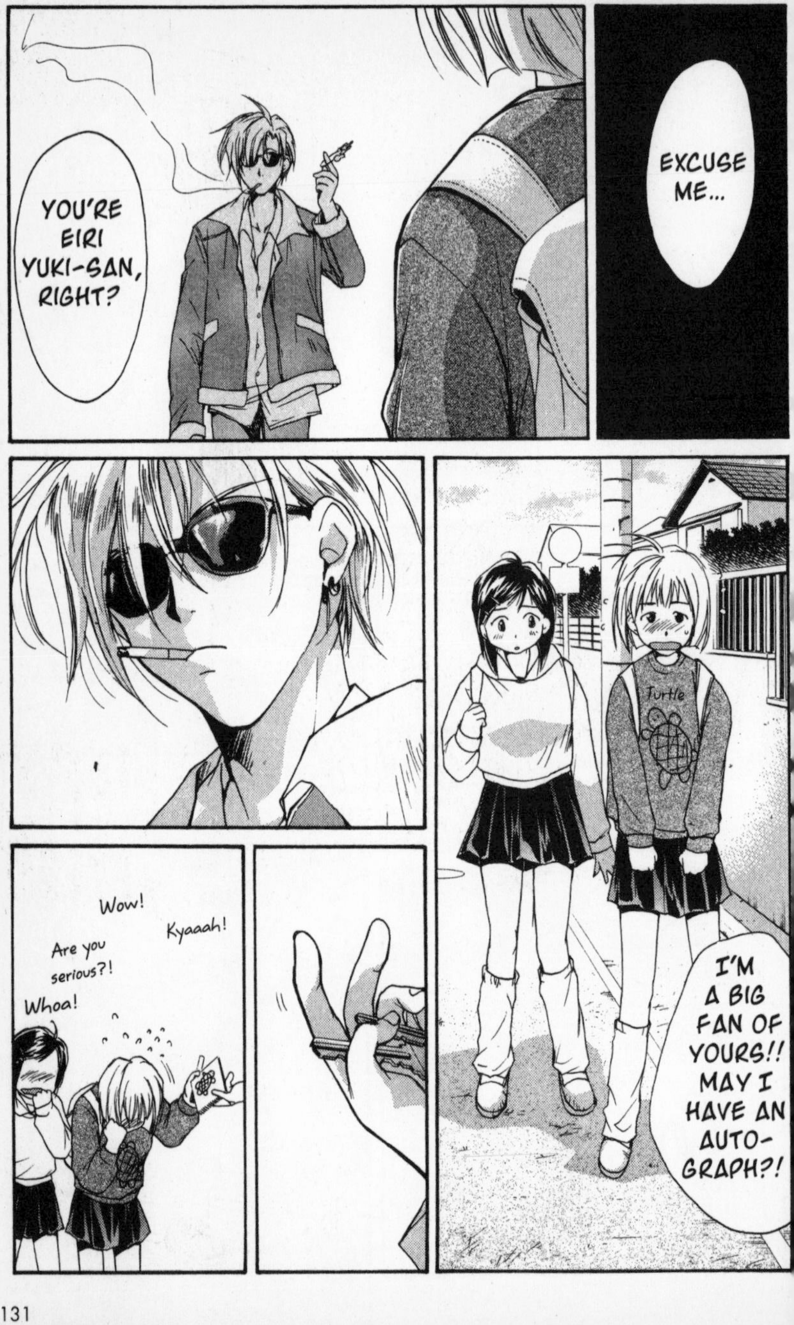
EXCUSE ME...
YOU'RE EIRI YUKI-SAN, RIGHT?
I'M A BIG FAN OF YOURS!! MAY I HAVE AN AUTO-GRAPH?!
Wow!
Kyaaah!
Are you serious?!
Whoa!

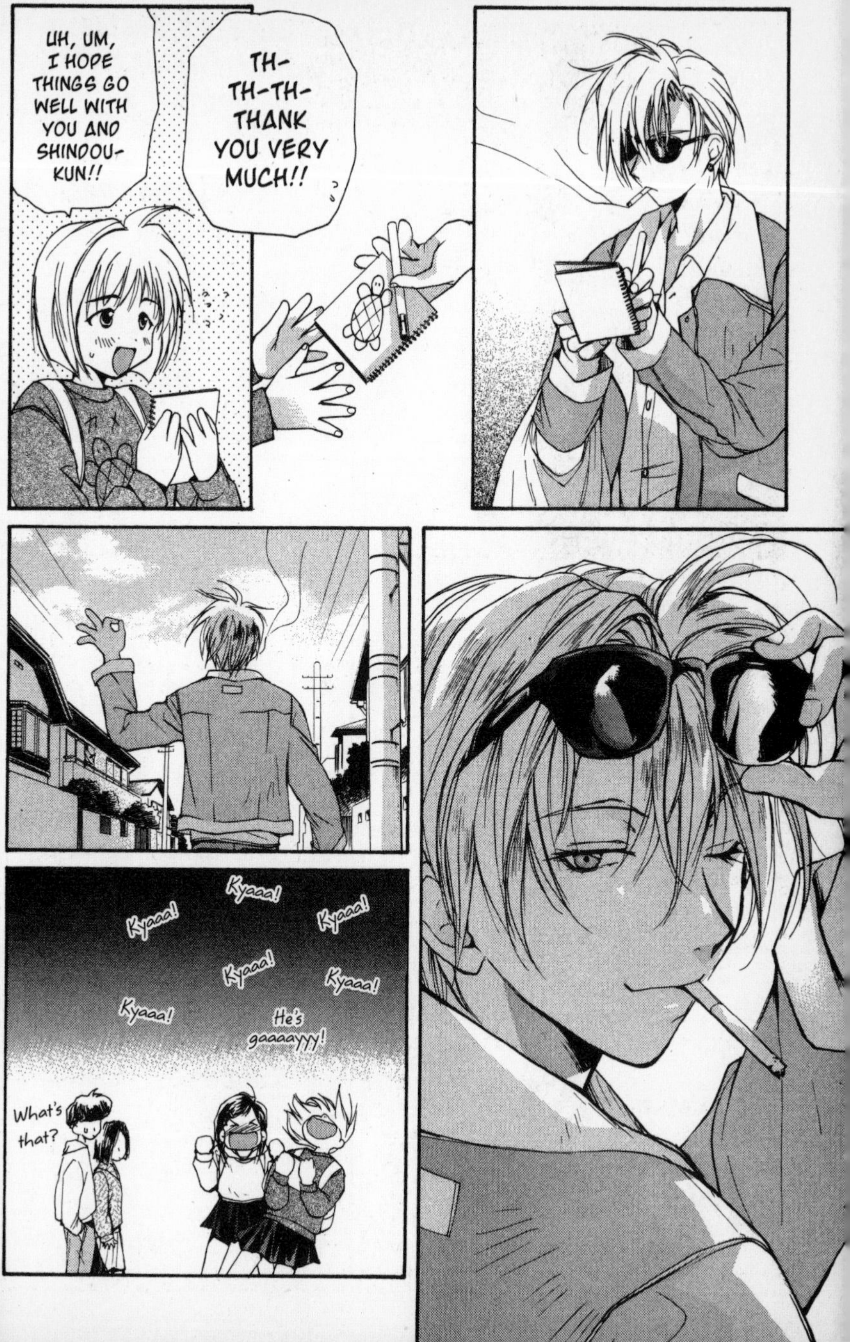
TH-TH-TH-THANK YOU VERY MUCH!!
UH, UM, I HOPE THINGS GO WELL WITH YOU AND SHINDOU-KUN!!
Kyaaa!
Kyaaa!
Kyaaa!
Kyaaa!
Kyaaa!
Kyaaa!
He's gaaaayyy!
What's that?

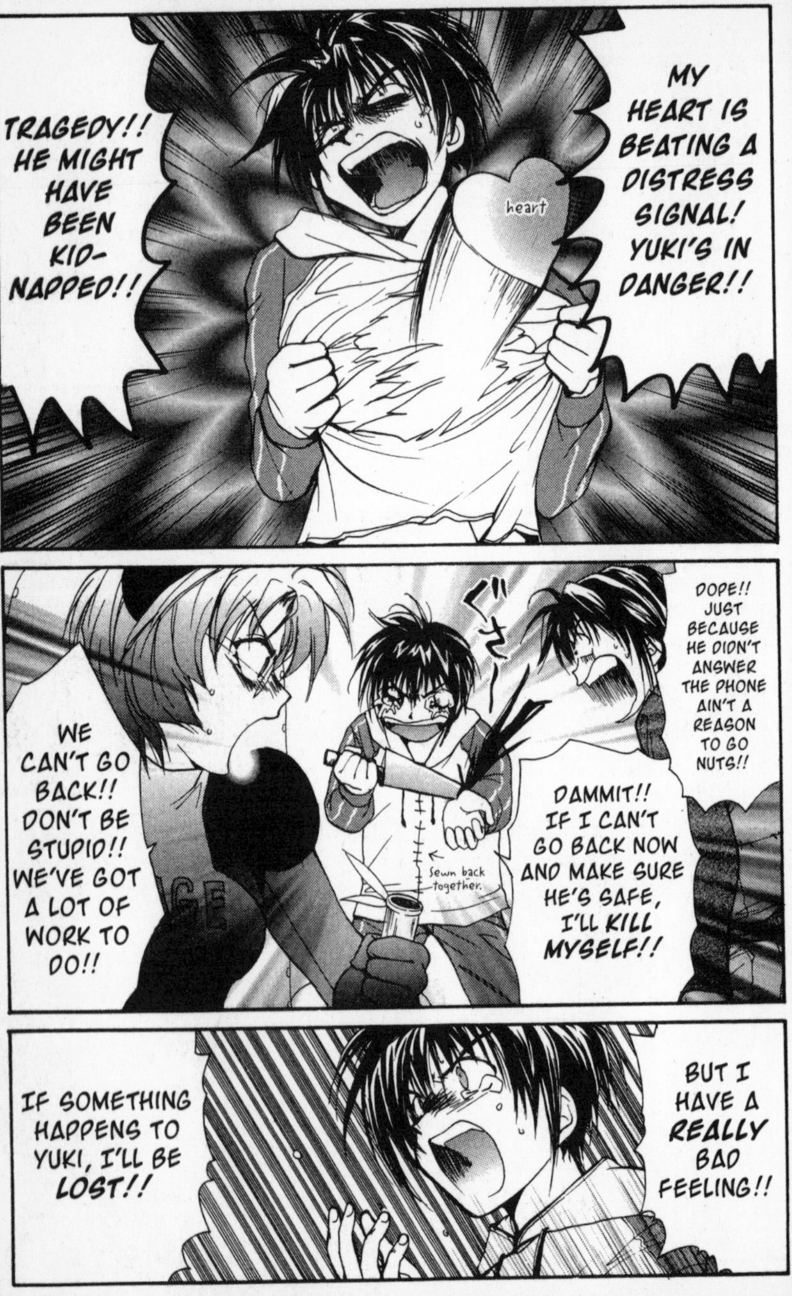
MY HEART IS BEATING A DISTRESS SIGNAL! YUKI'S IN DANGER!!
heart
TRAGEDY!! HE MIGHT HAVE BEEN KID-NAPPED!!
DOPE!! JUST BECAUSE HE DIDN'T ANSWER THE PHONE AIN'T A REASON TO GO NUTS!!
ぐさ
DAMMIT!! IF I CAN'T GO BACK NOW AND MAKE SURE HE'S SAFE, I'LL KILL MYSELF!!
WE CAN'T GO BACK!! DON'T BE STUPID!! WE'VE GOT A LOT OF WORK TO DO!!
Sewn back together.
BUT I HAVE A REALLY BAD FEELING!!
IF SOMETHING HAPPENS TO YUKI, I'LL BE LOST!!

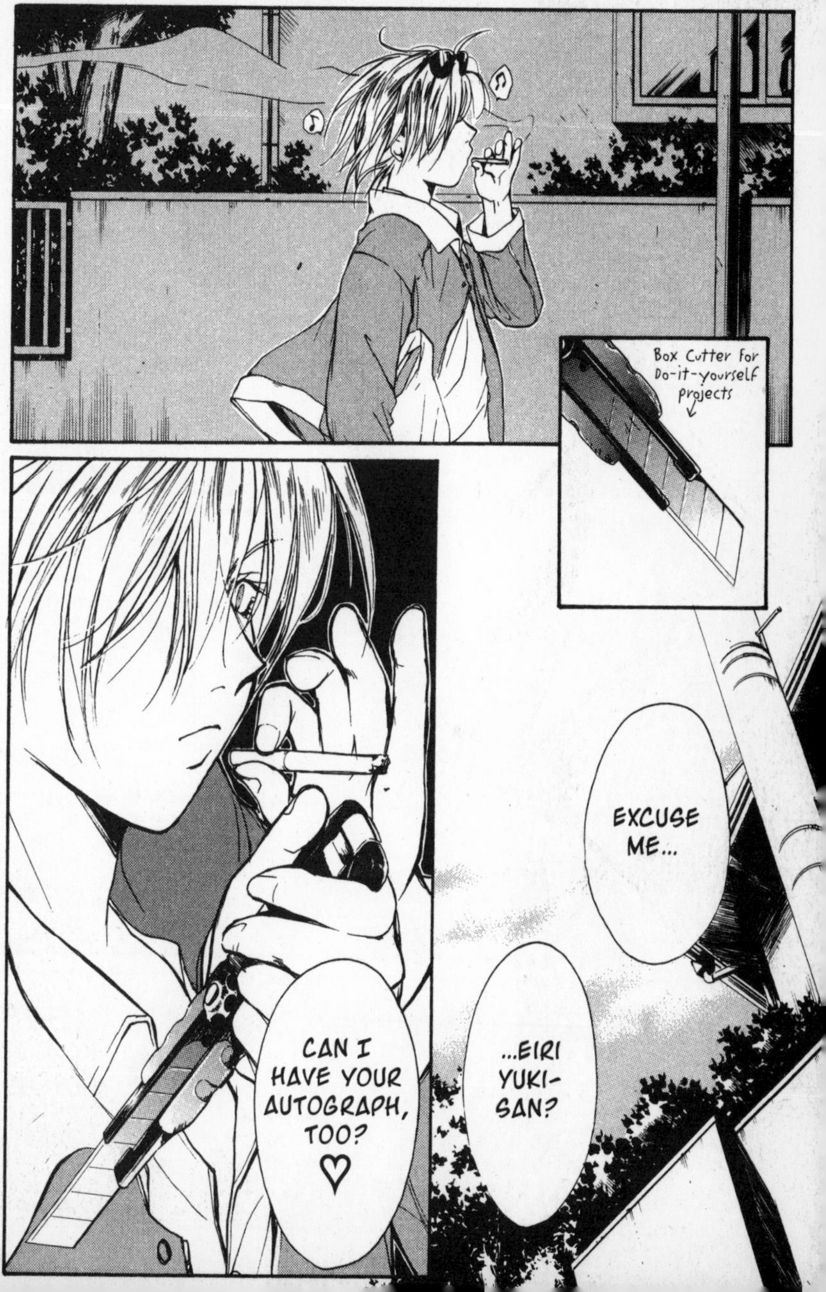
Box Cutter for Do-it-yourself projects
EXCUSE ME...
...EIRI YUKI-SAN?
CAN I HAVE YOUR AUTOGRAPH, TOO? ♡

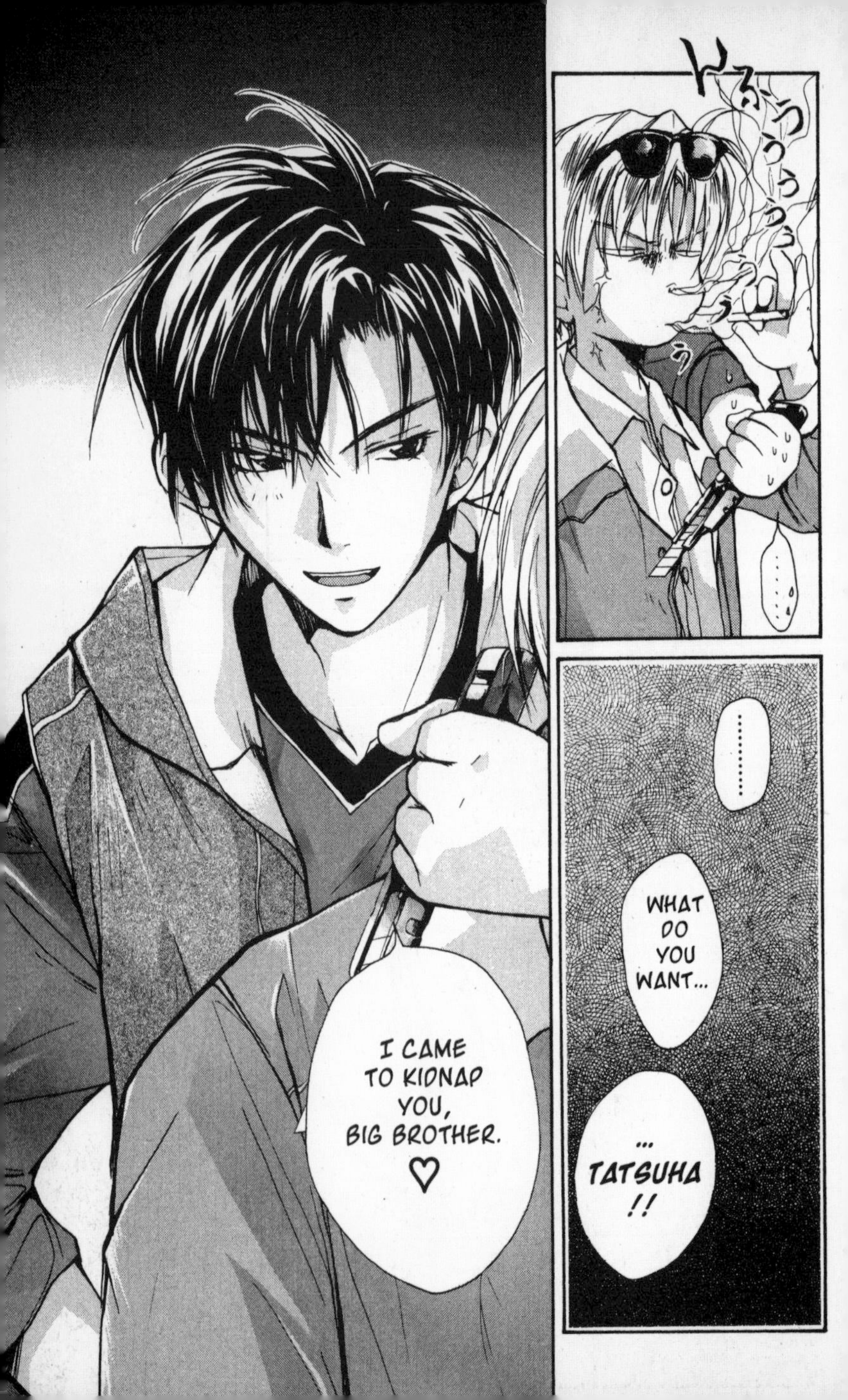
......
......
WHAT DO YOU WANT...
...TATSUHA!!
I CAME TO KIDNAP YOU, BIG BROTHER. ♡

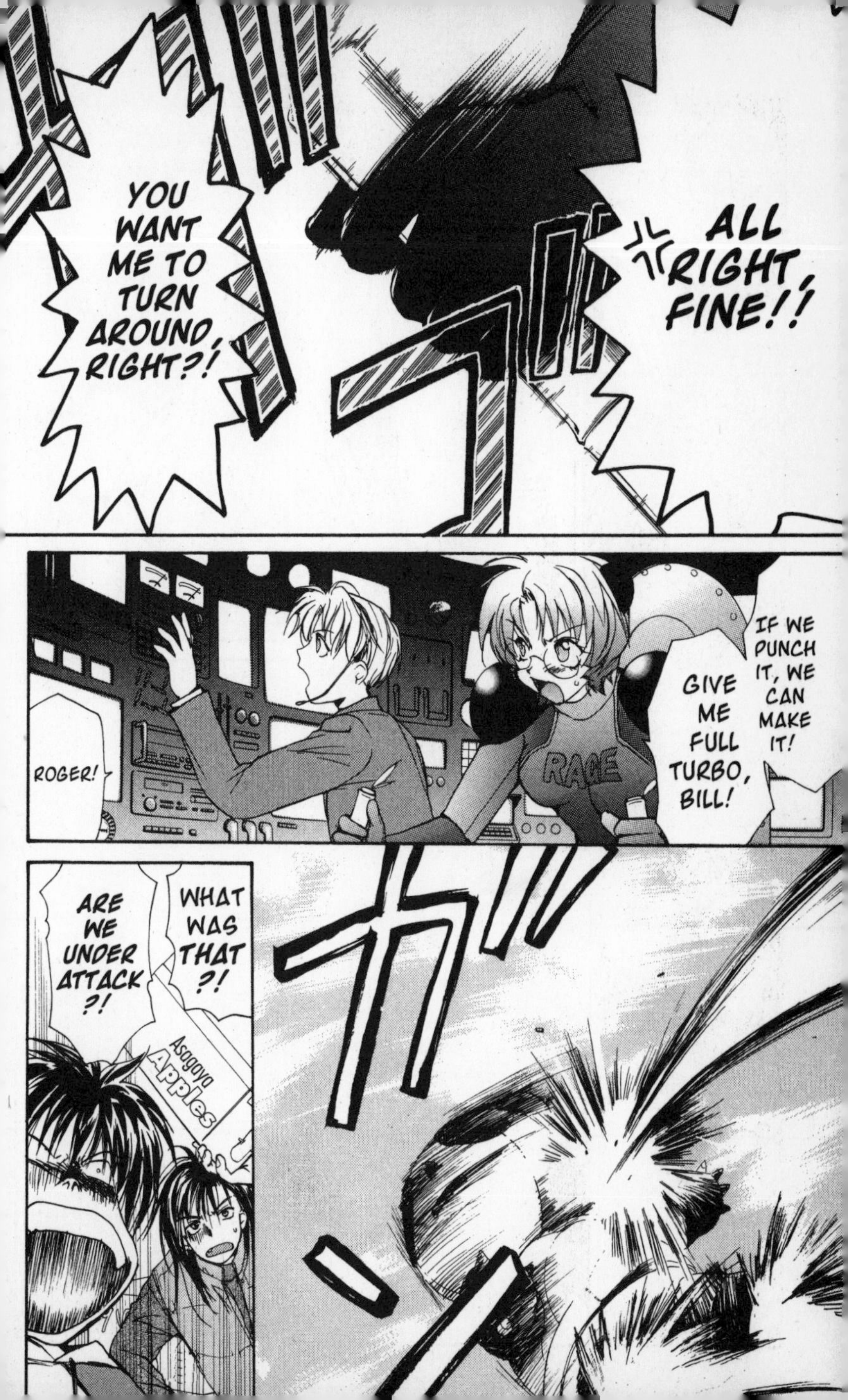
ALL RIGHT FINE!!
YOU WANT ME TO TURN AROUND, RIGHT?!
IF WE PUNCH IT, WE CAN MAKE IT!
GIVE ME FULL TURBO, BILL!
ROGER!
WHAT WAS THAT?!
ARE WE UNDER ATTACK?!
Asagaya Apples

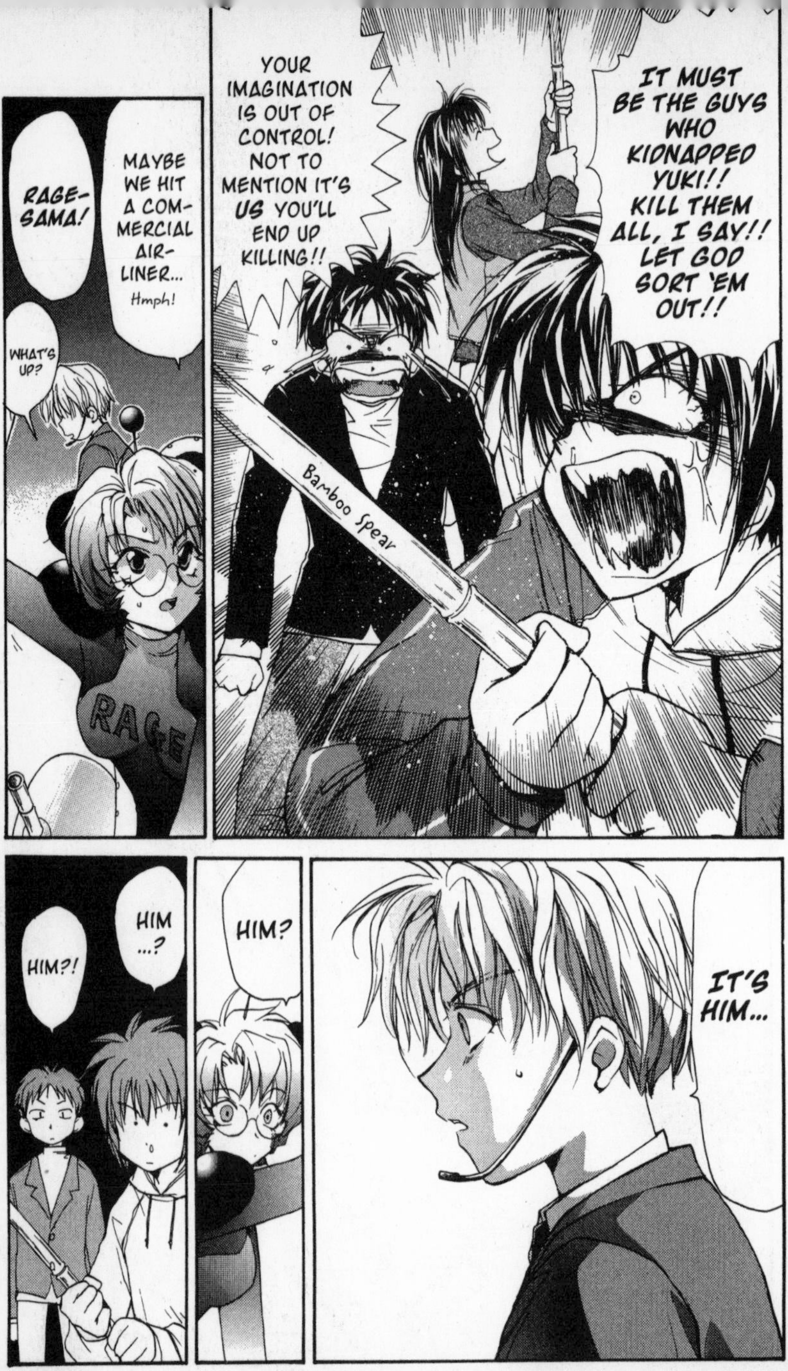
IT MUST BE THE GUYS WHO KIDNAPPED YUKI!! KILL THEM ALL, I SAY!! LET GOD SORT 'EM OUT!!
YOUR IMAGINATION IS OUT OF CONTROL! NOT TO MENTION IT'S US YOU'LL END UP KILLING!!
Bamboo Spear
MAYBE WE HIT A COMMERCIAL AIRLINER...
RAGE-SAMA!
Hmph!
WHAT'S UP?
RAGE
IT'S HIM...
HIM?
HIM ...?
HIM?!

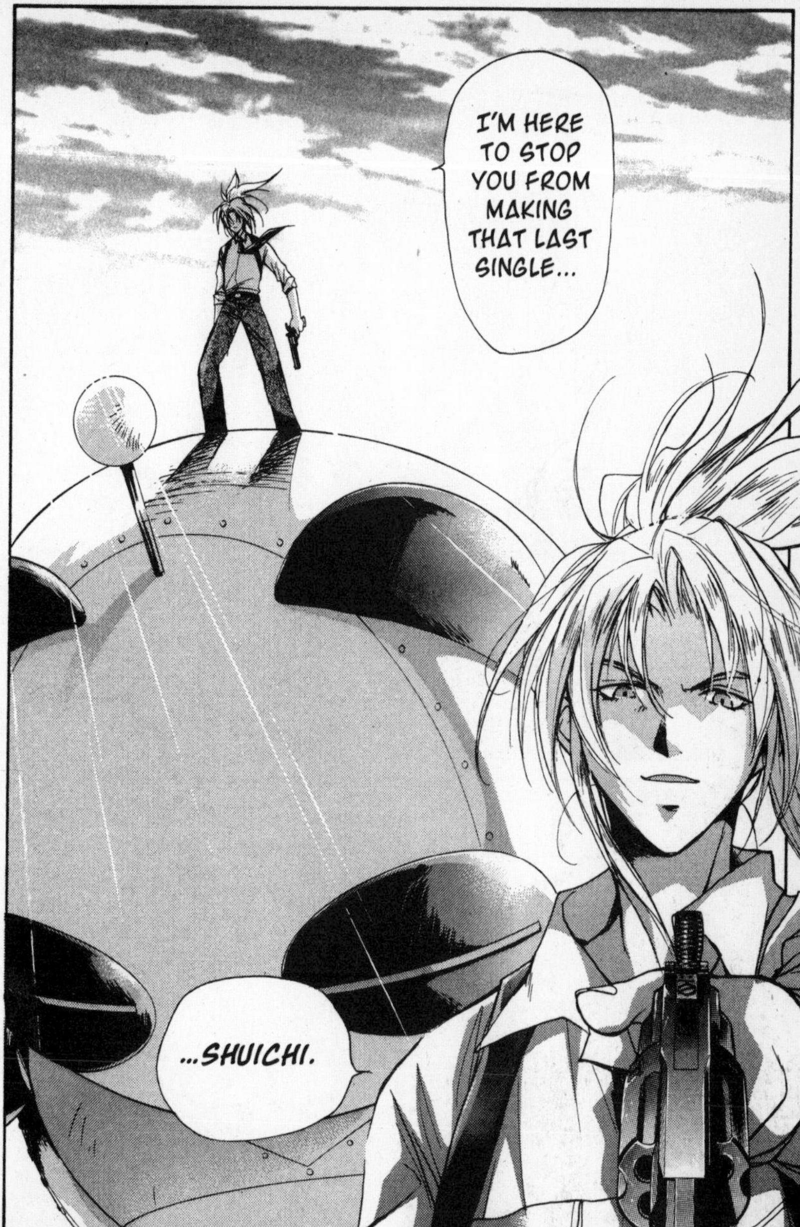
I'M HERE TO STOP YOU FROM MAKING THAT LAST SINGLE...
...SHUICHI.

track47 ▶ END

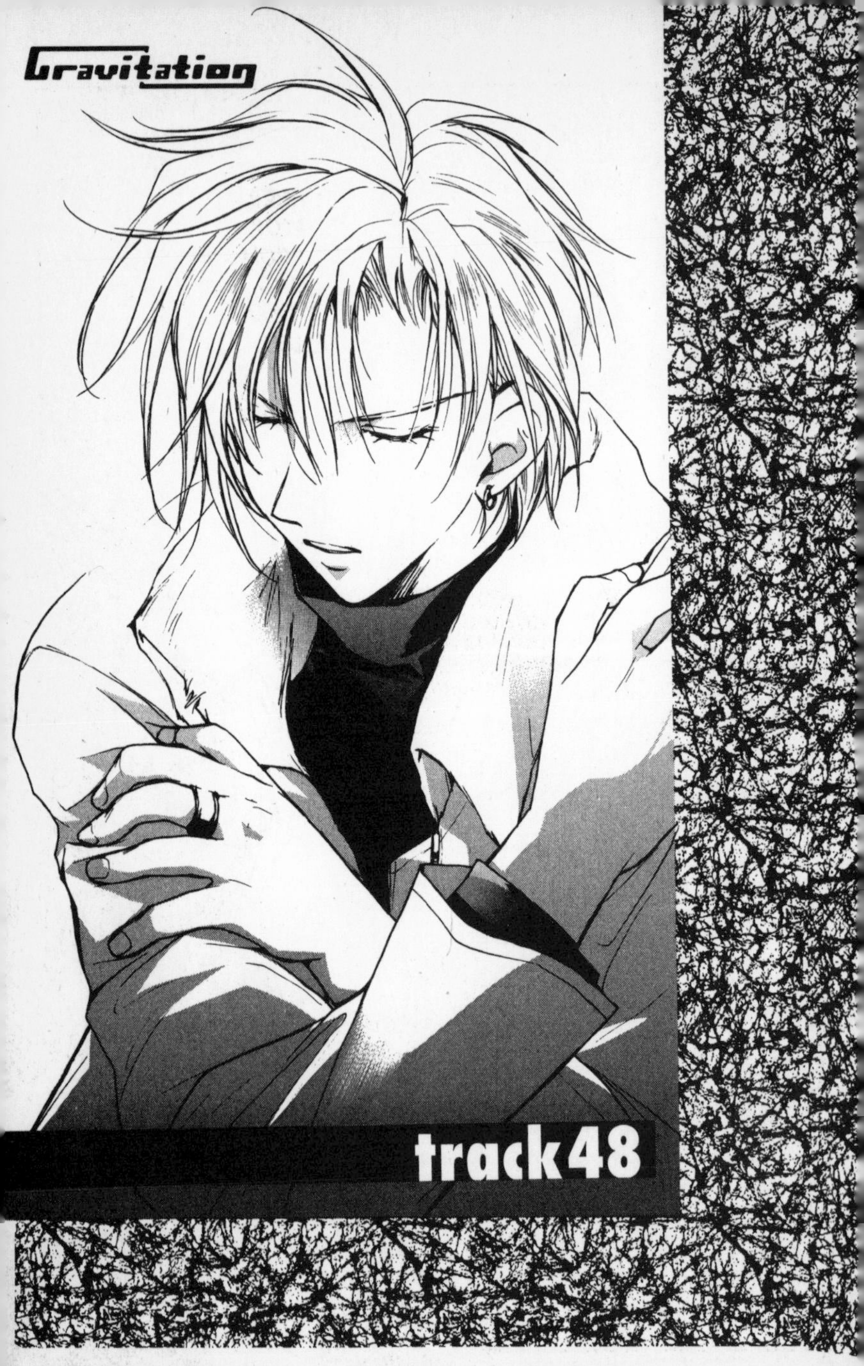
Gravitation
track 48

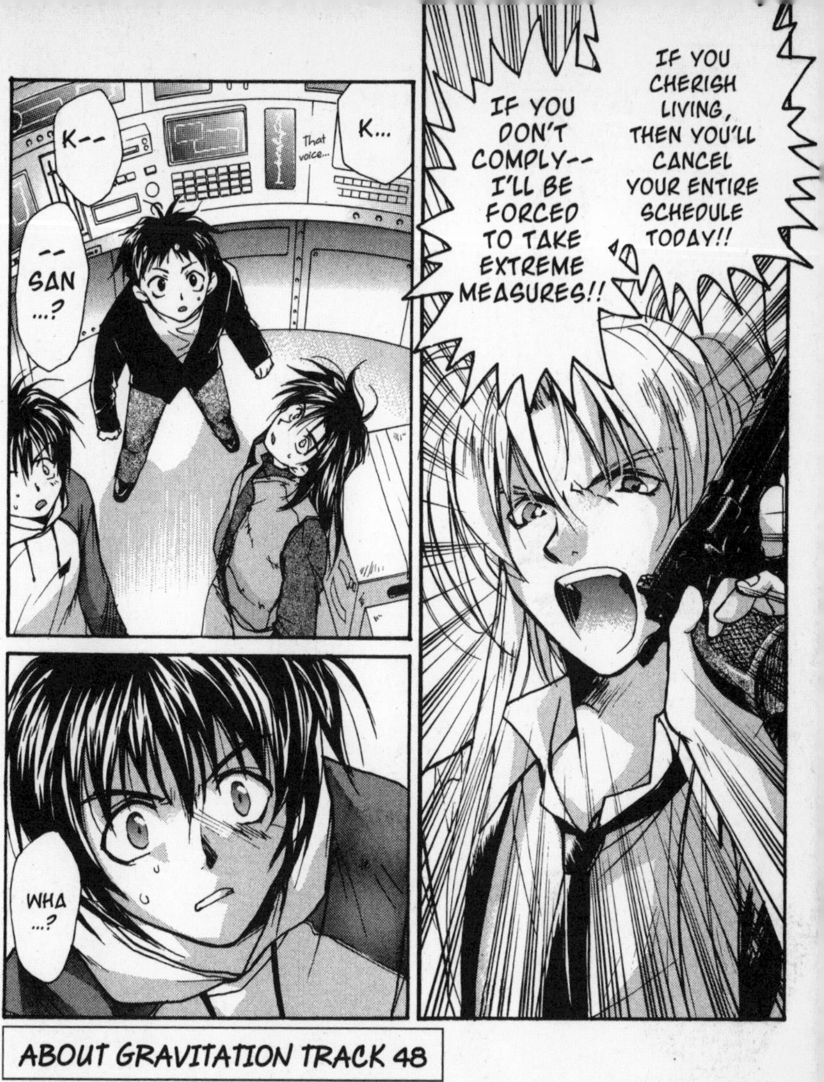
IF YOU CHERISH LIVING, THEN YOU'LL CANCEL YOUR ENTIRE SCHEDULE TODAY!!
IF YOU DON'T COMPLY-- I'LL BE FORCED TO TAKE EXTREME MEASURES!!
K...
That voice...
K--
--SAN ...?
WHA ...?

ABOUT GRAVITATION TRACK 48

Book 11 contains only three tracks!! (The extra track isn't included in that total.) Sucks, doesn't it?! But before you say "What's with this three track shit?" allow me to explain!! It's not enough!! The second track is 80 pages, but compared to that, the third track is only 24 pages!! Somehow, I made it to 100 pages, so I think I can just squeak by!! I worked hard to draw these pages, so please read track 48 as well! I'm going to be causing trouble for a lot of people from here on out. So please, don't give up on me...! Ughhh...

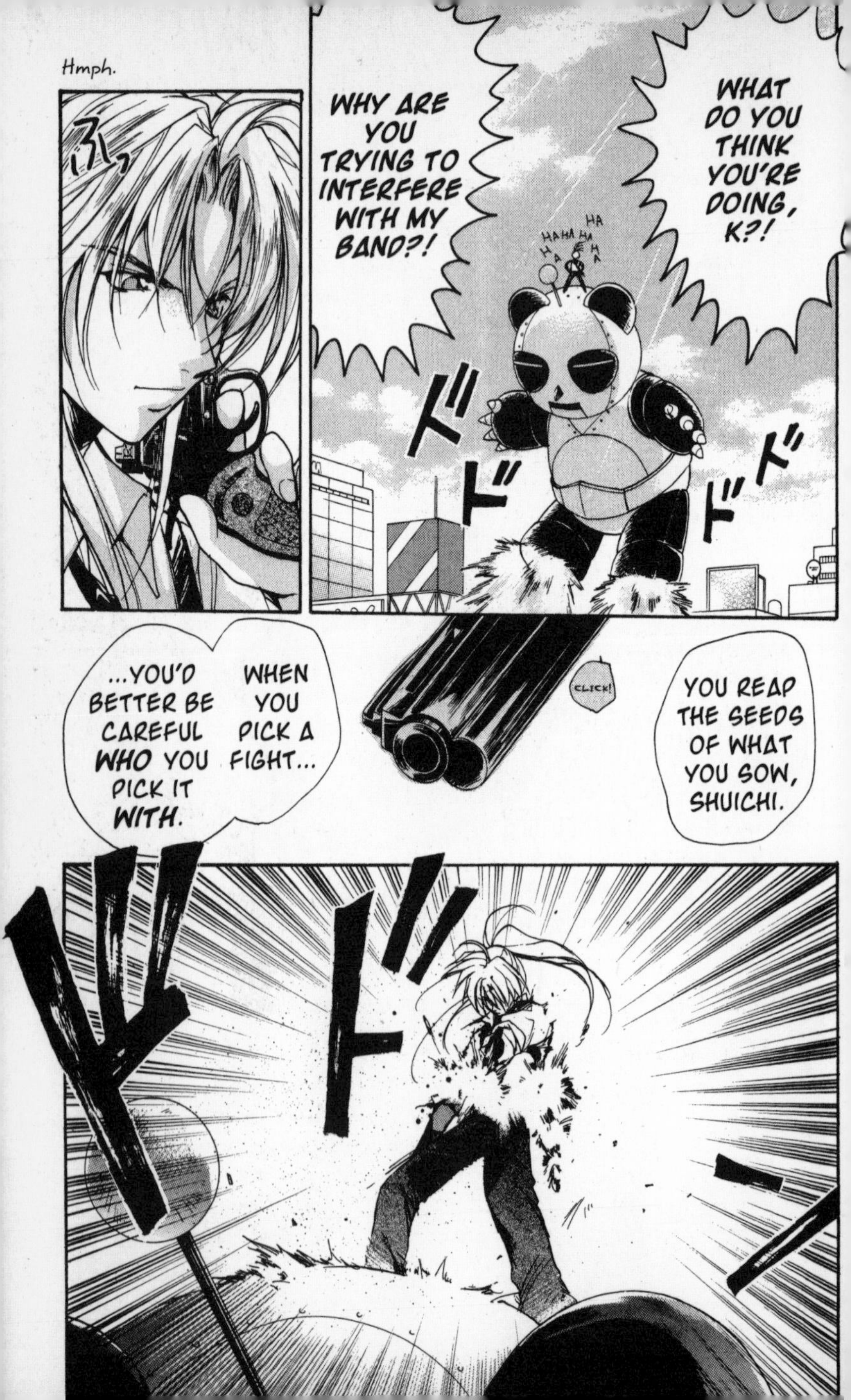
WHAT DO YOU THINK YOU'RE DOING, K?!
WHY ARE YOU TRYING TO INTERFERE WITH MY BAND?!
HA HA HA HA HA HA HA HA
Hmph.
YOU REAP THE SEEDS OF WHAT YOU SOW, SHUICHI.
CLICK!
WHEN YOU PICK A FIGHT...
...YOU'D BETTER BE CAREFUL WHO YOU PICK IT WITH.

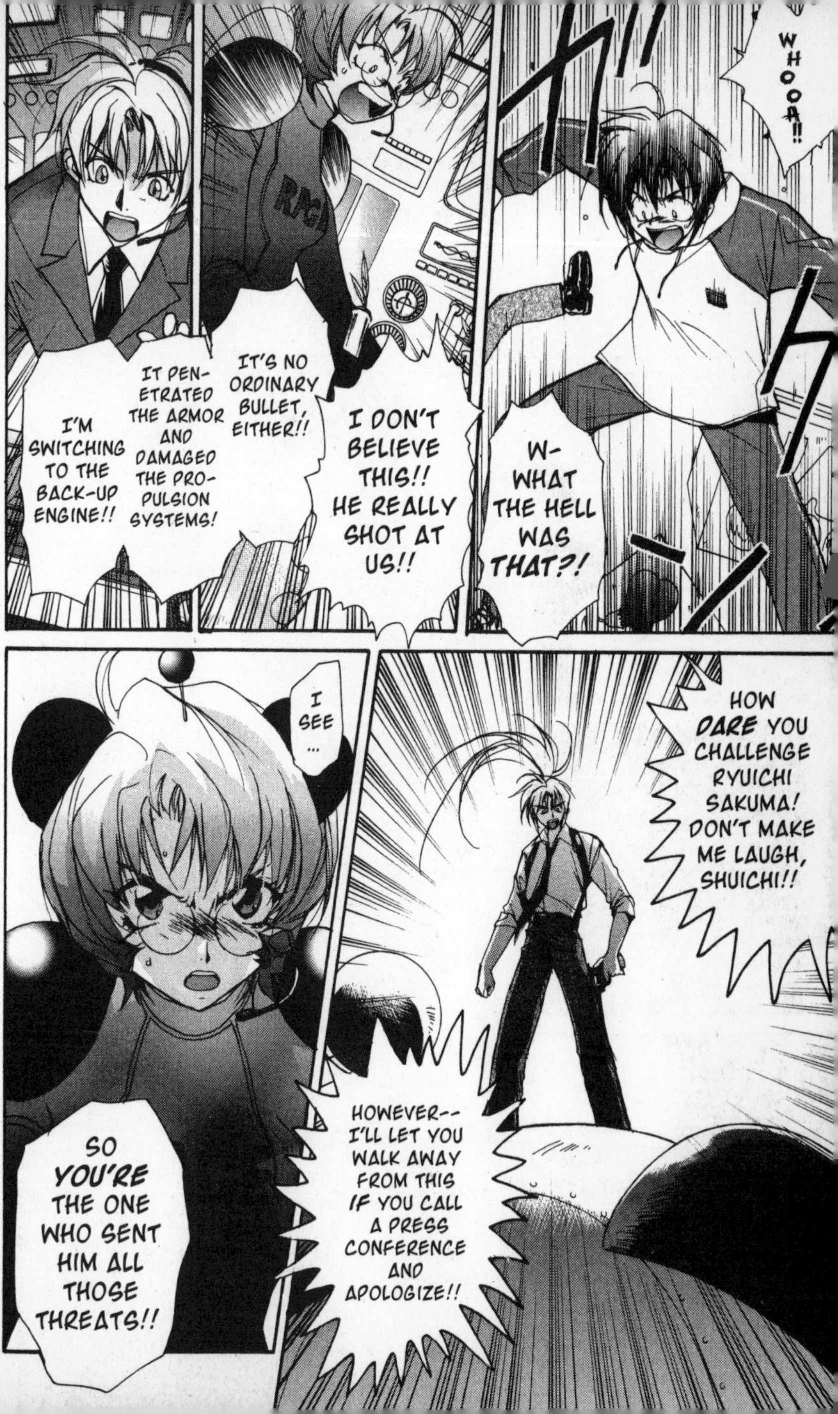
WHOOA!!
W-WHAT THE HELL WAS *THAT?!*
I DON'T BELIEVE THIS!! HE REALLY SHOT AT US!!
IT'S NO ORDINARY BULLET, EITHER!!
IT PEN-ETRATED THE ARMOR AND DAMAGED THE PRO-PULSION SYSTEMS!
I'M SWITCHING TO THE BACK-UP ENGINE!!
HOW *DARE* YOU CHALLENGE RYUICHI SAKUMA! DON'T MAKE ME LAUGH, SHUICHI!!
HOWEVER-- I'LL LET YOU WALK AWAY FROM THIS *IF* YOU CALL A PRESS CONFERENCE AND APOLOGIZE!!
I SEE...
SO *YOU'RE* THE ONE WHO SENT HIM ALL THOSE THREATS!!

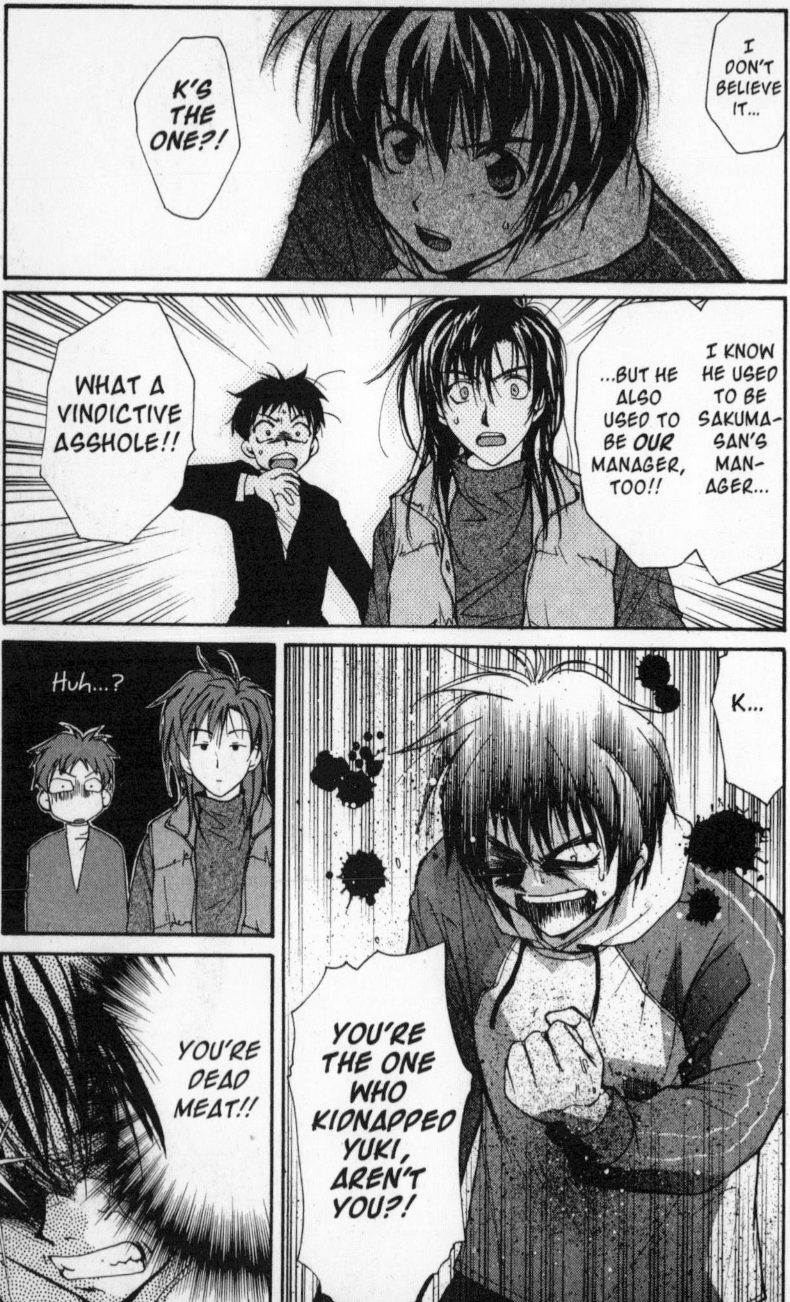
I DON'T BELIEVE IT...
K'S THE ONE?!
I KNOW HE USED TO BE SAKUMA-SAN'S MAN-AGER...
...BUT HE ALSO USED TO BE OUR MANAGER, TOO!!
WHAT A VINDICTIVE ASSHOLE!!
K...
YOU'RE THE ONE WHO KIDNAPPED YUKI, AREN'T YOU?!
Huh...?
YOU'RE DEAD MEAT!!

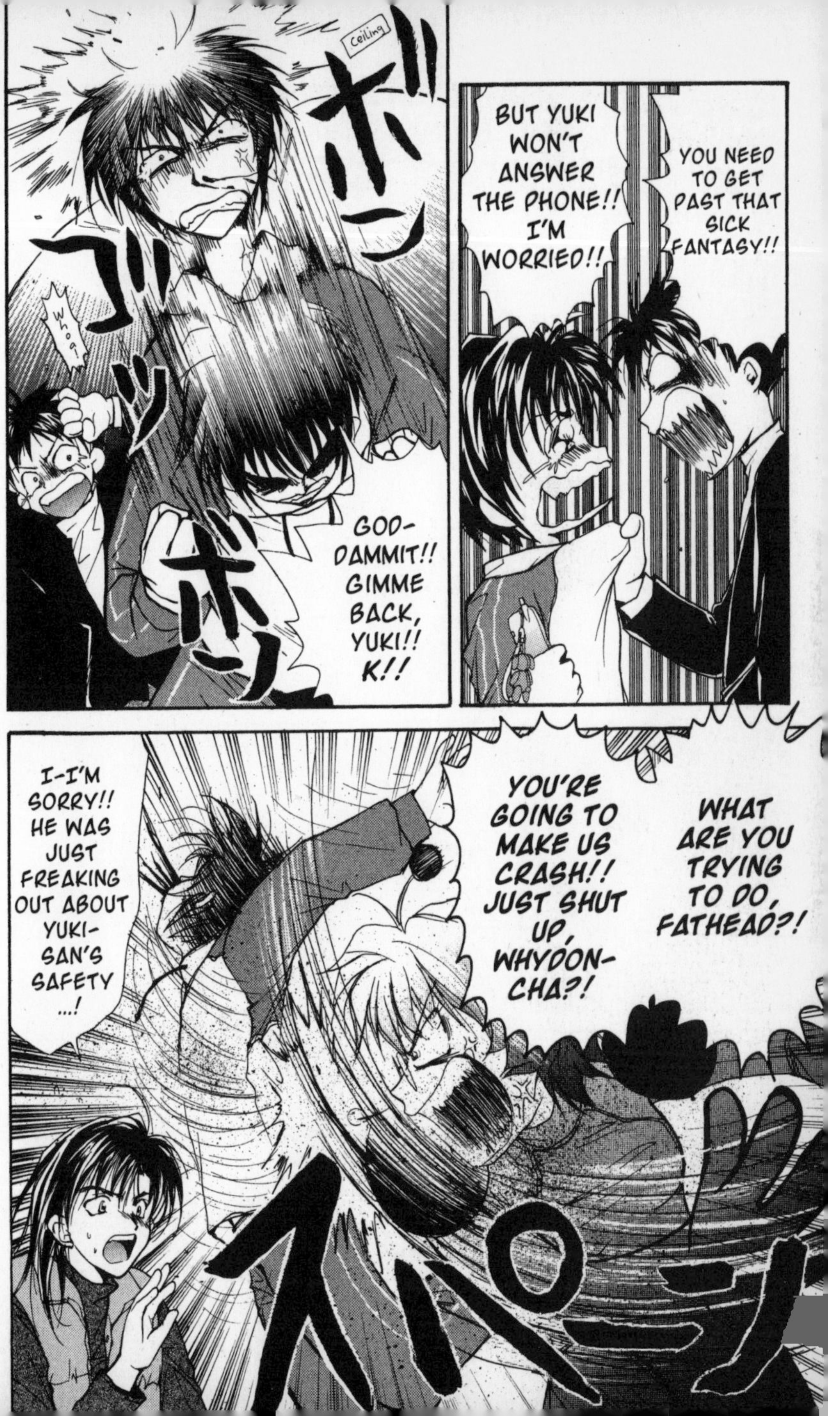
YOU NEED TO GET PAST THAT SICK FANTASY!!
BUT YUKI WON'T ANSWER THE PHONE!! I'M WORRIED!!
Ceiling
GOD-DAMMIT!! GIMME BACK, YUKI!! K!!
Whoa!
WHAT ARE YOU TRYING TO DO, FATHEAD?!
YOU'RE GOING TO MAKE US CRASH!! JUST SHUT UP, WHYDON-CHA?!
I-I'M SORRY!! HE WAS JUST FREAKING OUT ABOUT YUKI-SAN'S SAFETY ...!

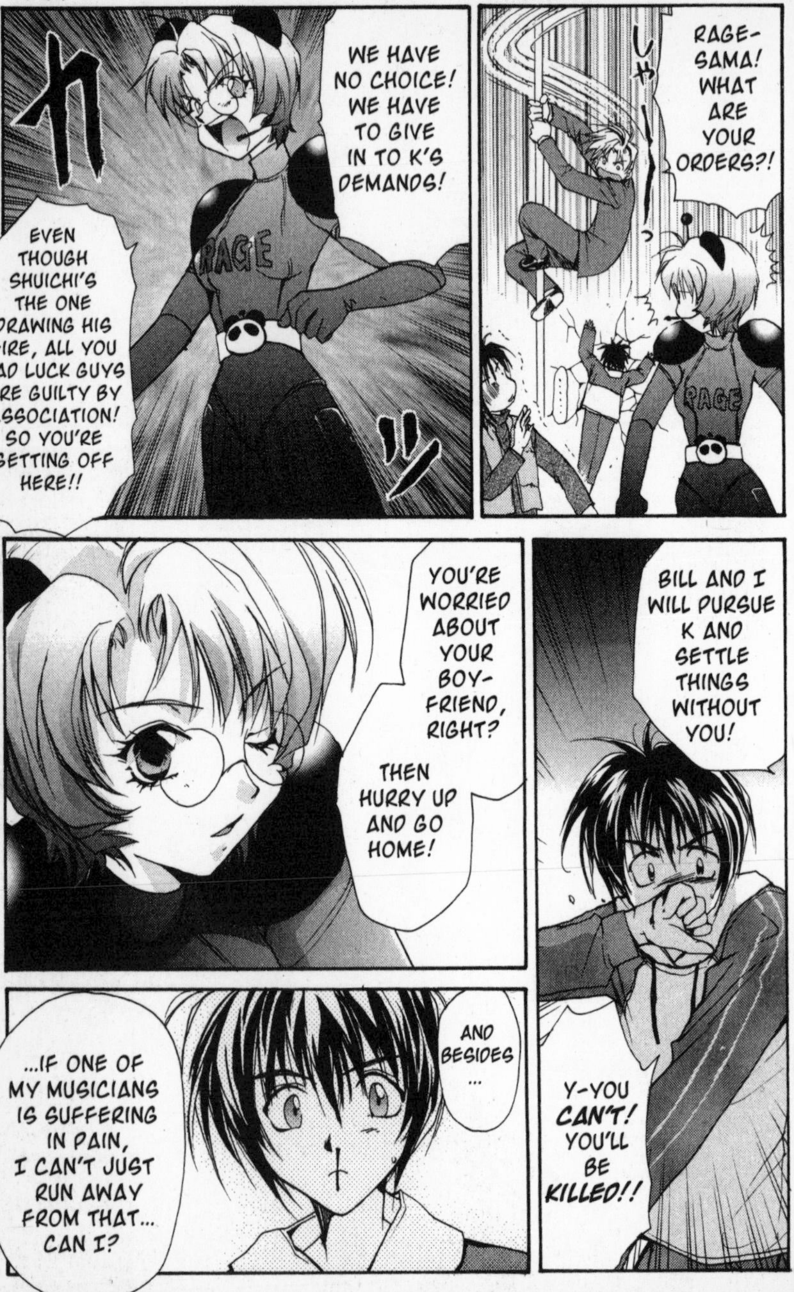
RAGE-SAMA! WHAT ARE YOUR ORDERS?!
RAGE
WE HAVE NO CHOICE! WE HAVE TO GIVE IN TO K'S DEMANDS!
RAGE
EVEN THOUGH SHUICHI'S THE ONE DRAWING HIS FIRE, ALL YOU BAD LUCK GUYS ARE GUILTY BY ASSOCIATION! SO YOU'RE GETTING OFF HERE!!
BILL AND I WILL PURSUE K AND SETTLE THINGS WITHOUT YOU!
Y-YOU CAN'T! YOU'LL BE KILLED!!
YOU'RE WORRIED ABOUT YOUR BOY-FRIEND, RIGHT?
THEN HURRY UP AND GO HOME!
AND BESIDES ...
...IF ONE OF MY MUSICIANS IS SUFFERING IN PAIN, I CAN'T JUST RUN AWAY FROM THAT... CAN I?

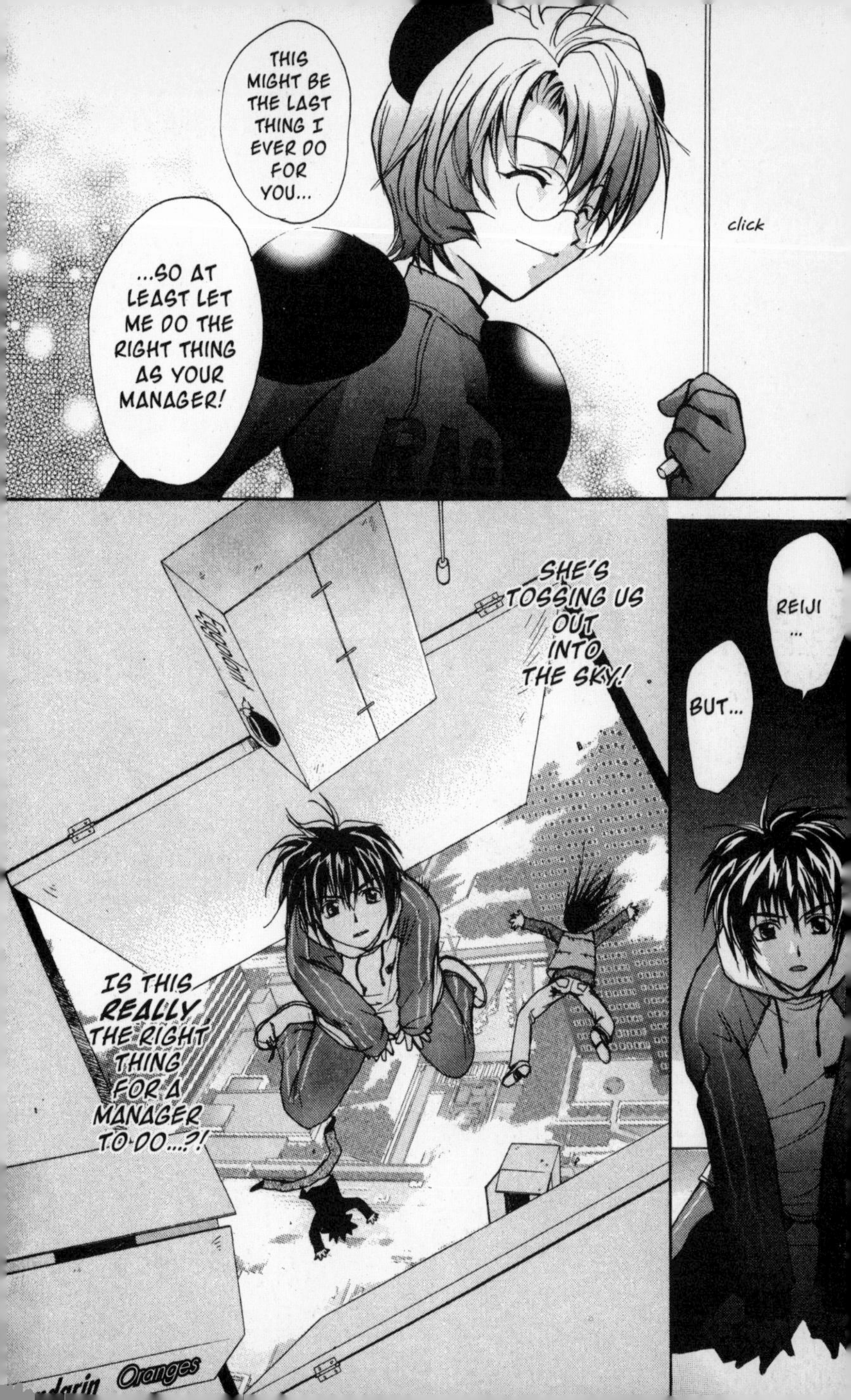
THIS MIGHT BE THE LAST THING I EVER DO FOR YOU...
...SO AT LEAST LET ME DO THE RIGHT THING AS YOUR MANAGER!
click
REIJI ...
BUT...
SHE'S TOSSING US OUT INTO THE SKY!
IS THIS REALLY THE RIGHT THING FOR A MANAGER TO DO...?!
Oranges

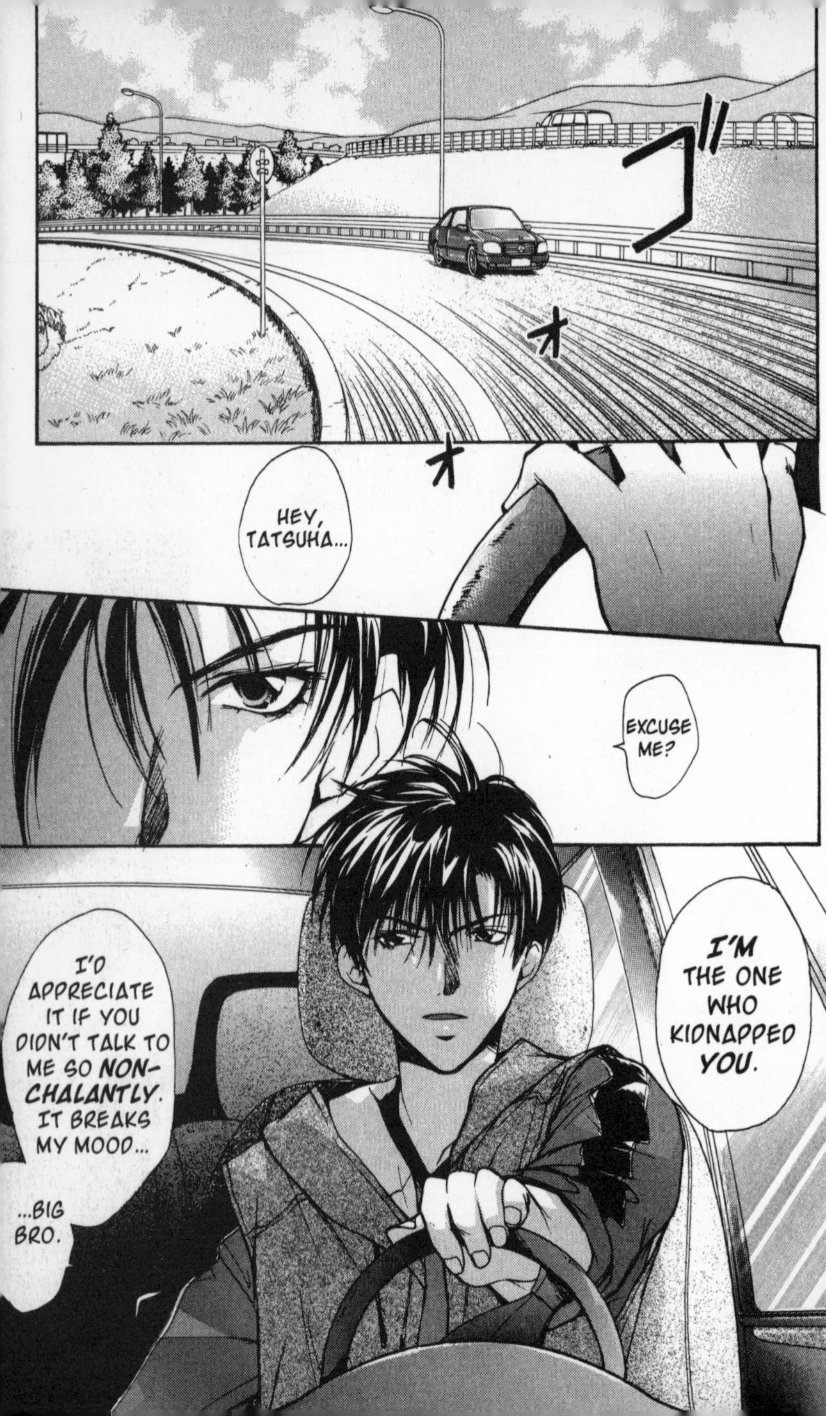
ゴ
オ
オ
HEY, TATSUHA...
EXCUSE ME?
I'M THE ONE WHO KIDNAPPED YOU.
I'D APPRECIATE IT IF YOU DIDN'T TALK TO ME SO NONCHALANTLY. IT BREAKS MY MOOD...
...BIG BRO.

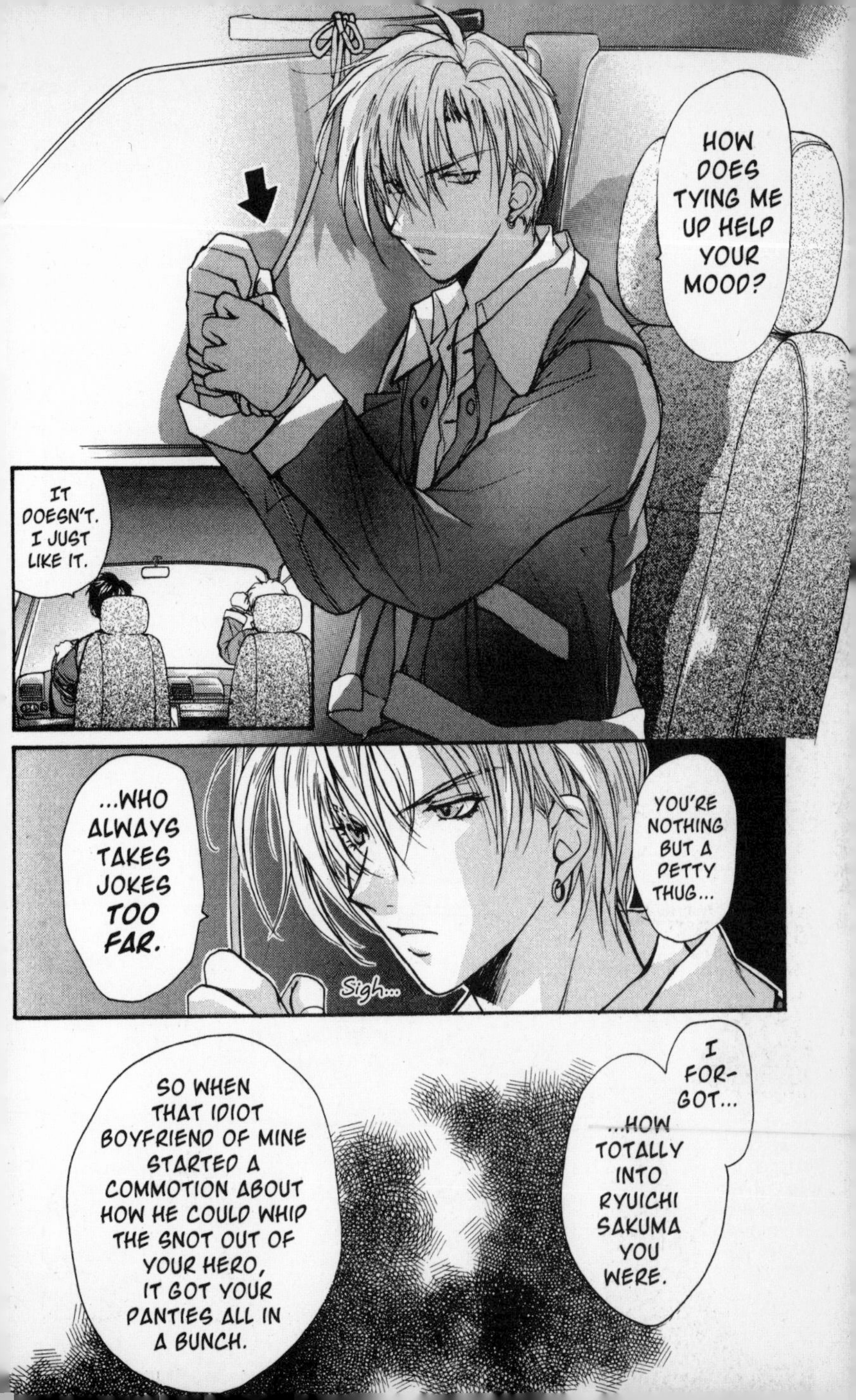
HOW DOES TYING ME UP HELP YOUR MOOD?
IT DOESN'T. I JUST LIKE IT.
YOU'RE NOTHING BUT A PETTY THUG...
...WHO ALWAYS TAKES JOKES TOO FAR.
Sigh...
I FOR-GOT...
...HOW TOTALLY INTO RYUICHI SAKUMA YOU WERE.
SO WHEN THAT IDIOT BOYFRIEND OF MINE STARTED A COMMOTION ABOUT HOW HE COULD WHIP THE SNOT OUT OF YOUR HERO, IT GOT YOUR PANTIES ALL IN A BUNCH.

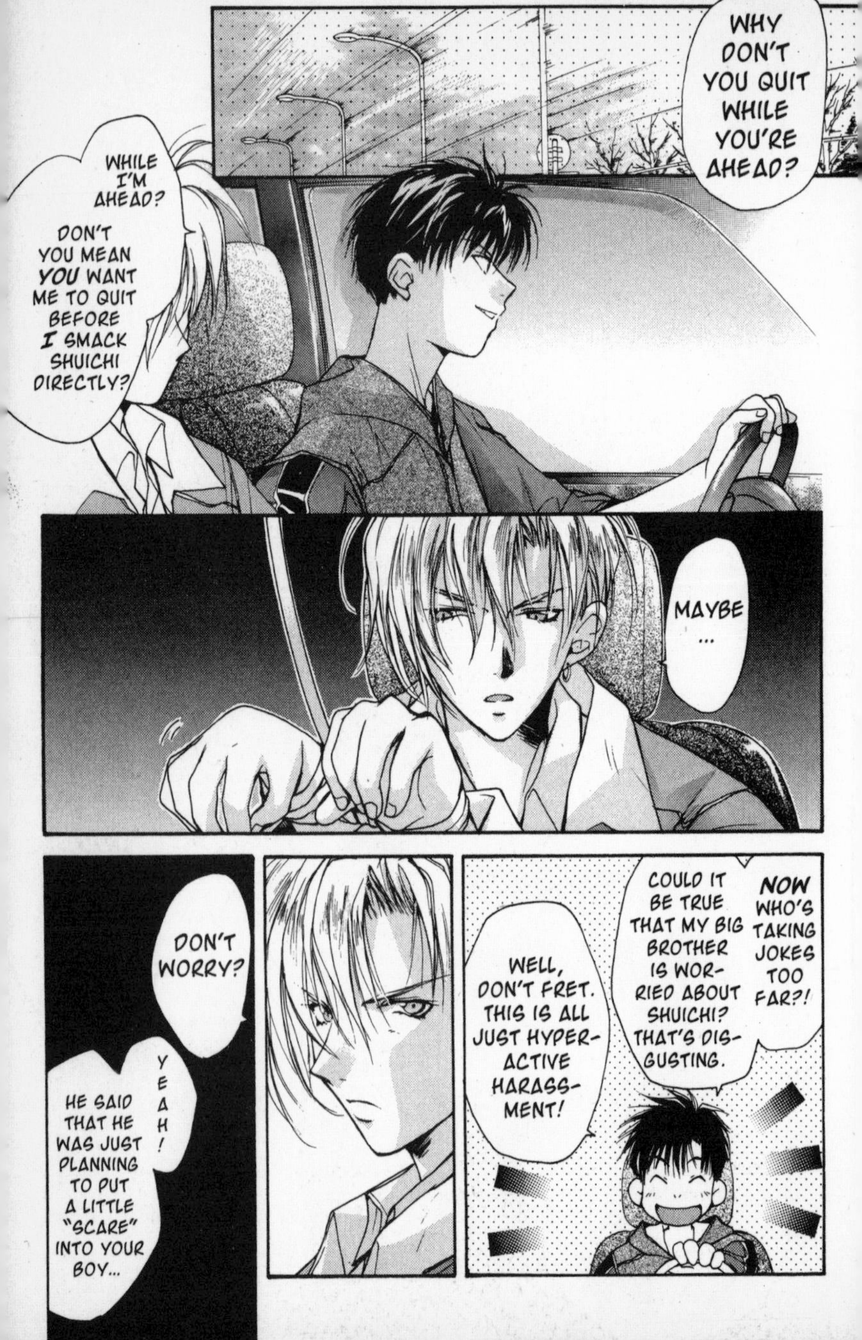
WHY DON'T YOU QUIT WHILE YOU'RE AHEAD?
WHILE I'M AHEAD? DON'T YOU MEAN *YOU* WANT ME TO QUIT BEFORE *I* SMACK SHUICHI DIRECTLY?
MAYBE ...
NOW WHO'S TAKING JOKES TOO FAR?!
COULD IT BE TRUE THAT MY BIG BROTHER IS WORRIED ABOUT SHUICHI? THAT'S DISGUSTING.
WELL, DON'T FRET. THIS IS ALL JUST HYPERACTIVE HARASSMENT!
DON'T WORRY?
YEAH!
HE SAID THAT HE WAS JUST PLANNING TO PUT A LITTLE "SCARE" INTO YOUR BOY...

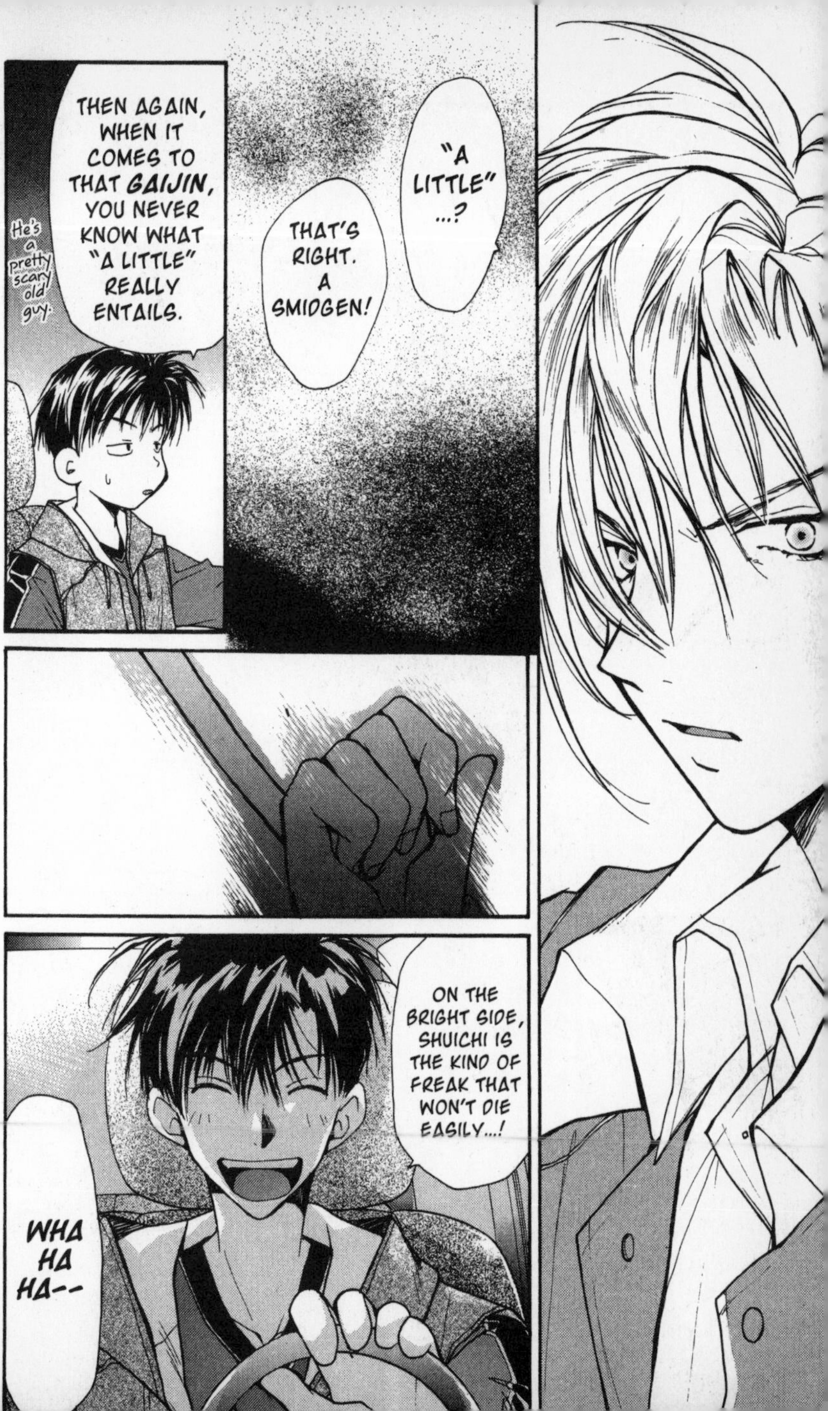
"A LITTLE" ...?
THAT'S RIGHT. A SMIDGEN!
THEN AGAIN, WHEN IT COMES TO THAT GAIJIN, YOU NEVER KNOW WHAT "A LITTLE" REALLY ENTAILS.
He's a pretty scary old guy.
ON THE BRIGHT SIDE, SHUICHI IS THE KIND OF FREAK THAT WON'T DIE EASILY...!
WHA HA HA--

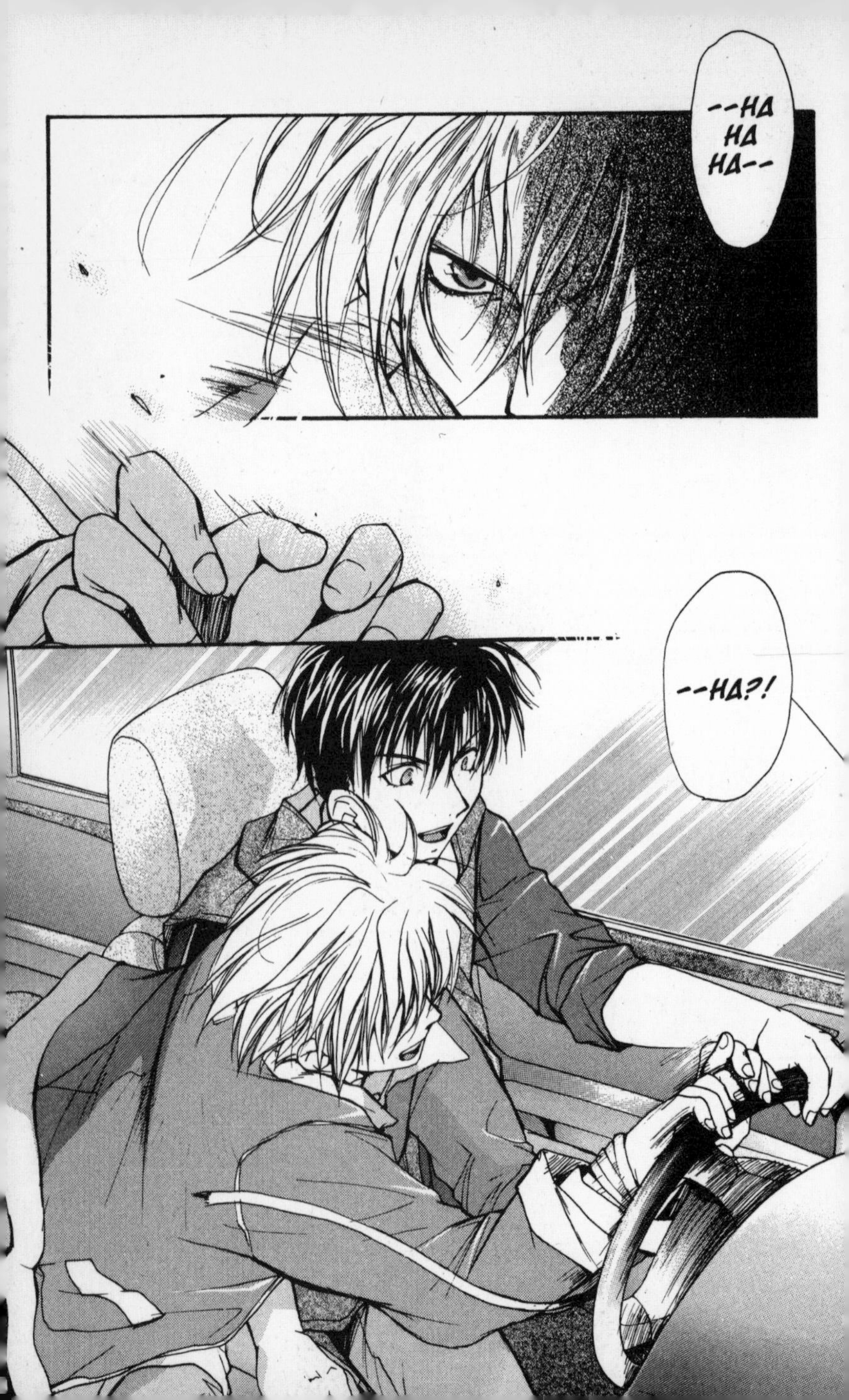
--HA HA HA--
--HA?!

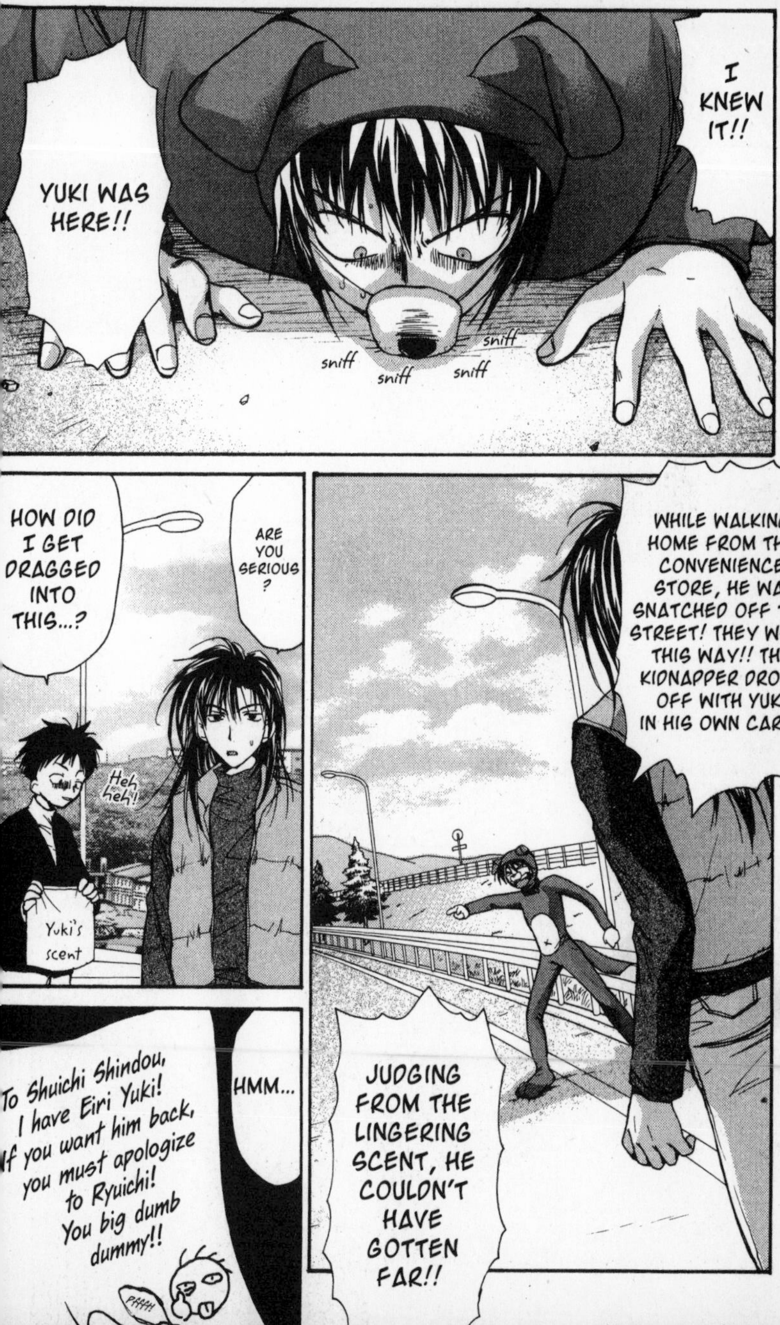
I KNEW IT!!
YUKI WAS HERE!!
sniff
sniff
sniff
sniff
WHILE WALKING HOME FROM THE CONVENIENCE STORE, HE WAS SNATCHED OFF THE STREET! THEY WENT THIS WAY!! THE KIDNAPPER DROVE OFF WITH YUKI IN HIS OWN CAR!!
JUDGING FROM THE LINGERING SCENT, HE COULDN'T HAVE GOTTEN FAR!!
ARE YOU SERIOUS?
HOW DID I GET DRAGGED INTO THIS...?
Heh heh!
Yuki's scent
HMM...
To Shuichi Shindou, I have Eiri Yuki! If you want him back, you must apologize to Ryuichi! You big dumb dummy!!

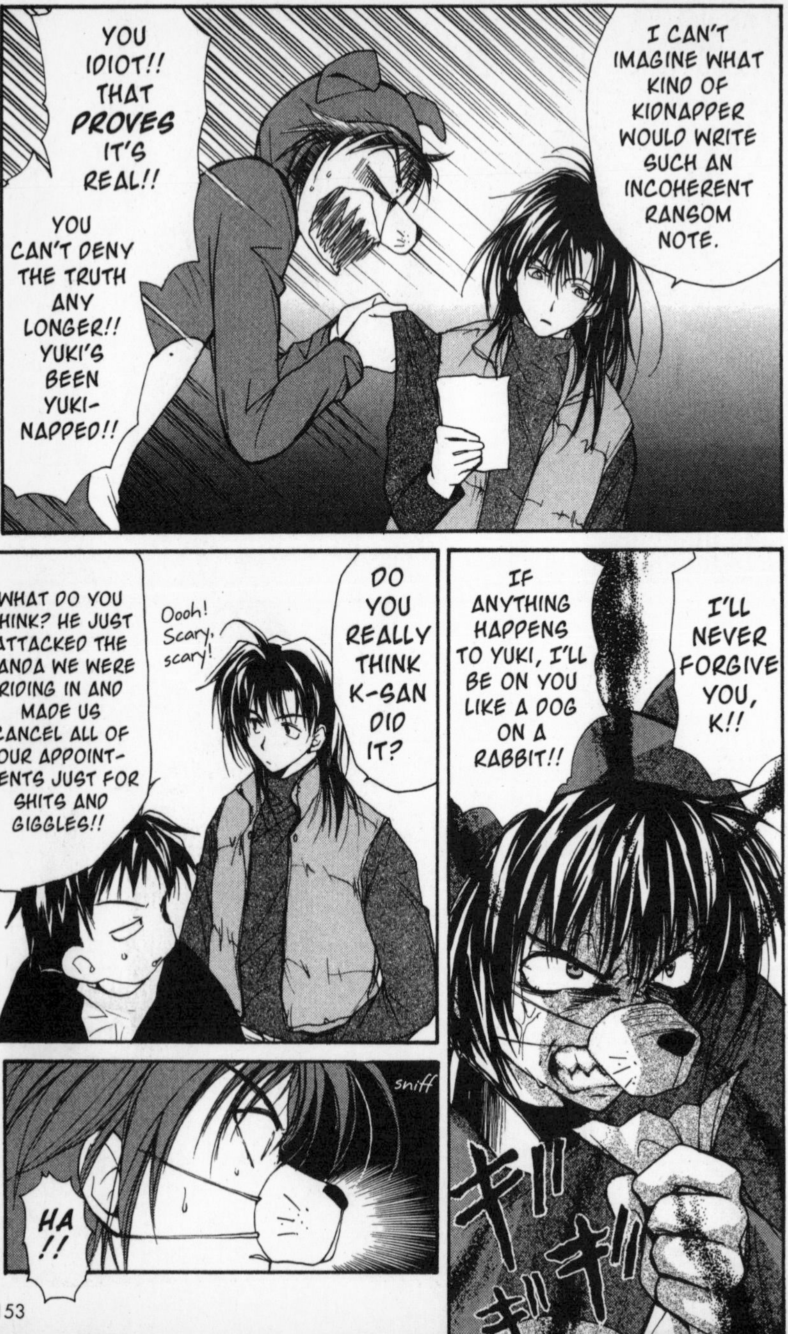
I CAN'T IMAGINE WHAT KIND OF KIDNAPPER WOULD WRITE SUCH AN INCOHERENT RANSOM NOTE.
YOU IDIOT!! THAT *PROVES* IT'S REAL!!
YOU CAN'T DENY THE TRUTH ANY LONGER!! YUKI'S BEEN YUKI-NAPPED!!
I'LL NEVER FORGIVE YOU, K!!
IF ANYTHING HAPPENS TO YUKI, I'LL BE ON YOU LIKE A DOG ON A RABBIT!!
DO YOU REALLY THINK K-SAN DID IT?
Oooh! Scary, scary!
WHAT DO YOU THINK? HE JUST ATTACKED THE PANDA WE WERE RIDING IN AND MADE US CANCEL ALL OF OUR APPOINT-MENTS JUST FOR SHITS AND GIGGLES!!
sniff
HA !!

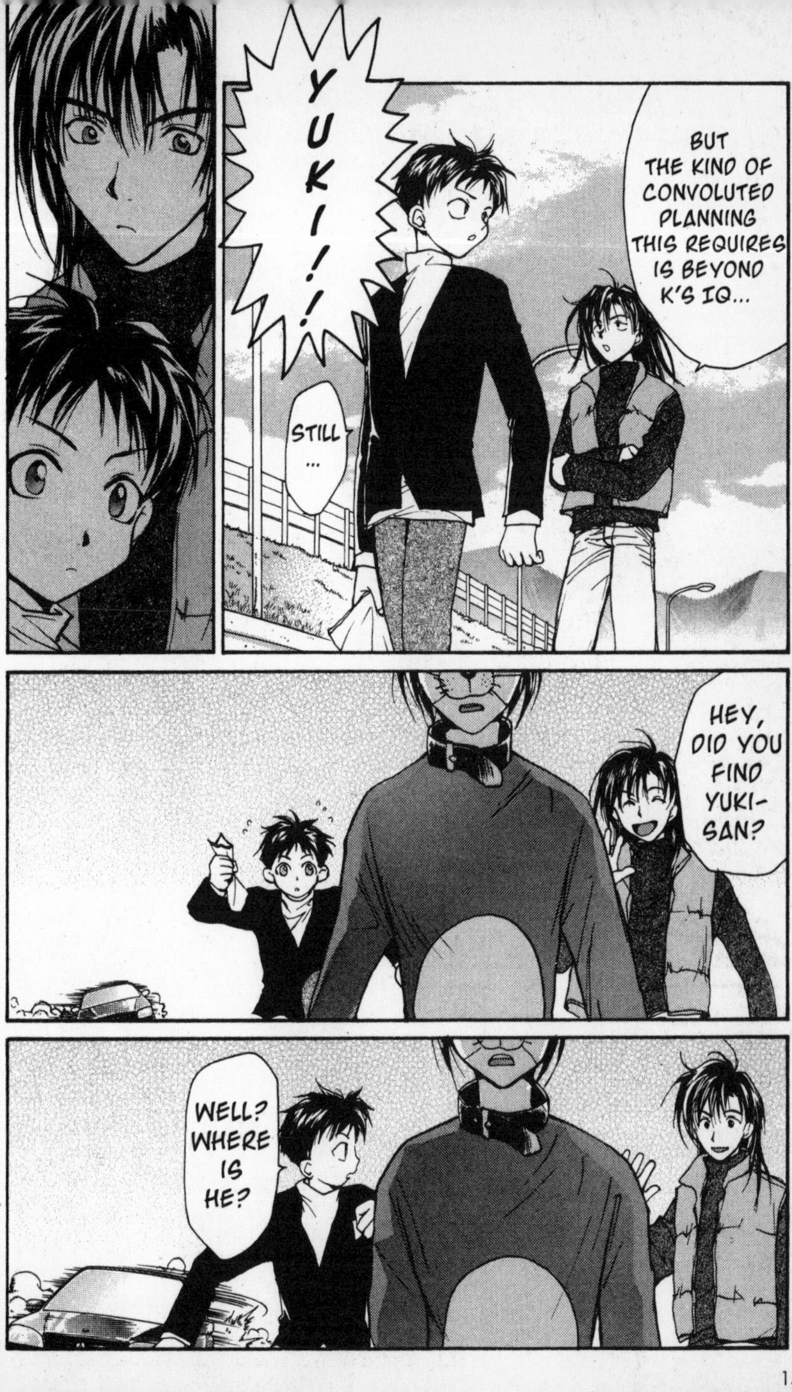
BUT THE KIND OF CONVOLUTED PLANNING THIS REQUIRES IS BEYOND K'S IQ...
YUKI!!!!
STILL ...
HEY, DID YOU FIND YUKI-SAN?
WELL? WHERE IS HE?

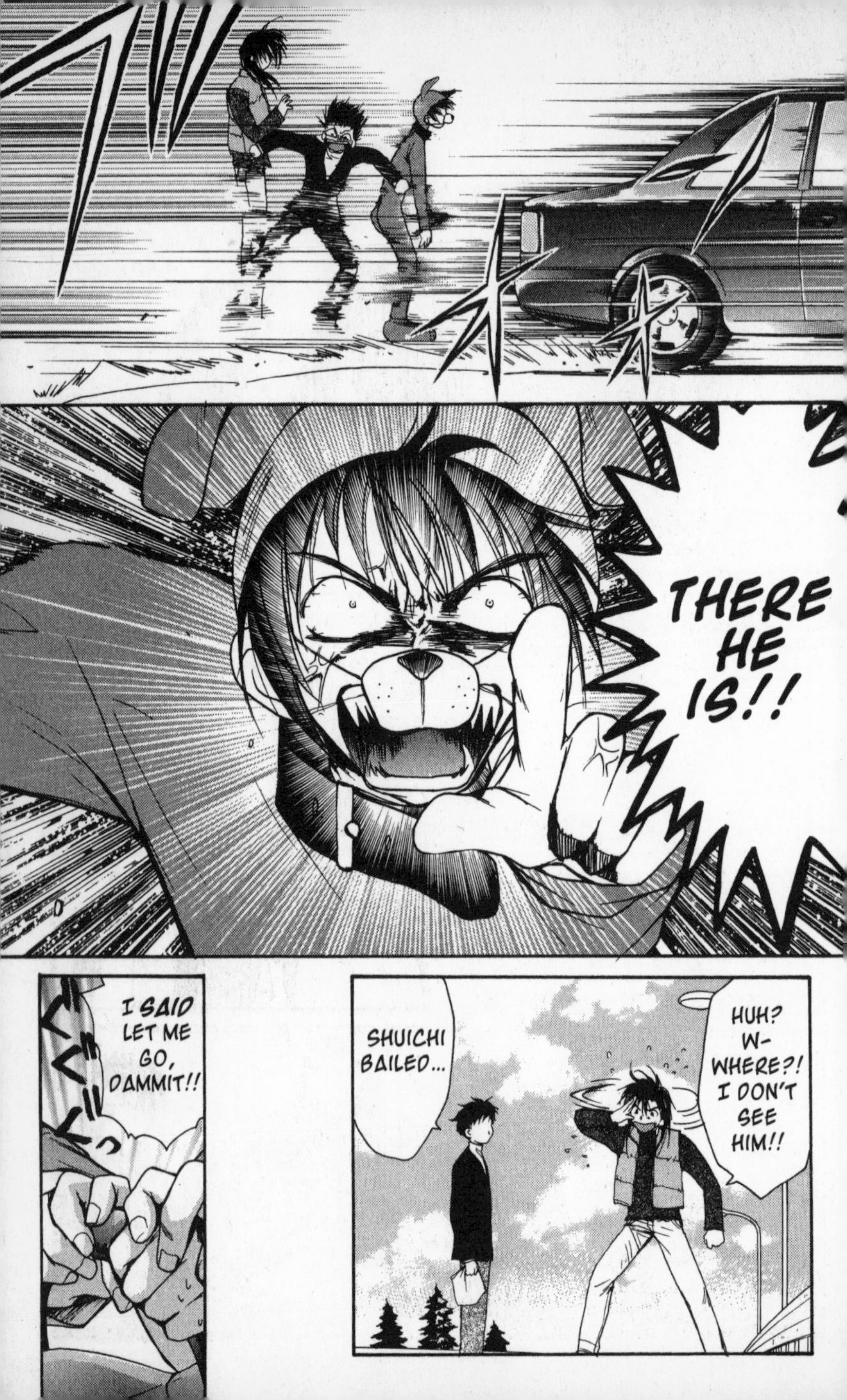
THERE HE IS!!
HUH? W-WHERE?! I DON'T SEE HIM!!
SHUICHI BAILED...
I SAID LET ME GO, DAMMIT!!

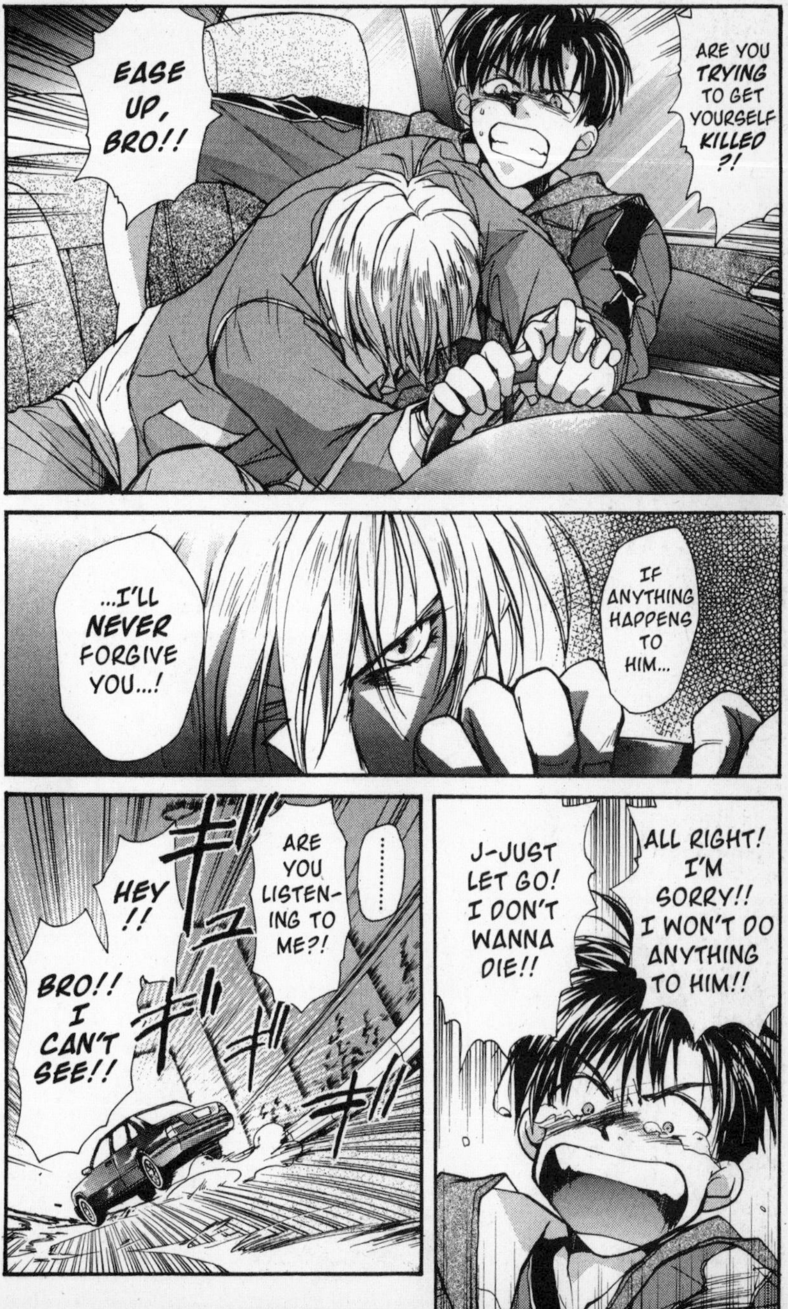
ARE YOU TRYING TO GET YOURSELF KILLED?!
EASE UP, BRO!!
IF ANYTHING HAPPENS TO HIM...
...I'LL NEVER FORGIVE YOU...!
ALL RIGHT! I'M SORRY!! I WON'T DO ANYTHING TO HIM!!
J-JUST LET GO! I DON'T WANNA DIE!!
......
ARE YOU LISTENING TO ME?!
HEY!!
BRO!! I CAN'T SEE!!

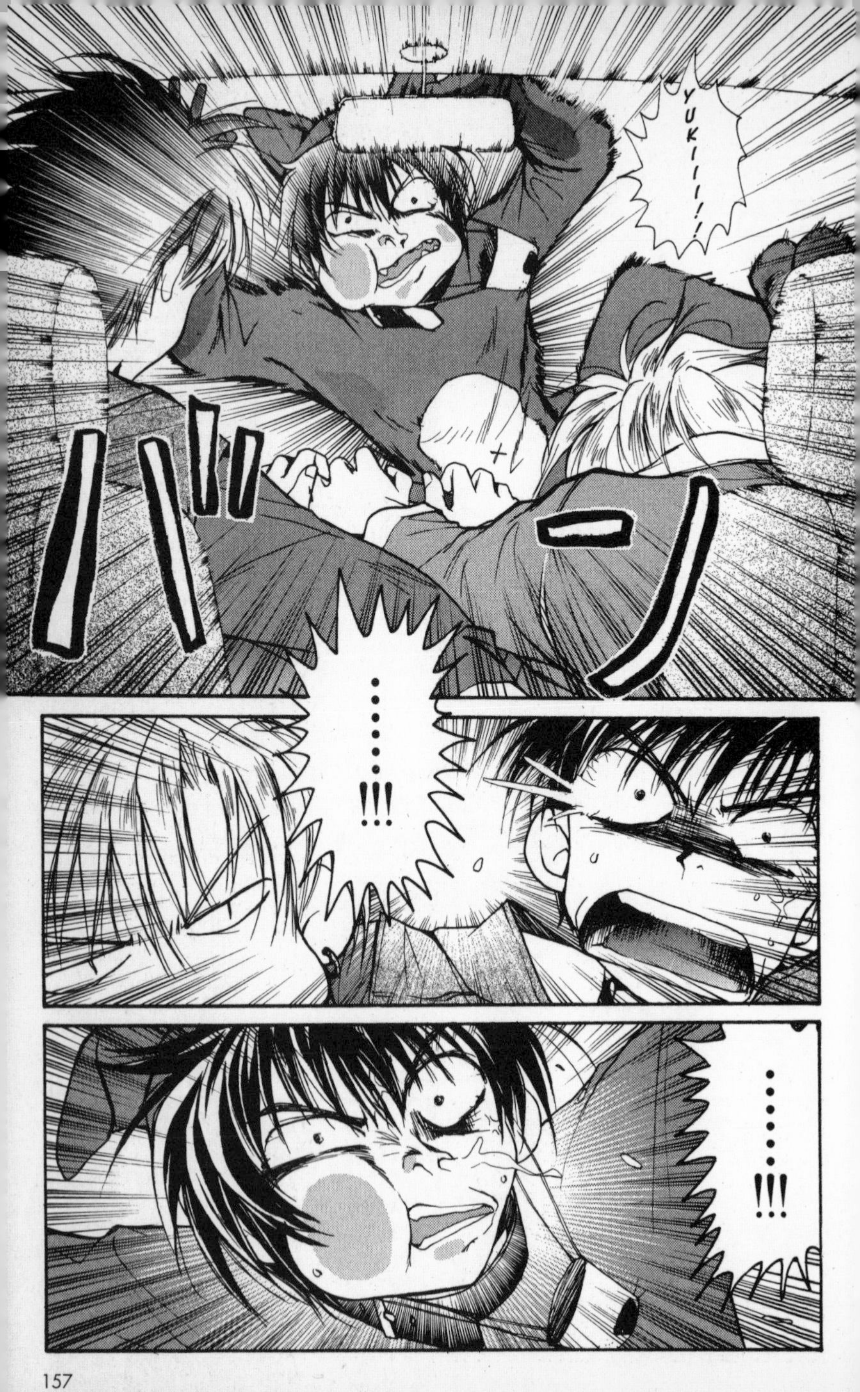
YUKIII!!
......!!!
......!!!

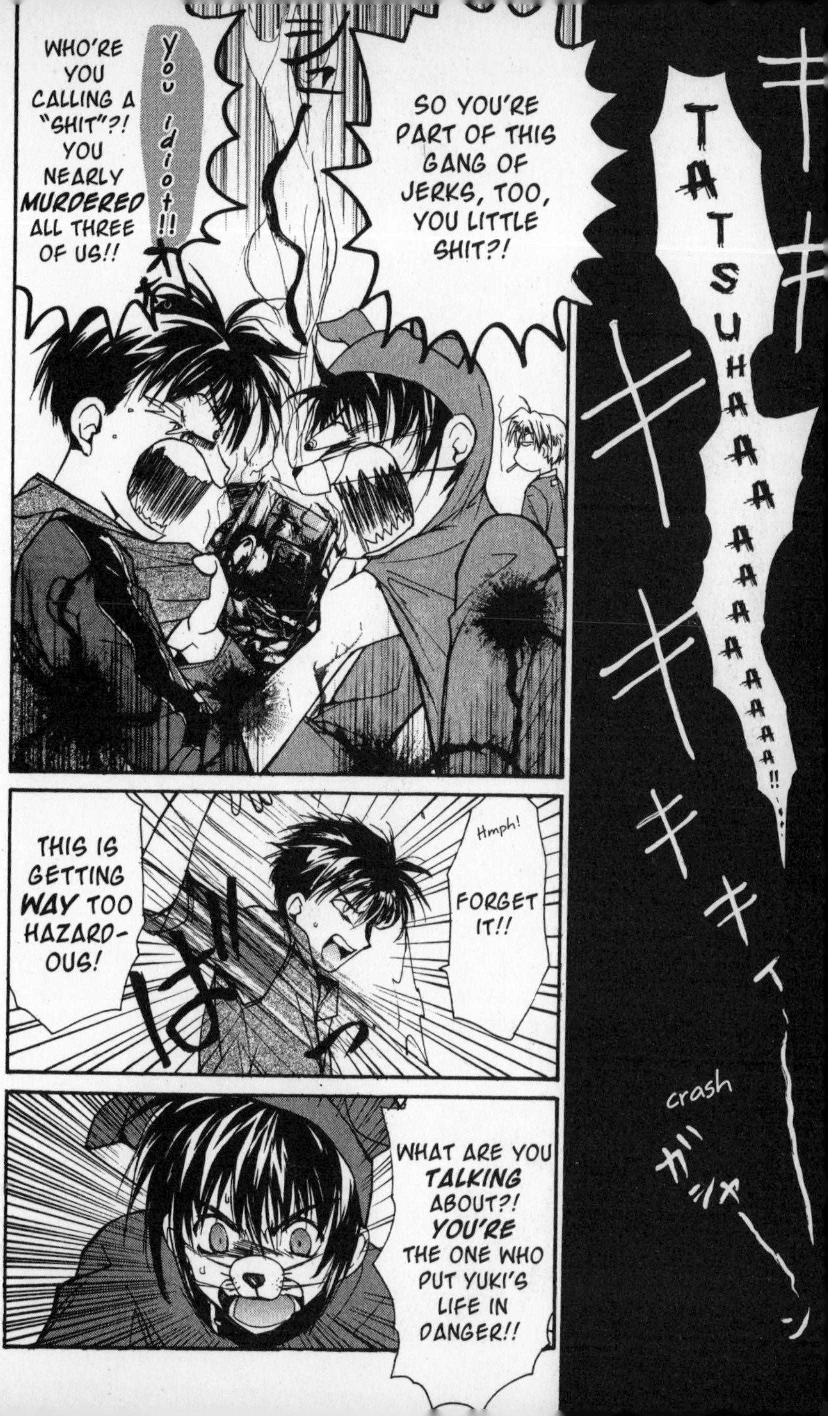
TATSUHAAAAAAAAAAA!!
crash
SO YOU'RE PART OF THIS GANG OF JERKS, TOO, YOU LITTLE SHIT?!
You idiot!!
WHO'RE YOU CALLING A "SHIT"?! YOU NEARLY MURDERED ALL THREE OF US!!
Hmph!
FORGET IT!!
THIS IS GETTING WAY TOO HAZARD-OUS!
WHAT ARE YOU TALKING ABOUT?! YOU'RE THE ONE WHO PUT YUKI'S LIFE IN DANGER!!

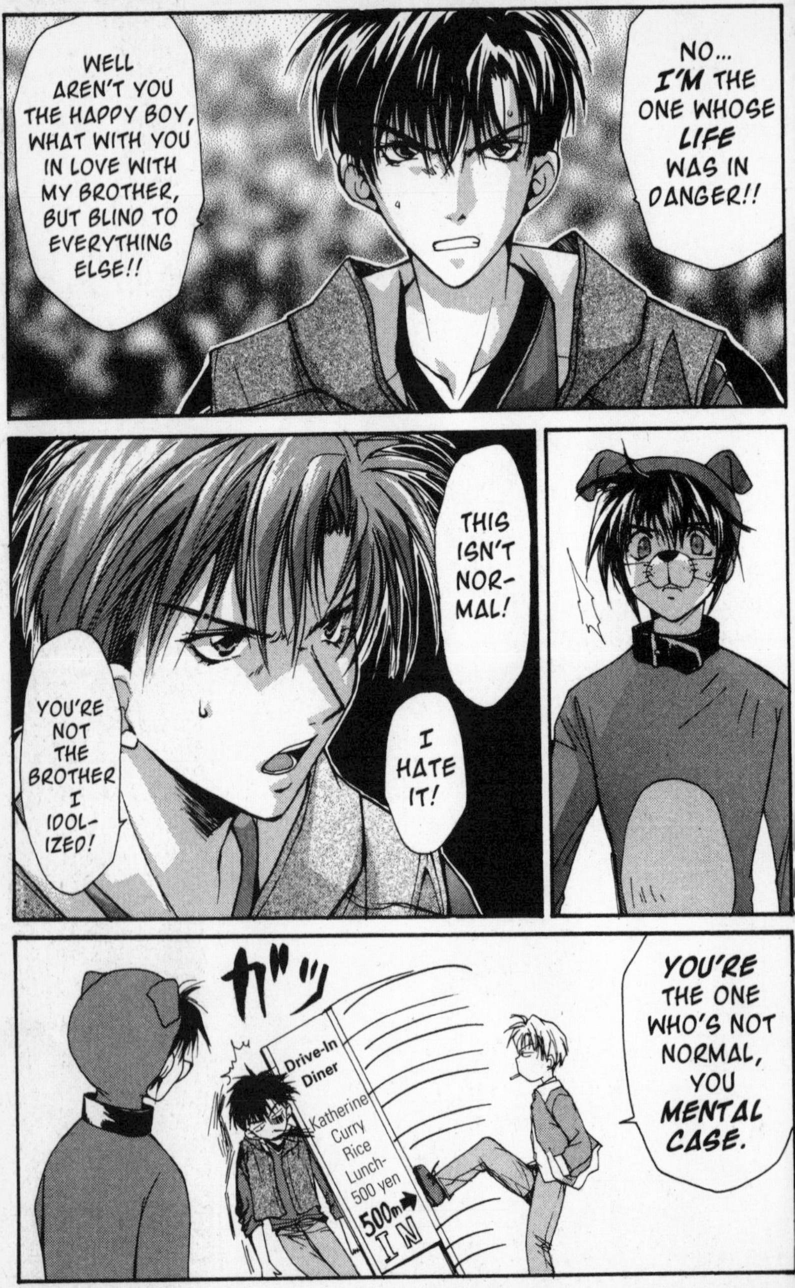
NO... I'M THE ONE WHOSE LIFE WAS IN DANGER!!
WELL AREN'T YOU THE HAPPY BOY, WHAT WITH YOU IN LOVE WITH MY BROTHER, BUT BLIND TO EVERYTHING ELSE!!
THIS ISN'T NOR-MAL!
I HATE IT!
YOU'RE NOT THE BROTHER I IDOL-IZED!
YOU'RE THE ONE WHO'S NOT NORMAL, YOU MENTAL CASE.
ガッ
Drive-In Diner
Katherine Curry Rice Lunch- 500 yen
500m
IN

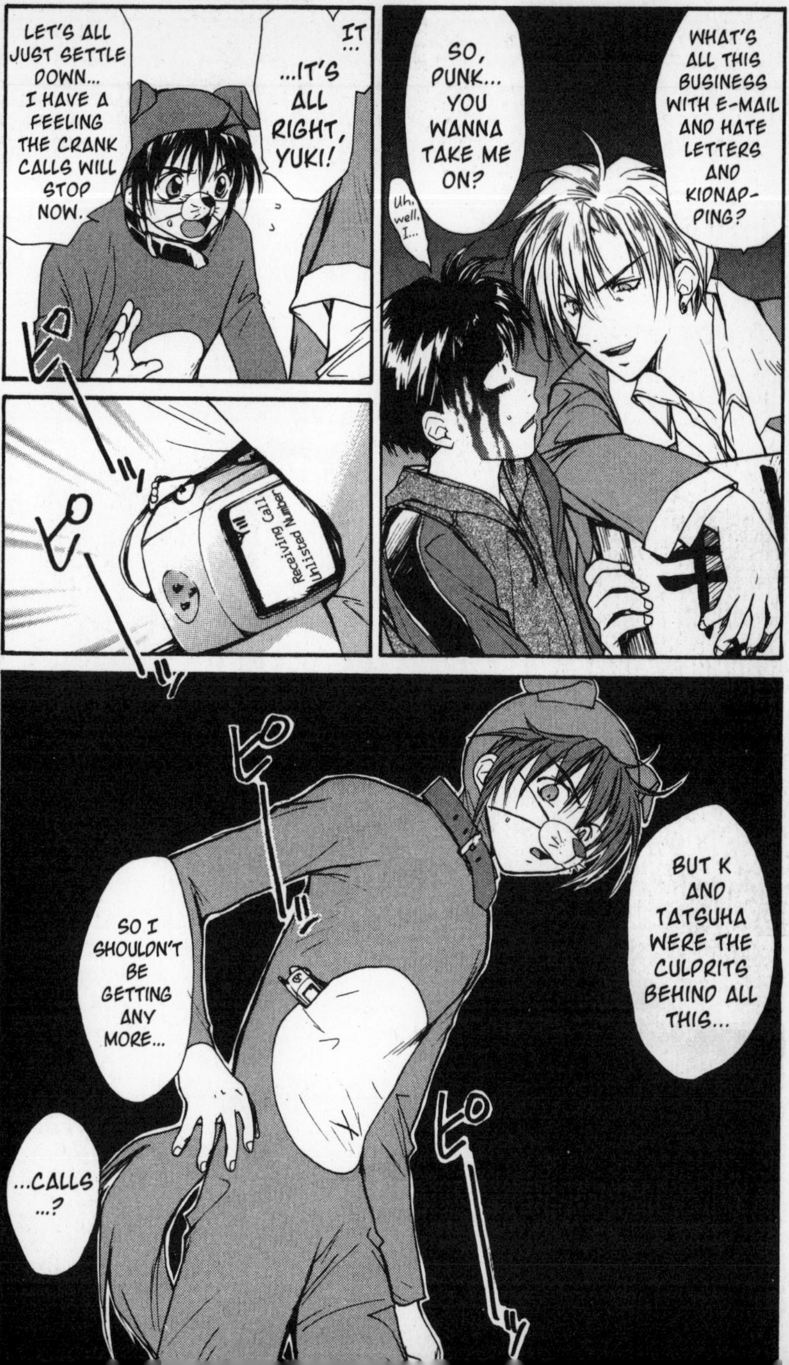
WHAT'S ALL THIS BUSINESS WITH E-MAIL AND HATE LETTERS AND KIDNAPPING?
SO, PUNK... YOU WANNA TAKE ME ON?
Uh, well, I...
IT...
...IT'S ALL RIGHT, YUKI!
LET'S ALL JUST SETTLE DOWN... I HAVE A FEELING THE CRANK CALLS WILL STOP NOW.
Receiving Call
Unlisted Number
BUT K AND TATSUHA WERE THE CULPRITS BEHIND ALL THIS...
SO I SHOULDN'T BE GETTING ANY MORE...
...CALLS...?

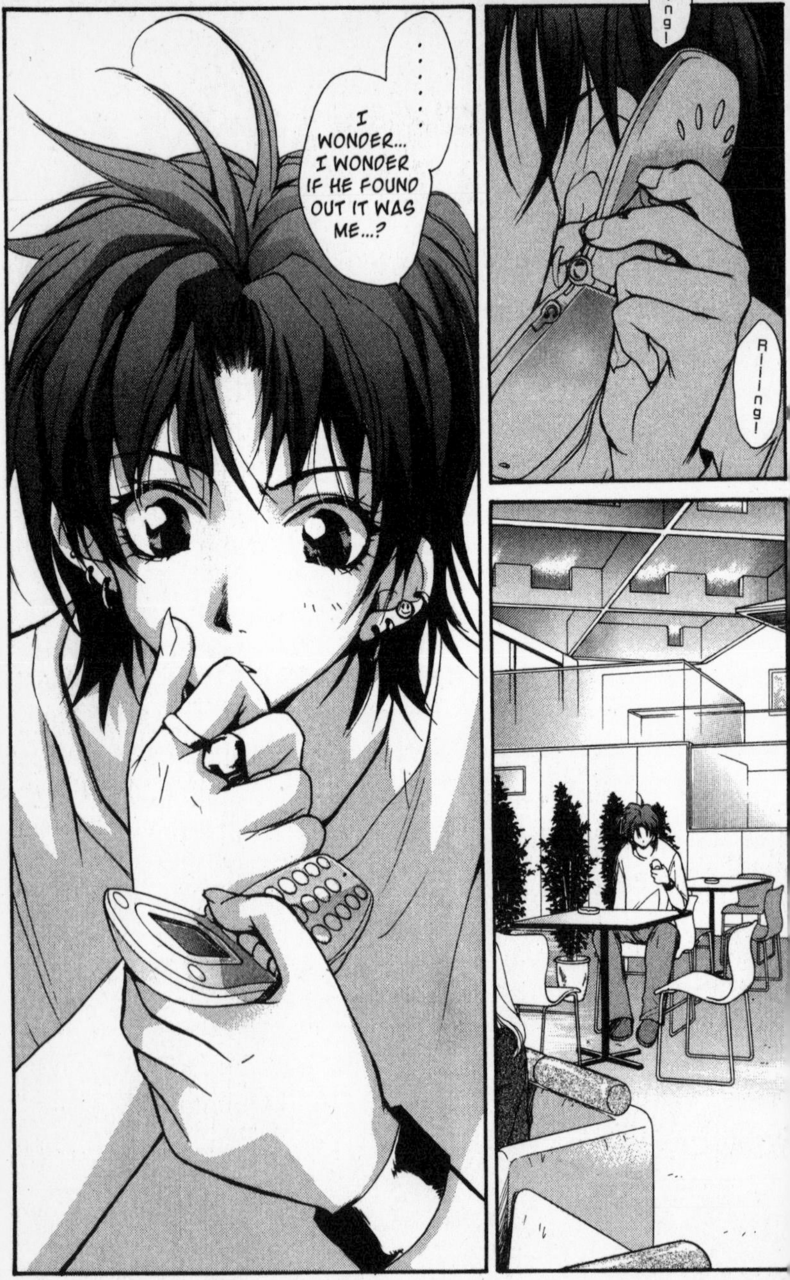
Riiing!
Riiing!
......
I WONDER... I WONDER IF HE FOUND OUT IT WAS ME...?

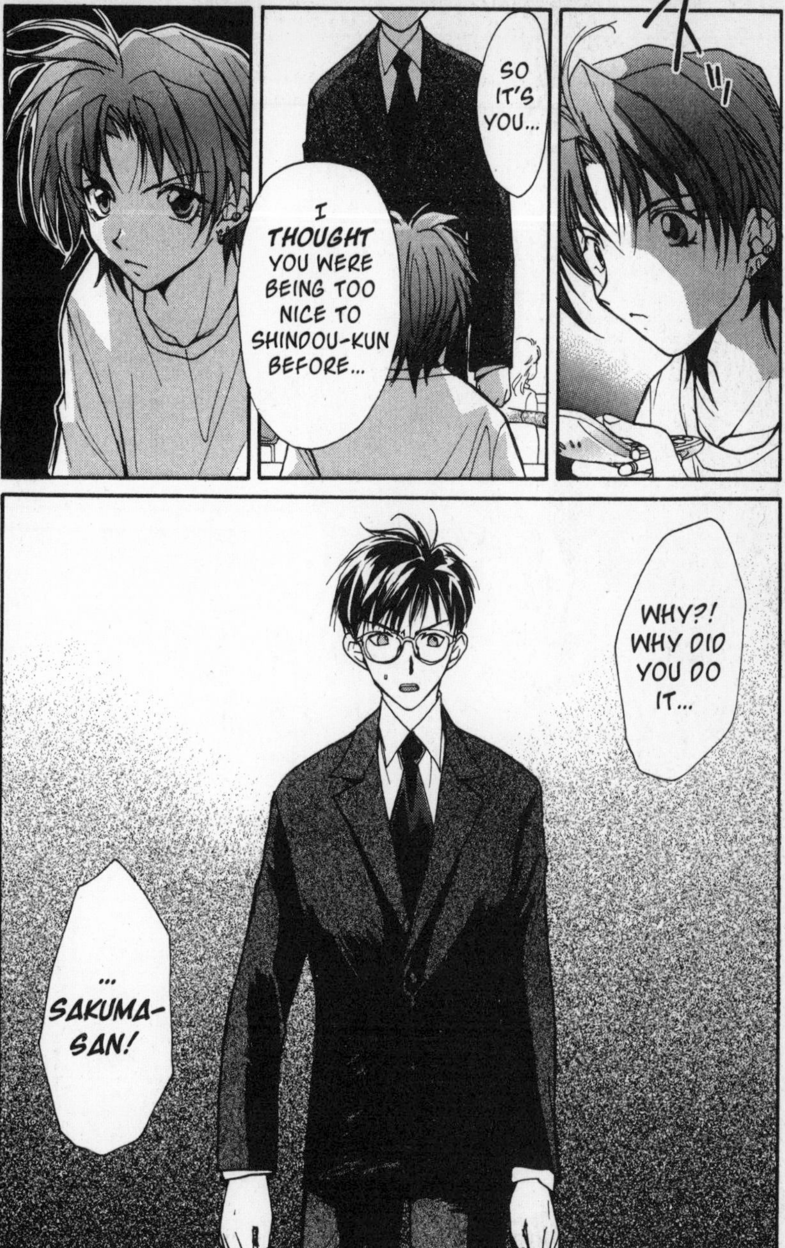
SO IT'S YOU...
I **THOUGHT** YOU WERE BEING TOO NICE TO SHINDOU-KUN BEFORE...
WHY?! WHY DID YOU DO IT...
... SAKUMA-SAN!

track48 ▶ END

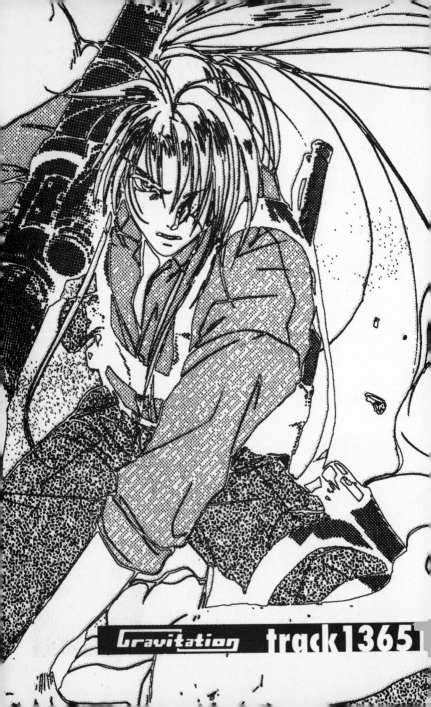

Gravitation track13651

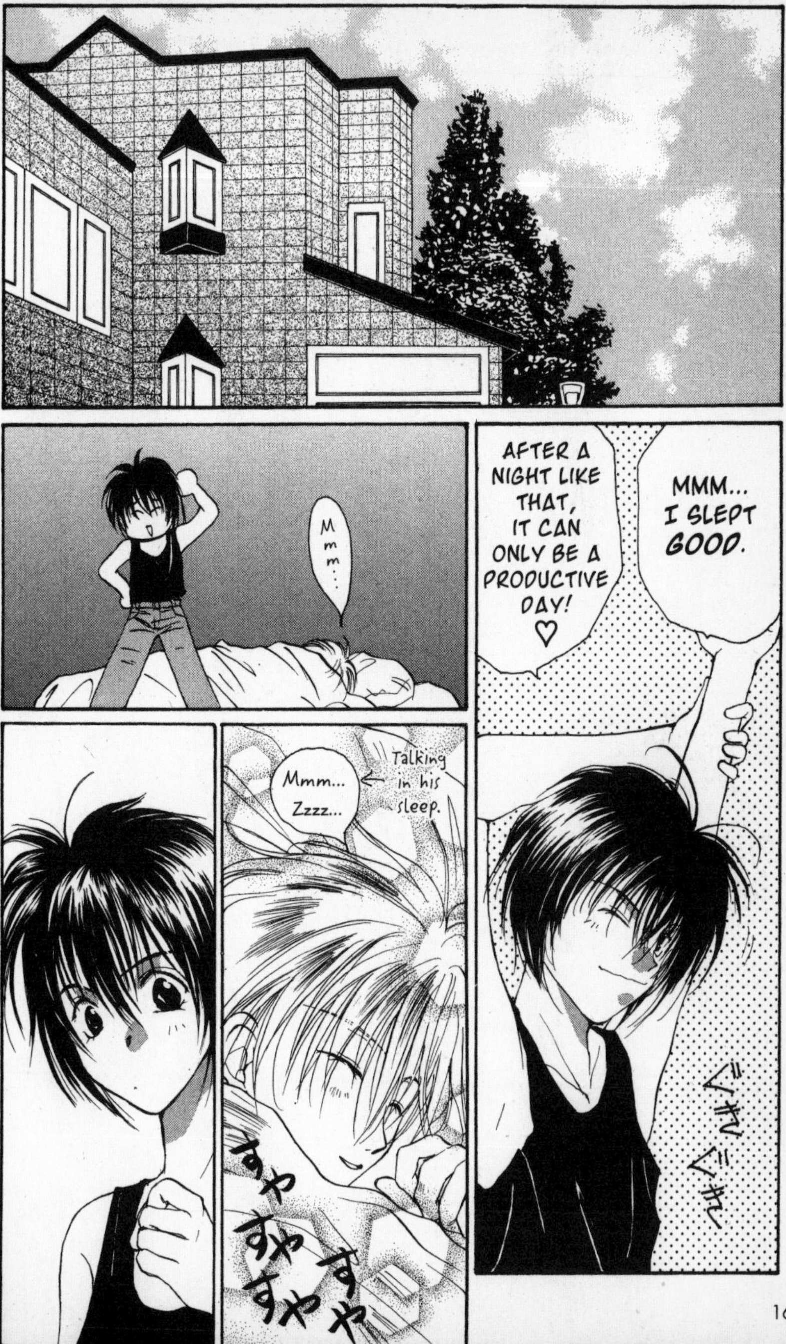
MMM... I SLEPT GOOD.
AFTER A NIGHT LIKE THAT, IT CAN ONLY BE A PRODUCTIVE DAY! ♡
ぐぃぐぃ
Mmm...
Mmm... Zzzz...
Talking in his sleep.
すやすや
すやすや

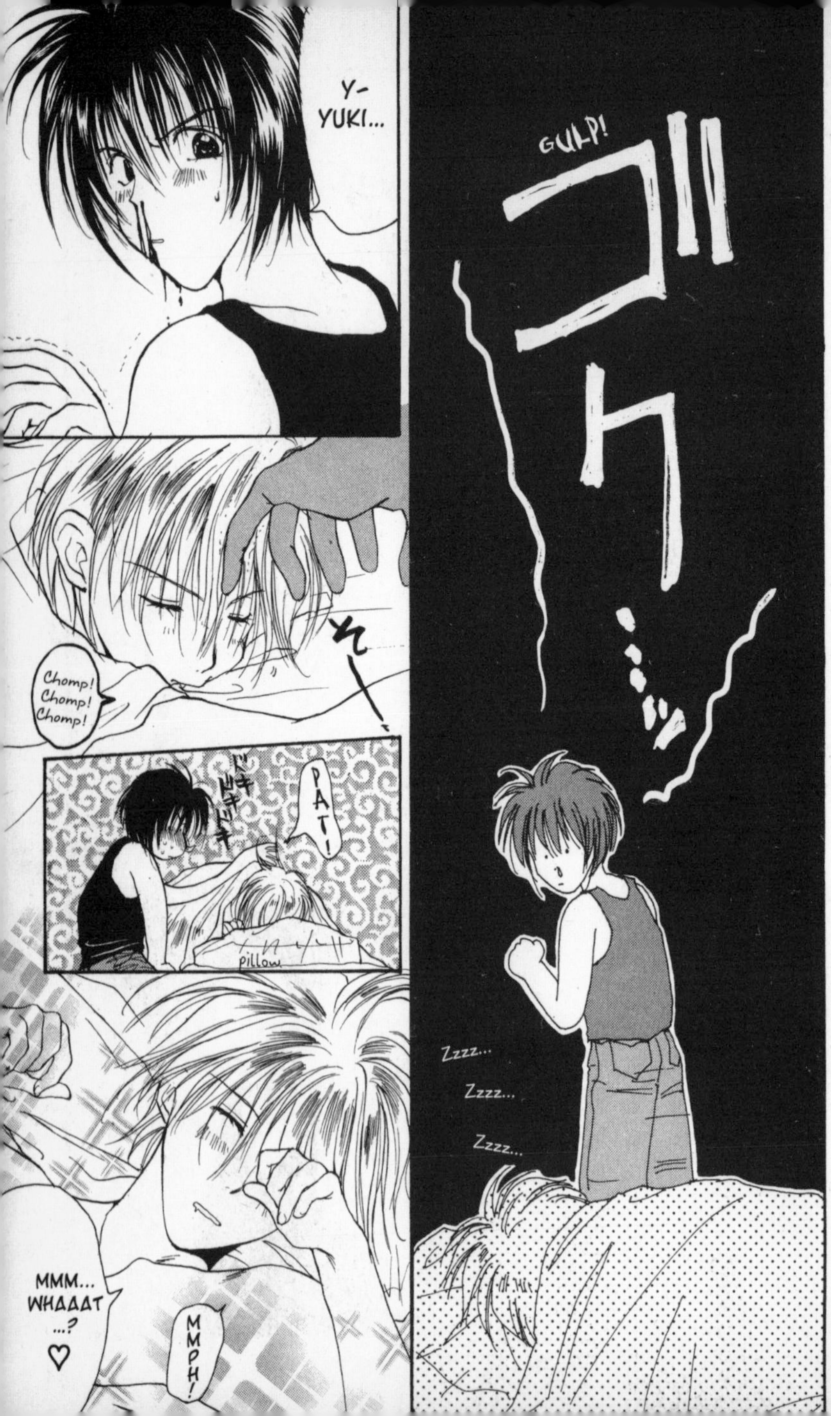
GULP!
ゴクッ
Zzzz...
Zzzz...
Zzzz...
Y- YUKI...
そー
Chomp! Chomp! Chomp!
ドキドキ
PAT!
pillow
MMPH!
MMM... WHAAAT ...? ♡

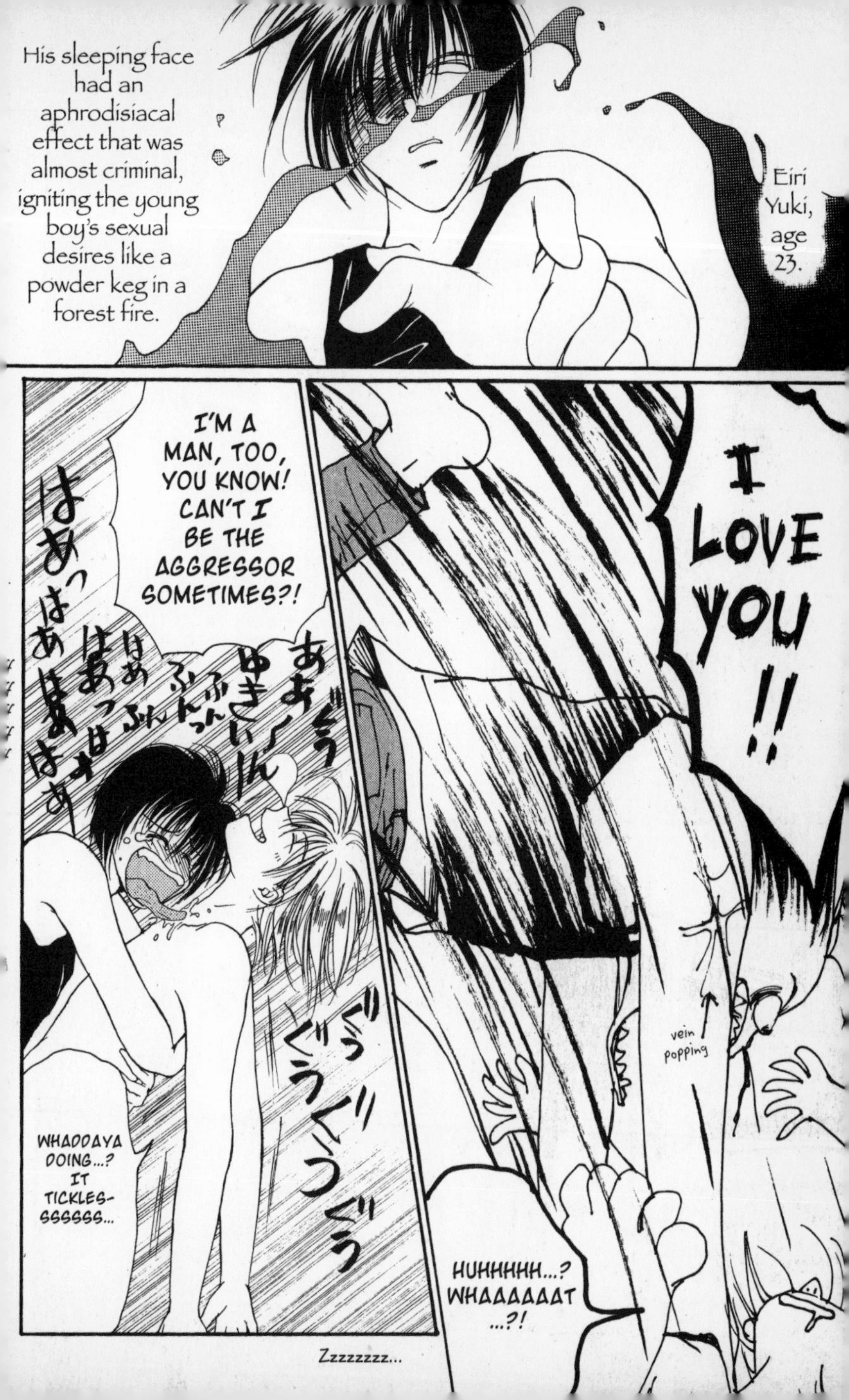

Eiri Yuki, age 23.
His sleeping face had an aphrodisiacal effect that was almost criminal, igniting the young boy's sexual desires like a powder keg in a forest fire.
I LOVE YOU!!
vein popping
HUHHHHH...? WHAAAAAAT ...?!
I'M A MAN, TOO, YOU KNOW! CAN'T I BE THE AGGRESSOR SOMETIMES?!
WHADDAYA DOING...? IT TICKLES-SSSSSS...
Zzzzzzzz...

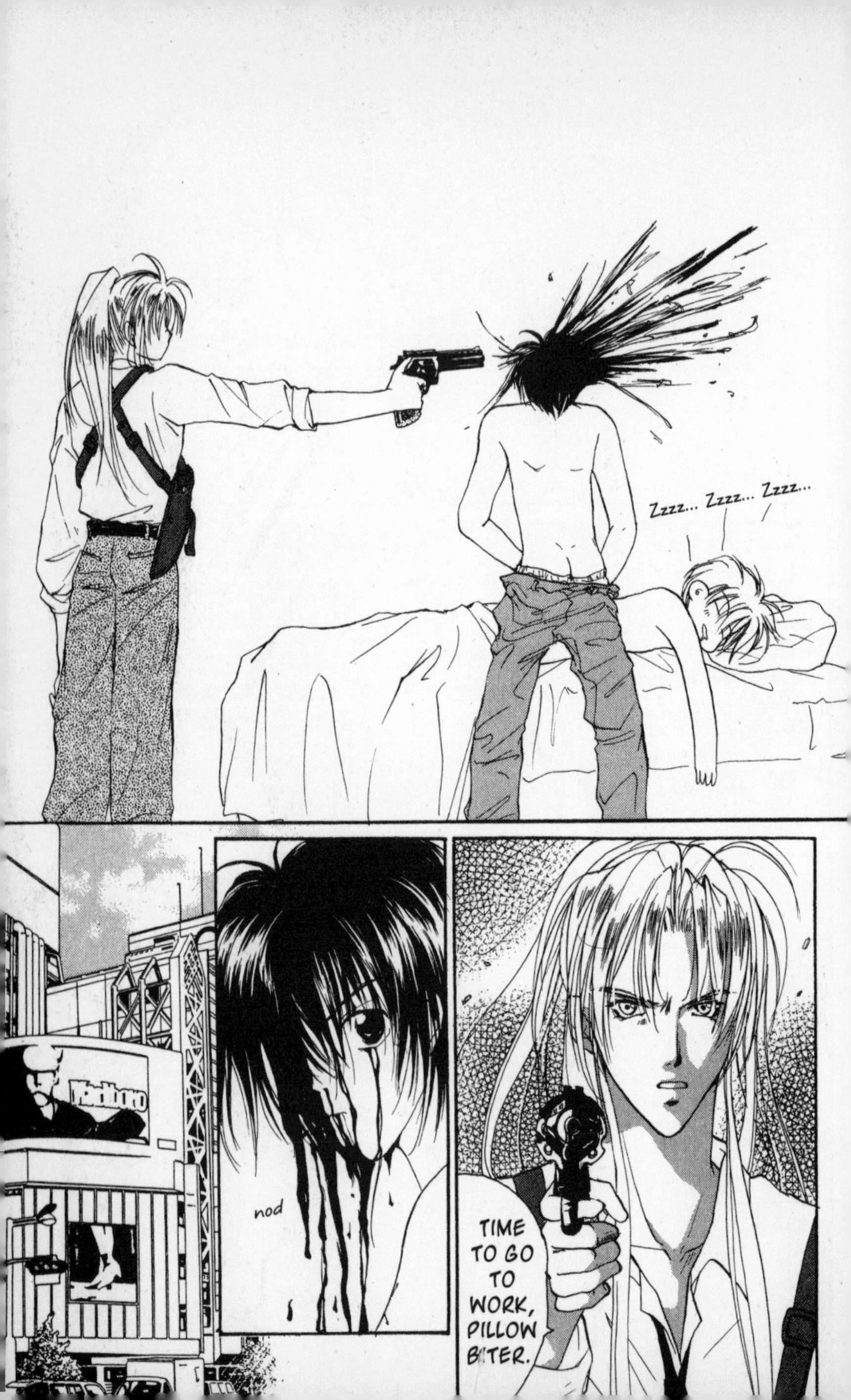
Zzzz... Zzzz... Zzzz...
TIME TO GO TO WORK, PILLOW BITER.
nod

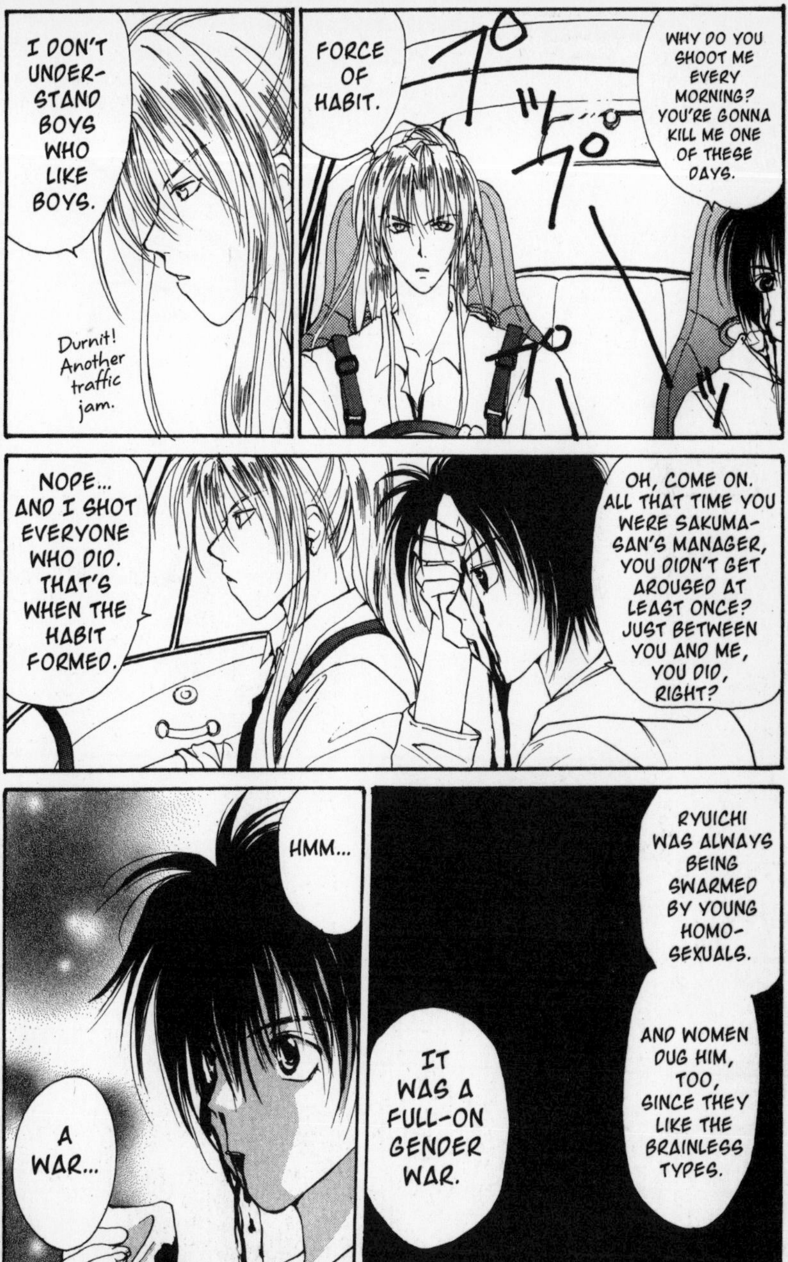
WHY DO YOU SHOOT ME EVERY MORNING? YOU'RE GONNA KILL ME ONE OF THESE DAYS.
FORCE OF HABIT.
I DON'T UNDER-STAND BOYS WHO LIKE BOYS.
Durnit! Another traffic jam.
OH, COME ON. ALL THAT TIME YOU WERE SAKUMA-SAN'S MANAGER, YOU DIDN'T GET AROUSED AT LEAST ONCE? JUST BETWEEN YOU AND ME, YOU DID, RIGHT?
NOPE... AND I SHOT EVERYONE WHO DID. THAT'S WHEN THE HABIT FORMED.
RYUICHI WAS ALWAYS BEING SWARMED BY YOUNG HOMO-SEXUALS.
AND WOMEN DUG HIM, TOO, SINCE THEY LIKE THE BRAINLESS TYPES.
IT WAS A FULL-ON GENDER WAR.
HMM...
A WAR...

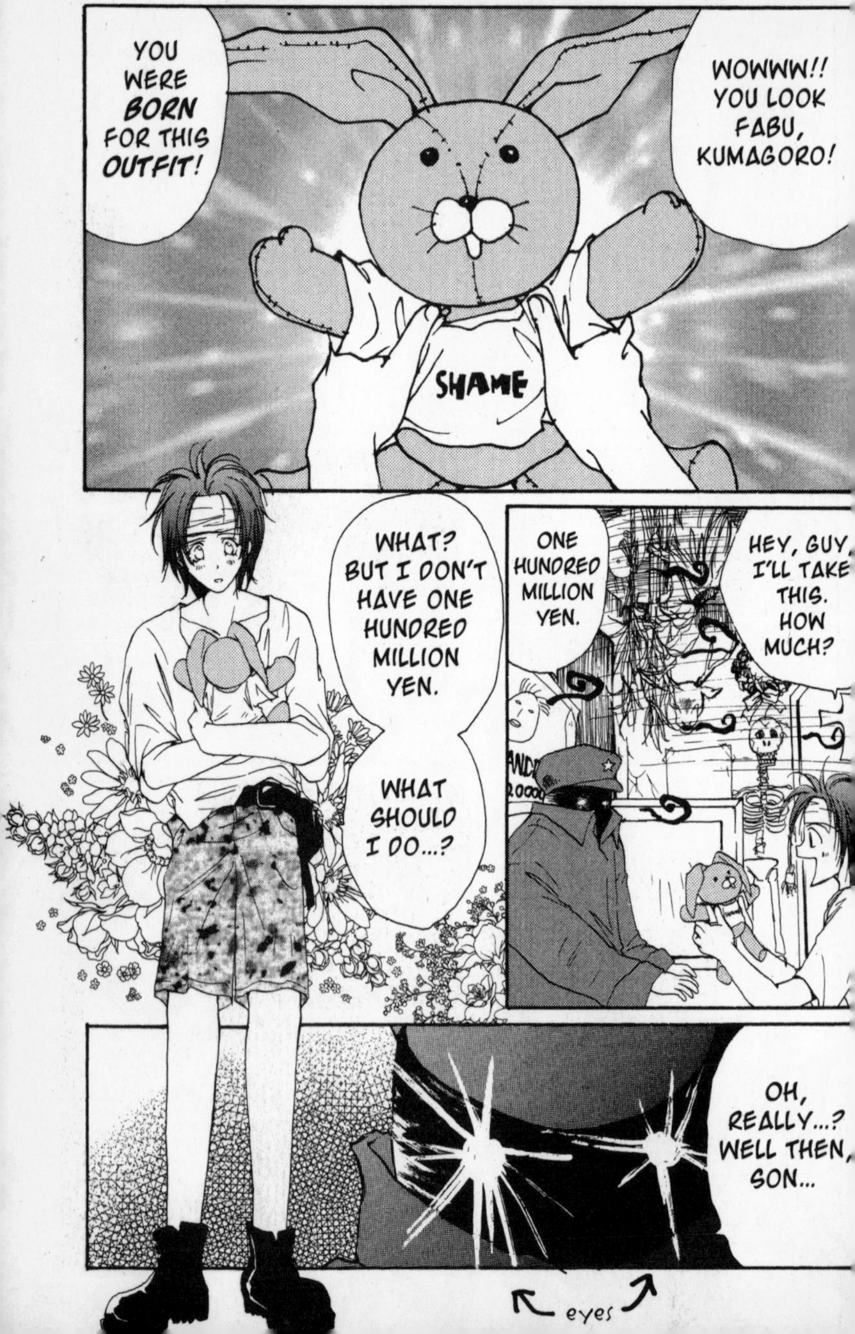
WOWWW!! YOU LOOK FABU, KUMAGORO!
YOU WERE BORN FOR THIS OUTFIT!
SHAME
HEY, GUY, I'LL TAKE THIS. HOW MUCH?
ONE HUNDRED MILLION YEN.
WHAT? BUT I DON'T HAVE ONE HUNDRED MILLION YEN.
WHAT SHOULD I DO...?
OH, REALLY...? WELL THEN, SON...
eyes

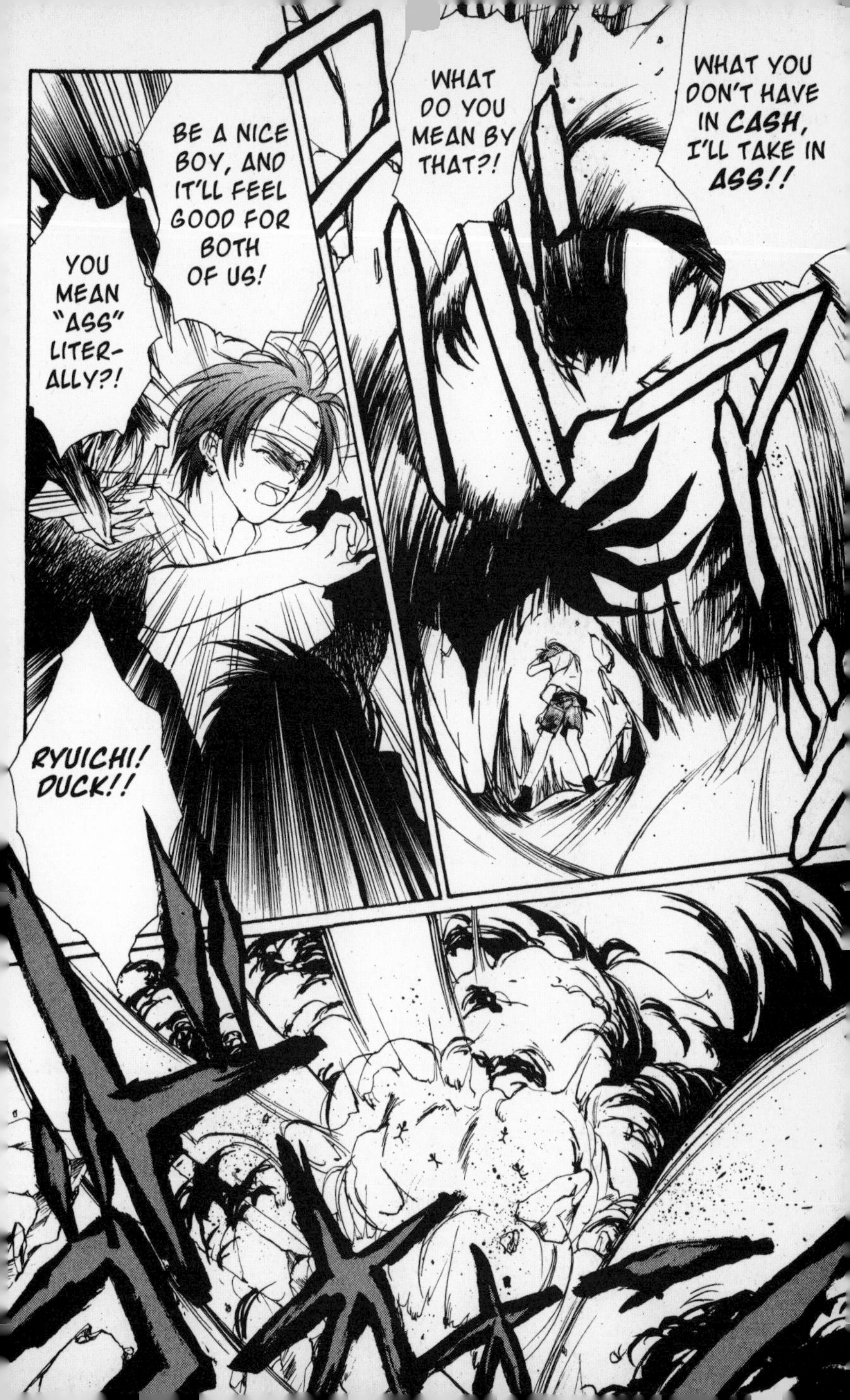
WHAT YOU DON'T HAVE IN CASH, I'LL TAKE IN ASS!!
WHAT DO YOU MEAN BY THAT?!
BE A NICE BOY, AND IT'LL FEEL GOOD FOR BOTH OF US!
YOU MEAN "ASS" LITERALLY?!
RYUICHI! DUCK!!

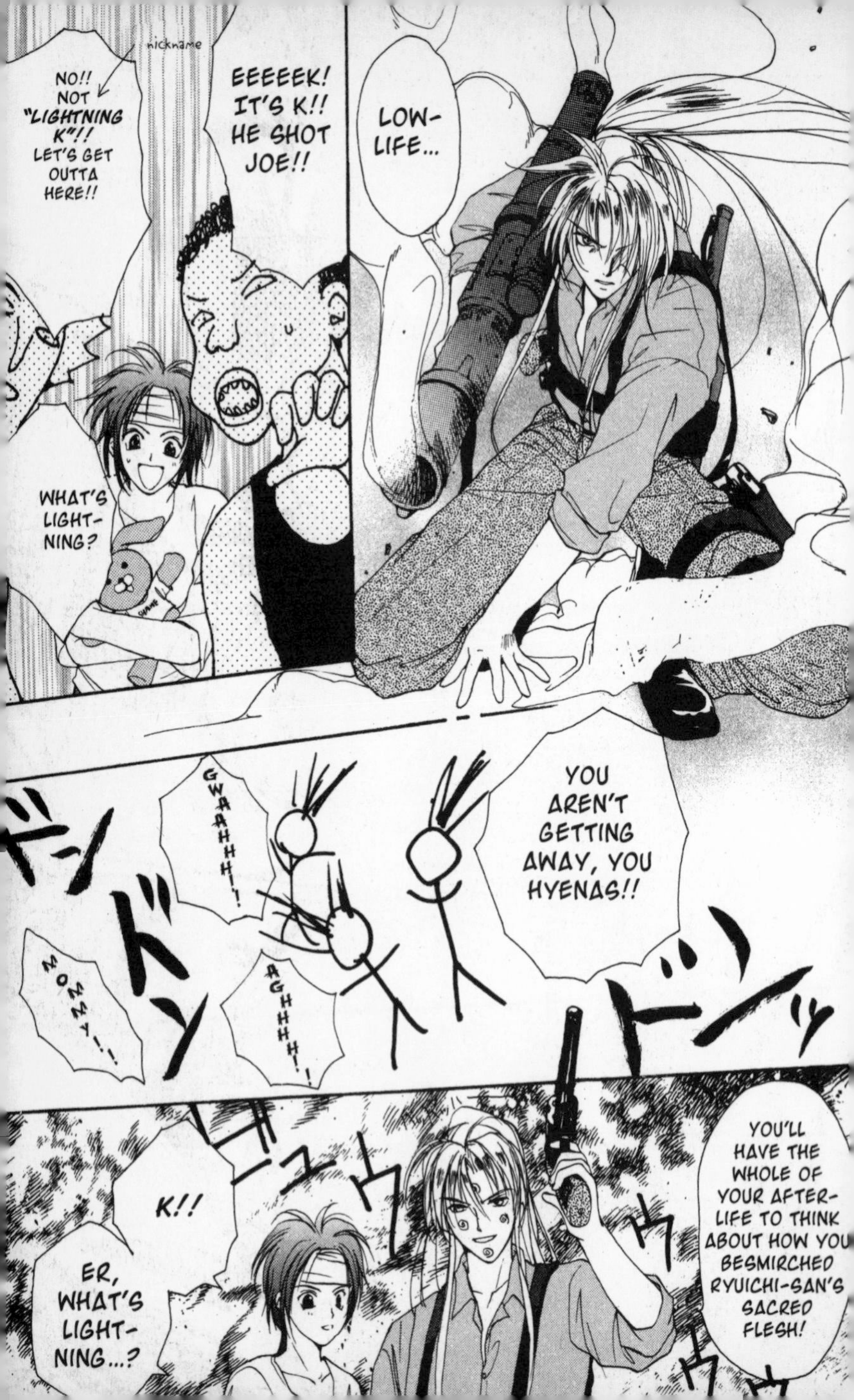
LOW-LIFE...
EEEEEK! IT'S K!! HE SHOT JOE!!
NO!! NOT "LIGHTNING K"!! LET'S GET OUTTA HERE!!
nickname
WHAT'S LIGHTNING?
YOU AREN'T GETTING AWAY, YOU HYENAS!!
GWAAHHH!!
AGHHHH!!
MOMMY!!
YOU'LL HAVE THE WHOLE OF YOUR AFTER-LIFE TO THINK ABOUT HOW YOU BESMIRCHED RYUICHI-SAN'S SACRED FLESH!
K!!
ER, WHAT'S LIGHTNING...?

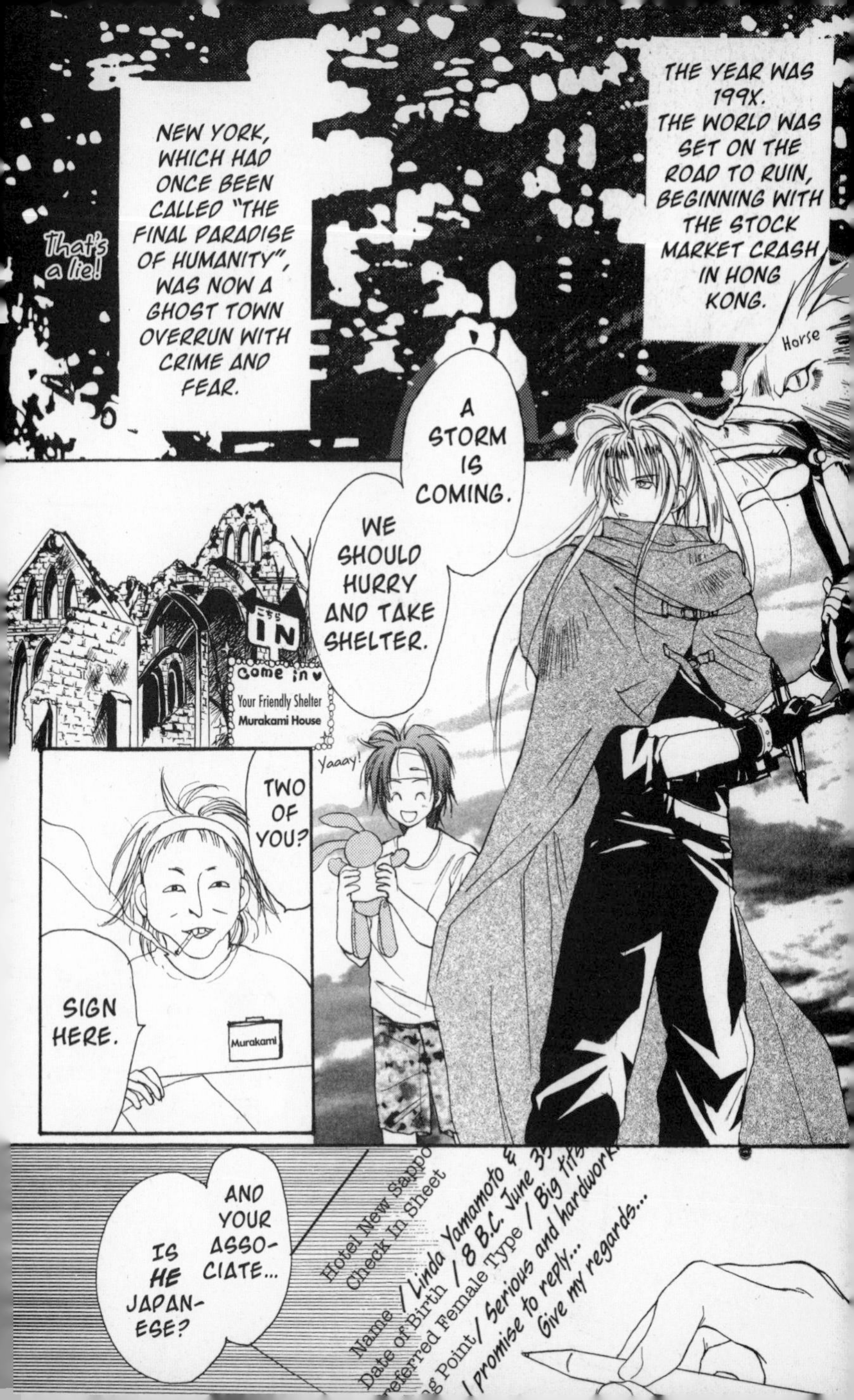
THE YEAR WAS 199X. THE WORLD WAS SET ON THE ROAD TO RUIN, BEGINNING WITH THE STOCK MARKET CRASH IN HONG KONG.
NEW YORK, WHICH HAD ONCE BEEN CALLED "THE FINAL PARADISE OF HUMANITY", WAS NOW A GHOST TOWN OVERRUN WITH CRIME AND FEAR.
That's a lie!
Horse
A STORM IS COMING.
WE SHOULD HURRY AND TAKE SHELTER.
IN
Come in ♥
Your Friendly Shelter
Murakami House
Yaaay!
TWO OF YOU?
SIGN HERE.
Murakami
Hotel New Sappo
Check In Sheet
Name / Linda Yamamoto &
Date of Birth / 8 B.C. June 3
eferred Female Type / Big tits
g Point / Serious and hardwork
I promise to reply...
Give my regards...
AND YOUR ASSOCIATE... IS HE JAPANESE?

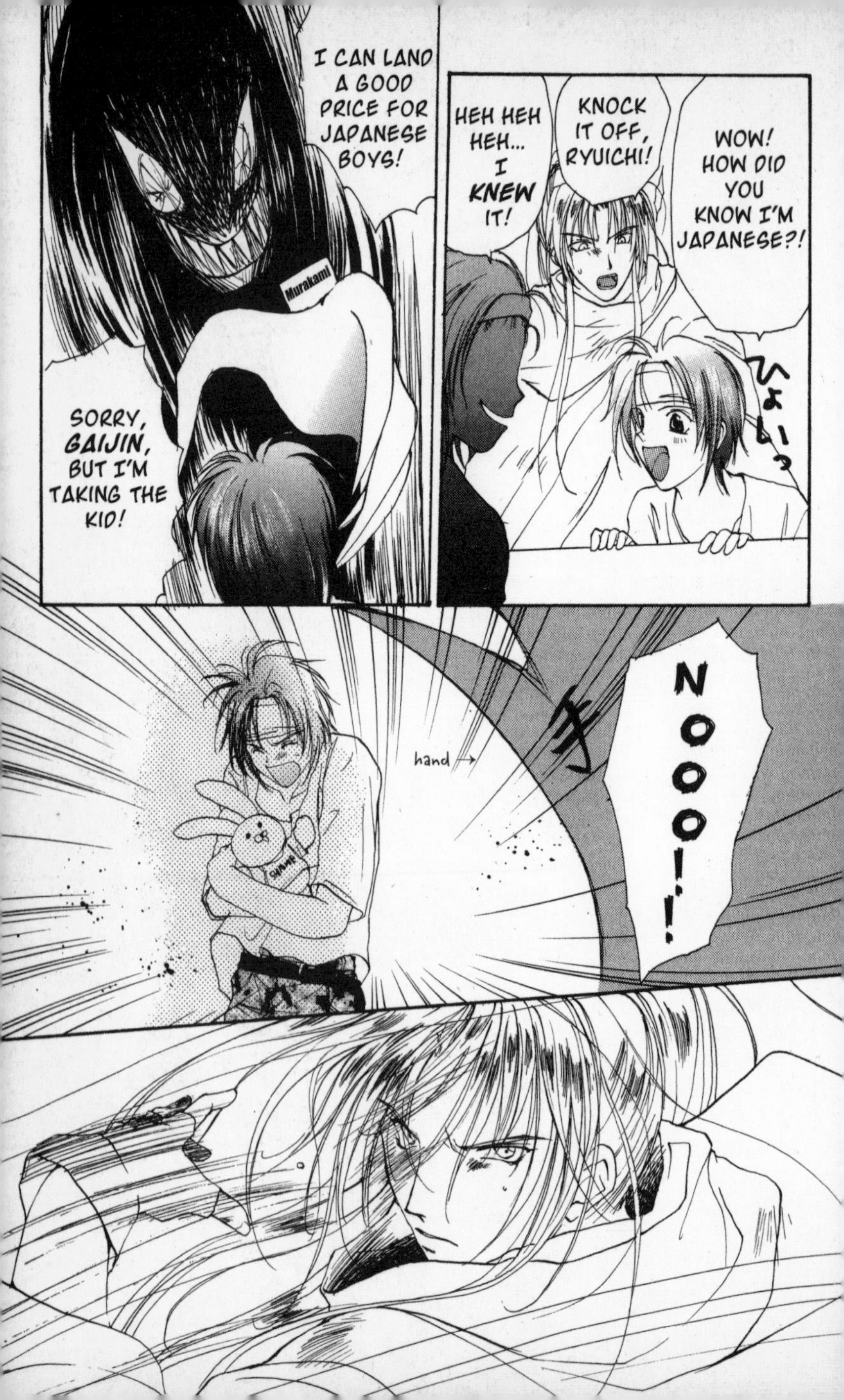
WOW! HOW DID YOU KNOW I'M JAPANESE?!
ひょいっ
KNOCK IT OFF, RYUICHI!
HEH HEH HEH... I KNEW IT!
I CAN LAND A GOOD PRICE FOR JAPANESE BOYS!
Murakami
SORRY, GAIJIN, BUT I'M TAKING THE KID!
NOOOO!!
手
hand →

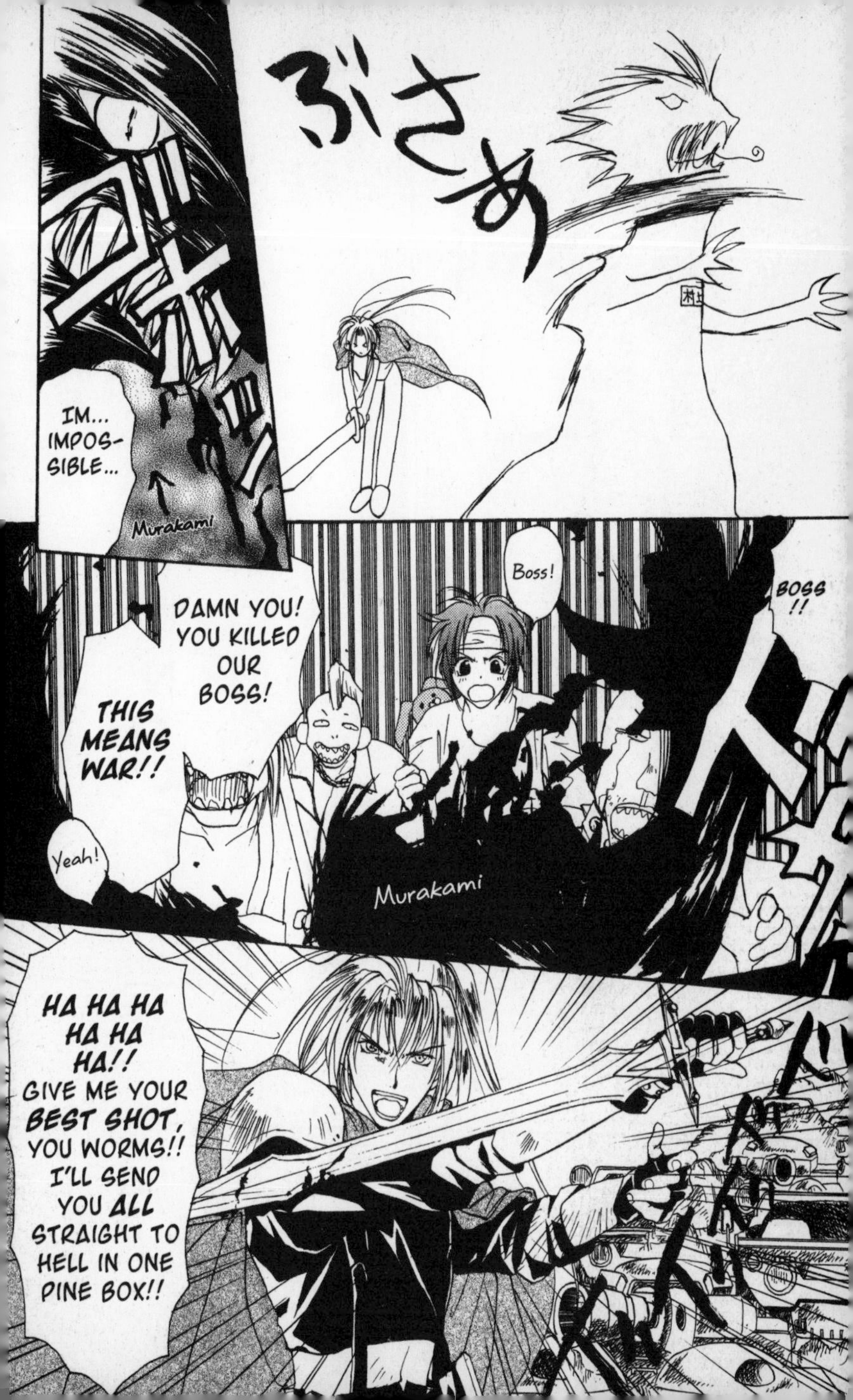
ぶさあ
IM... IMPOSSIBLE...
Murakami
BOSS!!
Boss!
DAMN YOU! YOU KILLED OUR BOSS!
THIS MEANS WAR!!
Yeah!
Murakami
HA HA HA HA HA HA!! GIVE ME YOUR BEST SHOT, YOU WORMS!! I'LL SEND YOU ALL STRAIGHT TO HELL IN ONE PINE BOX!!

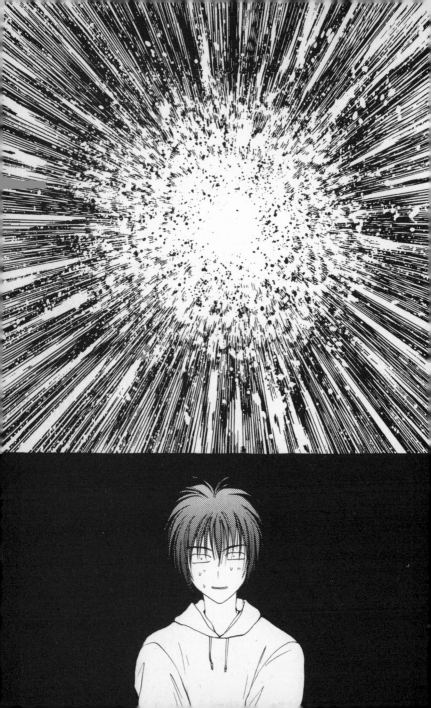

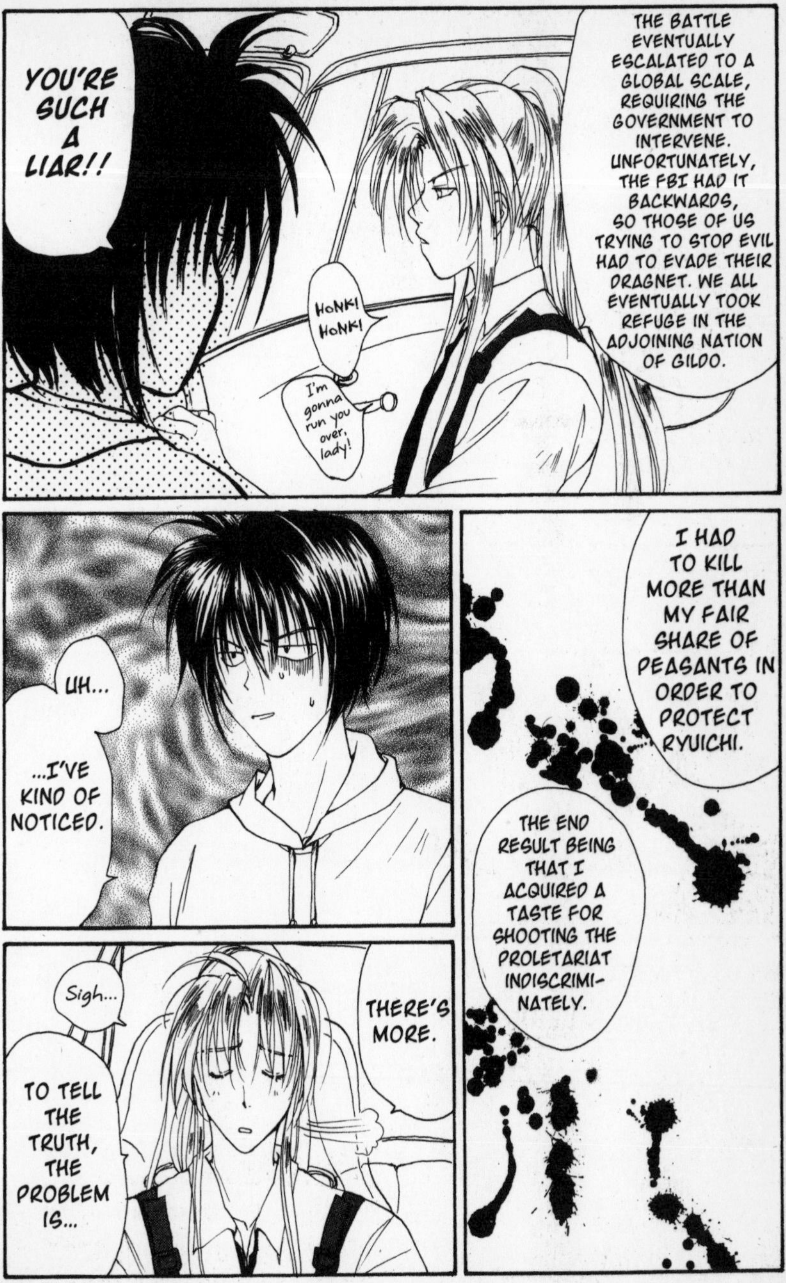
THE BATTLE EVENTUALLY ESCALATED TO A GLOBAL SCALE, REQUIRING THE GOVERNMENT TO INTERVENE. UNFORTUNATELY, THE FBI HAD IT BACKWARDS, SO THOSE OF US TRYING TO STOP EVIL HAD TO EVADE THEIR DRAGNET. WE ALL EVENTUALLY TOOK REFUGE IN THE ADJOINING NATION OF GILDO.
HONK! HONK!
I'm gonna run you over, lady!
YOU'RE SUCH A LIAR!!
I HAD TO KILL MORE THAN MY FAIR SHARE OF PEASANTS IN ORDER TO PROTECT RYUICHI.
THE END RESULT BEING THAT I ACQUIRED A TASTE FOR SHOOTING THE PROLETARIAT INDISCRIMI-NATELY.
UH...
...I'VE KIND OF NOTICED.
THERE'S MORE.
Sigh...
TO TELL THE TRUTH, THE PROBLEM IS...

So, where in the world is Gildo?

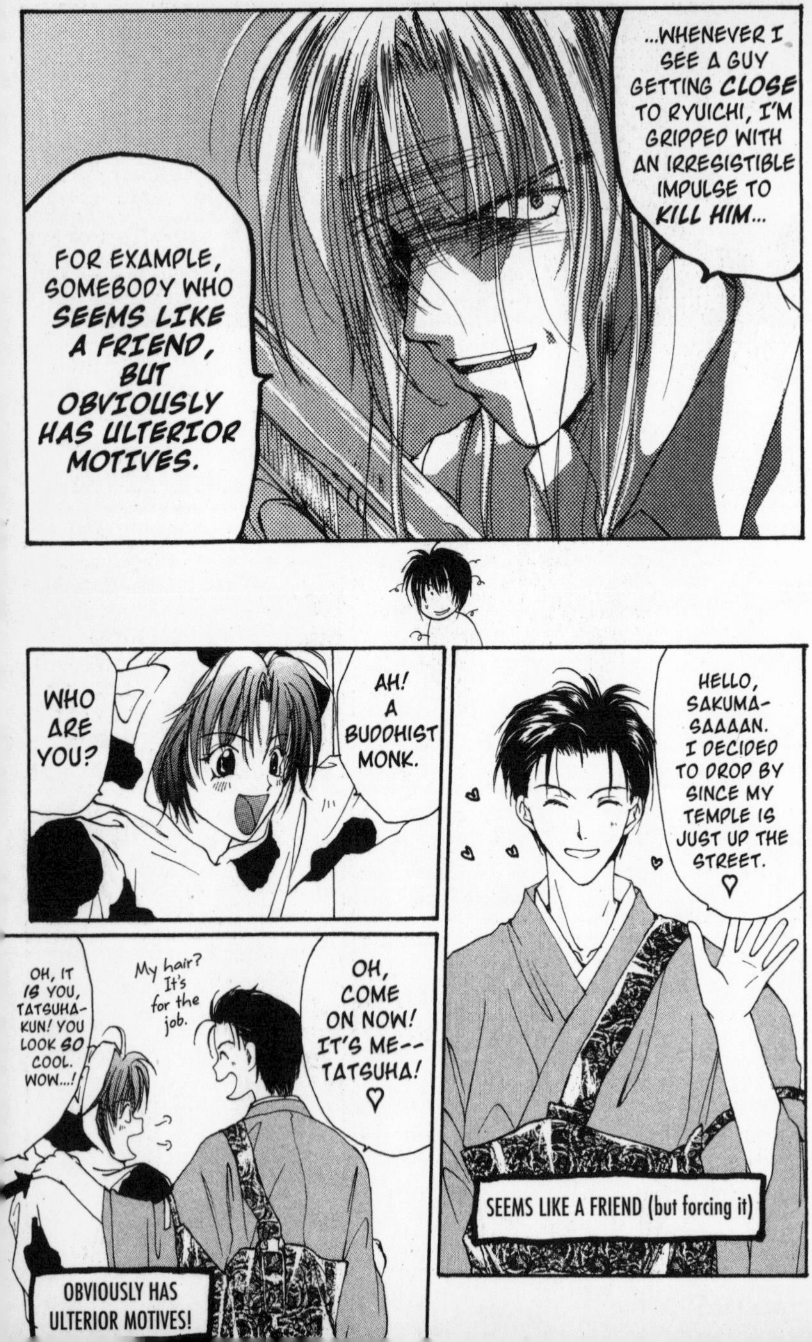
...WHENEVER I SEE A GUY GETTING CLOSE TO RYUICHI, I'M GRIPPED WITH AN IRRESISTIBLE IMPULSE TO KILL HIM...
FOR EXAMPLE, SOMEBODY WHO SEEMS LIKE A FRIEND, BUT OBVIOUSLY HAS ULTERIOR MOTIVES.
HELLO, SAKUMA-SAAAAN. I DECIDED TO DROP BY SINCE MY TEMPLE IS JUST UP THE STREET. ♡
SEEMS LIKE A FRIEND (but forcing it)
AH! A BUDDHIST MONK.
WHO ARE YOU?
OH, COME ON NOW! IT'S ME--TATSUHA! ♡
OH, IT IS YOU, TATSUHA-KUN! YOU LOOK SO COOL. WOW...!
My hair? It's for the job.
OBVIOUSLY HAS ULTERIOR MOTIVES!

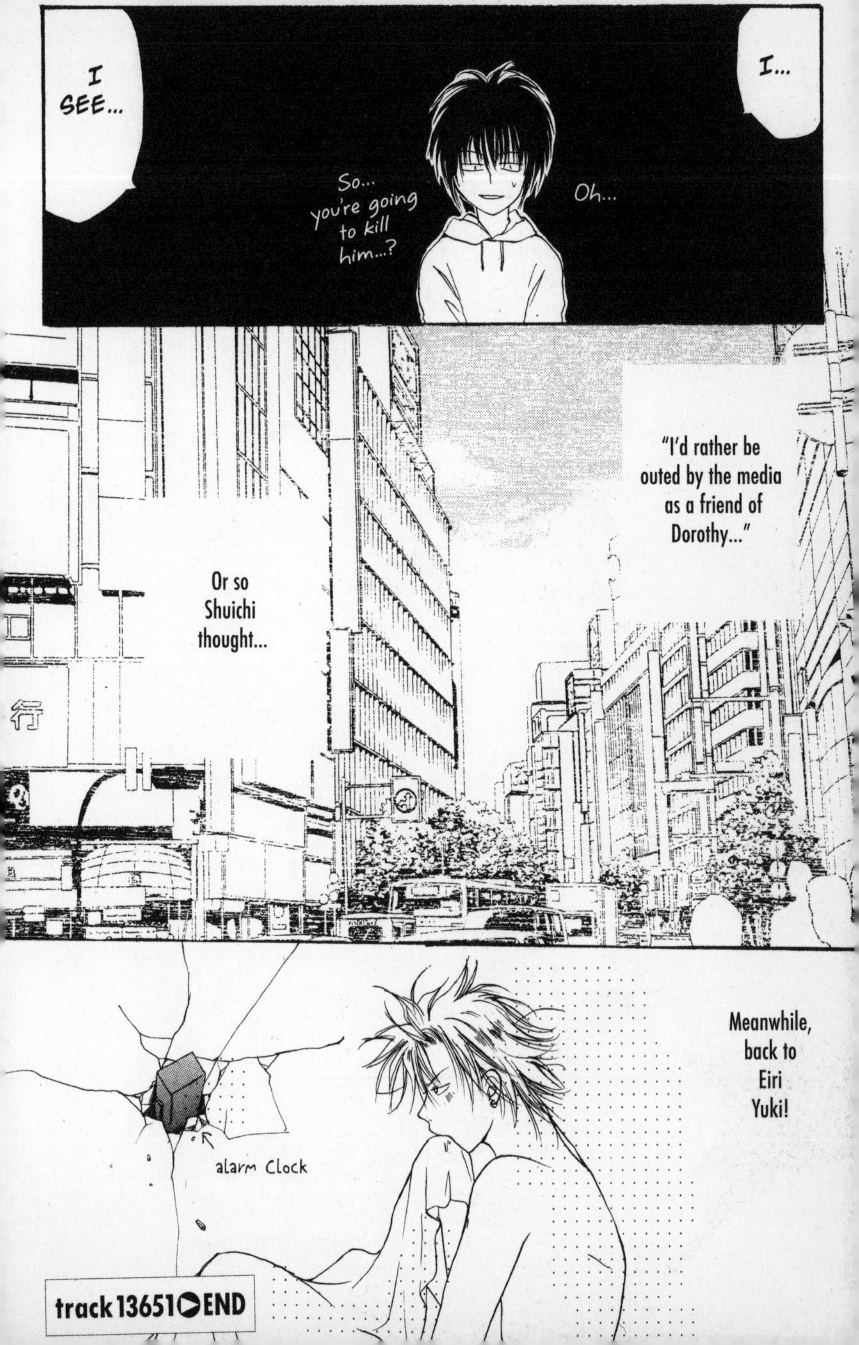
I...
Oh...
So... you're going to kill him...?
I SEE...
"I'd rather be outed by the media as a friend of Dorothy..."
Or so Shuichi thought...
Meanwhile, back to Eiri Yuki!
alarm Clock
track 13651 ▶ END

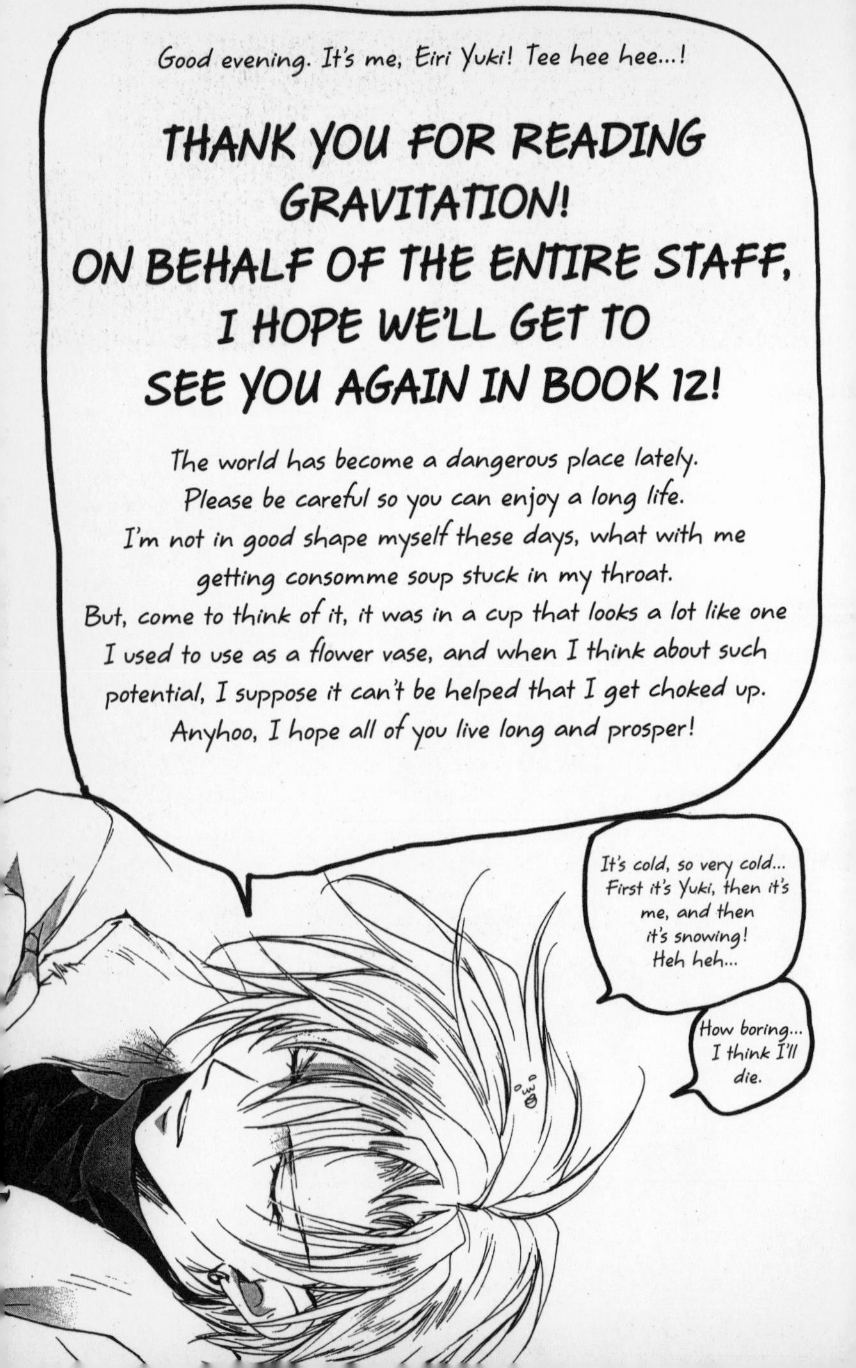
Good evening. It's me, Eiri Yuki! Tee hee hee...!
THANK YOU FOR READING GRAVITATION! ON BEHALF OF THE ENTIRE STAFF, I HOPE WE'LL GET TO SEE YOU AGAIN IN BOOK 12!
The world has become a dangerous place lately. Please be careful so you can enjoy a long life. I'm not in good shape myself these days, what with me getting consomme soup stuck in my throat. But, come to think of it, it was in a cup that looks a lot like one I used to use as a flower vase, and when I think about such potential, I suppose it can't be helped that I get choked up. Anyhoo, I hope all of you live long and prosper!
It's cold, so very cold... First it's Yuki, then it's me, and then it's snowing! Heh heh...
How boring... I think I'll die.

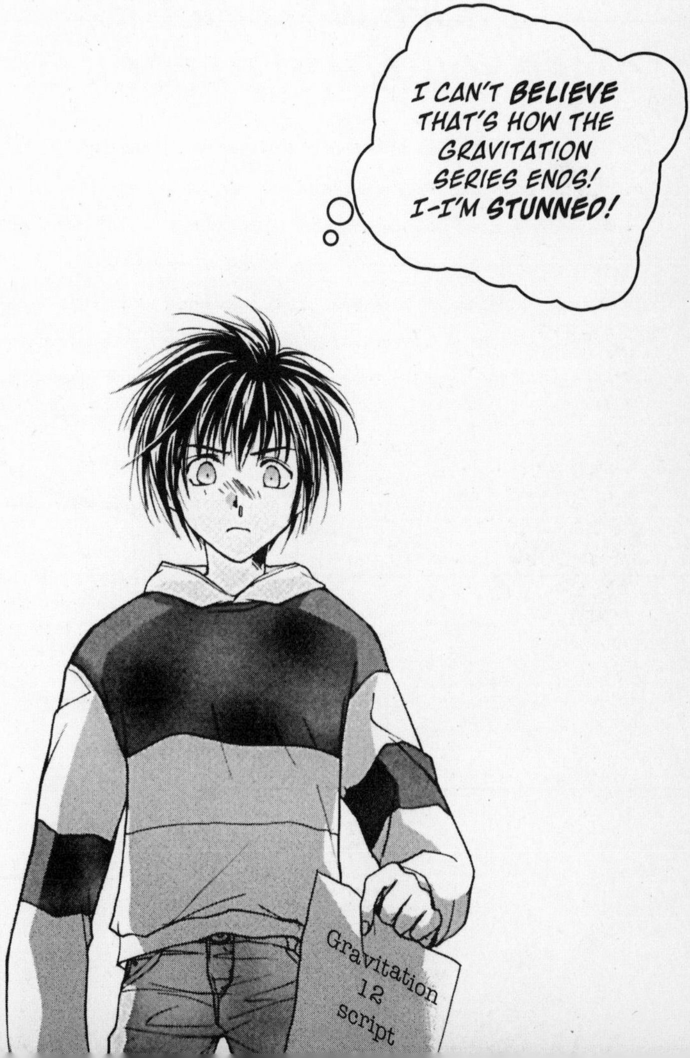
I CAN'T BELIEVE THAT'S HOW THE GRAVITATION SERIES ENDS! I-I'M STUNNED!
Gravitation 12 script

Gravitation

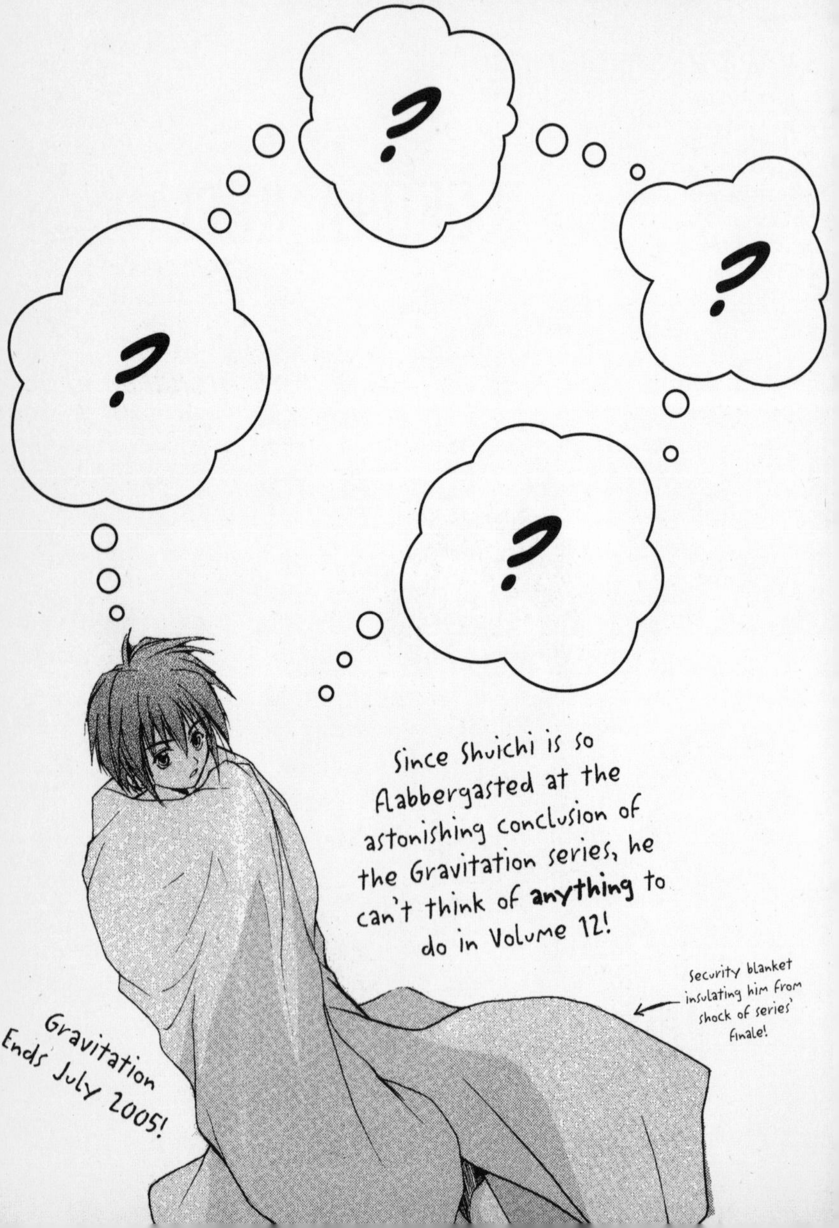
?
?
?
?
Since Shuichi is so flabbergasted at the astonishing conclusion of the Gravitation series, he can't think of **anything** to do in Volume 12!
Security blanket insulating him from shock of series' finale!
Gravitation Ends July 2005!

TOKYOPOP SHOP

SOKORA REFUGEES

PLANET BLOOD

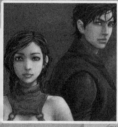

THE TAROT CAFÉ

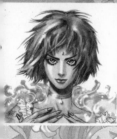

- LOOK FOR SPECIAL OFFERS
- PRE-ORDER UPCOMING RELEASES!
- COMPLETE YOUR COLLECTIONS

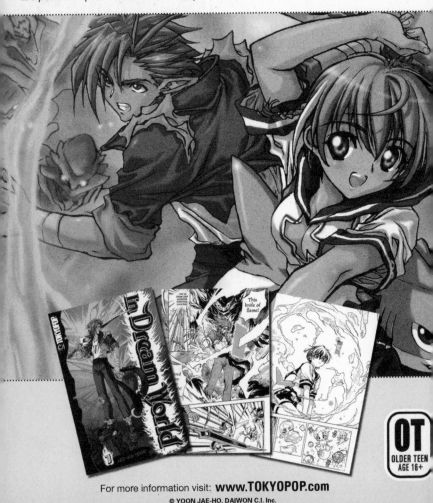

VAN VON HUNTER™

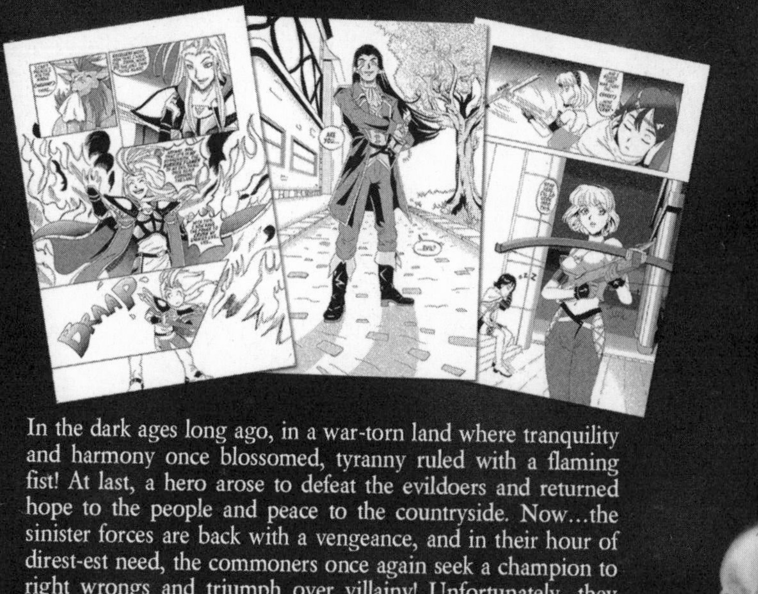

In the dark ages long ago, in a war-torn land where tranquility and harmony once blossomed, tyranny ruled with a flaming fist! At last, a hero arose to defeat the evildoers and returned hope to the people and peace to the countryside. Now...the sinister forces are back with a vengeance, and in their hour of direst-est need, the commoners once again seek a champion to right wrongs and triumph over villainy! Unfortunately, they could only get the mighty warrior Van Von Hunter, Hunter of Evil...Stuff!

Together with his loyal, memory-challenged sidekick, Van Von Hunter is on a never-ending quest to smite the bad guys—and believe us, they're real bad!

Preview the manga at:

www.TOKYOPOP.com/vanvonhunter
www.VanVonHunter.com

T TEEN AGE 13+

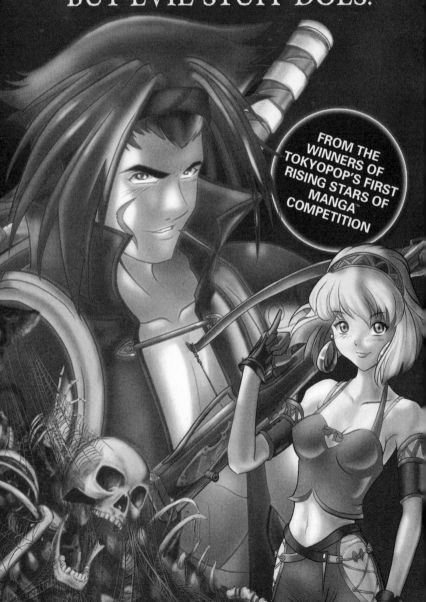

FAERIES' LANDING

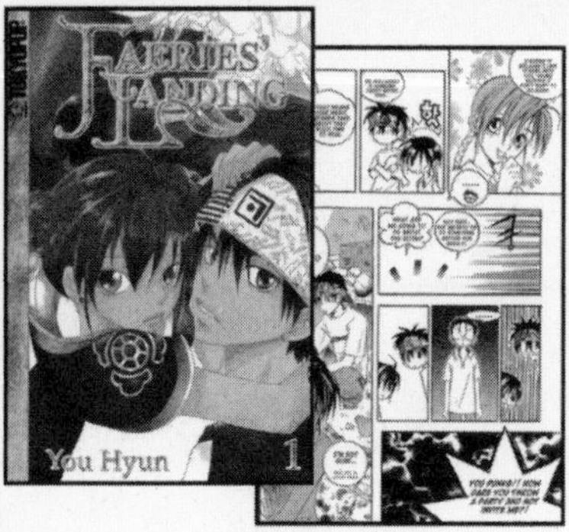
Faeries' Landing
You Hyun
1
TOKYOPOP

BY YOU HYUN

Following the misadventures of teenager Ryang Jegal and Fanta, a faerie who has fallen from the heavens straight into South Korea, *Faeries' Landing* is both a spoof of modern-day teen romance and a lighthearted fantasy epic. Imagine if Shakespeare's *A Midsummer Night's Dream* had come from the pen of Joss Whedon after about a dozen shots of espresso, and you have an idea of what to expect from You Hyun's funny little farce. Bursting with sharp wit, hip attitude and vibrant art, *Faeries' Landing* is guaranteed to get you giggling.

~Tim Beedle, Editor

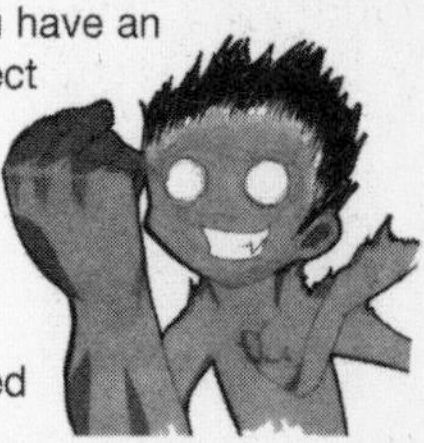

TRAMPS LIKE US

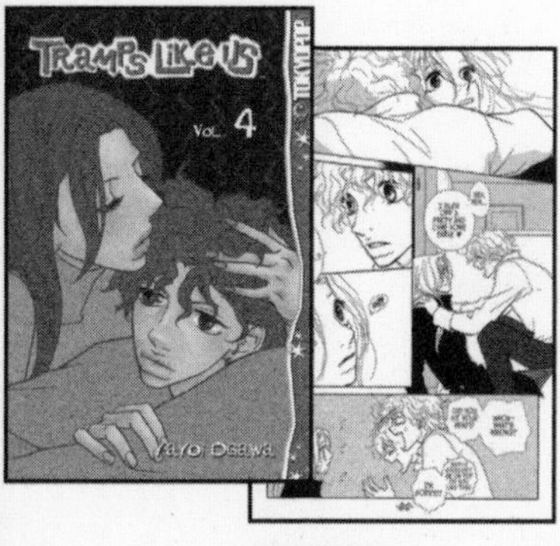
Tramps Like Us
Vol. 4
Yayoi Ogawa
TOKYOPOP

BY YAYOI OGAWA

Yayoi Ogawa's *Tramps Like Us*—known as *Kimi wa Pet* in Japan—is the touching and humorous story of Sumire, a woman whose striking looks and drive for success alienate her from her friends and co-workers...until she takes in Momo, a cute homeless boy, as her "pet." As sketchy as the situation sounds, it turns out to be the sanest thing in Sumire's hectic life. In his quiet way, Momo teaches Sumire how to care for another being while also caring for herself...in other words, how to love. And there ain't nothin' wrong with that.

~Carol Fox, Editor

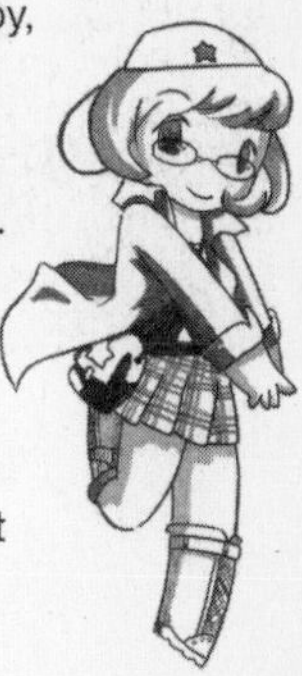

SGT FROG

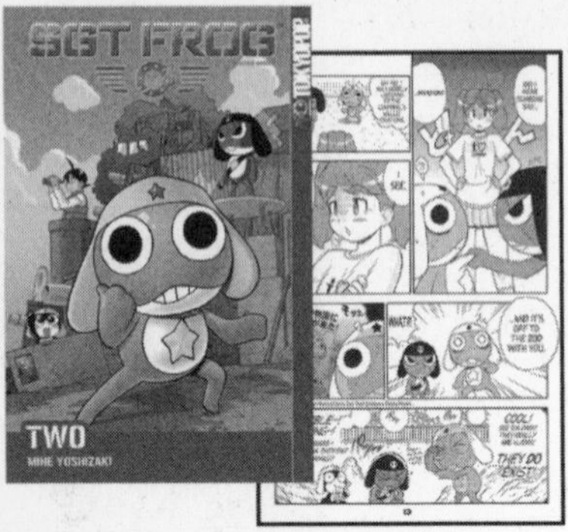
SGT FROG
TWO
MINE YOSHIZAKI

BY MINE YOSHIZAKI

Sgt. Frog is so absurdly comical, it has me in stitches every time I edit it. Mine Yoshizaki's clever sci-fi spoof showcases the hijinks of Sergeant Keroro, a cuddly looking alien, diabolically determined to oppress our planet! While some E.T.s phone home, this otherworldly menace has your number! Abandoned on Earth, Keroro takes refuge in the Hinata home, whose residents quickly take advantage of his stellar cleaning skills. But between scrubbing, vacuuming and an unhealthy obsession with Gundam models, Keroro still finds time to plot the subjugation of humankind!

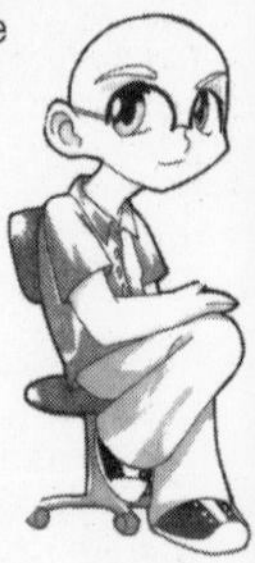

~ Paul Morrissey, Editor

@LARGE

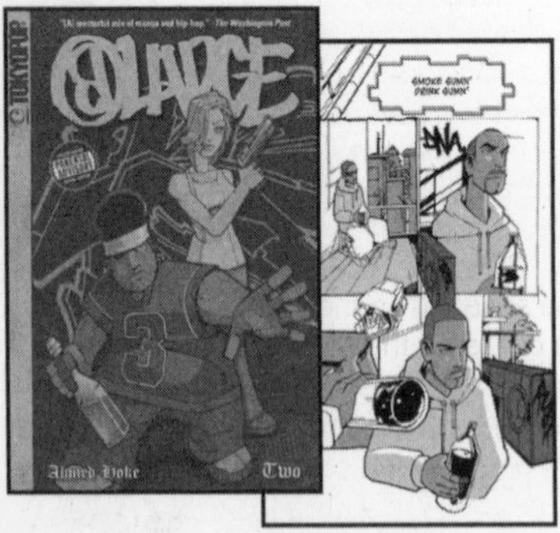
@LARGE
Ahmed Hoke
Two

BY AHMED HOKE

Ahmed Hoke's revolutionary hip-hop manga is a groundbreaking graphic novel. While at first glace this series may seem like a dramatic departure from traditional manga styles, on a deeper level one will find a rich, lyrical world full of wildly imaginative characters, intense action and heartfelt human emotions. This is a truly unique manga series that needs to be read by everyone—whether they are fans of hip-hop or not.

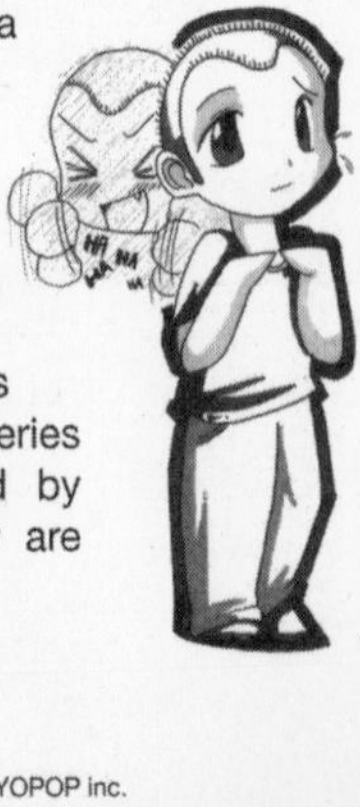

~Rob Valois, Editor

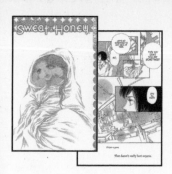

PASSION FRUIT
BY MARI OKAZAKI

Passion Fruit is a unique, unforgettable collection of stylish stories that touch upon our most private inhibitions and examine our deepest desires. This uncompromising blend of realism and raw emotion focuses on women exploring the vulnerability and frailty of the human condition. With uninhibited authenticity and pathos, passion proves to be stranger than fiction.

© Mari Okazaki

OT OLDER TEEN AGE 16+

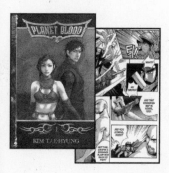

PLANET BLOOD
BY TAE-HYUNG KIM

Universal Century 0091. The Mars and Moon colonies fight for repatriation rights over the newly restored Earth. Amidst the bloody battle, one soldier, is rendered unconscious—only to awaken in an entirely different world enmeshed in an entirely different war...

© KIM TAE-HYUNG, DAIWON C.I. Inc.

T TEEN AGE 13+

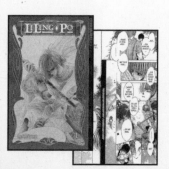

LILING-PO
BY AKO YUTENJI

Master thief Liling-Po has finally been captured! However, the government offers a chance for Liling-Po to redeem himself. All he has to do is "retrieve" some special items—eight mystic treasures that are fabled to grant their owners any wish!

© Ako Yutenji

T TEEN AGE 13+

The breakout manga that put CLAMP on the map!

RG VEDA
聖伝

At the dawn of creation, the world was a beautiful and tranquil place. When a powerful warlord rebelled against the king, a violent, chaotic age began.... Three hundred years later, a group of noble warriors embarks on a quest to find the prophesied Six Stars before the land is torn apart!

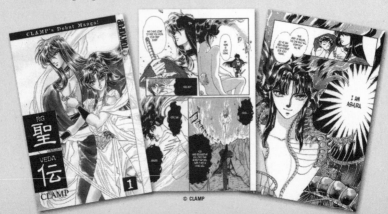

© CLAMP

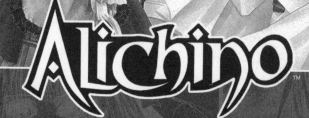
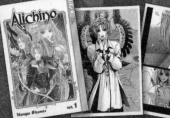

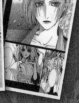

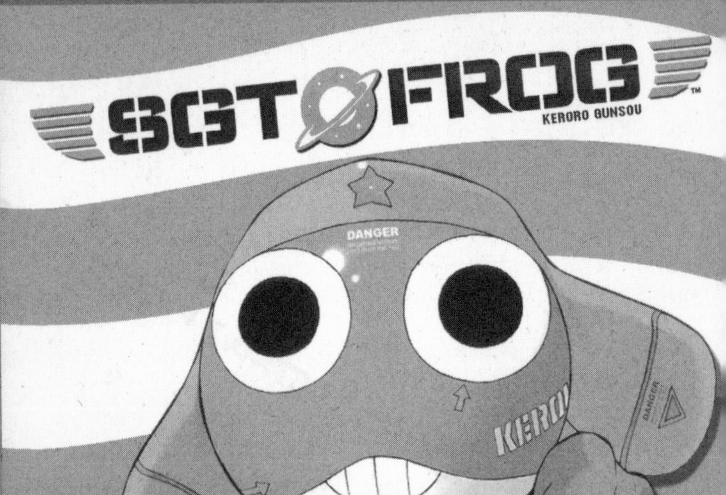
SGT FROG
KERORO GUNSOU
™
DANGER
KERO
DANGER
DANGER
KERORO
DANGER

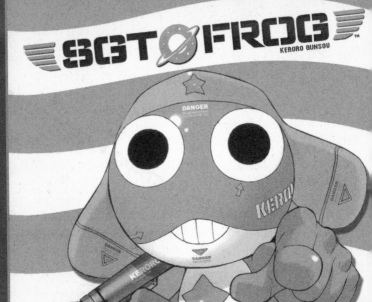

STOP!

This is the back of the book.
You wouldn't want to spoil a great ending!

This book is printed "manga-style," in the authentic Japanese right-to-left format. Since none of the artwork has been flipped or altered, readers get to experience the story just as the creator intended. You've been asking for it, so TOKYOPOP® delivered: authentic, hot-off-the-press, and far more fun!

DIRECTIONS

If this is your first time reading manga-style, here's a quick guide to help you understand how it works.

It's easy... just start in the top right panel and follow the numbers. Have fun, and look for more 100% authentic manga from TOKYOPOP®!

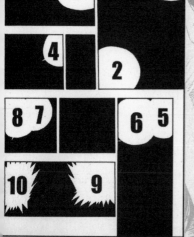

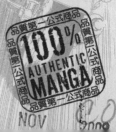